CONTENTS

Here are
*the **Michelin** maps*
to use with this
guide.

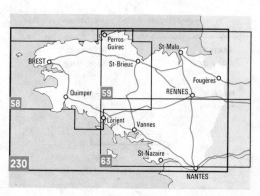

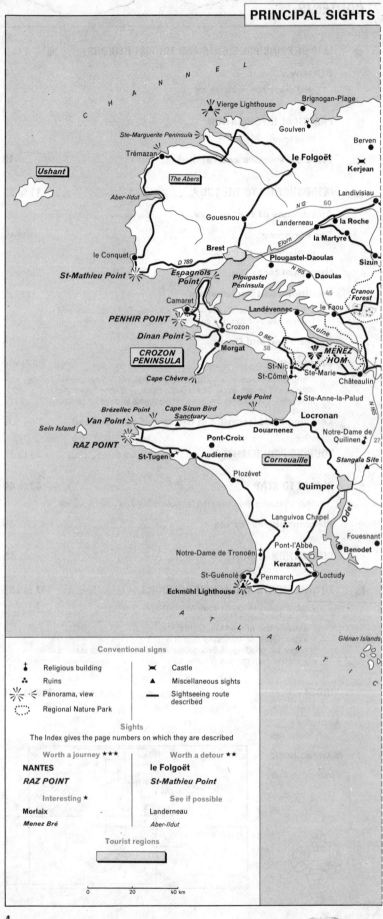

Conventional signs

✝	Religious building	✖	Castle
⁂	Ruins	▲	Miscellaneous sights
☀	Panorama, view	—	Sightseeing route described
⬚	Regional Nature Park		

Sights

The Index gives the page numbers on which they are described

Worth a journey ★★★	Worth a detour ★★
NANTES	**le Folgoët**
RAZ POINT	*St-Mathieu Point*
Interesting ★	See if possible
Morlaix	Landerneau
Menez Bré	*Aber-Ildut*

Tourist regions

0   20   40 km

AND TOURIST REGIONS

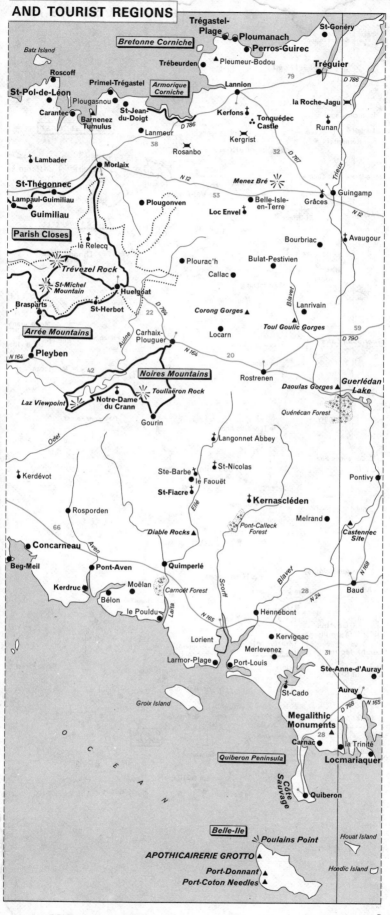

Batz Island

Bretonne Corniche

Trégastel-
Plage
Ploumanach
Perros-Guirec
St-Gonéry
Trébeurden
Pleumeur-Bodou
Tréguier
Roscoff
Primel-Trégastel
Armorique Corniche
Lannion
la Roche-Jagu
St-Pol-de-Léon
Plougasnou
Kerfons
Runan
Carantec
Barnenez
Tumulus
St-Jean-
du-Doigt
Tonquédec
Castle
D 786
79
D 786
Lanmeur
Kergrist
Lambader
Rosanbo
38
32
D 767
Morlaix
Menez Bré
Guingamp
St-Thégonnec
N 12
53
Belle-Isle-
en-Terre
Grâces
Lampaul-Guimiliau
Plougonven
Loc Envel
Trieux
N 12
Guimiliau
Bourbriac
Avaugour
Parish Closes
le Relecq
Bulat-Pestivien
Plourac'h
Callac
Trévezel Rock
St-Michel
Mountain
Huelgoat
Corong Gorges
Lanrivain
Braspars
St-Herbot
D 764
22
Locarn
Toul Goulic Gorges
59
Arrée Mountains
Aulne
Carhaix-
Plouguer
Blavet
D 790
N 164
Pleyben
N 164
20
Rostrenen
**Guerlédan
Lake**
42
Noires Mountains
Daoulas Gorges
Laz Viewpoint
Toullaëron Rock
Notre-Dame
du Crann
Quénécan Forest
Odet
Gourin
Langonnet Abbey
Kerdévot
Ste-Barbe
St-Nicolas
Pontivy
le Faouët
St-Fiacre
Ellé
Kernascléden
Rosporden
Melrand
**Castennec
Site**
66
Aven
Diable Rocks
Pont-Calleck
Forest
N 168
Concarneau
Quimperlé
Blavet
Baud
Beg-Meil
Pont-Aven
Moëlan
Carnoët Forest
Scorff
28
N 24
Kerdruc
Bélon
le Pouldu
Laïta
N 165
Hennebont
Lorient
Kervignac
Groix Island
Merlevenez
31
Larmor-Plage
Port-Louis
Ste-Anne-d'Auray
St-Cado
Auray
D 768
N 165
**Megalithic
Monuments**
28
O
Carnac
la Trinité
C
Locmariaquer
E
A
Quiberon Peninsula
N
Côte
Sauvage
Quiberon
Houat Island
Belle-Ile
Poulains Point
APOTHICAIRERIE GROTTO
Hoedic Island
Port-Donnant
Port-Coton Needles

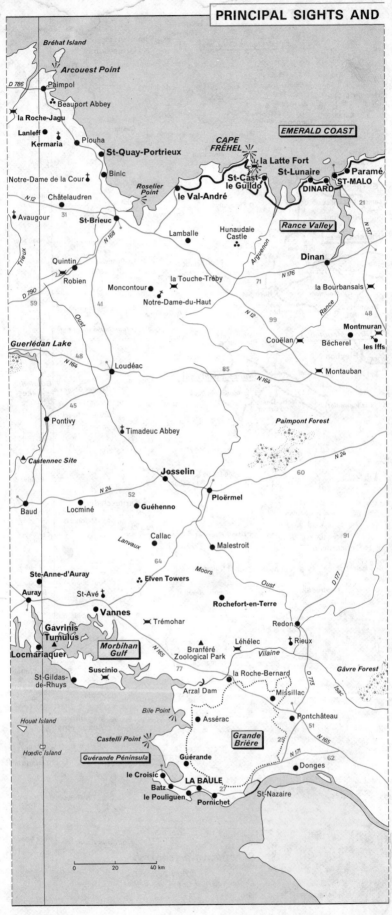

Bréhat Island

Arcouest Point

D 786

Paimpol

Beauport Abbey

la Roche-Jagu

Lanleff

Kermaria

Plouha

St-Quay-Portrieux

Binic

Notre-Dame de la Cour

Châtelaudren

N 12

Avaugour

31

St-Brieuc

N 168

Quintin

Robien

D 790

59

Oust

41

Moncontour

la Touche-Tréby

Notre-Dame-du-Haut

Trieux

Roselier Point

le Val-André

Lamballe

Hunaudaie Castle

Arguenon

CAPE FRÉHEL

la Latte Fort

St-Cast-le Guildo

St-Lunaire

DINARD

Paramé

ST-MALO

EMERALD COAST

Rance Valley

N 137

21

Dinan

N 176

la Bourbansais

N 12

99

Rance

48

Montmuran

Couëlan

Bécherel

les Iffs

71

Guerlédan Lake

N 164

Loudéac

85

N 164

Montauban

45

Pontivy

Timadeuc Abbey

Paimpont Forest

N 24

60

Castennec Site

Josselin

Baud

N 24

52

Locminé

Guéhenno

Ploërmel

Lanvaux

Callac

Malestroit

64

91

D 177

Ste-Anne-d'Auray

Elven Towers

Moors

Oust

Auray

St-Avé

Rochefort-en-Terre

Redon

Vannes

Trémohar

Rieux

Gavrinis Tumulus

Léhélec

Vilaine

Locmariaquer

Morbihan Gulf

N 165

Branféré Zoological Park

Gâvre Forest

St-Gildas-de-Rhuys

Suscinio

77

la Roche-Bernard

D 773

Isac

Arzal Dam

Missillac

Houat Island

Bile Point

Assérac

Pontchâteau

51

Hoedic Island

Castelli Point

Grande Brière

25

N 165

Guérande Péninsula

Guérande

N 171

62

le Croisic

Donges

Batz

LA BAULE

le Pouliguen

Pornichet

St-Nazaire

27

0   20   40 km

TOURIST REGIONS

Chausey Islands

Grouin Point

Cancale

MONT-ST-MICHEL

Dol Mound

St-Georges-de-Gréhaigne

Dol-de-Bretagne

Landal

Antrain

Bonne-Fontaine

Combourg

Lanrigan

Tremblay

le Rocher-Portail

State Forest of Fougères

Fougères

Hédé

Couesnon

St-Aubin-du-Cormier

Champeaux

Vitré

Rennes

les Rochers-Sévigné

Louvigné-de-Bais

Bruz

Bais

la Roche-aux-Fées

la Guerche-de-Bretagne

Retiers

Mottes Lake

Grand-Fougeray

Châteaubriant

la Meilleraye-de-Bretagne

Melleray Abbey

Vioreau Reservoir

Blain

NANTES

LA ROCHELLE

POITIERS

KU-762-112

CALVARIES

★★

Tronoën p 77
Guimiliau p 104
Pleyben p 139
Plougastel-Daoulas p 140
Plougonven p 127
St-Thégonnec p 175

CATHEDRALS

★★

Dol-de-Bretagne p 85
Quimper p 149
St-Pol-de-Léon p 174
Tréguier p 178

CASTLES

★★

Fort la Latte p 116
Fougères p 93
Josselin p 108
Nantes p 131
St-Malo p 169
Vitré p 184

RAMPARTS

★★★

St-Malo p 168

★★

Concarneau p 74
Mont-St-Michel p 123

BOAT TRIPS

★★★

Cape Fréhel p 85
St-Malo p 85

★★

Auray River and Morbihan Gulf pp 53, 125
Bréhat Island p 59
Brest Roadstead p 64
Rance Valley
from Dinard p 154
from St-Malo p 154
Dinan by the Rance p 154
Grande Brière p 98
Quimper by the Odet p 118
Down the Odet p 151
Up the Odet pp 59, 151

7

BRITTANY

BRIEF DESCRIPTION OF THE REGION

The Coast. – The most vivid memory left after a visit to Brittany is that of the coast, with its red, rosy, grey or mauve cliffs, scarred, rent and crumbled by a restless sea; a multitude of reefs and a chaplet of islands; tremendous piles of rocks; impressive headlands that seem truly to mark the ends of the earth; huge bays; gracious inlets and beaches of fine sand, sometimes narrow, sometimes spreading farther than the eye can reach.

The Islands. – The Breton islands, whether far out on the high seas or just offshore, all have their own special character be it a certain charm, solitude or wild beauty.

In the Channel **Bréhat** with its red rocks supports highly scented flora: mimosa, eucalyptus and fig trees. Opposite the 'pink granite coast' or Bretonne Corniche the group, **Archipel des Sept Iles**, surrounded by foam fringed reefs, is a birds' paradise, especially **Rouzic**, an extinct volcano bathed by a warm current and covered with a reddish coloured plant. **Batz**, near Roscoff, is known for its abundance of seaweed and shellfish.

The Atlantic islands are often bigger and placed further out to sea: **Ushant** rising above its sea pounded reefs, with its broken coastline, lighthouses and purple or yellow heaths. **Sein** off the Raz Point on the Cornouaille coastline is a flat, green, wind battered island. The **Glénan Islands** (Iles de Glénan), off Concarneau, evidence of a drowned continent (coastline) are reputed for their sailing facilities. **Groix** near Lorient with its beaches and cliffs, **Belle-Ile** and its varying aspects: threatening rocks, peaceful vales, immense beaches, gorse covered heaths and hydrangea filled gardens; finally two small isles **Houat** and **Hoedic**. The Morbihan Gulf is a sheltered haven for the peaceful **Moines Island** (Ile aux Moines) with its sea pines, broom and camellias, **Arz**, **Gavrinis** and **Er Lannic** all with megalithic monuments.

The Interior. – To the tourist who has had his fill of seascapes, the Breton hinterland offers strongly marked characteristics; fields bounded by wooded banks; melancholy heaths covered with brush and gorse; hilly forests; crests with rocky slopes, from which wide panoramas can be seen; short rivers flowing through green, narrow valleys which open out suddenly into great river estuaries.

Seaside resorts and towns. – There are two large, fashionable seaside resorts, Dinard on the Channel and La Baule on the Atlantic coast. There are many others, ideal for family holidays or little out of the way places for those who seek solitude. The chief fishing villages, except St-Malo, are on the Atlantic coast. There are also commercial ports of which two of the most important are Nantes and St-Nazaire and two naval bases, Brest and Lorient.

There are no large towns inland apart from Rennes. The regional centres are Quimper, Tréguier, Morlaix, Vannes and the market towns with their many old streets and ancient houses. Inland are scattered a great number of hamlets and isolated farms.

Agriculture, fishing and the tourist industry provide a living for most of the Breton population.

Industry's role is not to be despised: with maritime and agricultural based industries predominating although others such as electronics, car and rubber manufacturing have been established.

Mystical atmosphere. – Long before the Christian era, this was a land of religion; it contains more druidical remains (menhirs) than any other place in the world.

Nine cathedrals, thousands of churches and chapels consecrated to a host of local saints, crosses standing by the roadsides, the "parish closes" with their Calvaries and ossuaries and the sacred springs, show that Breton piety has flourished through the centuries.

Even today the *pardons*, though often accompanied by social festivals, give glimpses of the pious fervour which animates the people.

The Breton character. – At the beginning of the twentieth century the customs, dress and ideas of the time of Louis XIV were still to be found in many parts of Brittany.

Since the First World War there has been a more rapid advance. The picturesque old costumes are no longer worn every day, but *pardons* and the family festivities of baptism, confirmation, and weddings bring them out of the cupboards to make a spectacle in which tourists delight. In Finistère and Morbihan many of the older women still wear the traditional head-dress.

Many box beds, great wardrobes, chests and dressers have found their way to the antique dealers' shops and those that have remained have often been put to very different use from that for which they were designed.

In the west, Breton is still a living tongue, but French is spoken everywhere, while legends and simple beliefs are fading away. In spite of the efforts of the folklore societies, Breton life has lost much of its traditional character and the motorist who travels through the country at high speed may suffer some disappointment.

Yet the distinctive nature of Brittany remains. It is due chiefly to the sky which is often overcast and always changing, the sea, the landscape, the buildings and monuments so different from those in other parts of France.

Travellers from Britain will, however, notice many similarities with Cornwall and southwest Wales with which Brittany has innumerable ties.

The companion guides in English in this series on France are

Châteaux of the Loire, Dordogne,
French Riviera, Normandy, Provence,
Paris

Other Michelin Green Guides available in English

Austria, Germany, Italy,
Portugal, Spain, Switzerland,
London, New York City

PRACTICAL INFORMATION

The French Government Tourist Offices at 178 Piccadilly, London W1V 0AL, Tel (01) 493 31 71 and 610 Fifth Avenue, New York, Tel (212) 757 – 1125 will provide information and literature.

How to get there. – You can go directly by scheduled national airlines, by commercial and package tour flights, possibly with a rail or coach link-up or you can go by cross-Channel ferry or hovercraft and on by car or train. Brittany Ferries run daily services from Portsmouth to St-Malo and from Plymouth to Roscoff, and in summer only from Cork to Roscoff. Enquire at any good travel agent and remember if you are going in the holiday season or at Christmas, Easter or Whitsun, to book well in advance.

When to go there. – Brittany's climate is both mild and invigorating.

Spring. – This is the time when gorse and broom flare golden. The countryside, flowered and scented, noisy with birds of every species, is delightful – when the sun shines. It is the time when the nature lover can enjoy the country almost undisturbed.

Summer. – A characteristic of the Breton summer is its moderate warmth, due to the sea breeze. A few showers are enough to keep the fields and trees green and the moss alive. Rare spells of heat come with occasional light winds from the east. The light has a special quality. Scores of painters come to capture the Breton scenes.

Autumn. – The russet tints of the trees and the golden broom sometimes make splendid pictures at sunset. Northwesterly and southwesterly gales are frequent: for those who like to watch rough seas, the gales, however, provide a wonderful spectacle.

Winter. – The winter is mild, with a mean temperature like that of the Mediterranean coast. A bitter wind may come from the east, but not too often.

Before Leaving

Papers and other documents. – A valid national passport, identity card or British Visitor's Passport is all that is required in the way of personal documents.

For the car a valid Driving licence, international driving permit, car registration book and a nationality plate of the approved size. Insurance cover is compulsory and although the Green Card (an International Insurance Certificate) is no longer a legal requirement for France it is the most effective form of proof of insurance cover and is internationally recognized by police and other authorities.

Caravan owners must, in addition produce the caravan log-book and an inventory for customs clearance. Endorse the Green Card for caravan and trailer. A carnet is required to import temporarily certain vehicles: pleasure craft over 5.5 m long and motor boats.

Certain motoring organisations run accident insurance and breakdown service schemes for their members. Enquire before leaving. A red warning triangle is obligatory in case of a breakdown.

In France it is compulsory for the front passengers to wear seat belts if the car is equipped with them. Children under ten should be on the back seat.

Medical treatment. – For EEC countries it is necessary to have Form E 111 which testifies to your entitlement to medical benefits from the Department of Health and Social Security. With this you can obtain medical treatment in an emergency and after the necessary steps, a refund of part of the costs of treatment from the local Social Security offices (Caisse Primaire de Sécurité Sociale). It is however advisable to take out comprehensive insurance cover.

Customs

Currency. – There are no customs restrictions on what you take into France in the way of currency. To facilitate the export of currency in foreign bank notes, superior to the given allocation, visitors are advised to complete a currency declaration form on arrival. Unlimited amounts of travellers cheques may be exported.

Duly Arrived

Consulate: British – 6 Rue Lafayette, 44000 Nantes (Tel 48 57 47).

Local Tourist Information Centres or Syndicat d'Initiative (SI) are to be found in most large towns and many tourist resorts. They can supply large scale town plans, timetables and local information on entertainment facilities, sports and sightseeing *(see tables on pp 40-44)*.

Where to stay. – In the Michelin Red Guide France you will find a selection of hotels at various prices in all areas. It will also list local restaurants again with prices. If camping or caravanning consult the Michelin Guide Camping Caravaning France.

Electric Current. – Mostly 220/230 volts, in some places however it is still 110 volts. European circular two pin plugs are the rule – remember an electrical adaptor.

Poste Restante. – Name, Poste restante, Poste centrale, Department's postal number followed by the town's name, France.

Postage via air mail to: UK letter: 1.50F postcard: 1.00F
US aerogramme: 1.90F postcard: 1.50F

Public Holidays in France. – National museums and art galleries are closed on Tuesdays. The following are days when museums and other monuments may be closed or may vary their hours of admission:

New Year's Day	Whit Sunday and Monday	All Saints' Day, **1 November**
Easter Sunday and Monday	France's National Day, **14 July**	Armistice Day, **11 November**
May Day **(1 May)**	The Assumption, **15 August**	Christmas Day
Ascension Day		

PRINCIPAL PARDONS AND FESTIVALS

DATE	PLACE	Page in guide or no of section on Michelin map 230	NATURE OF FESTIVAL
Ascension Day	St-Herbot	50	Pardon*.
2nd Sunday in May	Quintin	154	Pardon of Our Lady of Deliverance (Notre-Dame-de-Délivrance).
Saturday (8.30pm) to Whit Monday	Moncontour	120	Pardon of St-Mathurin.
Whit Sunday	Carantec	67	Pardon of Our Lady of Callot (Notre-Dame-de-Callot).
19 May	Tréguier	178	Pardon of St-Yves.
Trinity Sunday	Notre-Dame-du-Crann Chapel	135	Pardon.
—	Rumengol	50	Pardon**.
Sunday before St-John's Day	St-Tugen	77	Pardon* (3pm).
Last Sunday in June	Le Faouët	92	Pardon of St. Barbara.
—	Plouguerneau	47	Pardon of St. Peter and St. Paul.
—	St-Jean-du-Doigt	166	Pardon of the Fire.
Eve of 1st Sunday in July	Guingamp	105	Pardon* of Our Lady of Succour (Notre-Dame-de-Bon-Secours) (10pm to midnight).
2nd Sunday in July	Locronan	117	Petite Troménie.
3rd Sunday in July and week before	Douarnenez	87	Festival Mouez ar mor (the voice of the sea).
26 July	Ste-Anne-d'Auray	176	Grand Pardon**.
4th Saturday and Sunday in July	Le Vieux Marché	⑥	Islamo-Christian pilgrimage to the Chapel of the Seven Saints.
4th Sunday in July	Bubry	㉟	Pardon* of St. Helen.
	Quimper		Great festival of Cornouaille*.
3rd Sunday in July	Carantec	67	Pardon of St-Carantec (10am).
—	Persquen	㉑	Pardon of Our Lady of Pénéty (Notre-Dame-de-Pénéty).
—	Pont-Aven	142	Festival of the Golden Gorse.
Sunday after 26 July	Fouesnant	93	Pardon of St. Anne.
15 August	Perros-Guirec	138	Pardon of Our Lady of Light (Notre-Dame-de-la-Clarté).
—	Quelven	145	Pardon of Our Lady.
—	Vannes	181	Festival of Arvor (in front of the ramparts).
Sunday after 15 August	Carantec	67	Pardon of Our Lady of Callot (Notre-Dame-de-Callot).
—	Ploërdut	186	Pardon of Our Lady of Crénénan (Notre-Dame-de-Crénénan).
—	Concarneau	73	Festival of Blue Nets* (Fête des Filets Bleus).
—	Ste-Anne-la-Palud	117	Grand Pardon**.
1st Sunday in September	Camaret	66	Pardon of Our Lady of Rocamadour (Notre-Dame-de-Rocamadour). Blessing of the Sea.
—	Le Folgoët	92	Grand Pardon**.
—	Penhors	77	Pardon of Our Lady of Penhors (Notre-Dame-de-Penhors).
8 September	Josselin	108	Pardon* of Our Lady of the Rosebush (Notre-Dame-du-Roncier).
2nd Sunday in September	Carnac	69	Pardon of St-Cornély.
3rd Sunday in September	Notre-Dame-de-Tronoën	77	Pardon.
Last Sunday in September	Hennebont	106	Pardon of Our Lady of the Vow (Notre-Dame-du-Vœu).
—	Plouguerneau	47	Pardon* of St. Michael.
Sunday nearest to 29 September	Mont-St-Michel	121	Festival of the Archangel St. Michael.
4 December	Le Faouët	92	Pardon of St. Barbara.

You will find an **index** at the back of the guide listing all subjects referred to in the text or illustrations (monuments, picturesque sites, points of interest, historical or geographical items, etc.).

INTRODUCTION TO THE TOUR

APPEARANCE OF THE COUNTRY

Relief. – The map below shows the relief of Brittany in a general way. The coast is jagged. The interior does not rise to a great altitude (384 m - 1 288 ft at its highest point, the Toussaines Beacon – Tuchenn Gador – in the Arrée Mountains), but consists of undulating plateaux which slope by stages towards the sea, where they die away. There are a few dominating ridges (the Arrée, Noires and Menez Mountains), several hilly areas (the Sillon de Bretagne); two depressions (the basins of Châteaulin and Rennes) and numerous rivers ending in estuaries.

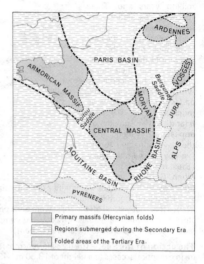

The Breton earth. – The subsoil consists chiefly of hard primary formations, granite and closely bound sandstone, with some softer rocks and schists (hardened or flaky clay).

During the primary period, which began some 600 million years ago, water covered the whole land mass of France. It was at this period that the earth's crust was forced upwards: the fold, known as the "Hercynian fold" which appears in the form of a V and is shown by shading on the map, made great mountains rise up (Armorican Massif, Massif Central, the Vosges and Ardennes). These mountains of impermeable, crystalline rock – granite, gneiss and mica-schist mixed with volcanic rock such as porphyry – appeared in Brittany as two massive chains stretching from east to west and separated by a central furrow.

Erosion has since that time almost levelled these former mountains, exposing the older and harder primaeval rocks which formed their foundation. On the other hand, the central furrow, being lower, was less affected by the destructive process of erosion and the primaeval schists and sandstone rocks which formed it often remain undisturbed.

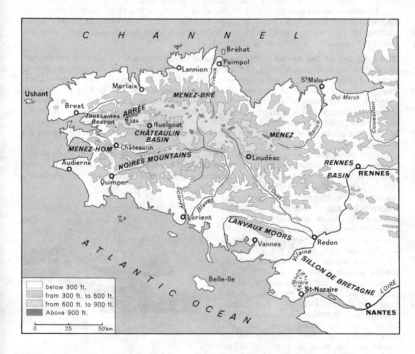

The tremendous work of erosion. – Erosion, or the constant destruction of the soil by alternating rain, sun, frost and the action of running water, attacked these high mountains. This wearing away, which affects rocks as hard as granite or sandstone, has gone on for millions of centuries; peaks more than 4 000 m - 12 800 ft high were progressively reduced to less than 400 m - 1 280 ft. Later the deep valleys (Rance, Trieux, Aulne, Blavet, etc.), which cut into the plateaux on a scale different from that of the present day rivers, were hollowed out. They are among the characteristic features of the land, especially towards the north; as they approach the sea the valleys become true gorges, ending in deep estuaries known in Breton as *abers (details p 47)*.

11

THE ARMOR

This name of **Armor**, which means "country near the sea", was given to the coastal region by the Gauls: the interior was Argoat (country of wood). The Breton coast is extraordinarily indented; this makes it 1 200 km - 750 miles long whereas it would be half that without its saw-teeth. The jaggedness of this coastline with its islands, islets and reefs is due only in part to the action of the sea.

Origin of the coastline indentation. – The deep cuts into the coast were formed by rocking movements of the earth in the tertiary era which began 50 million years ago. There followed oscillations of both the sea and the earth.

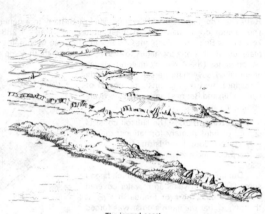

As changes in the land level took place the sea swept into the valleys and so prevented their being silted up. These estuaries, which are so characteristic and where the tide flows as much as 12 km - 19 miles inland, differ greatly in appearance, varying from the bay connected to the sea by a narrow gully (Brest roadstead, the Morbihan Gulf) to the wide

The jagged coast.
Grouin Point and its surroundings.

open bay such as that at Douarnenez or Quiberon.

The inland mountains have become steep cliffs (Cape Fréhel, Penhir Point, Raz Point). The islands that today stand off the coast were once part of the mainland, but they were joined by low strips of land that the sea has now covered completely or has left partially exposed as islets or reefs linking the islands to the shore (Ushant).

The action of the Sea. – The tides are very great in Brittany. On the north coast, the tide sweeps in, in exceptional cases to a height of 13.50 m - 43 ft in the Bay of St-Malo and of 15 m - 48 ft in the Bay of Mont-St-Michel. When the wind blows, the battering ram effect of the sea is tremendous. Sometimes the shocks given to the rocks of Penmarch are felt as far off as Quimper, 30 km - 19 miles away.

Attacking the softest parts of the cliffs, the sea makes fissures and brings down slabs of rock. In this way caves (Morgat), tunnels and arches (Dinan "Château") are formed. Peninsulas joined to the mainland by strips of softer material are turned gradually into islands.

The waves do not only destroy; they also build. The sand they carry, added to the alluvial deposits brought down by the rivers, forms beaches, silts up the bays (Mont-St-Michel Bay is a striking example), and connects islands with the mainland; this is the case at Quiberon and it will probably be the same, in due course, at Bréhat.

The beauties of the Armor. – The most typical seascapes are to be found at the western extremity of the peninsula. Sombre cliffs, rugged capes 50 to 70 m - 160 to 224 ft high, islands, rocks and reefs give the coast a grimness which is reflected in local names: the channel of Great Fear (Fromveur), the Bay of the Dead (Baie des Trépassés), the Hell of Plogoff (Enfer de Plogoff). There are many other impressive features, too: piles of enormous blocks of pink granite sometimes rising as much as 20 m - 64 ft as at Ploumanach and Trégastel; the red sandstone promontory of Cape Fréhel standing 57 m - 182 ft above the sea; the brightly coloured caves at Morgat. The roadstead of Brest, the Bay of Douarnenez, the Morbihan Gulf and its islands are unforgettable.

The successive estuaries between the Rance and the Loire offer magnificent views at high tide as one crosses the bridges that span them (Albert-Louppe and Térénez bridges).

Some low lying sections of the coast contrast with the more usual rocks. In the north, the Bay of Mont-St-Michel is bordered by a plain won from the sea; in the south, the inhospitable Bay of Audierne, the coast between Port-Louis and the base of the Quiberon Peninsula, the beach at La Baule give a foretaste of the great expanses of sand which predominate south of the Loire.

Wherever the coast is directly open to the sea winds it is completely barren. This is so on the points and on the summits of the cliffs: the salt with which the winds are impregnated destroys vegetation. But in sheltered spots magnificent flowering shrubs bloom profusely. Arum lilies, camellias, hydrangeas and rhododendrons which would be the pride of many a skilled

Ploumanach. — The " tortoise ".

gardener, bedeck the smallest gardens. The climate is so mild that plants from hot countries grow in the open and mimosas, agaves, pomegranates, palms, eucalyptus, myrtles, oleanders and figs may be seen.

The times indicated in this guide

when given with the distance allow one to enjoy the scenery
when given for sightseeing are intended to give an idea of
the possible brevity or length of a visit.

THE LURE OF THE SEA

To savour the charm of Brittany to the full, take note of the sea.

The waves. – Waves are an undulating movement produced by the wind. Even after the wind has dropped, the movement continues: this is the swell. The impression that the water moves forward is an optical illusion; by watching a floating cork one can see that the up and down movement does not displace the water. Near the shore the undulation of the waves, which reaches to a depth of about 30 m - 100 ft is braked by the bottom. The balance is upset and the crest collapses, forming long rollers of foam and giving out a dull, rhythmic sound: this is surf. When the wave meets a steep obstacle, such as rocks or cliffs, it seems to recoil, shoots up, flinging spray into the air, and then falls with all its weight. On stormy days the spectacle can be awe-inspiring.

The tides. – You should first learn the rhythm of the tides, a division of time as regular as that of the sun. Twice every twenty-five hours the sea advances on the coast – this is the rising tide. It reaches high water mark, stays for some time at full stretch and then drops back – this is the falling or ebb tide – until it reaches low water mark. After remaining flattened for some time, the cycle begins again.

You will find tide timetables displayed in hotels, on the quays and in the local papers. Look at them before choosing what to do, bearing in mind how long you have to spend.

It is at high tide that the coast of Brittany is most beautiful. The waves advance on the coast, break on the rocky outspurs and surge in parallel crests into the bays: a shining, liquid carpet fills the estuaries. This is the time when a journey along a coast road or a walk to the harbour is the most rewarding; it is also the time for aquatic sports and pastimes.

At low water the uncovered rocks, stained with algae and seaweed which is often dirty, can be disappointing. At the mouths of the coastal rivers there is only a poor thread of water winding between mudflats. The greater the tide and the gentler the slope, the greater is the extent of shore uncovered; in Mont-St-Michel Bay the sea retreats 15 to 20 km - 9 to 12 miles. On the other hand, low tide is the joy of anyone fishing for crabs, shrimps, clams, mussels, etc.

Life by the sea. – Learn how the fishermen live; watch the traffic of the ports, great and small. Go to the early morning fish auction, watch for the return of the fishing boats. Even if you are not a good sailor do not be afraid to leave dry land in a fishing smack or excursion boat. The sight of the coast from the sea will be a revelation to you.

Amateur fishing. – Fishing for molluscs and crustaceans is free except near the cultivation beds. The fishermen may go out waist deep in the water and the angler may use a line with one or two hooks; if more are used the Harbour Office (*Inscription Maritime*) must be told. A permit is necessary if a net is used. Float fishing, using a line with a lead sinker is allowed from rocks and quays and from the shore. Minimum sizes for fish that may be caught are laid down. Shrimps and prawns are caught with a long-handled net; the best time is at low tide. You may dig for clams, cockles and sand eels with a spade or rake and among the rocks you may hunt for mussels, sea-urchins, crabs and conches.

Sailing. – The indented coast-line provides many sheltered bays which are ideal for this sport. Plenty of sailing clubs, such as the well known centre on Glénans Islands, provide instruction during the summer. Large resorts hold regattas throughout the season.

Skin diving. – This pastime is gaining in popularity in Brittany. The southern coasts (from Port-Manech, Port Goulphar to Belle-Ile, etc.) with creeks of crystal clear water, an abundance of fish and seaweeds, provide an ideal setting to practice underwater fishing or swimming to marvel at the beauty of it all.

(After Yvon photo, Paris)

Trébeurden. — The Tresmeur beach.

Seaside cures. – The special characteristics of sea water and the mildness of the climate are particularly beneficial for certain illnesses: rheumatism, arthritis and certain states of shock. Salt water and sea air cure centres are found on the Channel coast at Paramé and Roscoff and on the Atlantic at Douarnenez, Bénodet and Quiberon.

Natural beauties. – Follow the changing moods of the sea and sky. Remember to look at the sunsets – they are unforgettable. Go for a walk by the sea at the full moon; or, when there is no moon, take a look at the lighthouse beams as they pierce the darkness.

By day these lighthouses make wonderful observation points even if the climb to the top by circular stairs gives one cramp in the calf muscles! A tour of the lighthouse equipment is an added attraction when it is allowed.

Become hardened to the wind. Sea going folk smile when landsmen call what seems to be a fresh breeze, a gale.

In windy weather do not stay shut up in the hotel or in your car. Walk boldly along the points or the capes. Take the lash of sea spray with a smile; enjoy the salty taste on your tongue when you lick your lips. It is a great thing to have seen from close to, a rough sea dashing itself on a world's end cape: it verges on the sublime.

Guarded beaches: Many beaches along the Brittany coast are entirely safe for bathing - many are guarded. If flags are hoisted - green for safe bathing, red for too dangerous to bathe - obey them; if the beach is unguarded take local advice in case there are currents, hidden rocks or shelving.

THE ARGOAT

In the Breton tongue the interior is called the **Argoat**, or "wooded country". But, in fact, in spite of appearances to the contrary, there has been so much clearing that Brittany is one of the least wooded areas of France.

The plateaux. – Plains cover most of the country, although you must not expect to find great expanses, extending, without a break, to far horizons. Instead you cross a series of rises without any clear idea of their general direction. Between these uplands flow deeply sunken rivers with brown, rushing waters. The land is usually cut up into a chessboard pattern by banks or walls of uncemented stone which form the boundaries of fields and pastures. Pollarded oaks grow on most of the banks, and it is these which make the countryside, seen from a distance, seem heavily wooded.

(After Lapie photo)

The Breton chess-board.

The mountains. – Mountains! The word rather overpowers the Breton hills. But that is what the coast dwellers call the central part of Brittany. It must be said that in many places the barrenness and loneliness of the heights, the saw-toothed crests contrasting with the undulating plains that they overshadow and the strong wind give an impression of high altitude. In clear weather a vast expanse of Breton country can be seen from Trévezel Rock (384 m - 1 229 ft), the Ménez-Hom (330 m - 1 056 ft) and the Menez-Bré (302 m - 966 ft).

The rivers flowing down from the hills to the Channel or the Atlantic offer pretty scenery. The fresh vegetation in their valleys contrasts with the barren lands of the heights.

Forests and moors. – Brittany once had immense forests of oak and beech. Successive generations since the Romans have wielded the axe in these woods, and there are now only scattered strips of woodland: the forests of Paimpont, Loudéac, Huelgoat, Quénécan, etc. These woodlands are very hilly and intersected by gorges, ravines and tumbled rocks. This type of country is to be seen to perfection at Huelgoat. Unfortunately most of the woodlands would appear to be neglected and brushwood predominates. The fine forests so familiar to those who know the great woods of the Ile-de-France are rare and these Breton woodlands owe their picturesque quality more to their relief than to their trees.

(After Le Doaré photo, Châteaulin)

The Trévezel Rock.

Untilled moors succeeded the forests. Near the summits they still form great empty stretches whose gloom is relieved for a time only when the gorse wears its golden cloak and the heather spreads a purple carpet on the hills. Elsewhere, moors have yielded to the efforts of the peasants and have become tilled fields. Such are the Lanvaux Moors, where the stranger, misled by the name and expecting rough ground, finds reclaimed land, rich in promise for the future.

The attraction of the Argoat. – This region was off the beaten track for so long that it remained silent, melancholy and rural in character, but schemes like the Armorique Regional Nature Park (1969) in the Arrée Mountains should draw an ever increasing number of tourists.

And yet it is the ideal stopping place for lovers of nature to stand and stare, for naturalists to watch hundreds of birds and find a wide variety of plant life and for those who like to walk alone. To these, turning off the beaten track will often reveal a former seignorial manor now become a farm, or, following a scarcely perceptible path across the fields, the presence of a megalith or a little chapel standing alone and noticeable from a distance only by its pointed steeple. There are gorges, too, where waters leap from rock to rock before disappearing into depths below. Poets and romantics who love the simple charm of nature will be transported into a world of fantasy and, often in hazy surroundings conducive to dreams and mystery, will be able, at leisure, to weave anew the rich store of Breton legends.

Michelin main road maps *(scale 1:1 000 000)*

986 *Great Britain, Ireland*
987 *Germany, Austria, Benelux*
988 *Italy, Switzerland*
989 *France*
990 *Spain, Portugal*
991 *Yugoslavia*

THE ECONOMY

"Brittany is almost an island" – this phrase of Jules Michelet (French historian, 1798-1874) aptly describes the Breton economy which is marked by its proximity to the sea and its separation from France as a whole.

Brittany is a land of sailors where the sea is still very basic to the way of life and prosperity of the people. From the end of the 18C to 1960 Brittany remained peripheral to the development of the national economy, particularly the industrial sector, a fact which was often attributed to the lack of local mineral and energy resources.

This underdevelopment was aggravated by the great loss of human life during the First World War and the material destruction wreaked by the Second World War. Although used to being a subsistence area and being jealous of her individuality, Brittany's plight became acute and was manifested in a constant outflow of the younger generation to the bigger regional urban centres or to the Paris region.

The reversal of these tendencies, and subsequent improvement of the economic and social structure of the region, has been achieved by means of a supreme joint effort by government agencies and the people themselves. Measures taken include: the modernisation of the communication network and the fishing fleet and the mechanisation of agriculture; implantation of new industries and a search for new energy sources (tidal and nuclear); growth of the tertiary sector which now employs 45 per cent of the working force and the tourist industry (this is the most popular region in France after the Mediterranean coast). It is no longer essential for the younger generation to leave the region, some in fact have returned home.

The Breton miracle of improved economic structure of the region, although incomplete and still fragile, has incurred changes which would appear to be irreversible.

AGRICULTURE

Although Brittany is said to be a hard and poor land it is, nevertheless, one of France's foremost agricultural regions. Breton agriculture with a labour force of 20 % (50 % in 1954) grows a variety of top quality products and achieves some of the best returns on a national level.

The land. – The **bocage**: there is water everywhere in this green countryside where fields shelter behind banks topped by hedges; picturesque, sunken roads wander as they link the scattered farms and hamlets.

The soil. – This is very varied since it ranges from the moorland crests of quartzite of the interior to the rich loam of the Golden Belt (Ceinture Dorée). In general, however, the soil is poor siliceous clay which needs enriching, particularly with lime. Modern mixed fertilisers replace the traditional marine fertilisers.

Current projects. – The policy of regrouping land holdings that has been in operation for some years has been accompanied by considerable improvement such as ameliorating the soil, levelling, removing some of the dividing embankments, land clearance and reafforestation. Land under cultivation, which elsewhere in France occupies a third of the total area, now covers half of the area of Brittany.

The people. – The **village**: the wide dispersal of the population is due both to the Breton temperament which is highly individualistic and to the natural conditions of the country. The local market town with its church, cemetery, town hall, school and the majority of the tradesmen and craftsmen often only numbers a tenth of the people living in the area, the others being scattered in the neighbourhood in little hamlets consisting of three or four farms.

The **farmstead**: there are still some of the old houses left where men and beasts live together in the large only room, but, more often the house has been modernised and enlarged and outhouses have been built round it. The old furniture has gone and the picturesque box beds, where they still exist, serve as cupboards or wardrobes.

Two Breton farms.

Arable farming. – The main crops are cereals, fodder crops and fruit and vegetables.

Cereals. – These have been the basis of agricultural production and have always held pride of place, today nearly half the land under cultivation is given over to their production.

Wheat occupies a quarter of the land given over to cereals and the Ille-et-Vilaine department has the largest area under wheat.

The growing of **maize** has shown a tremendous increase: in 1976 the area devoted to this crop was more than ten times the 1966 figure.

Buckwheat porridge was for a long time the staple diet of country folk, but nowadays it is only used to make the traditional *crêpes* or thin, light pancakes and biscuits.

Rye is now only to be found in the most unfavourable parts of the country: the last twenty years have seen a considerable drop in the production.

Fodder crops. – Gorse which was once the lucerne of the country, has been superseded for livestock feed by fodder crops (cabbage, beetroot) and maize.

Market gardening. – This brings wealth to those living in the sheltered rich, alluvial, coastal areas between St-Malo and the mouth of the Loire, which is known as the Golden Belt (Ceinture Dorée). Potatoes, early vegetables representing 40 per cent of the national production, cauliflowers (57 per cent), artichokes (69 per cent), peas, French beans, carrots, cabbage, onions and garlic are all grown in the open fields. Part of the production is sent to the local canneries while the remainder supplies wider markets, notably the Paris region. Two of the more important crops are the strawberries of Plougastel-Daoulas and the seed potatoes of the Côtes-du-Nord, Morbihan and, in particular, Finistère which amount to two thirds of the total French yield.

Apple orchards. – There are still many in Ille-et-Vilaine but a certain decline is noticeable in Morbihan. They are used in the making of cider, apple juice and concentrate. A thriving trade has developed around the parasite mistletoe on the apple trees. Quantities are despatched via Redon to the British Isles for the Christmas period.

Stock raising. – Though all types of stock are raised in Brittany, it is especially known for its dairy cattle, which produce 15 per cent of French dairy produce.

Cattle. – Great efforts have been made over the years to improve the different breeds which provide 18 per cent of the total beef production. Local breeds have been replaced by more productive ones with a special emphasis on the milkers. Hence the French Frisian is now the most common breed; next comes the Normandy beef and dairy cow. The small piebald Brittany Pie Noire which was once so popular is now the object of special protection measures. The Armorican now crossed with other breeds gives the Pie Rouge.

Pigs. – The subsistence farm style of pig rearing has been replaced by intensive rearing systems with pig units of up to 300 animals. Pig rearing has become so important that Brittany is now France's greatest pig producing region with a third of the total pork meat production. Originally for local consumption the fresh pork is now despatched to meet national requirements and to the many small firms which produce fresh and canned pork meat, *charcuterie*.

Horses. – Once famous, horse breeding has now considerably decreased. Colts are sold as draught animals or, as foals, to the butchers for meat. The most prized of the draught animals are the Léon post horses, formerly a great attraction at the Landivisiau and Morlaix horse fairs.

Poultry. – Poultry farming is suitable to the smallholdings and abundant labour to be found in the region and has been increasingly successful in recent years (one third of the national production) often becoming fully commercial units. The Côtes-du-Nord, where there are most farms, has a poultry research centre at Ploufragan and heads the list with Finistère in the production of chickens and eggs.

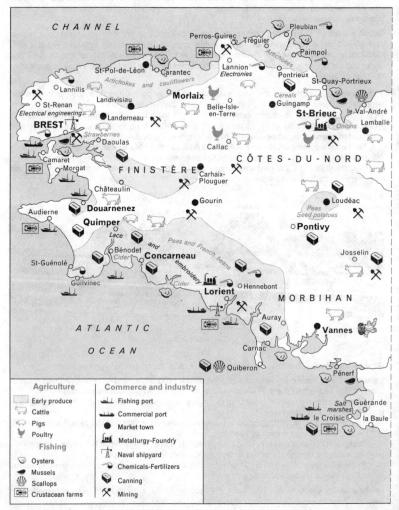

FISHING AND THE PRODUCTS OF THE SEA

Though not as important as agriculture, the contribution made by the sea is an essential part of the Breton economy, and the Bretons themselves, if one is to believe a well known proverb, "are born with the waters of the sea flowing round their hearts".

Lorient and Concarneau are the two most important fishing ports in France after Boulogne, and Brittany is the greatest fishing region both in monetary value and size of the catch (percentage of total French catch: 41 per cent for fish; 67 per cent for crustaceans). Modern methods have been adopted: deep sea trawling, purse seiners for sardines and tunny, and trawler freezers.

The fishing ports. – There are countless little harbours along the Breton coast where just a few boats lie stranded on the sand at low tide, for the peninsula is rich in natural harbours. But, with the exception of St-Malo, the big harbours – namely Concarneau, Lorient, Douarnenez, Guilvinec, Camaret, Quiberon and St-Guénolé – are on the south coast. Even though nearly all the sailing ships now have engines and modern trawlers have replaced the tunny boats with their coloured sails and the sardine boats with their characteristic blue nets, the fishing ports still have a great appeal, particularly the smaller ones.

In the larger ports, modernisation of the boats has been accompanied by modernisation of the harbour installations: erection of warehouses linked to the main railway system and cold stores; means of storage and fuel, loading, construction of additional anchorages and breakwaters and the modernisation of handling gear.

Modern methods have often led to changes in the running of the industry. The head of each business is the owner or part owner of the boat whose crew are paid on a percentage basis of the catch. Recently, however, owners and builders in the big harbours have often combined to compete in a difficult market with severe competition especially from the Russians.

Coastal fishing. – All along the coast there is inshore fishing. Boats which sail and return on the tide, bring in fresh fish such as sole, mullet, turbot, skate, bass, sea-bream, mackerel, crustaceans, scallops, etc. Even so the catch is not nearly enough for local needs, and a town like St-Brieuc on the north side of the peninsula receives supplementary supplies from Lorient in the south.

On the Atlantic coast the season for sardine fishing lasts from June to September some 50 to 80 per cent depending on the size of the catch, is despatched to the canneries. In winter the sardine boats are used for trawling, lobster and crab fishing.

Deep sea fishing. – Trawlers operating in the Bay of Biscay, Irish Sea and off the coasts of Iceland bring in most of the fresh fish especially the kinds of fish in great demand. Trawling is the main activity of big ports like Lorient, Concarneau and Douarnenez.

For **tunny** fishing both live bait and nets are used in the Bay of Biscay and seine nets along the African coasts.

The white tunny is fished from June to October: starting somewhere between Portugal and the Azores, the season ends in the Bay of Biscay.

Tropical or albacore tunny is the quarry of a fleet of over thirty boats with refrigerated holds, equipped at Concarneau and operating from the ports of West Africa during the season.

Cod fishing. – The cod fishing fleets operate in the fisheries of Newfoundland, Labrador and Greenland. Paimpol and St-Malo were once renowned for their cod fleets but now only St-Malo has connections with the cod fishing. The fleets are currently undergoing reorganization since public preference has shifted from salted to frozen cod. The trawlers have become veritable factories with mechanical filetting and freezing equipment on board. Frozen fish represents one quarter of the total cod catch. St-Malo is the number one port for frozen cod and third in importance for the salted product.

Crustaceans. – Much crustacean fishing takes place along the rocky coasts using lobster pots and traps, but long distance fishing using all the modern equipment is also common.

The lobster boats with refrigeration plants, from Camaret, Audierne and Douarnenez leave for the coast of Mauretania for several months at a time. The boats are equipped with tanks as well as freezing plants.

When the boats return to harbour, part of the catch is put into storage beds. These are situated at many points round the coast, the most important lying between Primel and Audierne.

17

(After Yvon photo, Paris)

Tunny boats put to sea, before motorisation.

Oysters and shellfish. – Oysters, mussels, scallops, cockles, clams, razor-clams, limpets and winkles are to be found everywhere along the shore.

Conchyliculture or oyster and mussel breeding has now become commercially important. Oysters are ready for harvesting in three to five years.

Brittany, which has for long been the great production region for flat oysters (Belons) and which has increased that production considerably since the 1950s, has also developed its Portuguese oyster beds and, above all, its mussel beds. The positions of the different cultivation beds has been strictly laid down because of the incompatibility biologically of oysters and mussels on the one hand and the flat and Portuguese oysters on the other.

Oysters. – The beds in the Morbihan specialise in breeding. However, some of the brood-oysters have been imported from Japan. The tiny oysters, measuring about three-tenths of a millimetre each, float with the current until they reach and attach themselves to the specially placed lime washed tiles. Eight months later they are taken off the tiles and placed in the beds – this operation is known as the *détroquage*. After two or three years when they have attained the correct size, they are sent to the "nurseries" or maturing centres where after another year they will go through the purifying centre (*dégorgeoir*) and the *trompage* which accustoms the oysters to hold sea water in their shells when they close their valves.

The biggest maturing beds on the Channel coast lie off Cancale and Morlaix and on the Atlantic in the Bélon and Pénerf river estuaries.

Mussels. – Mussel breeding was originally introduced to the region in 1235 by Walton, an Irish navigator, in the Aiguillon Bay. Reintroduced in 1957 it was taken up in the Mont-St-Michel Bay and in the region lying between the Rance Estuary and Cape Fréhel (the Bay of La Fresnaye). The mussel spawn is collected *captage* and transplanted to the upstanding poles known as *bouchots*, where they mature. Growth is regular and they are harvested eighteen to thirty months afterwards.

In the harbour of Douarnenez. — A tunny boat, a trawler and a lobster boat.

Algae and marine fertilisers. – Algae a raw material for the chemical industry (iodine, soda, alginates, etc.), and above all ordinary seaweed, have for long been harvested and used as fertilisers. The Bretons also use shelly sand from beaches, sea mud and maërl (sand from banks containing calcified algae, found around Paimpol) to improve the soil. According to a local saying these sands change "gorse to clover and rye grass to wheat"; they can be used either in their natural form or as a processed product.

18

INDUSTRY

Till recently *(p 15)* Brittany, with the exception of the Loire Estuary, was recognised as an under-industrialised region. Any existing industry was generally linked to the sea, agriculture, passing maritime traffic and the construction industry (building and public works).

In an astonishingly short time a great stimulus was given to the industrial development of the region when many large firms decentralised and engaged in training schemes and research programmes often assisted by local universities. Industrial growth was further encouraged by the enterprising spirit of the local younger generation thus disproving the statement of their compatriot Renan: "That never was a race more unsuited to industry or commerce."

The new industries were often of a technically very advanced nature: space electronics at Pleumeur-Bodou, tidal generated electricity at La Rance and nuclear energy at Brennilis. Further possibilities for expansion are offered by the renewed exploration for petrol oil in the Iroise Sea off Finistère (earlier tentative searches had been made in 1975-6) and the exploitation of recently discovered mineral deposits: copper; zinc and iron in the Noires Mountains; titanium in the south of the Ille-et-Vilaine department.

Recent development means that apart from the tertiary sector, industry is the most active one in the regional economy.

Building industry and public works. – Although stationary this remains the dominant sector.

Metallurgy. – Apart from the steelworks at St-Brieuc and Ploërmel there is little metallurgy although foundries exist at Lorient, Nantes and St-Brieuc. There are a greater number of metal processing industries and these are widely dispersed: they include tins for the canning industry and agricultural implements. Châteaubriant, for example, manufactures nearly one third of all French ploughs. The more important industries are often of recent growth: boiler making at St-Nazaire, Michelin at Vannes; domestic hot water boilers at St-Brieuc; gas lighters at Redon; and two Citroën plants at Rennes employing 14 000 workers.

Naval shipyards. – Half of all the ships built in France come from the Breton yards. The Atlantic Dockyard at St-Nazaire can now build vessels up to 500 000 tons. Most of the fishing boats (of smaller tonnage and steel built) come from Lorient and St-Malo. Pleasure craft are built in a variety of places. Ships for the French Navy come from the yards at Brest (8 000 workers) or Lorient (4 300 workers).

Agricultural food products. – The industry based on local agricultural food products holds a most important place in the national economy with more than half the total output of the country and provides a natural outlet for local produce.

Fish canneries. – Brittany enjoys superiority in this field, producing two thirds of the national total. Sardines, mackerel, white and albacore tunny are all canned in the factories round the coast, particularly in the Penmarch region, at Douarnenez, Concarneau, Quiberon and Nantes.

Vegetable canneries. – These are equally important and lie round the coast near the areas producing the early vegetables. The best known products are canned peas, French beans, artichoke hearts and mixed vegetables.

Meat canneries. – These are almost all concerned with the canning of pork products. There is an ever growing number of curing (salting) plants. The factories are mostly in the interior.

Creameries are numerous in Ille-et-Vilaine and Finistère, while other plants make pork and poultry based products.

Wood, paper and packaging materials. – Wood based activities and furniture making are both expanding industries. In Finistère, and especially at Rennes, there are factories making packaging materials/products. Cigarette paper is made at Scaër, Quimperlé and Ergué-Gabéric. Printers are also fairly numerous, the main centre being at Rennes.

Textiles and leather. – The manufacturing of ready to wear clothes and hosiery is localised in the east (Ille-et-Vilaine) and west (Finistère) of the country. Tanneries are sited in the north of Finistère, fancy leather goods are produced at Plancoët and the declining shoe manufacturing trade is centred on Fougères and Rosporden.

Mining industries. – Though there are only a few such industries, they have maintained a certain importance. The most noteworthy are the kaolin works, and slate quarries particularly those of the Châteaulin and Carhaix-Plouguer areas, the tin mines of St-Renan (Finistère), and the granite quarries of which the best known is the Kersanton near Logonna (Finistère) – its stone was much used in Breton statuary.

The ancillary industries include glass making at Fougères, ceramics at Quimper, and building materials (bricks, cement and reinforced concrete) at Rennes and elsewhere.

Chemicals and marine products. – The main products are fertilisers, dyes, varnish, perfume and rubber (St-Brieuc). Immense modern plants – the largest is at Pleubian – process seaweed for alginates which are found in a diverse range of products such as foodstuffs (biscuits), cosmetics and plastics. Other small plants along the coast manufacture iodine and soda, refine marl *(p 18)* and process fish offal for use in fertilisers, animal feed and chemical products.

Other industries. – Whether State controlled or private the other industries, all of a diverse nature, are highly scattered throughout the region and include military workshops at Rennes and Bruz (Ille-et-Vilaine), a tobacco plant at Morlaix and factories manufacturing plastic goods, toys, etc.

LOCAL CRAFTS

The list below gives a general idea of the range:
Brush-making: St-Brieuc
Dolls in regional costumes: Pont-Aven, Pont-l'Abbé, St-Brieuc.
Handwoven linen: Dinan, Locronan.
Hosiery: Dinan, Rennes.
Lace and fine embroidery: Pont-L'Abbé, Quimper, Rennes.
Porcelain: Quimper.
Wrought iron work: Lannion, Quimper, Rennes, Vitré.

HISTORICAL FACTS

British and American historical events

BC	

Ancient Armor

6C	The Gauls arrive in the peninsula. They give it the name of Armor (country of the sea). A little known people who set up many megaliths were there before them.
56	Caesar destroys the fleet of the Veneti, the most powerful tribe in Armor (details p 124), and conquers the whole country.
AD	
	For four centuries Roman civilisation does its work. Then the barbarian invasions wreck Armor, which returns almost to savagery.

Armor becomes Brittany

460	Arrival of the first Celts from Britain, driven from their homes by the Angles and Saxons. Immigration continues for two centuries. These colonists revive and convert Armor and give it a new name, Little Britain, later shortened to Brittany. The Breton people make saints of their religious leaders, who become the patrons of many towns in the peninsula (details p 22). The political state, made up of innumerable parishes, remains anarchic.
799	Charlemagne subjugates all Brittany.

The Duchy of Brittany

826	Louis the Pious makes Nominoé, a noble of Vannes, Duke of Brittany (details p 181).
845	Nominoé throws off Frankish suzerainty by defeating Charles the Bald, near Redon. He brings all of Brittany under his sway and founds an independent ducal dynasty which lasts for more than a century.
851	Erispoë takes the title, King of Brittany. He was later assassinated by his cousin Salomon who reigned from 857.
874	Assassination of Salomon. During his reign the kingdom of Brittany reached its zenith embracing both Anjou and Cotentin.
919	Great Norman invasion. Rapine and pillage.
939	Duke Alain Barbe-Torte drives out the last Normans.
952	Death of Alain, the last King of Brittany, in the fortresses built all over the country to resist the Normans, the nobles defy the successors of Barbe-Torte. There follows a period of disorder and poverty which lasts until nearly the end of the 14C.
1066	William the Conqueror lands in England.
1215	Magna Carta.
1337	Start of the Hundred Years War ending in 1453.
1341	The War of Succession begins at the death of Duke Jean III. His niece, Jeanne de Penthièvre, wife of Charles de Blois, supported by the French, and her brother Jean of Montfort, ally of the English, contend for the Duchy.
1351	Battle of the Thirty (details p 108).
1364	Charles of Blois, though aided by Du Guesclin, is defeated and killed at Auray (details p 52). Brittany emerges ruined from this war.

The Montforts

1364-1468	The Dukes of the House of Montfort restore the country. This is the most brilliant period of its history. The arts reach their highest development. The dukes are the real sovereigns and pay homage only in theory to the King of France. Constable de Richmont (p 183), the companion in arms to Joan of Arc succeeded his brother in 1457 as Duke of Brittany.
1488	Duke François II, who has entered into the federal coalition against the Regent of France, Anne of Beaujeu, is defeated at St-Aubin-du-Cormier and dies. His daughter, Anne of Brittany, succeeds him.

Reunion of Brittany with France

1491	Anne of Brittany marries Charles VIII (details p 156) but remains Duchess and sovereign of Brittany.
1492	Christopher Columbus discovers America.
1498	Charles VIII dies accidentally. Anne returns to her Duchy.
1499	Anne again becomes Queen of France by marrying Louis XII, who had hastily repudiated his first wife. The Duchy remains distinct from the Crown (details p 181).
1514	Anne of Brittany dies. Her daughter, Claude of France, inherits the Duchy. She marries François of Angoulême, the future François I.
1532	Claude cedes her Duchy to the Crown. François I has this permanent reunion of Brittany with France ratified by the Parliament at Vannes.

French Brittany

1534	Jacques Cartier discovers the St. Lawrence estuary (details p 167).
1588	Brittany rebels against its governor, the Duke of Mercœur, who wants to profit by the troubles of the League to seize the province. Bandits like the famous La Fontenelle ravage the country (details p 87).
1598	By the Edict of Nantes, Henri IV puts an end to religious strife (details p 128).
1675	The "Stamped Paper" revolt (details p 145) which develops into a peasants' rising.
1711	Duguay-Trouin (details p 167) takes Rio de Janeiro.
1764	The Rennes parliament and its Public Prosecutor, La Chalotais, oppose Governor of Aiguillon (p 157). The authority of the Crown is much weakened. The Revolution is near.

1765	Arrival on Belle-Ile of many Canadian families of French origin from Nova Scotia (*p 56*).
1773	Birth of Surcouf, the Breton pirate (*p 168*).
1776	American Declaration of Independence.
1789	The Bretons welcome the Revolution with enthusiasm.
1793	Carrier executes thousands by drowning in the Loire near Nantes (*details p 128*).
1794	The Laws against the priests and the mass levies give rise to the *Chouannerie* (revolt of Breton Royalists).
1795	A landing by Royalists exiles is defeated at Quiberon (*details p 147*).
1804	Cadoudal (*details p 52*), who tried to revive the *Chouannerie*, is executed.
1832	Another attempted revolt, organised by the Duchess de Berry, fails (*details p 128*). This was the last rising.
1861	Start of American Civil War.
1909	Strikes and riots among the Concarneau cannery workers.
1914-18	Brittany pays a heavy toll in loss of life during the First World War.

Brittany today

1927-28	The Morbihan aviator Le Brix, accompanied by Costes, are the first to fly round the world.
1940	The islanders of Sein (*p 176*) are the first to rally to General de Gaulle's call.
1942	An Anglo-Canadian commando raids the St-Nazaire submarine base (*p 172*).
1944-45	The end of the German Occupation period witnesses a wake of destruction, especially at Brest, Lorient, St-Nazaire.
1951	Formation of the organisation Comité d'Etudes et de Liaison des Intérêts Bretons to safeguard Breton interests, is an initial step towards the rejuvenation of the local economy.
1962	First transatlantic transmission by satellite of a television programme by the station at Pleumeur-Bodou (*p 139*).
1966	The opening of the Rance tidal power scheme (*p 155*) and the Arrée Mountains nuclear station near Brennilis.
1967	The *Torrey Canyon* disaster off the English coast, causes great oil slicks to hit the beaches of Brittany.
1969	Creation of the Armorique Regional Nature Park (*p 49*).
1975	First search for oil in the Iroise Sea off the Finistère coast.
1978	Establishment of a charter and council to safeguard the Breton cultural heritage. *Amoco Cadiz* oil spill on Brittany beaches.

Principal Campaigns of Du Guesclin

Bertrand du Guesclin, born at La Motte-Broons Castle, near Dinan, was one of France's greatest warriors. Entering the King's service, he was dubbed knight on the capture of Rennes (1356). Subsequent victories (*see map below*) brought further titles: Governor of Pontorson (1360), Count of Longueville (1364), Duke of Molina and Transtamarre (1366), King of Granada (1369), High Constable of France (1370). His campaigns, mostly against the English and their allies had brought about considerable expansion of the crown lands by his death in 1380 (*p 82*).

① **1356** Capture of Rennes.

② **1359** Liberation of Dinan.

③ **1363** Capture of Breton towns. From St-Pol-de-Léon Du Guesclin sends ships against the English.

④ **1364** Capture of Mantes and Meulan.

⑤ (May 16) Victory of Cocherel.

⑥ (Sept. 29) Defeat of Auray. Du Guesclin made prisoner.

⑦ **1366** "The Great Companies", commanded by Du Guesclin, march into Spain. A series of victories over Peter the Cruel and the English brings the French to Seville.

1367 (April 3) Defeat of Najera: Du Guesclin made prisoner and taken by the English to Bordeaux.

1369 (Jan. 17) Du Guesclin ransomed and returns to Spain.

(March) Siege of Montiel Castle; Peter the Cruel killed; Du Guesclin returns to France.

⑧ **1370** Capture of Moissac and liberation of Périgord.

⑨ Liberation of Le Mans. Victory of Pontvallain. Liberation of Maine and Anjou.

⑩ Capture of Bressuire.

⑪ Defeat of Pont de Juigné. Du Guesclin made prisoner.

⑫ **1371** Capture of Briouze.

⑬ **1372** Victory of Mortain. The Norman Bocage is freed.

⑭ **1372-3** Capture of towns in Poitou, Saintonge and Angoumois.

⑮ **1373** All Brittany conquered except Brest and Derval.

⑯ **1374** Capture of St-Sauveur-le-Vicomte.

⑰ **1378** All Normandy conquered except Cherbourg.

⑱ **1380** (June 27) Capture of Chaliers.

⑲ (July 13-14) Capture of Châteauneuf-de-Randon. Death of Du Guesclin.

(From documents supplied by the Museum of French Monuments at the Palais de Chaillot, Paris)

21

TRADITIONS AND REGIONALISM

A LAND OF LEGENDS

The Breton soul has always been inclined to the dreamy, the fantastic and the supernatural. This explains the astonishing abundance and persistence of legends in the Armor country.

The Round Table. – After the death of Christ, Joseph of Arimathea, one of His disciples, left Palestine, carrying away a few drops of the divine blood in the cup from which the Redeemer drank during the Last Supper. He landed in Britain according to some legends, in Brittany according to others, lived for some time in the forest of Brocéliande (now the forest of Paimpont) before vanishing without trace. The precious cup was lost.

In the 6C King Arthur and fifty knights set out to find it. For them it was the Holy Grail, which only a warrior whose heart was pure could win. Perceval (Wagner's Parsifal) was such a man. In the Middle Ages the search for the Grail gave rise to the endless stories of adventure which formed the Cycle of the Round Table. The most famous version of the tale in English being, of course, Sir Thomas Malory's *Morte d'Arthur* (1471) and Alfred Lord Tennyson's *Idylls of the King* (1859).

Merlin and Viviane. – One of Arthur's companions, Merlin the sorcerer, came to the forest of Brocéliande to live there in seclusion. But he met the fairy Viviane, and love inflamed them both. To make sure of keeping Merlin, Viviane enclosed him in a magic circle. It would have been easy for him to escape, but he joyfully accepted this romantic captivity for ever.

Tristan and Iseult. – Tristan, Prince of Lyonesse, being sent to Ireland by his Uncle Mark, King of Cornwall, brought back Iseult, whom Mark was to marry. On board their ship Tristan and Iseult accidentally drank a philtre which was intended to bind Iseult to her husband in eternal love. Passion stronger than duty sprang up in both their hearts. There are several versions of the end: sometimes Tristan is slain by Mark, furious at his betrayal; sometimes he marries and dies in his castle in Brittany. But Iseult always follows him to the grave. Wagner's opera has made the love story famous.

The town of Is. – At the time of good **King Gradlon**, about the 6C, Is was the capital of Cornouaille; finds claimed as belonging to Is have been discovered in Trépassés and Douarnenez Bays and off Penmarch Peninsula. The town was so beautiful that according to a Breton tradition the inhabitants of Lutetia, seeking a name for their own proud city, chose Par-is ("like Is"), whence the name: Paris. The town was protected from the sea by a dyke, opened by locks to which the King always carried the golden key.

His daughter, the beautiful Dahut, also called Ahès, who led a dissolute life, met the Devil in the form of an attractive young man. To test her love he asked her to open the sea gate. Dahut stole the key while the King was asleep, and soon the sea rushed into the town. King Gradlon fled on horseback, with his daughter on the crupper. But the waves pursued him and were about to swallow him up. At this moment a celestial voice ordered him, if he would be saved, to throw the demon who was riding behind him into the sea. With aching heart the King obeyed and the sea withdrew at once, but Is was destroyed.

For his new capital Gradlon chose Quimper; this is why his statue stands between the two towers of the cathedral. He ended his days in the odour of sanctity, guided and sustained by St. Corentin. As for Dahut, she turned into the mermaid, who is known as Marie-Morgane and, by her beauty, still lures sailors to the bottom of the sea. Everything will stay exactly as it is until the Good Friday when Mass is celebrated in one of the churches of the drowned city. Then Is will cease to be accursed and Morgane will no longer be a siren.

THE SAINTS OF BRITTANY

Brittany, with its magicians, spirits, fairies and demons – both masculine and feminine – has also known more haloes than any other part of France. Its saints are counted by hundreds; their painted wooden statues adorn chapels and churches. Truth to tell, those (St. Yves for example) who were canonised by the Vatican authorities can be counted on one's fingers. The most "official" among them were simply recognised by the bishops; the people adopted others. Their fame goes no farther than the borders of the province, or even the limits of the villages where they are venerated.

(For the purposes of this guide the names of saints of purely local standing have been left in their original form.)

Patrons of towns. – The Celtic religious leaders who landed from Britain in the 5C *(p 20: Historical Facts)* became the patron saints of the seven former bishoprics: St-Malo, St-Brieuc, St-Pol-de-Léon, Dol (St. Samson), Tréguier (St. Tugdual), Quimper (St. Corentin) and Vannes (St. Patern). The same applies to many other localities: St-Efflam, St-Lunaire, St-Briac, St-Gildas, etc.

Until the 16C, tradition demanded that every Breton should make a pilgrimage to the cathedrals at least once in his life; this was called the Tro Breiz (tour of Brittany). Whoever failed to observe this rite was bound to make the journey after his death, when he could cover only the length of his coffin every seven years!

The "healing saints". – The Bretons have always been on trustful, friendly and even familiar terms with their saints.

There are saints who are invoked on all occasions. Innumerable others are invoked against specified ailments: rheumatism, baldness, etc. For centuries they took the place of doctors. Horses and oxen also have their appointed saints (St. Cornély and St. Herbot).

" Healing " saints.

(Moncontour and Cast)

On the left, St. Mamert (cures colic) ; in the centre, St. Tugen (any key that has touched the key he carries will drive away mad dogs) ; on the right, St. Livertin (cures headaches).

Saint Yves. – "Monsieur Saint Yves" is the most popular saint in Brittany. He is the righter of all wrongs: whoever suffers injustice turns to him. He is the comfort of the poor.

Yves Helori, the son of a country gentleman, was born at Minihy-Tréguier in 1253. When quite young he had a taste for the ascetic life. He came to Paris to study law, and unravelled its subtleties for thirteen years. On his return to Brittany he became a priest, and at the bishop's palace of Tréguier acted as a magistrate in one court and as an advocate in others.

He won unheard-of popularity by his spirit of justice and conciliation, the rapidity of his judgments and the brevity of his pleas. One day a *bourgeois* summoned before him a beggar who came every day to the grating of his kitchen to enjoy the smell of cooking. Yves took a coin, made it ring on the bench and dismissed the plaintiff, saying: "The sound has paid for the smell." In order not to "cut out" the barristers Yves always chose the most wretched cases, and thus became known as the "poor man's counsel". In fact, he was a precursor of free legal aid. He was canonised in 1347.

As the patron saint of advocates and men of law, his cult has spread all over Europe. And within the last few years delegations of barristers from Britain, Belgium, Holland, Luxembourg and even America have joined the unceasing stream of pilgrims who attend the blessing of the poor *(pardon des pauvres)* at Tréguier *(p 10)*.

(After Arthaud photo, Nantes)

Huelgoat. — St-Yves.

He receives the poor man's petition and refuses the rich man's purse.

(After Hamonic photo, St-Brieuc)

St. Apolline.
(La Houssaie Chapel, near Pontivy)

The executioner begins her martyrdom by pulling out one of her teeth.

The calendar saints. – Mystical Brittany has made a place among its innumerable saints for the great figures of the Church. Statues of the Apostles line church porches and stand on Calvaries; St. Michael is the patron of high places; St. James, that of sailors; St. Fiacre of gardeners. St. Barbara, who is invoked in stormy weather, is the patroness of corporations which handle explosives (her father, who had her martyred, was killed by lightning). St. Apolline protects people from toothache *(see illustration above)*, and many others have an established cult. The Virgin Mary is the most fervently invoked of the saints.

(After CAP photo, Paris)

Open   Closed

Morlaix. — Opening statue of the Virgin.

Saint Anne. – The cult of Saint Anne was brought to western Europe by those returning from the Crusades. Her eager adoption by the Bretons was in part due to the popularity of the Duchess, Anne of Brittany and her later renown. Patroness of Brittany and mother of the Virgin Mary, Saint Anne was originally invoked for a good harvest. The most famous *pardon* in Brittany, that of Ste-Anne-d'Auray, is dedicated to her, so is the very important one of Ste-Anne-la-Palud and hence the local saying, "Whether dead or alive, every Breton goes at least once to Saint-Anne."

A doubtful legend makes St. Anne a Cornouaille woman of royal blood who was taken to Nazareth by angels to save her from her husband's brutality. After having given birth to the Virgin Mary she returned to Brittany to die. It was Jesus who, when visiting his grandmother, called forth the sacred spring of Ste-Anne-la-Palud.

The statues usually portray her alone or teaching Mary to read, very often wearing a green cloak symbolising hope for the world.

THE PARDONS

The Breton *pardons* are above all a manifestation of religious fervour. They take place in the churches and chapels, sometimes consecrated by the tradition of a thousand years. There the faithful come to seek forgiveness for their sins, to fulfil a vow or to beg for grace.

The great *pardons* are most impressive, while the smaller, though less spectacular, are often more fervent. It is well worth the tourist's while to arrange his trip so that he may be present at one of them *(list p 10)*.

It is also one of the rare occasions when he will see the old costumes, occasionally slightly modernised.

The procession, which begins in the afternoon, is the most curious ceremony: candles, banners and statues of saints are carried by men and girls; with pilgrims singing hymns, priests, the Blessed Sacrament, and sometimes even several bishops.

After the procession, the lay festival is given free rein. As a rule this is a rather ordinary fair. Modern dances are taking the place of the gavotte but bagpipes and bombards still hold their own against accordions and jazz. Sometimes there are wrestling matches, for **wrestling** is a traditional sport of the Breton peasants. The wrestlers, wearing short cloth breeches and blouses with cloth belts, exchange three loud kisses and then seize

(After Dr le Thomas photo)

Pardon at Penhors. — Bigouden procession.

one another by the back of the neck, trip one another and struggle in silence before breathless and attentive audiences.

COSTUMES AND HEAD-DRESSES

Costumes. – Brittany possesses costumes of surprising richness and variety. The fine clothes passed down from one generation to another were to be seen at every family festivity. It was customary for a girl at her marriage to acquire a costly and magnificent outfit that would last many years. Today the traditional costumes are only brought out on great occasions such as *pardons*, First Communions, weddings, baptisms and sometimes High Mass on feast days, and even then few young women are to be seen in them.

In spite of attempts to modernise the dress, and the efforts of regional societies over the last few years – and they have had some success – to make the young appreciate the old finery the tourist who travels quickly through Brittany is not likely to see many of the rich, traditional dresses made familiar by picture postcards and books on the subject.

Here and there a few old men have remained faithful to their beribboned felt hats, and more rarely, to their embroidered waistcoats. The usual costume for the women is a plain black dress.

The women's traditional costumes attract above all by the brilliance of their aprons which reveal how well off the family are by the richness of their decoration. The aprons are made of satin or velvet, are brocaded or embroidered or are edged with lace and are of every size and shape: at Quimper they have no bib, at Pont-Aven they have a small one, while at Lorient the bib reaches to the shoulders. Ceremonial dresses are usually black and are often ornamented with bands of velvet. The finest are at Quimper with their many coloured embroideries.

(After Jean photo)

Plougastel   Pont-l'Abbé   Quimper   Pont-Aven

Head-dresses. – The most original feature of the Breton costume is the *coiffe* or head-dress, now most worn in Finistère and Morbihan. One of the most attractive is the *coiffe* of Pont-Aven which has as an accessory a great starched lace collar. The **Bigoudène** *coiffe* from the **Pont-l'Abbé** area, well known to people in Paris, is one of the most curious: it used to be quite small but has recently become huge. In **Quimper** the *coiffe* is much smaller and is worn on the crown of the head; in **Plougastel**, where tradition is still strong, the *coiffe* has a mediaeval appearance, and in **Tréguier** the plainest of materials is allied to the most original of shapes. The **Douarnenez** *coiffe* is small and fits tightly round the bun on the back of the head, that of **Auray** shades the forehead and that of **Huelgoat** is almost like a lace hair-net.

In order to get a complete picture of the richness and variety of Breton costume the tourist should visit the museums of Quimper, Guérande, Rennes, Dinan, etc., all of which have fine collections of traditional dress.

EVOLUTION AND REGIONALISM

The two Brittanies.–The map below delimits **Upper Brittany** (Haute-Bretagne), or the "Gallo" country, and **Lower Brittany** (Basse-Bretagne), or the Breton-speaking country. French is spoken in the first, French and Breton in the second.

Lower Brittany has four regions, each of which has its customs and brings shades of diversity to the Breton Language. These are: the district of Tréguier or Trégorrois, the district of Léon, the district of Cornouaille and the district of Vannes or Vannetais.

Apart from the language, these limits conform with tradition. It is in Lower Brittany that one is more likely to find the old customs; in Upper Brittany they have hardly left a trace. And the delimitation has not remained fixed.

(After A. Dauzat)

The two Brittanies.

The Breton language. –
From the ethnic and linguistic point of view the Bretons are nearer to the Welsh than to the French. This is because in the 5 and 6C *(p 20)* Armorica (present day Brittany) was invaded by Britons driven from Britain by the Anglo-Saxon invasion. Brittany was founded, and the Breton language opposed the French language, derived from Low Latin.

In the 9C the dynasty of Nominoé *(p 181)* marked the apogee of the Breton nation and the farthest advance of its language *(see map)*. The Norman invasions that followed and feudal rule harmed the unity of Brittany. The annexation of the province to France in the 15C and the French Revolution enhanced the trend in favour of French still further so that nowadays, in Lower Brittany, the domain of the Breton language, only a few of the older peasants still do not understand French.

An association called U.D.B. (Union for the Defence of the Breton Language), after a campaign for the optional teaching of Breton in Lower Brittany, secured this in the secondary and teachers' training schools. The University of Rennes has a chair of Celtic Language and there is a demand for the creation of an Institute of Celtic languages. Can Breton, thanks to regionalism, become, once more, a vital tongue? In the face of emigration, military service, the cinema, radio and the tourist trade, what will be the fate of Breton as a living language?

Rapid development of Brittany. – Brittany changed more in the first half of the 20C than in the two previous centuries. Contacts of Breton soldiers with men from other provinces, and especially the return to their homeland of men who had held administrative or executive posts in the navy, the civil service, commerce and industry, hastened the evolution started by the tourists. The distinctive character of customs, dress and furniture faded away. Villages no longer kept alive a mass of traditional customs and traditional beliefs. Only half the population still know their own language. We hardly ever seen the blind, the maimed, the deaf-and-dumb and the feeble-minded standing in a rather frightening line at the exit from church and gravely accepting, without begging for it, the charity that, traditionally, is their due.

Modern life, which makes originality expensive, has hastened the evolution in furniture and dress. How can one compare the price of a box bed with that of an ordinary brass or iron bedstead; the great, decorated grandfather-clock with the alarm clock; a dresser with shelf units fixed to the wall? How can one compare the price of the costume worn by the women of Pont-Aven, which is one of the finest in Brittany, with that of a ready made dress? For all these reasons, picturesqueness in daily life is losing ground. But the sea, nature, the sky, the light, the traces of the past, the very foundations of the race are everlasting. With a little patience and imagination, especially in the Argoat, it is possible to recapture the simple, mystic and characteristic atmosphere of the Brittany of former days.

Regionalism and Celtic Clubs. – For the past twenty years the provinces have cultivated regionalism. In Brittany a few folklore groups were active, but the movement did not spring from the soil. Before 1939 the Bretons of Paris – who founded the first Celtic Club in 1917 – made it their business to spread an interest in Breton gatherings. At the Liberation the clubs grew; today more than sixty in Brittany revive and bring fame once more to Breton dances, music and costume. Sometimes girls, who want to look their best, wear the *coiffe* and embroidered skirt and apron. The "ringers" (bagpipe and bombard players), who numbered sixty-three in 1939, are now 2 000.

The Congress of Bleun-Brug (a Breton Catholic cultural association) and the folk festivals give opportunities to bring these groups together and to make them compete and give displays greatly enjoyed by those who see them. The vitality of clubs like these is being proved in every part of France and overseas. There are ninety-four associations in Paris and its environs. The Bretons of New York elect a "Duchess Anne" every year.

An ever fruitful race. – Brittany has about 3 000 000 inhabitants (Paris 2 600 000). The excess of births over deaths is very great and is superior to the average figures for the whole of France. Population numbers tend to be stable, in spite of emigration to seek work.

Paris, where colonies of Bretons live around the Gare Montparnasse, and neighbouring regions which are richer but with a lower birthrate such as Anjou, Maine, Normandy and especially Aquitaine and Périgord, welcome these sturdy workers, farm hands, quarrymen, labourers and traders.

If you love natural beauty leave no litter,
no trace of where you have been.

BRETON NAMES

Place-names. – In Brittany, as in other French provinces, place-names have meanings that are often easy to find. Most of them are formed from a root to which the name of a saint is added.

Ploe, plou, plo, or **pleu,** which means parish, has given us: Ploudaniel (Daniel's parish), Plogoff (parish of St. Cof), Ploërmel (parish of St. Armel), Plougastel (parish of the castle), Pleumeur (great parish), Plounevez (new parish), etc.

Tre or **Tref** (parish subdivision) has given: Tréboul, Trégouet, etc.

Loc (holy place) gives: Locmaria (Mary's place), Locronan (place of St. Renan), Locquirec (place of St. Guirec), Locminé (place of monks), etc.

Lann (church) gives: Lannion (church of St. Yon), Lampaul (church of St. Paul), Landerneau (church of St. Ternoc), Langoat (church in the woods), etc.

Ker (village or house) gives: Kermaria (Mary's village), Kerjean (John's village), Kerguen (white village), etc.

Guic, gui (town) gives: Guimiliau (town of St. Méliau), Guisseny (town of St. Seny).

Traon, trou, tro (valley) gives: Tromelin (valley of the mill), Tromeur (great valley), etc.

Coat, goat, goët, hoët (wood) appears in: Huelgoat (high wood), Kergoat (house in the woods), Penhoët (end of the wood), Toulgoët (hollow in the wood), etc.

Family names. – Many are formed from the word Ker (house) followed by a distorted Christian name: Kerber (House of Peter), Kerbol (House of Paul), Kerjean (House of John), Kertanguy (House of Tanguy), etc.

Other names indicate professions: Le Barazer (cooper), Le Goff (blacksmith), Le Goffic (tinker), Le Gonidec (ploughman), Quémeneur (tailor), Le Tocquer (hatter), Le Trocquer (second-hand dealer), etc.

Nicknames are also widely used: Le Bihan (small), Le Braz (big), Le Bail (marked on the forehead), Cudenec (mournful), Cosmao (jolly old man), Le Fur (wise man), Gallouédec (powerful), Le Moigne (one-armed), Le Troadec (man with big feet), Le Guen, Guennec, Guennoc (white man), Le Dantec (toothy), Le Cornec (horned), Le Pennec (obstinate), etc.

BRETON FOOD AND DRINK

Breton cooking is characterised more by the quality of the materials used than by fine preparation. Some of the local dishes may be eaten at tea-time.

Sea food, crustaceans and fish. – Shellfish, crustaceans and fish are all first class. Particularly outstanding are the lobsters, grilled or stuffed clams, scallops, shrimps, crisp batter covered fried fish morsels and crab pasties. Belon oysters, Armorican oysters from Concarneau, La Forêt and Ile-Tudy, and Cancale oysters are all well known in France, but are not at their best until the end of the tourist season.

In Breton hotels the king of the table is the lobster. It is served grilled or with cream and especially in a *coulis*, the rich hot sauce which makes the dish called "Armoricaine" or "a l'Américaine" (the latter name is due to a mistake made in a Paris restaurant).

Try also *cotriade* (a Breton fish soup like *bouillabaisse*), the Aulne or Élorn salmon, trout from the Arrée and the Noires Mountains, or pike and shad served with "white butter" in the district near the Loire. This is a sauce made from slightly salted butter, vinegar and shallots, and its preparation requires real skill. Finally, there are *civelles* (eel roes), which are a speciality of Nantes.

Meat, vegetables and fruit. – The salt pasture sheep of the coast are famous. Breton leg of mutton (with white beans) is part of the great French gastronomic heritage. Grey partridges and heath hares are tasty as are the chickens from Rennes and Nantais ducks. Pork butchers' meat is highly flavoured: Morlaix ham, bacon, black pudding, smoked sausage from Guéméné-sur-Scorff and chitterlings from Quimperlé.

Potatoes, artichokes, cauliflowers and green peas are the glory of the Golden Belt. There are also strawberries from Plougastel and many other fruits.

Pancakes, cakes and sweetmeats. – Most towns have *crêperies* (pancake shops) where pancakes made of wheat or buckwheat are served with cider or, for those who like it, with yoghurt. In some of the smaller picturesque shops you may see them made. Others, more modern and with Breton furniture, offer more handsome surroundings, perhaps, but not better pancakes. There is the plain, bare pancake the Breton has enjoyed for centuries, and also modern variations with jam, cheese, eggs, ham, salad, etc. The buckwheat pancake is eaten with salt and the wheat one with sugar.

Other cakes (lace pancakes at Quimper, Breton *galettes* or flat scones, Nantes biscuits, Quintin oat and cream cakes) find many devotees as do Rennes pralines, and Nantes *berlingots* (sweet drops).

Cider, Muscadet and Rhuys wine. – The local drink is cider. Except for that made at Fouesnant and Beg-Meil, however, it is inferior to Normandy cider. The only Breton wine is Muscadet which is found all over Brittany. The people of Nantes guard it jealously and have founded the "Order of Bretvins" in its honour. The grapes are grown only around Nantes, on the slopes that border the Sèvre. This white wine, dry and fruity, is specially recommended to drink with oysters and shellfish. The Muscadet Tour *(see Michelin Green Guide Côte de l'Atlantique – in French only)* takes in the best producing districts.

Vines still grow on the Rhuys peninsula, but the wine drawn from them is a subject of Breton humour. "To drink it", the Bretons say, "you need four men and a wall: one man to pour it out, one to drink, two to hold him up and the wall to stop him from falling backwards." Distilled, on the other hand, it produces an excellent brandy.

If you like crêpes, sea food ... consult the table p 45.

BRETON ART

PREHISTORIC MONUMENTS

The megaliths or "great stones". – More than 3 000 "great stones" are still to be found in the Carnac district alone. These monuments were set up between 5000 and 2000 BC by the little known race who preceded the Gauls. They must have had a certain degree of civilisation to be able to move and set upright stones which weigh up to 350 tons. To give a simple comparison, the Luxor obelisk in the Place de la Concorde in Paris, weighs only 220 tons.

(After Basuyau photo)

Single menhir.

(After TCF Records)

A dolmen.

The **menhir**, or single stone was set up at a spring near a tomb and more often on a slope. It must have had a symbolic meaning. In Brittany there are about twenty menhirs over twenty feet high; the biggest is at Locmariaquer *(p 116)*.

The **lines of menhirs** are probably the remains of religious monuments associated with the worship of the sun or moon. Most are formed by only a few menhirs set in line (many of the menhirs now isolated are the remains of more complicated groups). There are, however, especially in the Carnac area *(p 69)* fields of menhirs arranged in parallel lines running from east to west and ending in a semicircle or **cromlech**. In the Lagatjar area *(p 79)* the lines intersect. The lines of the menhirs appear also to be astronomically set, with an error of not more than one degree, either by the cardinal points of the compass, or in line with sunrise and sunset at the solstices from which it has been concluded that sun worship had something to do with the purpose of the monuments.

(After Yvon photo, Paris)

Carnac. — Kermario Lines.

As for the **dolmens** (the best known is the Merchants' Table at Locmariaquer – *p 116*), these are considered to have been burial chambers. Some known as **passage graves** are preceded by an ante-chamber or corridor. Originally all were buried under mounds of earth or dry stones called **tumuli** but most of them have been uncovered and now stand in the open air. The round tumuli found in the interior are of more recent date than the tumuli with closed chambers like the one of St-Michel at Carnac *(p 69)* and the former were probably built up to 1000 BC. **Cairns** are tumuli composed entirely of stones such as the ones at Barnenez *(p 53)* which dates back over 5000 BC and at Gavrinis *(p 97)* which is not so old.

In northern Brittany **gallery graves** or **covered alleyways**, are formed of a double row of upright stones with flat slabs laid on them, sometimes engraved.

Mystical tradition. – For long centuries the menhirs were connected with the mystic life of Brittany. The Romans adapted some to their rites, carving pictures of their gods upon them. When the Christian religion was established, it sanctified many raised stones that people still venerated by crowning them with a cross or cutting symbols on them.

CHURCHES AND CHAPELS

Nine cathedrals or former cathedrals, about twenty large churches and thousands of country churches and chapels make up an array of religious buildings altogether worthy of mystical Brittany.

The edifices were built by the people and designed by artists who transmitted to them an inspired faith. This faith appeared in a richness that was sometimes excessive – the exaggeratedly decorated altarpieces are an example – and a realism that was at times almost a caricature – as, for instance, the carvings on certain capitals and many church beams. Only affected in part by outside influences, they always preserved their individuality and remained faithful to their own traditions.

Cathedrals. – These are inspired by the great buildings in Normandy and the Ile-de-France, although they do not rival their prototypes either in size or ornamentation. The little towns that built them had limited means. Moreover, their erection was influenced by the use of granite, a hard stone, difficult to work. The builders had to be content with rather low vaulting and simplified decoration.

Financial difficulties dragged out the work for three to five centuries. Owing to this, every phase of Gothic architecture is found in the buildings, from the bare and simple arch of early times to the wild exuberance of the Flamboyant style; and the Renaissance often added the last touches.

The most interesting cathedrals are those of St-Pol-de-Léon, Tréguier, Quimper, Nantes and Dol-de-Bretagne.

The corresponding Gothic period in England, lasted until the end of the 13C and included in whole or in part the cathedrals of Wells (1174), Lincoln (chancel and transept: 1186), Salisbury (1220-58), Westminster Abbey (c 1250) and Durham (1242).

Country churches and chapels. – In the Romanesque period (11 and 12C) Brittany was miserably poor. Buildings were few and small. Most of them were destroyed or transformed in the following centuries. It was during the Gothic and the Renaissance periods, under the Dukes and after the union with France, that the countryside saw the growth of churches and chapels.

Buildings constructed before the 16C are usually rectangular, though one also frequently sees the disconcerting T plan in which the nave, usually without supporting aisles, ends in a chancel flanked by often disproportionately large chapels. The apse is flat; there are no side windows – light comes through openings pierced right at the east end of the church. Stone vaulting is rare and is nearly always replaced by wooden panelling, often painted, whose crocodile headed tie beams (cross beams dividing the roof timbers), wooden cornices at the base of the vaulting and timber heads on which the beams rest, are frequently carved and painted. When there is no transept a great stone arch separates the chancel from the nave.

From the 16C onwards there was a complete transformation: there had to be a transept which, inevitably, gave rise to the Latin Cross outline. The central arch disappeared; the east end became three sided; the nave was lit by windows in the aisles.

The tourist will be surprised to find in hamlets of a few houses only, and even in dreary wastes, chapels of which large places might be proud (Notre-Dame-du-Folgoët, Kernascléden, Notre-Dame-du-Crann, St-Fiacre-du-Faouët, etc.). The faith of the Breton communities has worked miracles.

Nevertheless there are many chapels where services are held only, perhaps, once a year on the occasion of a *pardon* or local festival, which leave a marked impression of spiritual as well as material neglect.

The belfries. – The Bretons are proud of their belfries. The towers do not serve only to hold bells; they also symbolise both religious and civic life. In olden days the people prized them, and it was a terrible punishment for them when an angry king had them laid low.

Usually square in outline, their position on the building varies considerably.

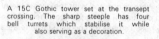

(After Nédelec photo, Morlaix)

St-Pol-de-Léon. — The Kreisker.

A 15C Gothic tower set at the transept crossing. The sharp steeple has four bell turrets which stabilise it while also serving as a decoration.

(After TCF Records)

Le Folgoët. — Belfry.

Gothic tower (15C), standing on west front. Derived from the Kreisker, but with the addition of a pierced bell gallery.

(After TCF Records)

Pleyben. — Belfry.

Renaissance tower (16C), built against the side of the church. The steeple consists of a dome and small lantern over a gallery. Some Renaissance towers have a double gallery.

Small churches and chapels were often given the lighter and less costly gable tower in preference to a belfry. The tower was placed either on the west front gable or on the roof itself, at the intersection of the chancel and the nave.

It is reached by outside steps or by stairs in the turrets that flank it and are linked to it by a gallery.

Sometimes these little belfries become so reduced as only to be walls in gable form, pierced by arcades. This form of architecture, while fairly widespread in southwest France, is somewhat rare in Brittany.

Porches. – Breton churches have a large porch on the south side. For long it was used as a meeting place for the parish notables, who sat on stone benches along the walls.

(After TCF Records)

Penmarch. — 16C Gable-tower.

(After TCF Records)

Landivisiau. — Gothic Porch (16C).

(After Bertault photo, Paris)

Landerneau. — Renaissance Porch (17C).

A double row of Apostles often decorates the porch. They can be recognised by their attributes: St. Peter holds the key of Heaven; St. Paul, a book or a sword; St. John, a chalice; St. Thomas, a set square; St. James the Elder, a pilgrim's staff. Others carry the instruments of their martyrdom: St. Matthew, a hatchet; St. Simon, a saw; St. Andrew, a cross: St. Bartholomew, a knife.

THE FOUNTAINS

There are numberless fountains in Lower Brittany. Most of them are sacred.

Nearly all places used for *pardons* have a fountain by the chapel where pilgrims come to drink. It is placed under the protection of a saint or of the Virgin, whose statues are set in small sanctuaries. For great pilgrimages like that at Ste-Anne-d'Auray the spring has been arranged in modern fashion, with basins, troughs and staircases.

Many fountains which were once venerated are now used for domestic purposes.

(After FT photo, Brest)

Le Folgoët. — Fountain.

(After Hamonic photo, St-Brieuc)

St-Nicolas-du-Pélem. — Fountain.

RELIGIOUS FURNISHINGS

Sculpture. – From the 15 to the 18C an army of Breton sculptors in stone and especially in wood supplied the churches with pulpits, organ casings, baptistries and fonts, choir screens, rood-screens, rood-beams, altarpieces, triptychs, confessionals, shrines, Holy Sepulchres, statues, etc.

The tourist in the humblest chapel will always find some piece to arrest his attention.

These works are usually more highly developed than the figures on the Calvaries since it is much easier to work in oak, chestnut or alabaster than in granite.

Visits to the churches of Guimiliau, Lampaul-Guimiliau, St-Thégonnec, St-Fiacre at Le Faouët and Tréguier Cathedral (stalls) will give a good general idea of Breton religious furnishings.

The many **rood-screens** (*jubés*) to be found in the churches of Brittany are often of unparalleled richness. Some are cut in granite, as in the church at Le Folgoët, but most are carved in wood which makes them peculiar to Brittany. Their decoration is very varied and is different on both sides. The screen serves two purposes: it separates the chancel from the part of the church reserved for worshippers and completes the side enclosures of the chancel;

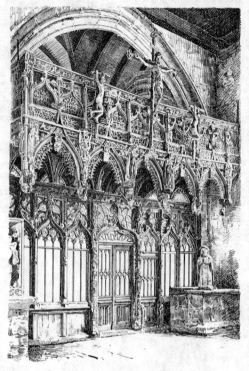

Le Faouët. — Rood-screen in St-Fiacre.

the upper gallery may also be used for preaching and reading prayers. (The name derives from the first word of a prayer sung from the gallery.)

The screen is usually surmounted by a large Crucifix flanked by statues of the Virgin and St. John facing the congregation.

The **rood-beam** *(see illustration opposite)* or *tref*, which supported the main arch of the church was the origin of the rood-screen. To prevent the beam from bowing it had to be suppported by posts which eventually were replaced by a screen carved to a greater or lesser degree. It is to be seen mostly in the small chapels and churches where it serves as a symbolic boundary for the chancel; is usually decorated with scenes from the Passion and always carries a group of Jesus Christ, the Virgin and St. John.

Renaissance works are numerous and very elaborate. **Fonts** and **pulpits** are developed into richly decorated monuments.

Altarpieces, or retables, show an interesting development which can be traced through many stages in Breton churches. Originally the altar was simply a table; as the result of decoration it gradually lost its simplicity and reached a surprising size. In the 12 and 14C altars were furnished with a low step and altarpiece, the same length as the altar. Sculptors took possession of the feature and added groups of figures in scenes drawn from the Passion. From the 15C onwards the altarpiece became a pretext for twisted columns, pediments, niches containing statues and sculptured panels, which reached their highest expression in the 17C. Finally the main subject was lost in decoration consisting of angels, garlands, etc., and the altarpiece occupied the whole of the chapel reserved for the altar, and sometimes even, joined up with the retables of side altars, decorated the whole wall of the apse as is the case at Ste-Marie-du-Ménez-Hom *(p 72)*.

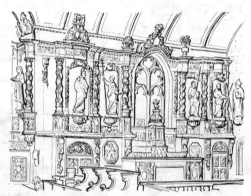

(After le Doaré photo, Châteaulin)

Ste-Marie-du-Ménez-Hom. — Altarpieces.

It is curious to find in Breton altarpieces of the 15C the influence of the Flemish craftsmen who excelled in this work, producing tiny figures in the minutest detail.

Devotion to the Rosary, due to Alain de la Roche, a 15C Breton Friar of the Dominican Order, gave rise from 1640 onwards to the erection of many altarpieces in which Our Lady is shown giving the chaplet to St. Dominic and St. Catherine of Siena.

Of less importance but equally numerous are the triptychs which, when the two panels are open, reveal a Tree of Jesse. Jesse, who was a member of the tribe of Judah, had a son, David, from whom was descended the Virgin Mary. Jesse is usually shown lying on his side; from his heart and his body come the roots of the tree whose branches bear the figures, in chronological order, of the kings and prophets who were Christ's forebears. In the centre is the Virgin representing the branch which bears the flower: Jesus Christ.

Among the many statues ornamenting the churches, such as the Trinity of St. Anne and the Virgin and Child, are often to be found portraits of real people and items of great importance in the study of the history of costume in Brittany. Such representation, seen frequently in Central Europe, is rare in France.

The Entombment. – The Entombment which is often shown as part of a Calvary group in other parts of France is not often so seen in Brittany. The best depictions of the Placing in the Tomb or Holy Sepulchre with the group of seven round the dead Christ are at Lampaul-Guimiliau and St-Thégonnec.

Funeral statuary is represented in most masterly manner by the tomb of François II at Nantes and Olivier de Clisson at Josselin.

Stained glass windows. – Whereas the altarpieces, beams and statues were often coloured, paintings and frescoes, as such, were

(After CAP photo, Paris)

Lampaul-Guimiliau. — 17C Rood-beam.

rare; almost the only exception are those at Kernascléden. In contrast there are a great many stained glass windows, often Italian or Flemish inspired but always made in Brittany. Some are really fine: Dol Cathedral has a beautiful 13C window. The three workshops at Rennes, Tréguier and Quimper produced stained glass between the 14 and 16C which should be seen; the most remarkable windows are in the churches of Notre-Dame-du-Crann, La Roche and St. Fiacre at Le Faouët.

Gold church plate. – In spite of considerable losses, Brittany still possesses many wonderful pieces of gold church plate. This was made by local craftsmen, most of them from Morlaix. Though fine chalices and shrines may be hidden away from the covetous, magnificent reliquaries, chalices, richly decorated patens and superb processional crosses may be seen at St-Jean-du-Doigt, St-Gildas-de-Rhuys, Paimpont and Locarn.

THE PARISH CLOSE

The parish close is the most typical monumental grouping in Breton communities.

The tourist should not leave Brittany without having seen a few examples, and we therefore describe a tour of parish closes taking in the most interesting *(p 137)*.

The centre of the close was the cemetery which was very small and with gravestones of uniform size. This is tending to disappear. Around the cemetery which is often reached through a **triumphal arch** are grouped the **church** with its small **square** *(placître)*, the **Calvary**, and the **charnel house** or ossuary. Thus the spiritual life of the parish is closely linked with the community of the dead. Death, *Ankou*, was anyway a familiar idea to the Bretons who often depicted it.

(After Bertault photo, Paris)

Triumphal arch   Charnel house   Calvary   Church

St-Thégonnec. — Parish close.

The extraordinary rivalry between neighbouring villages explains the richness of the closes which grew up in Lower Brittany at the time of the Renaissance and in the 17C. Competition between Guimiliau and St-Thégonnec went on for two centuries: a Calvary answered a triumphal arch, a charnel house a porch, a tower replied to a belfry, a pulpit to a font, an organ loft to a set of confessionals, an Entombment to chancel woodwork. The two finest closes in Brittany sprang from this rivalry.

Triumphal arches. – The entrance to a cemetery is often ornamented with a monumental gateway. This is treated as a triumphal arch to symbolise the entry of the just into immortality.

Some arches built during the Renaissance, like those of Sizun and Berven, are surprisingly reminiscent of antique triumphal arches.

Charnel houses. – In the tiny Breton cemeteries of olden days, bodies often had to be exhumed to make room for new dead. The bones were piled in small shelters with ventilating openings, built against the church or cemetery wall. Then these charnel houses became separate buildings, larger and more carefully built and finally reliquaries which could be used as funeral chapels.

Calvaries. – In these small, essentially Breton, granite monuments, episodes of the Passion are represented around Christ on the Cross. Many of them were built to ward off in 1598 a plague epidemic, or as an act of thanks after it ended. They served for religious teaching in the parish. The priest preached from the dais, pointing out with a wand the scenes which he described to his flock.

The distant forebears of the Calvaries were Christianised menhirs *(p 27)*, which were still fairly common, and their immediate predecessors were the crosses, plain or ornate. Crosses along roads in this countryside are legion; there have been tens of thousands. In the 16C a Bishop of Léon boasted that he alone had had 5 000 erected. Ornate crosses were common in the 14C; many were destroyed. The oldest remaining Calvary is that of Tronoën, which dates from the end of the 15C. They were being erected as late as the end of the 17C.

The most famous are those of Guimiliau with 200 figures, Plougastel-Daoulas with 180 and Pleyben.

1. Cross of Christ. This is sometimes alone or flanked by one thief's cross.
2. Thieves' crosses. Usually T-shaped and on either side of the Crucifix.
3. Horsemen (Roman guards) or the Holy Women, or St. Peter, St. John or St. Yves.
4. Virgin of Pity (Mary holding the body of Jesus removed from the Cross) or angels catching His Blood in chalices.
5 and 6. Dais and frieze encircling the base of the Cross. They carry many figures, either isolated (Apostles, saints and holy women) or in scenes from the Passion. The four Evangelists are usually set in niches at the corners.
7. Altar on which is the statue of the saint to whom the Calvary is dedicated (sometimes there are several).

(After TCF Records photo)

Plougastel-Daoulas. — Typical calvary.

The sculpture is rough and naïve – the work of a village stonemason – but it shows a great deal of observation and is often strikingly lifelike and expressive. Many figures, notably soldiers, wear the costumes of the 16 and 17C.

A lesson in sacred history. – Walking round a large Calvary, we see the history of the Virgin and Christ pass before our eyes: the Virgin's marriage, the Annunciation, the Visitation, the Nativity, the Adoration of the Shepherds, the Adoration of the Magi, the Presentation at the Temple, the Circumcision, the Flight into Egypt, the Baptism of Jesus, the Entry into Jerusalem, the Last Supper, the Washing of Feet, the Garden of Olives, the Kiss of Judas, the Arrest of Jesus, Jesus before Caiaphas, Jesus before Herod, Pilate washing his hands, the Scourging, the Crown of Thorns, the Carrying of the Cross, Jesus falling beneath the Cross, the Descent from the Cross, the Embalming, the Entombment, the Resurrection and the Descent into limbo.

Catell-Gollet. – The story of Catell-Gollet (Catherine the Lost) appears on several Calvaries (Plougastel-Daoulas, Guimiliau). Catherine, a young servant girl, has concealed her misbehaviour at confession. Embarked on the slippery slope, she steals a consecrated Host to give it to the Devil, who appears in the guise of her lover. The culprit is condemned to eternal fire. She is seen above (at the corner of the platform, below the right-hand cross) in the jaws of Hell; devils hold her neck with a fork and tear her naked body with their claws. The priest, when preaching, would draw a terrible lesson for flirtatious girls from this adventure.

No Calvary has all these scenes. The sculptor chose those that inspired him most, and arranged them without any regard for chronological order. Some can be recognised at a glance, others, more or less damaged or treated too sketchily, are a tax to sagacity.

What is a Calvary ?

Calvary is the name given to the hill, also known as Golgotha, where Christ was crucified. The hill took its name from its skull form (Skull: calvaria in Latin).

Breton Calvaries representing scenes from the Passion and Crucifixion are not to be confused with wayside crosses often erected at crossroads or near churches to mark the site of a pilgrimage or procession.

BRETON DOMESTIC FURNITURE

For centuries Breton artisans made box beds, chests, sideboards, dressers, wardrobes and clock cases. Repetition of the same models, differing only in small ornamental details, developed true mastery in them.

The box bed, an essential characteristic of Breton furnishing, is still used in some parts of Lower Brittany. It sometimes has two storeys or bunks, one above the other, and a bench chest is often added which makes it easier to get into. Its sliding doors, decorated with pierced designs, sometimes bear the monogram of Christ.

As in most parts of France, the linen chest plays a great part. Some are remarkable for their

Chest.

Box bed.

fine carving in the form of interlaced or adjoining geometrical figures, known as "compass decoration".

In the 17C the wardrobes succeeded the chests and their decoration varies according to the regions. In Lower Brittany they were carved with balusters and in Upper Brittany with heart or bird motifs.

There are fine beds and chests in the museums of Quimper, Rennes and Nantes and the Château of Kerjean; also reconstructions of old interiors.

CASTLES AND FORTRESSES

Breton granite is somewhat daunting to the tourist coming to Brittany for the first time. Clean cut and hard, it does not age or weather and it would therefore not be possible to give a date to the grey buildings that blend perfectly into the landscape were it not for the architectural design and methods employed in construction. With the exception of the fortresses, most of which stood guard on the eastern border in fear of the kings of France or along the coast to ward off the raids of English invaders, there are few great castles in Brittany. This lack conveys perfectly the Breton character that turned all its artistic endeavour to the service of religion.

Nevertheless it is easy to imagine Brittany in the Middle Ages. Few regions, in fact, had such fortresses and though many have been destroyed or have fallen into ruin, many are still standing. Before these walls can be conjured up the problems of war in the Middle Ages. Although some fortresses fell at once to a surprise attack, it was not unusual for a siege to go on for several months. The attacker then sapped the ramparts, brought up machines which could hurl stones weighing over 100 kg - 200 lb, and tried to smash the gates with battering rams before launching the final assault.

In the middle of the 15C, artillery brought about new methods of attack and changes in military architecture.

(After CAP photo, Paris)

Josselin Castle.

At St-Malo and at Guérande the stone walls that encircled these towns can be seen in their entirety. Remains of ramparts of varying extent can be seen in many other places. Vannes, Concarneau and Port-Louis have ramparts that are almost complete. There are many fortresses: those of Fougères and Vitré are among the finest in France. Dinan and Combourg have fortified castles still standing; Suscinio, Tonquédec, etc., have impressive ruins; La Hunaudaye, though of lesser importance, the towers of Elven, of Oudon and Châteaugiron still stand proudly upright. La Latte Fort, standing like a sentinel far ahead, has a magnificent site.

Buildings, half fortress and half palace, like Kerjean, Josselin and the ducal castle at Nantes, are interesting to see, but are few. The fact is that the Breton nobility, except for the Duke and a few great families, were poor. The included many country gentlemen who lived in very simple manors, which nevertheless retained their watchtower defences. The cultivated their own land, like the peasants, but they did not give up their rank and they continued to wear the sword.

In some places these manor farms give a great deal of character to the Breton countryside. This is the case in Léon where they are numerous and where Kergonadéac'h, Kerouzéré, Kerouarz, Kergroadès and Tronjoly together form a background setting to Kerjean, pride of the province. Certain other châteaux, such as Rocher-Portail, were built later, and lack all appearance of being fortresses, but impress by their simplicity of outline and the grouping of the buildings; alternatively at such places as Lanrigan and La Motte-Glain it is the detail that charms the visitor.

Landal is one of those that gain enormously from their surroundings; others take great pride in a well laid out garden or a fine park – these include Bonne-Fontaine, Caradeuc, Rosanbo and Couëlan.

OLD STREETS AND OLD HOUSES

One of the charms of travelling in Brittany is to stroll in the old quarters of the towns. There is hardly a town or village which has not kept whole streets, or at least a few single houses, just as they were 300 or 400 years ago.

There you can conjure up the life of other days. On the ground floors of the houses the shops of tradesmen and artisans are indicated by sheet metal signs which creak on their hinges. Linen hangs out to dry on poles fixed to the windows along the façades. Heavy objects are hauled up with pulleys fixed to the gables.

In the narrow streets, the roofs of overhanging houses almost meet; the roads are dark but at the back the dwellings give on yards which bring air and light to the living rooms and the backs of the shops.

People worked long and hard: wages were very low. At the crack of dawn the watchman on the tower gave a trumpet call and the workers jumped out of bed. Every trade was thoroughly organised in a corporation which had its own street, its banner, its patron saint and its annual feast-day. There was no night life; at 8pm in winter and 9pm in summer the curfew rang from the belfry, the watch fastened chains across the streets, the lights went out and the town went to sleep.

(After le Doaré photo, Châteaulin)

Dinan. — Place des Merciers.

Sunday brought rest. In a deafening chorus, the bells called the faithful to church. Masses, vespers and processions followed one another. Great occasions were the fairs, the harvest festival, the vintage, the corporation feast-days, the *pardons* and theatricals.

People amused themselves with games of skill, like the *papegault* (a wooden bird to be shot at with a cross-bow) and the *quintaine*, in which a jouster mounted on a donkey and armed with a lance charged a wooden dummy which he had to strike in the middle of its body. If he aimed badly, the dummy pivoted on its axis and hit the clumsy fellow with its staff.

Some picturesque old streets

Dinan: Rue du Jerzual (p 82)
Guingamp: Place du Centre (p 105)
Morlaix: Grand'Rue (p 127)
Pontivy: Rue du Fil (p 144)
Quimper: Rue Kéréon (p 149)
Quimperlé: Rue-Dom-Morice (p 152)
Vitré: Rue Beaudrairie (p 185)

Modern towns. – It is difficult to find any basis of comparison between the old towns with their historical associations and the modern towns. And yet to cite only the chief ones, if Dinan, Locronan, Vitré, Morlaix and Quimper, as well as St-Malo which has been admirably reconstructed, have an undeniable appeal, it is impossible not to be struck also by the planning and grouping of buildings in such towns as Brest and Lorient. The wide streets and huge, airy squares are elegant and have obviously been built to achieve harmony and unity.

The visitor may well be surprised by certain buildings, but he will find something to admire in the upward sweep of a tall bell-tower, the simple lines of a concrete façade, the successful decorative effect of stone and cement combined. Above all, if he has some slight appreciation of colour harmony, and goes inside any building he will be struck by the present day artist's skill in lighting and the use of light.

LEARNING AND LITERATURE IN BRITTANY

The Middle Ages and the Renaissance. – Learning was centred on the monasteries; the language used was Latin; the subjects studied were concerned, for the most part, with the history of the Church or of Brittany, moral philosophy and the lives of the saints. A life of St. Guénolé was written by Wurdistein, Abbot of Landévennec in the 9C. Authors are rarely known by name, but there are some exceptions as, in the 12C: **Peter Abelard**, one of the most brilliant figures of the Middle Ages, who was born at Pallet near Nantes and became Abbot of St-Gildas-de-Rhuys *(p 168)*; **Etienne de Fougères** whose *Livre des manières* (Book of Manners) gave him free rein to lecture his contemporaries; and **Guillaume Le Breton**, poet and historian at the court of Philippe-Auguste.

Students from Brittany first went to the University in Paris, and then to Nantes when that was founded in the 15C; schools were established to supplement the teaching provided by the churches and monasteries in out of the way parishes and yet it is not until the 15 and 16C that one begins to hear of names such as those of the historians Pierre Le Baud, Alain Bouchard and Bertrand d'Argentré, of the poet Meschinot from Nantes who wrote a series of ballads entitled *Les lunettes des princes* (the Princes' Spectacles), which became well known in his own time, of Noël du Fail, Councillor of the Rennes Parliament who depicted the world around him so well and of the Dominican, Albert Legrand, who wrote the *Vie des saints de la Bretagne armoricaine* (Life of the Saints of Armorican Brittany).

17 and 18C. – The best known figures of the 17 and 18C are Mme de Sévigné – Breton by marriage – who addressed many of her letters from her Château des Rochers *(p 161)*. **Lesage**, the witty author of *Gil Blas* who came from Vannes, and Duclos, moralist and historian who was Mayor of Dinan. There were also Fréron *(p 149)* and Trubet who became known only through their disputes with Voltaire and, finally, the Benedictines, Dom Lobineau and Dom Morice, historians of Brittany.

The Romantics and Contemporary Writers. – Three figures dominated literature in the 19C in Brittany:

François-René de Chateaubriand *(p 168)* who had an immense influence on French literature. The effect he had over his contemporaries arose from his sensitivity, his passionate eloquence, his fertile imagination, all of which were displayed with brilliant and powerful style; in his *Mémoires d'Outre-Tombe* (Beyond the Tomb) he recounts his childhood at St-Malo and his youth at the Combourg Castle.

Lamennais *(p 168)*, fervent apologist of theocracy who became a convinced democrat, reflects in his philosophical works the evolution of his thought.

Ernest Renan *(p 178)*, philologist, historian and philosopher was a thinker who maintained that he had faith only in science. He wrote many books in an easy and brilliant prose and in one, *Souvenirs d'enfance et de jeunesse* (Recollections of Childhood and Youth), described his native Brittany.

Less important but nevertheless true interpreters of the native soil and turn of mind of Brittany are the sensitive poet **Auguste Brizeux**, author of *Marie* and the poems *Telen Arvor*; Émile Souvestre who wrote such stories as *Les derniers bretons* (The Last Bretons); Hersart de la Villemarqué who published a collection of poems based on popular folk songs; Frédéric Le Guyader, a poet who sang the praises of cider; **Anatole Le Braz** the folklorist; **Charles Le Goffic** the novelist; and **Théodore Botrel** the song writer.

Others came from Brittany and should be noted though they did not write in praise of their native province are: the Symbolist poets, Villiers-de-l'Isle-Adam and Tristan Corbière; the novelists, Paul Féval, author of *Bossu*; **Jules Verne**, precursor of modern scientific discoveries; Zénaï de Fleuriot whom young people still read; Louis Hémon who became known through his *Maria Chapdelaine*, and finally **Pierre Loti** with his *Pêcheur d'Islande* and *Mon frère Yves*. **Alphonse de Chateaubriant** born in Rennes in 1877, depicts the Brière. **Jean-Pierre Calloch** native of the Groix Island *(p 99)*, a lyrical poet writes in the Breton language. The Surrealist poet **Saint-Pol-Roux**, Marseilles born but undying lover of Brittany, wrote works touched with Romanticism, *Les Féeries intérieures*.

Today **Henry Queffélec** is one of the authors who have most lauded Brittany in his *Le recteur de l'île de Sein*, *Un homme d'Onessant*, *Au bout du monde*, *Franche et Secrète Bretagne* and *Promenades en Bretagne*.

Unfortunately few Breton authors have been translated into English.

BOOKS TO READ

In English

BRITTANY   **René Jacques**   *Panorama Books*

BRITTANY AND NORMANDY   **Mary Elsy**   *Johnson*

UNKNOWN FRANCE – THE VALLEY OF THE LOIRE: BRITTANY   **Georges Pillement**   *Johnson*

THE CELTIC REALMS   **Dillon and Chadwick**   *Weidenfeld & Nicolson*

THE CELTS   **T. D. E. Powell**   Ancient Peoples and Places Series   *Thames & Hudson*

ACCESS IN BRITTANY **(Disabled Tourist's Guide)** *Obtainable from Mr G. R. Couch, 68B Castlebar Road, Ealing, London W5 2OO*

In French

PÊCHEUR D'ISLANDE   **Pierre Loti**   *Calman-Lévy, Paris*

PROMENADES EN BRETAGNE   **Henri Queffélec**   *A. Balland*

PRESTIGES DU FINISTÈRE (old myths and legends)   **Yann Brekilien**   *France Empire*

GUIDE DE BRETAGNE MYSTÉRIEUSE   **Le Scouëzec**   *Tchou*

TOURING PROGRAMMES

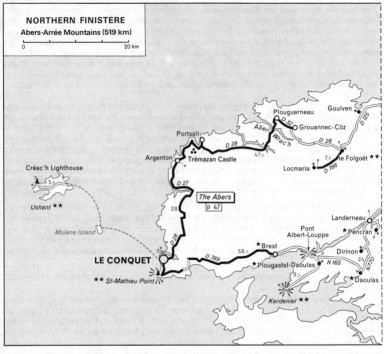

NORTHERN FINISTERE
Abers-Arrée Mountains (519 km)

0   20 km

Plouguerneau
Goulven
Aber Wrac'h
Grouannec-Côz
D 32
D 125
Portsall
D 28
47.5
D 28
le Folgoët ★★
Argenton
Trémazan Castle
7.5
Locmaria
D 788
D 27
The Abers
p 47
Landerneau
28
Pont Albert-Louppe
Pencran
Créac'h Lighthouse
5
D 28
Dirinon
Ushant ★★
Molène Island
38.5
★ Brest
N 165
24
N 170
D 789
★ Plougastel-Daoulas
LE CONQUET
9.5
★ Daoulas
★★ St-Mathieu Point
Kerdeniel ★★

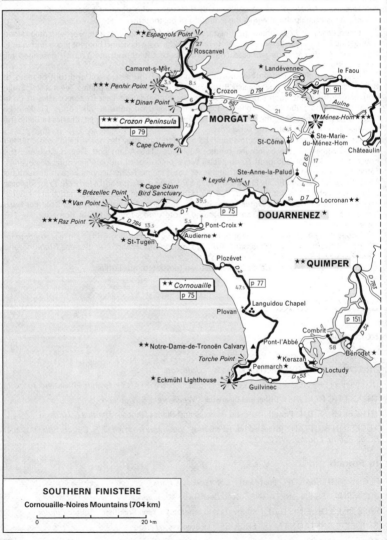

★★ Espagnols Point
27
Roscanvel
★ Landévennec
le Faou
Camaret-s-Mêr
8.5
3.5
D 791
p 91
★★★ Penhir Point
Crozon
D 791
Aulne
★★ Dinan Point
6
D 887
56
★★★ Crozon Peninsula
3
21
★★ Ménez-Hom ★★★
p 79
MORGAT ★
★ Cape Chèvre
7.5
St-Côme
4.5
Ste-Marie-du-Ménez-Hom
Châteaulin
D 63
17
Ste-Anne-la-Palud
★ Leydé Point
★ Cape Sizun Bird Sanctuary
4
★ Brézellec Point
39.5
14
D 7
Locronan ★★
★★ Van Point
D 7
p 75
★★★ Raz Point
D 784
13.5
5.5
DOUARNENEZ ★
2
Pont-Croix ★
★ St-Tugen
Audierne ★
★★ QUIMPER
Plozévet
D 2
D 785
★★ Cornouaille
47.5
p 77
p 75
Languidou Chapel
Plovan
p 151
Combrit
★★ Notre-Dame-de-Tronoën Calvary
Pont-l'Abbé
58
D 54
Torche Point
★ Kerazan
Bénodet ★
Penmarch ★
Loctudy
★ Eckmühl Lighthouse
D 53
Guilvinec

SOUTHERN FINISTERE
Cornouaille-Noires Mountains (704 km)

0   20 km

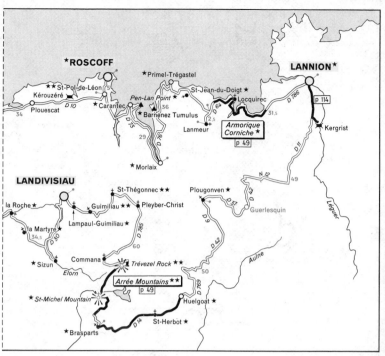

★ROSCOFF

★★St-Pol-de-Léon
Kérouzéré ★
D 10
34 Plouescat
D 75
D 76
★ Carantec
Pen-Lan Point ★
36
★ Primel-Trégastel
★ St-Jean-du-Doigt ★
64
Locquirec
31,5
D 786
Kergrist ★
★ Barnenez Tumulus
2,5
Lanmeur ★
Armorique Corniche ★
p 49
LANNION ★
p 114
D 11
29 ★ Morlaix
Léguer

LANDIVISIAU
la Roche ★
★★St-Thégonnec ★★
Plougonven ★
D 37
Guerlesquin
N 12
49
la Martyre ★
34,5 D 30
Guimiliau ★★
Lampaul-Guimiliau ★
★ Pleyber-Christ
D 785
D 9
D 42
★ Sizun
Commana ★
60
Elorn
★ Trévezel Rock ★★
Arrée Mountains ★★
p 49
50
D 769
Aulne
★ St-Michel Mountain ★
Huelgoat ★
D 14
St-Herbot ★
★ Brasparts

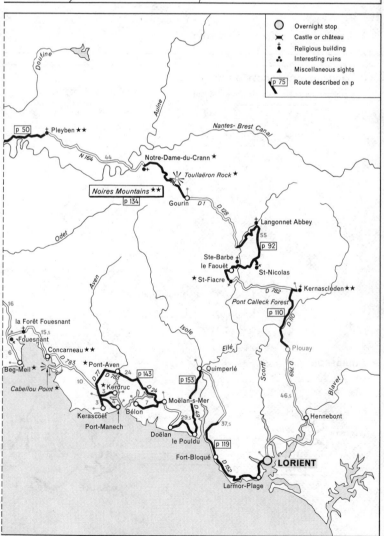

| | Overnight stop |
| Castle or château |
| Religious building |
| Interesting ruins |
| Miscellaneous sights |
| p 75 | Route described on p |

Douron
Aulne
Nantes- Brest Canal
p 50 ★ Pleyben ★★
N 164
44
★ Notre-Dame-du-Crann ★
★ Toullaëron Rock ★
Noires Mountains ★★
p 134
Gourin
D 1
D 128
Langonnet Abbey
55
p 92
Odet
Ste-Barbe
le Faouët
St-Nicolas
★ St-Fiacre ★
D 782
Kernascléden ★★
Pont Calleck Forest
p 110
D 110
Aven
Isole
16
la Forêt Fouesnant
Ellé
Plouay
15,5
Fouesnant
6
Concarneau ★★
D 783
★ Pont-Aven
D 77
24
p 143
Quimperlé
p 153
Scorff
D 769
46,5
Beg-Meil ★
10
D 783
★ Kerdruc
D 24
D 24
Cabellou Point ★
3
7
Moëlan-s-Mer
Bélon
29,5
D 49
37,5
Kerascoët
Port-Manech
Doëlan
le Pouldu
p 119
Hennebont
Fort-Bloqué
D 152
LORIENT
Larmor-Plage

37

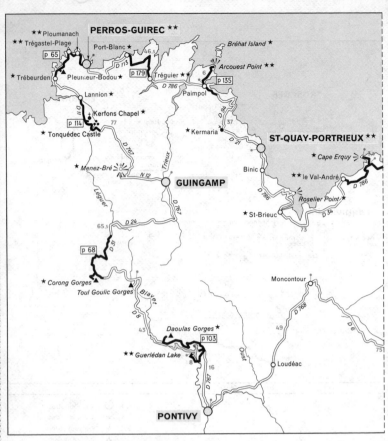

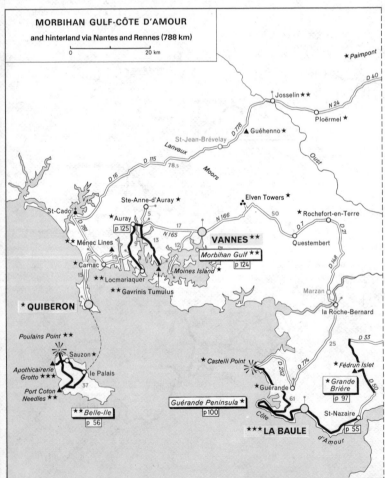

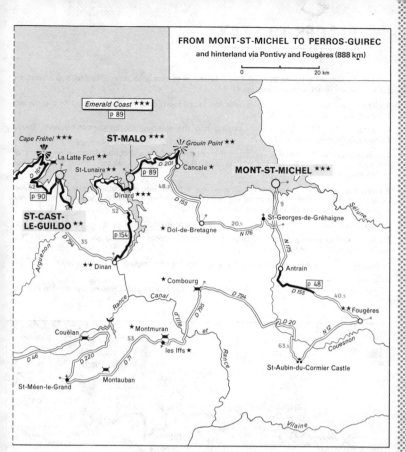

Emerald Coast ★★★
p 89

Cape Fréhel ★★★

St-MALO ★★★

Grouin Point ★★

La Latte Fort ★★

D 16¹

St-Lunaire ★★

D 201

Cancale ★

MONT-ST-MICHEL ★★★

42

p 90

Dinard ★★★

48.5

Sélune

ST-CAST-
LE-GUILDO ★★

52

D 155

9

St-Georges-de-Gréhaigne

D 794

35

p 154

★ Dol-de-Bretagne

N 176

20.5

N 175

Antrain

p 48

Arguenon

★★ Dinan

★ Combourg

D 794

D 155

40.5

Rance

Canal

D 795

D 20

★★ Fougères

Couëlan

★ Montmuran

d'Ille

N 12

les Iffs ★

ef

63.5

Couesnon

D 46

D 220

53

D 71

Rance

St-Aubin-du-Cormier Castle

St-Méen-le-Grand

Montauban

Vilaine

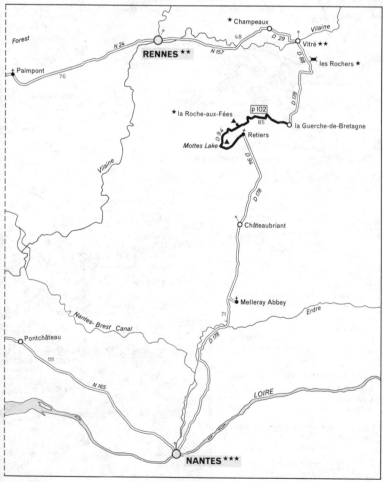

Forest

★ Champeaux

Vilaine

N 24

48

D 29

Vitré ★★

RENNES ★★

N 157

D 88

les Rochers ★

Paimpont

76

D 178

★ la Roche-aux-Fées

p 102

Vilaine

D 94

la Guerche-de-Bretagne

Mottes Lake

★ Retiers

D 94

D 178

Châteaubriant

Nantes-Brest Canal

★ Melleray Abbey

Erdre

71

Pontchâteau

D 178

111

N 165

LOIRE

NANTES ★★★

PLACES TO STAY

On the following pages you will find a selection of places to stay. The facilities offered by each town are listed on the tables pp 41-44.

Hotels. — The letter H denotes that a selection of the town's hotels is to be found in the current Michelin Red Guide **France** *(1)*.

Camping. — The letter C shows a camping and site selected by the current Michelin Guide **Camping Caravaning France** *(1)*.

Tourist centres. — The letter T indicates the presence of a local tourist information centre or Syndicat d'Initiative *(1)*. For the address and telephone number see the current Michelin Red Guide **France**.

Pleasure boat harbours. — The symbol ⚓ indicates a basin with a constant water level, berthing places and other facilities *(see table opposite)*; the symbol ⚓ denotes anchorage possibilities (vessels may be left aground at low tide).

Cinemas. — Cinemas with at least one showing per day are indicated by ▥.

Swimming pool or bathing place. — Heated swimming pool ⌇ ; other swimming pools ⌇ ; guarded bathing place ≌.

Angling club. — The symbol ⚲ indicates the existence of an angling club in the town.

---

(1) For further information see the Michelin Red Guide France and Camping Caravaning France.

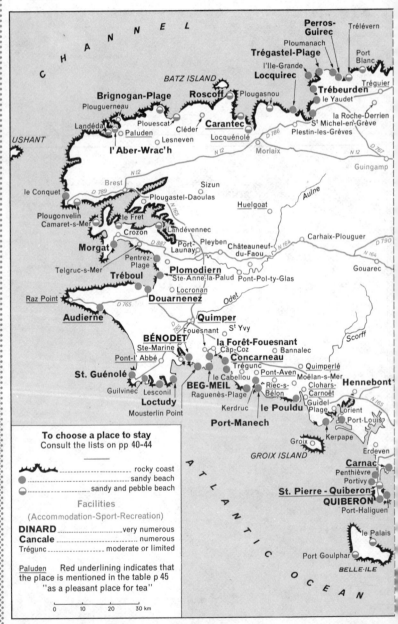

To choose a place to stay
Consult the lists on pp 40-44

〜〜〜〜 rocky coast
● sandy beach
◗ sandy and pebble beach

Facilities
(Accommodation-Sport-Recreation)

DINARD very numerous
Cancale numerous
Trégunc moderate or limited

Paluden   Red underlining indicates that the place is mentioned in the table p 45 "as a pleasant place for tea"

0   10   20   30 km

Facilities provided in pleasure boat harbours

MAIN HARBOURS	Capacity	Refuelling points = ●	Drinking water	Electric points	Toilets and showers	Handling facilities (crane, lift) = H	Repair facilities = R	Warden in attendance = W
La Baule - Le Pouliguen	800	●	●	●	●	H	–	–
Bénodet	445	●	●	●	●	H	–	W
Concarneau	255	●	●	●	●	–	R	W
Le Croisic	276	●	●	●	●	H	R	W
Dinard	386	●	●	●	–	H	–	–
La Forêt-Fouesnant	510	●	●	●	●	H	R	W
Morgat	367	–	●	●	●	–	–	–
Perros-Guirec	480	●	●	●	●	H	R	–
Pléneuf - Val-André	380	–	●	●	–	H	R	–
Port-Haliguen	430	●	●	●	●	H	R	W
St-Cast-le-Guildo	250	●	●	●	●	H	–	W
St-Malo	1150	–	●	–	●	H	–	W
St-Quay-Portrieux	371	●	●	●	●	H	R	W
La Trinité-sur-Mer	800	●	●	●	●	H	R	W

More detailed information can be obtained from tourist centres and specialized publications.

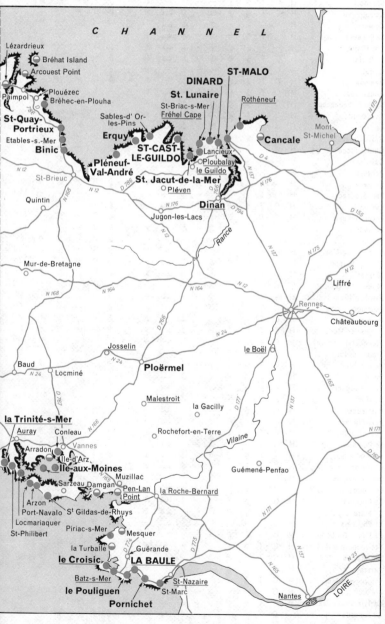

ATLANTIC COAST

	Hotels = H	Camping site = C	Tourist centre = T	Doctor	Chemist	Pleasant site	Particularly attractive town = ◇	Pleasure boat harbour	Fishing port	Cinema	Swimming pool	Sailing school	Boats for hire = B	Skin diving	Tennis	Horse riding	Page in guide or no of section on Michelin map 230
Arradon	H	–	–	✓	✓	✓	◇	✓	–	–	–	✓	B	✓	–	–	125
Arz (Island)	H	–	–	–	–	✓	–	–	✓	–	–	✓	–	–	✓	–	125
Arzon	–	C	T	✓	–	–	–	–	–	–	–	✓	B	–	✓	✓	125
Audierne	H	–	T	✓	✓	–	–	–	✓	▦	–	✓	B	✓	✓	–	51
Batz-sur-Mer	H	–	T	✓	✓	–	–	–	–	▦	–	✓	–	✓	✓	–	54
La Baule	H	C	T	✓	✓	✓	–	✓	–	▦	⛵	✓	B	–	✓	✓	55
Beg-Meil	H	C	T	–	✓	✓	–	✓	✓	–	–	–	B	–	✓	✓	56
Belle-Ile : Le Palais	H	C	T	✓	✓	✓	◇	✓	✓	▦	–	✓	B	✓	✓	–	57
Port Goulphar	H	–	–	–	–	✓	–	–	–	–	–	–	–	–	–	–	57
Bénodet	H	C	T	✓	✓	✓	–	✓	✓	▦	⛵	✓	B	✓	✓	–	58
Le Cabellou	H	C	–	–	–	✓	–	✓	–	–	–	–	–	–	–	–	75
Camaret-sur-Mer	H	C	T	✓	✓	✓	–	✓	✓	▦	–	✓	B	✓	✓	–	66
Carnac	H	C	T	✓	✓	–	–	–	–	▦	–	✓	–	✓	✓	✓	73
Concarneau	H	C	T	✓	✓	✓	◇	✓	✓	▦	⛵	–	–	✓	✓	–	183
Conleau	H	–	–	–	–	✓	–	✓	–	–	⛵	–	–	–	✓	–	48
Le Conquet	H	–	T	✓	✓	✓	–	✓	✓	–	–	–	–	✓	✓	✓	66
Coz (Cape)	H	–	T	✓	✓	✓	–	✓	✓	–	–	–	–	✓	✓	✓	(32)
Le Croisic	H	C	T	✓	✓	✓	◇	✓	✓	▦	–	✓	B	✓	✓	–	78
Crozon	–	C	T	–	–	–	–	–	✓	▦	–	✓	B	✓	✓	✓	79
Damgan	H	C	T	✓	✓	–	–	✓	–	–	–	✓	–	✓	✓	✓	(51)
Douarnenez	H	C	T	✓	✓	✓	◇	–	✓	▦	⛵	✓	–	✓	✓	–	87
La Forêt-Fouesnant	H	C	T	✓	✓	✓	–	✓	✓	–	–	✓	B	–	✓	–	93
Fouesnant	H	C	T	✓	✓	–	–	–	–	▦	–	✓	–	–	✓	✓	93
Le Fret	H	C	–	–	–	✓	–	✓	✓	–	–	✓	–	–	–	–	80
Groix (Island)	H	C	T	✓	✓	✓	–	✓	✓	–	–	✓	–	✓	–	✓	99
Guidel-Plage	H	C	–	–	–	–	◇	✓	–	–	–	✓	–	✓	✓	–	(34)
Guilvinec	H	–	–	✓	✓	–	–	–	✓	–	–	–	–	✓	✓	–	78
Kerdruc	–	–	–	–	–	✓	–	–	✓	–	–	–	–	–	–	–	143
Kerpape	–	–	T	✓	✓	–	–	✓	✓	–	–	✓	B	✓	✓	✓	(34)
Landévennec	H	–	–	–	–	✓	–	✓	✓	–	–	–	–	–	✓	–	113
Lesconil	H	C	T	✓	✓	–	◇	–	✓	–	–	✓	–	–	✓	–	78
Locmariaquer	H	C	T	✓	✓	✓	–	✓	–	–	–	✓	B	–	–	–	116
Loctudy	H	C	T	✓	✓	✓	–	✓	✓	–	–	✓	B	–	✓	✓	117
Mesquer	–	C	–	✓	–	–	–	–	✓	–	–	–	–	–	✓	✓	(51)
Moëlan-sur-Mer	H	–	T	✓	✓	✓	–	✓	✓	–	–	–	–	–	✓	✓	153
Moines (Island)	H	–	T	✓	✓	✓	–	✓	✓	–	–	✓	B	✓	✓	✓	125
Morgat	H	C	T	✓	✓	✓	–	✓	✓	▦	–	✓	B	✓	✓	✓	126
Mousterlin (Point)	H	C	–	–	–	✓	–	✓	✓	–	–	–	–	–	–	–	59
Pen-Lan (Point)	H	–	–	–	–	✓	–	–	–	–	–	–	–	–	–	–	(51)
Penthièvre	H	C	T	–	–	✓	–	–	–	–	–	✓	–	–	–	–	148
Pentrez-Plage	H	C	T	–	–	–	–	✓	–	▦	–	–	–	–	–	–	(17)
Piriac-sur-Mer	H	C	T	✓	✓	–	◇	✓	✓	▦	⛵	✓	–	✓	✓	✓	101
Plougastel-Daoulas	–	C	T	✓	✓	–	–	–	–	–	–	–	–	✓	✓	–	140
Plougonvelin	–	C	T	✓	✓	–	–	–	–	–	–	–	–	✓	✓	✓	(16)
Pont-l'Abbé	H	C	T	✓	✓	–	◇	✓	–	▦	–	–	–	–	✓	✓	145
Pornichet	H	C	T	✓	✓	✓	–	✓	✓	▦	⛵	✓	B	–	✓	✓	146
Port-Haliguen	H	–	–	–	–	✓	–	✓	✓	–	–	✓	B	–	–	–	148
Portivy	H	–	–	–	–	✓	–	✓	–	–	–	–	–	✓	–	–	148
Port-Louis	H	C	T	✓	✓	✓	◇	–	✓	–	–	✓	–	✓	✓	–	146
Port-Manech	H	–	T	✓	✓	✓	–	✓	–	–	–	✓	–	–	–	–	143
Port-Navalo	H	C	T	✓	✓	✓	–	✓	✓	–	–	✓	B	–	✓	✓	126
Le Pouldu	H	C	T	✓	–	–	–	–	–	–	–	✓	–	–	✓	✓	153
Le Pouliguen	H	–	T	✓	✓	–	–	✓	✓	–	–	✓	–	✓	–	✓	146
Quiberon	H	C	T	✓	✓	–	◇	✓	✓	▦	⛵	✓	B	✓	✓	✓	147
Raguenès-Plage	H	C	–	–	–	✓	–	–	–	–	–	–	–	–	–	–	(33)
St-Gildas-de-Rhuys	–	C	–	✓	✓	–	–	✓	–	–	–	–	–	–	✓	–	165
St-Guénolé	H	C	T	✓	✓	✓	–	–	✓	–	–	–	–	–	✓	✓	165
St-Marc	–	C	T	✓	✓	–	–	–	–	▦	–	–	–	–	✓	✓	55
St-Philibert	H	C	–	–	–	–	–	–	–	–	–	–	B	–	–	–	(35)(36)
St-Pierre-Quiberon	H	C	–	–	–	✓	–	–	✓	–	–	✓	B	–	–	✓	(49)
Ste-Anne-la-Palud	H	C	–	–	–	✓	–	–	–	▦	–	–	–	–	✓	✓	117
Ste-Marine	H	C	T	✓	✓	✓	–	–	–	–	–	✓	B	✓	✓	✓	125
Sarzeau	H	C	T	✓	✓	✓	–	✓	✓	–	–	✓	B	–	✓	✓	125
Telgruc-sur-Mer	–	C	T	✓	✓	–	–	–	✓	▦	–	–	–	–	✓	✓	(17)
Tréboul	H	C	–	–	–	✓	◇	✓	✓	✓	–	✓	–	–	✓	–	88
La Trinité-sur-Mer	H	C	T	✓	✓	–	–	✓	✓	–	–	✓	B	✓	✓	✓	179
La Turballe	–	C	T	–	–	–	–	✓	✓	–	–	✓	–	–	✓	–	101

CHANNEL COAST

	Hotels = H	Camping site = C	Tourist centre = T	Doctor = ⚕	Chemist = ℞	Pleasant site = ◁	Particularly attractive town = ◇	Pleasure boat harbour = ⚓	Fishing port = 🎣	Cinema = ▦	Swimming pool = 🏊	Sailing school = ⛵	Boats for hire = B	Skin diving = 🤿	Tennis = 🎾	Horse riding = 🐎	Page in guide or no of section on Michelin map
The Aber-Wrac'h	H	–	–	–	–	◁	–	⚓	🎣	–	–	⛵	B	–	🎾	–	43
Arcouest (Point)	H	C	–	–	–	◁	–	⚓	🎣	–	–	–	–	–	–	–	135
Binic	–	C	T	–	℞	◁	–	⚓	🎣	–	▦	🏊	⛵	–	🎾	–	175
Bréhat (Island)	H	–	T	⚕	℞	◁	–	⚓	🎣	–	–	⛵	–	🤿	–	–	60
Bréhec-en-Plouha	H	–	–	–	–	◁	–	⚓	🎣	–	–	⛵	–	–	–	–	141
Brignogan-Plage	H	–	T	⚕	℞	◁	–	–	🎣	–	–	⛵	–	–	🎾	–	65
Cancale	H	–	T	⚕	℞	◁	–	⚓	🎣	–	–	⛵	–	🤿	🎾	–	66
Carantec	H	C	T	⚕	℞	◁	–	⚓	🎣	–	–	⛵	–	🤿	🎾	–	67
Cléder	–	C	T	⚕	℞	–	–	–	–	–	–	–	–	–	🎾	–	④
Dinard	H	C	T	⚕	℞	◁	–	⚓	🎣	▦	🏊	⛵	B	–	🎾	🐎	84
Erquy	H	C	T	⚕	℞	◁	–	⚓	🎣	▦	–	⛵	–	–	🎾	🐎	91
Etables-sur-Mer	H	C	T	⚕	℞	◁	–	–	🎣	▦	–	⛵	–	–	🎾	🐎	175
Ile-Grande	H	C	T	–	–	–	–	⚓	🎣	–	–	⛵	–	🤿	–	–	65
Lancieux	H	C	T	⚕	℞	◁	–	⚓	–	–	–	⛵	B	–	🎾	–	90
Landéda	–	C	T	⚕	℞	–	–	–	–	–	–	–	–	–	🎾	–	③
Lézardrieux	H	–	–	⚕	℞	–	–	⚓	–	–	–	⛵	–	–	–	–	⑧
Locquirec	H	C	T	–	℞	◁	–	–	🎣	–	–	⛵	B	🤿	🎾	–	49
Paimpol	H	C	T	⚕	℞	–	–	⚓	🎣	▦	🏊	⛵	–	🤿	🎾	–	135
Perros-Guirec	H	C	T	⚕	℞	◁	–	⚓	🎣	▦	–	⛵	B	–	🎾	–	138
Pléneuf-Val-André	H	C	T	⚕	℞	◁	–	⚓	🎣	▦	🏊	⛵	B	–	🎾	🐎	181
Plestin-les-Grèves	H	C	T	⚕	℞	◁	–	–	–	–	–	⛵	–	–	🎾	–	49
Plouescat	–	C	T	⚕	℞	◁	–	–	🎣	▦	–	⛵	–	–	🎾	–	186
Plouézec	–	C	–	⚕	℞	◁	–	⚓	–	▦	🏊	⛵	–	–	–	–	⑧
Plougasnou	H	C	T	⚕	℞	–	–	–	–	–	🏊	⛵	–	–	🎾	–	140
Plouguerneau	H	C	T	⚕	℞	–	–	–	🎣	–	–	–	–	–	🎾	–	47
Ploumanach	H	C	T	–	–	◁	–	–	–	–	–	–	–	🤿	🎾	–	142
Port-Blanc	H	–	–	–	–	◁	◇	⚓	🎣	–	–	⛵	–	–	–	–	179
Roscoff	H	C	T	⚕	℞	–	◇	–	🎣	–	–	⛵	–	–	–	🐎	162
Sables-d'Or-les-Pins	H	–	T	–	–	◁	–	–	–	–	–	⛵	–	–	🎾	–	91
St-Briac-sur-Mer	H	C	T	⚕	℞	◁	–	⚓	–	–	–	⛵	–	–	🎾	–	90
St-Cast-le-Guildo	H	C	T	⚕	℞	◁	–	⚓	🎣	▦	🏊	⛵	B	🤿	🎾	🐎	164
St-Jacut-de-la-Mer	H	–	T	⚕	℞	◁	–	⚓	–	–	–	⛵	–	–	🎾	–	90
St-Lunaire	–	C	T	⚕	℞	◁	–	⚓	–	–	–	⛵	–	–	🎾	–	166
St-Malo and Paramé - Rothéneuf-St-Servan	H	C	T	⚕	℞	◁	◇	⚓	🎣	▦	🏊	⛵	–	–	🎾	🐎	167
St-Michel-en-Grève	H	C	T	–	–	–	–	⚓	🎣	–	–	⛵	–	–	🎾	–	49
St-Quay-Portrieux	H	C	T	⚕	℞	◁	–	⚓	🎣	▦	🏊	⛵	B	–	🎾	–	175
Trébeurden	H	C	T	⚕	℞	◁	–	⚓	🎣	–	🏊	⛵	–	🤿	🎾	🐎	177
Trégastel-Plage	H	C	T	⚕	℞	◁	–	–	–	–	–	⛵	B	–	🎾	🐎	177
Tréguier	H	–	T	⚕	℞	◁	◇	⚓	🎣	–	🏊	⛵	–	–	🎾	–	178
Trélévern	–	C	–	⚕	–	–	–	⚓	🎣	–	–	–	–	–	–	–	⑦
Le Yaudet	H	–	–	–	–	◁	–	–	🎣	–	–	⛵	–	–	–	–	115

TOURS WITH A SELECTION OF PLACES TO STAY

Listed below is a selection of places to stay *(from the tables on pp 42-44)* which are situated on or at close proximity to the towns described, and accompanied by maps on pp 47-187.

The **Abers** *(p 47)*. – Aber-Wrac'h, le Conquet, Landéda, Lesneven, Plougonvelin, Plouguerneau.

Armorique Corniche *(p 74)*. – Locquirec, Plestin-les-Grèves, Plougasnou, St-Michel-en-Grève, le Yaudet.

Arrée Mountains *(p 49)*. – Huelgoat, Pleyben, Port-Launay, Sizun.

Belle-Ile *(p 56)*. – Le Palais, Port Goulphar, Quiberon.

Bretonne Corniche *(p 64)*. – Ile-Grande, Perros-Guirec, Ploumanach, Trébeurden, Trégastel-Plage.

Carnac Region *(p 70)*. – Carnac, Erdeven, Penthièvre, Port-Haliguen, Portivy, Quiberon, St-Philibert, St-Pierre-Quiberon, la Trinité-sur-Mer.

Cornouaille *(p 75)*. – Audierne, Douarnenez, Guilvinec, Lesconil, Locronan, Loctudy, Pont-l'Abbé, St-Guénolé, Ste-Anne-la-Palud, Ste-Marine, Tréboul.

Emerald Coast *(p 89)*. – Cancale, Dinard, Erquy, Lancieux, Pléneuf-Val-André, Sables-d'Or-les-Pins, St-Briac-sur-Mer, St-Cast-le-Guildo, St-Jacut-de-la-Mer, St-Lunaire, St-Malo.

Crozon Peninsula *(p 79)*. – Camaret-sur-Mer, Crozon, le Fret, Morgat, Telgruc-sur-Mer.

Grande Brière *(p 97)*. – La Baule, Guérande, Pornichet, St-Marc.

Guérande Peninsula *(p 100)*. – Batz-sur-Mer, la Baule, le Croisic, Guérande, Mesquer, Piriac-sur-Mer, le Pouliguen, la Turballe.

continued overleaf

	Hotels = H	Camping site = C	Tourist centre = T	Doctor	Chemist	Pleasant site	Particularly attractive town	Lake or artificial Stretch of water = ●	Park or public garden	Cinema	Swimming pool / Bathing place	Footpaths	Tennis	Horse riding	Bicycles for hire = B	Angling club	Page in guide or no of section on Michelin map

INLAND

	H	C	T	Doc	Chem	Pleas	Attr	●	Park	Cin	Swim	Foot	Tennis	Horse	B	Angl	Page
Bannalec	–	C	T	●	●	–	–	–	–	–	–	–	✕	–	–	✦	33
Baud	–	C	T	●	●	–	–	–	–	▦	↗	☎	✕	–	B	✦	54
Carhaix-Plouguer	H	–	T	●	●	◁	◇	–	☞	▦	↗	☎	✕	–	–	✦	68
Châteaubourg	H	–	–	●	●	–	–	●	–	–	–	–	✕	–	–	✦	27
Châteauneuf-du-Faou	H	C	T	●	●	◁	–	–	☞	▦	–	☎	✕	●	B	–	135
Dinan	H	C	T	●	●	◁	◇	●	–	▦	↗	–	✕	–	–	✦	81
Erdeven	H	C	–	–	–	–	–	–	–	–	–	–	–	–	–	–	35
La Gacilly	H	–	T	●	●	◁	–	–	☞	–	↗	☎	✕	●	B	✦	38 39
Gouarec	H	C	–	●	●	–	◇	–	☞	–	–	☎	✕	–	–	✦	21
Guéméné-Penfao	H	C	T	●	●	–	–	–	☞	–	↗	–	✕	–	–	✦	39 40
Guérande	H	C	T	●	●	◁	◇	–	☞	–	–	–	✕	–	B	–	99
Hennebont	H	–	T	●	●	–	–	●	☞	▦	–	☎	✕	–	–	✦	106
Huelgoat	H	–	T	●	●	◁	–	●	–	–	–	☎	✕	–	–	✦	107
Josselin	H	C	T	●	●	◁	◇	●	–	▦	–	☎	✕	–	–	✦	108
Jugon-les-Lacs	–	C	–	●	●	◁	◇	●	–	–	≈	☎	✕	–	–	✦	24
Lesneven	H	–	T	●	●	–	◇	–	☞	▦	–	–	✕	–	–	✦	3 4
Liffré	H	–	–	●	●	–	–	●	–	–	–	–	✕	●	–	✦	27
Locminé	H	C	T	●	●	–	–	●	–	▦	↗	–	✕	–	–	✦	186
Locronan	H	C	T	●	●	◁	◇	–	–	–	–	☎	✕	–	●	–	117
Mur-de-Bretagne	H	C	–	●	●	◁	–	●	–	–	–	–	✕	●	B	–	103
Muzillac	H	C	T	●	●	–	–	–	☞	–	–	☎	✕	–	–	✦	51
Pléven	H	–	–	–	–	–	–	–	–	–	–	☎	✕	–	B	✦	24
Pleyben	–	C	T	●	●	◁	◇	–	–	–	–	–	✕	–	–	✦	139
Ploërmel	H	C	T	●	●	◁	–	●	☞	▦	↗	☎	✕	–	B	–	139
Plomodiern	H	C	T	●	●	◁	–	–	–	▦	–	☎	✕	●	–	✦	18
Pont-Aven	–	C	T	●	●	◁	◇	–	☞	–	–	–	✕	–	–	✦	142
Pont-Pol-Ty-Glas	H	–	–	–	–	◁	–	–	–	–	–	–	–	●	–	✦	19
Port-Launay	H	–	–	–	–	–	●	–	☞	–	–	–	–	–	–	✦	50
Quimperlé	H	–	T	●	●	◁	◇	–	☞	▦	–	☎	✕	●	B	✦	152
Quintin	H	C	T	●	●	◁	◇	–	☞	▦	–	☎	✕	–	–	✦	154
Riec-sur-Belon	H	C	T	●	●	–	◇	–	–	▦	–	–	–	–	–	✦	33
La Roche-Derrien	H	–	T	●	●	◁	◇	–	☞	–	–	–	✕	–	–	✦	7
Rochefort-en-Terre	–	C	T	●	●	◁	◇	–	–	–	≈	☎	✕	–	–	✦	161
St-Yvi	–	C	T	●	●	–	–	–	–	–	–	–	✕	–	–	✦	32 33
Sizun	H	–	T	●	●	◁	◇	●	☞	▦	↗	–	✕	–	–	✦	138
Trégunc	H	C	T	●	●	◁	–	–	☞	–	–	–	–	–	B	–	33

TOURS WITH A SELECTION OF PLACES TO STAY

Guerlédan Lake *(p 103)*. – Gouarec, Mur-de-Bretagne.

Lannion Region *(p 114)*. – St-Michel-en-Grève, Trébeurden, le Yaudet.

Morbihan Gulf *(p 128)*. – Arradon, Arz (Island), Arzon, Conleau, Locmariaquer, Moines (Island), Port-Navalo, St-Gildas-de-Rhuys, St-Philibert, Sarzeau, la Trinité-sur-Mer.

Noires Mountains *(p 134)*. – Carhaix-Plouguer, Châteauneuf-du-Faou, Pont-Pol-Ty-Glas.

Parish Closes *(p 137)*. – Huelgoat, Locquénolé, Sizun.

Plougastel Peninsula *(p 140)*. – Plougastel-Daoulas.

Pontivy Region *(p 144)*. – Baud, Mur-de-Bretagne.

Quiberon Peninsula *(p 147)*. – Carnac, Erdeven, le Palais, Penthièvre, Port-Haliguen, Portivy, Quiberon, St-Pierre-Quiberon.

Quimper Region *(p 150)*. – Bénodet, Fouesnant, Ste-Marine.

Quimperlé Region *(p 153)*. – Guidel-Plage, Moëlan-sur-Mer, le Pouldu, Quimperlé.

Rance Valley *(p 154)*. – Cancale, Dinan, Dinard, Lancieux, St-Briac-sur-Mer, St-Lunaire, St-Malo.

Tréguier Region *(p 178)*. – Port-Blanc, la Roche-Derrien, Tréguier.

Join us in our never ending task of keeping up to date.

Send us your comments and suggestions, please.

Michelin Tyre Co. Ltd
Tourism Department
81 Fulham Road, LONDON SW3 6RD.

	Page in guide or no of section on Michelin map 230	ESTABLISHMENTS Name and telephone number	Comfort	Characteristics ≼ Extensive view or pleasant view	P = Pancakes S = Sea food
Audierne	51	Aux Bonnes Crêpes de la Chaumière, along the corniche road to the beach	●●	....	P ..
Auray	52	Crêperie Quintin, Rue Père-Eternel ...	●	Breton interior, paintings .	P S
Batz-sur-Mer	54	Crêperie du Derwin	●	≼ St-Gildas Point	P S
Baule (La)	54	L'Espadon, 2 Avenue de la Plage ☎ 60.05.63	●●●	≼ bay and coast	P S
Bénodet	58	Ferme du Letty, Letty ☎ 91.01.27	●●	Country style	P S
		Au Bon Vieux Temps, 35 Ave Plage ☎ 91.01.41		Breton furniture	P ..
Boël (Le)	160	Auberge du Vieux Moulin ☎ 52.81.25	●	≼ the Vilaine and old mill	P S
Cape Fréhel	96	Relais de Fréhel ☎ 41.43.02.........	●	An old farm in a shaded garden	.. S
Carnac	69	Chez Yannik, 8 Rue Tumulus	●●	Country style, garden	P S
		Chez Marie, 3 Place de l'Eglise ☎ 52.07.93	●●	Country style	P S
Clohars-Carnoët	㉞	Crêperie St-Maurice (E : 5 km-3 miles by D 224) ☎ 96.67.05		≼ the Laïta	P ..
Concarneau	73	Noz-Ha-Deiz, 18 Place St-Guénolé	●●●	17C house, Breton furniture	P ..
Croisic (Le)	78	Océan, in Port-Lin ☎ 23.00.03	●●	≼ ocean	.. S
		Crêperie Le Bot, 6 Rue Marine	●●		P ..
		Chez Tante Germaine ☎ 23.06.90	●	Rural Breton interior	P ..
		Crêperie Jan, 10 Quai Aiguillon ☎ 23.05.75	●		P ..
Dinan	81	Crêperie « Le Connétable », Rue Apport ☎ 39.06.74	●●	15C house, country style ..	P S
Douarnenez	87	Au Goûter Breton, 36 Rue J.-Jaurès ☎ 92.02.74	●●	....	P ..
Guildo (Le)	104	Manoir du Guildo ☎ 41.04.85	●	Manor in a park	P ..
Huelgoat	107	Crêperie de l'Argoat, Rue Lac ☎ 93.71.72	●	≼ lake	P ..
		Crêperie Gallou, Rue Lac ☎ 93.70.55 .	●	≼ lake	P ..
Josselin	108	A la Bonne Crêpe ☎ 22.21.98	●●	....	P ..
Locquénolé	⑤	Kerliviou ☎ 67.21.04	●●●	Park, ≼ bay	P S
Locronan ;	117	Ty Coz, Place Eglise ☎ 91.70.79......	●●	Breton setting	P ..
		Manoir de Moellien (N W : 3 km-2 miles by VO) ☎ 92.50.40	●●		P ..
Malestroit	119	Crêperie du Corps de Garde ☎ 22.41.57	●	Country style, fire places .	P ..
Nantes ;	128	Au Bon Vieux Temps, 11 Rue Ste-Croix ☎ 47.01.83	●●	....	P ..
Paluden	③	Relais de l'Aber ☎ 84.01.21	●	≼ the Aber...........	.. S
Pen-Lan (Point)	㊿	Auberge de Pen-Lan ☎ 26.60.16......	●●●	Old house, flowered terrace, ≼ sea	P S
Pleven	㉔	Manoir de Vaumadeuc (W : 1.5 km-1 mile by D 28 and D 16) ☎ 27.14.67	●●●	15C manor, park	.. S
Plomodiern	44	Ferme de Pors Morvan ☎ 81.53.23....	●	Country style	P ..
Ploubalay	90	Panoramic ☎ 27.21.89	●	≼ over the coast	P ..
Pont-Aven	142	Chez Candide	●●	....	P ..
Pont-l'Abbé	145	Courot, route Penmarch ☎ 87.02.61 ..	●	....	.. .
		Crêperie des Douves, 2 Rue Burdeau ☎ 87.01.50	●	....	P ..
Quimper	149	Taverne des Cariatides, 4 Rue Guéodet ☎ 95.44.17	●●	Old house, Breton interior	P ..
		Au Vieux Quimper, 20 Rue Verdelet ..	●	Rural Breton interior	P ..
		Le Minuellou, 10 Rue Sallé ☎ 95.39.49	●	16C house, Breton furniture	P S
Quimperlé	152	Auberge de Toulfoën (S : 3 km-2 miles by D 49) ☎ 96.00.29	●●	≼ forest	P S
		Ty Breiz, 13 Rue La Tour-d'Auvergne ☎ 96.05.33	●	....	P S
Raz (Point)	76	Ty Breiz ☎ 70.07.02	●	....	P S
Riec-sur-Belon	㉝	Chez Mélanie ☎ 06.91.05	●●●	Old furniture, paintings, garden	.. S
Roche-Bernard (La)	160	Steak House (N W : 1 km-1/2 mile on N 165) ☎ 08.60.69	●	≼ the Vilaine	P S
Rothéneuf	171	Rochers Sculptés ☎ 58.22.07	●	≼ sea	.. S
St-Pierre-Quiberon	148	Ty Breiz, 23 Boulevard Chanard ☎ 50.09.90	●●	Country style	P S
		Le Courlis ☎ 52.21.14	●	≼ bay	P S
Ste-Marine	151	La Crémaillère ☎ 56.36.65	●	Garden	P ..
Tréguier	178	Crêperie du Cloître ☎ 20.33.18	●	....	P ..
Trinité-sur-Mer (La)	179	Restaurant Le Rouzic ☎ 52.72.06	●●	≼ harbour	.. S

CONVENTIONAL SIGNS

*** ST MALO	Worth a journey	N	National road
** Dinan	Worth a detour	D	Department road
* St Servan	Interesting	RF	Forest road
Rothéneuf	See if possible	Rtn	Return, Round trip
Antrain	Reference point		

230 8 Number and section of Michelin map (scale: 1 inch = 3.15 miles)
Pop 2750 = Population

Maps and Plans

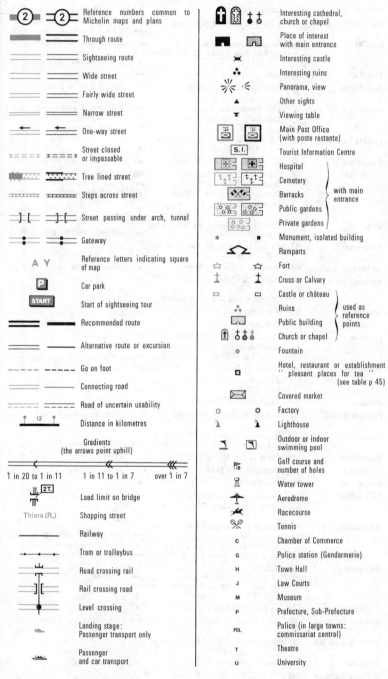

Reference numbers common to Michelin maps and plans	Interesting cathedral, church or chapel
Through route	Place of interest with main entrance
Sightseeing route	Interesting castle
Wide street	Interesting ruins
Fairly wide street	Panorama, view
Narrow street	Other sights
One-way street	Viewing table
Street closed or impassable	Main Post Office (with poste restante)
Tree lined street	S.I. Tourist Information Centre
Steps across street	Hospital
Street passing under arch, tunnel	Cemetery
Gateway	Barracks — with main entrance
Reference letters indicating square of map	Public gardens
Car park	Private gardens
Start of sightseeing tour	Monument, isolated building
Recommended route	Ramparts
Alternative route or excursion	Fort
Go on foot	Cross or Calvary
Connecting road	Castle or château
Road of uncertain usability	Ruins — used as reference points
Distance in kilometres	Public building
Gradients (the arrows point uphill)	Church or chapel
1 in 20 to 1 in 11 — 1 in 11 to 1 in 7 — over 1 in 7	Fountain
Load limit on bridge	Hotel, restaurant or establishment "pleasant places for tea" (see table p 45)
Thiers (R.) Shopping street	Covered market
Railway	Factory
Tram or trolleybus	Lighthouse
Road crossing rail	Outdoor or indoor swimming pool
Rail crossing road	Golf course and number of holes
Level crossing	Water tower
Landing stage: Passenger transport only	Aerodrome
Passenger and car transport	Racecourse
	Tennis
	C Chamber of Commerce
	G Police station (Gendarmerie)
	H Town Hall
	J Law Courts
	M Museum
	P Prefecture, Sub-Prefecture
	POL. Police (in large towns: commissariat central)
	T Theatre
	U University

Campers...

The Michelin Guide Camping Caravaning France
describes in detail the resources and amenities of selected sites.
Use the current edition.

46

TOWNS, SIGHTS
AND TOURIST REGIONS

The ABERS

Michelin map **230** 2, 3

The northwest coast of Finistère, still known as the Coast of Legends, is broken up by estuaries called *abers* (Aber-Wrac'h, Aber-Benoît, Aber-Ildut), which make a fine sight at high tide.

The *abers* are different from the estuaries on the north coast (rivers of Morlaix or Tréguier, Trieux): their beds are much less deep and their slopes less steep. Beyond high-tide mark the *aber* is prolonged upstream not by a small coastal river but by a tiny brook too small to dig a channel in the muddy estuary. There is no great port at the head of the estuary, as there is at Morlaix or Dinan.

The whole of this low and rocky coast, dotted with small islands, is particularly rich in varieties of seaweed. Factories process most of it: the brown species in the manufacture of alginates and mannitel, the fucus and floating weed as stock-feed; the remainder is sold as fertiliser *(details p 18)*.

ROUND TOUR STARTING FROM BREST

146 km - 91 miles – about 8 hours – Local map below

Leave Brest (p 61) by ② on the map, the D 788.

Gouesnou. – Pop 3 056. The 17C church suffered badly in the war. The belfry has been restored and the 1615 polygonal chevet is surmounted by three pediments. In the shade of the tree, the fine Renaissance fountain is adorned by a statue of St Gouesnou.

St-Jaoua. – *4 km - 2½ miles from Plabennec.* Standing in the centre of a shady parish close is a charming 15C chapel which contains the tomb of St. Jaoua.

Locmaria Chapel. – *1.5 km - 1 mile from the D 788.* This detour is worth while only to tourists interested in archaeology. In front of the 16-17C chapel there is a fine **crucifix*** with figures.

Le Folgoët★★. – *Description p 92.*

Grouannec-Coz. – Charming village church with many wooden statues and ceramic crosses marking the stations of the Cross. The fountain, Notre-Dame-de-la-Clarté, may be seen 100 m from the church.

Plouguerneau. – Pop 5 471. *Facilities p 43. Pardon on the last Sunday in June.*

Vierge Lighthouse (Phare de la Vierge). – *5 km - 3 miles from Plouguerneau.* Tourists wishing to visit the lighthouse and see the view from the top should take the D 71 to the landing stage where they will leave the car *(car park)*. Several boats cross to the island and the lighthouse which is the tallest in France (75 m - 246 ft – Bishop Rock lighthouse, Scilly Isles, 146 ft). *Information from Mme Riou at the Hôtel Castel Ac'h, Lilia Beach or telephone 84 70 20.*

The ABERS

The road across the **Aber-Wrac'h** and the valley is winding and picturesque. At high tide the view of the *aber* is very fine.

The Aber-Wrac'h. – *Facilities p 43*. This little port, yachting anchorage and seaside resort is at the mouth of the estuary, here over a mile wide. On the left bank are the ruins of the convent of Notre-Dame-des-Anges, near the Restaurant de la Baie des Anges.

Ste-Marguerite Peninsula (Presqu'île de Ste-Marguerite). – ¼ *hour on foot Rtn*. Before returning to Lannilis go on to Landéda and then to the Tresmenguy dam where the path divides: the fork on the right leads up to a point overlooking the sea and from which there is a view of Cézon Fort, the lighthouse on the Île de la Vierge, Plouguerneau and the Baie des Anges. The fork to the left goes to the Ste-Marguerite dunes: turn right and right again and leave the car opposite the Hôtel des Dunes. Walk round the hotel, bearing right to reach the Dunes and Ste-Marguerite beach. There is a wide view out over the sea: to the left is the Aber-Benoît and in the distance the Portsall Rocks.

Landéda. – Pop 2 250. *Facilities p 43*.

Aber-Benoît. – A pretty spot. There is a bridge over the *aber*.

    Lampaul-Ploudalmézeau. – Pop 551. *1 km - ½ mile from the D 28*. The church is modern apart from the north door which dates from the Renaissance. It also has a magnificent 17C belfry-porch which is crowned by a dome above which rise three little lantern-towers one above the other.

Portsall. – Small harbour in a sheltered bay.

Kersaint. – Near this village are the ruins of the feudal castle of Trémazan.

Trémazan. – Extensive view of the sea.

Beyond Trémazan, the corniche road approaches Landunvez Point.

Argenton. – A small fishing port.

Aber-Ildut. – The road continues beyond the village round the picturesque estuary of the same name which marks the theoretical boundary between the Channel and the Atlantic.

    Trézien Lighthouse (Phare de Trézien). – *4 km - 2½ miles from Plouarzel*. From the top (*182 steps*) there is a wide **panorama★**. You can go on to **Corsen Point** *(1 km - ½ mile – plus 1 hour Rtn on foot)*. This 50 m - 160 ft cliff is the most westerly point in France.

Le Conquet. – Pop 1 881. *Facilities p 42*. This is a fishing port for crawfish and lobsters and departure point for the islands of Ushant and Molène. The church has a fine 16C stained glass window.

St-Mathieu Point★★. – *Description p 171*.

ANTRAIN

Michelin map **230** 27 – Pop 1 626

    Antrain overlooks rich farmlands bordered by hedges and trees and green valleys, lying as it does high on the promontory before the confluence of the Couesnon and Loisance Rivers. It is a market town with steep little streets.

    Of its former Romanesque church there still remains a fine portal with a semicircular arch and buttresses on either side.

EXCURSION

Bonne-Fontaine; Tremblay; Le Rocher-Portail. – *16 km - 10 miles – about ½ hour. Leave Antrain by the Tremblay road to the south. Just 1 500 m - 1 mile farther along turn right.*

    Bonne-Fontaine Castle (Château de Bonne-Fontaine). – *The park may be visited between Easter and All Saints' Day to 7pm. Leave the car at the gate.*
    Built in 1547 as a feudal castle, Bonne-Fontaine, whose fortifications disappeared in the 19C, rises in the centre of a beautifully maintained park. The elegant turrets adorning the massive main part of the building, the great windows and the carved dormer windows balance the severity of the squat, machicolated pepper-pot towers.

    Tremblay. – Pop 1 810. The church, which was built in the 11 and 12C and modified in the 16C, is a good example of Romanesque architecture. There is only a single aisle; the solid square tower that rises above the transept crossing is topped by a pierced bell-turret. Notice the elegance of the canopy and the glory radiating outwards from the top of the great cross on the high altar which bears three heads symbolising the Holy Trinity at its centre, and at its foot the symbols of the four Evangelists. The beam is ornate, entwined by a vine and ears of corn being pecked by birds. There are interesting old wooden statues.

Follow the D 796 for 2 km - 1 mile and then the D 155 towards St-Brice-en-Coglès. At St-Brice turn left into the D 102 and after 2 km - 1 mile turn left and then shortly after right. The way to the castle branches off to the right a little before you reach the river.

    Le Rocher-Portail Castle (Château du Rocher-Portail). – It is amazing to find this homogeneous and impressive building set in the heart of the country.
    Gilles Ruellan, one-time pedlar who became a councillor of state, built the castle in 1608. A long façade and two wings at right angles to it enclose a big courtyard; along its fourth side runs a granite balustrade and beyond it is the moat spanned by a bridge which serves as the entrance. The ground floor of the wing on the left forms a beautiful arcaded gallery whose outer side looks out over a pool. An arched passageway through the right wing leads to a second courtyard.

Return to Antrain by La Selle-en-Coglès, Coglès and the D 15 road.

    If you intend to combine your tour of Brittany
    with journeys through Normandy or the Loire Valley
    remember to take
    the Michelin Green Guides Normandy, Châteaux of the Loire

ARMORIQUE CORNICHE ★

Michelin map 🔟230 6

This short section of the Channel coast should be seen by all tourists who visit northern Brittany. The Lieue de Grève, a long, majestic stretch of sand, is followed by steep capes skirted from a distance by the Armorican coast road proper.

FROM ST-MICHEL-EN-GRÈVE TO POUL RODOU

18 km - 11 miles – about ½ hour – Local map below

St-Michel-en-Grève. – Pop 382. *Facilities p 43.* A small seaside resort. The church and cemetery are well sited near the sea.

Lieue de Grève★. – This magnificent beach, 4 km - 2½ miles long, lies across the base of a bay which runs dry to a depth of over 2 km - 1 mile at low tide. Trout streams run into the sea through small green valleys. The road, which is very picturesque, follows the wooded coast and skirts the rocky mass of the Grand Rocher.

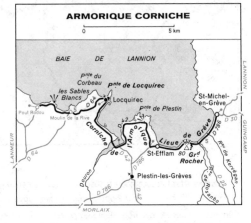

Climbing the Grand Rocher★. – ½ hour on foot Rtn. A steep path, starting from the west slope (on the St-Efflam side), leads to this 80 m vantage point - 261 ft. There is a very fine **view★** of the Lieue de Grève; at high tide, especially with a north-westerly blowing in winter, the sight of the endless foaming rollers breaking on the beach and dashing against the seawall that protects the D 786 gives an excellent idea of the undertow *(see details on waves p 13).*

St-Efflam. – Next to the St-Efflam Chapel, half hidden by lush vegetation, is a fountain, surmounted by a massive dome. Efflam, a hermit who came from Ireland and landed with seven companions in 470 in the neighbouring bay of Porzmellec, settled in a place called Coz Iliz, 2 km - 1 mile beyond the Grand Rocher. Efflam died there in 512.

Plestin-les-Grèves. – Pop 3 241. *Facilities p 43.* Its 16C church, mined and burnt by the Germans in 1944, has since been rebuilt. The building contains the tomb of St. Efflam. A statue shows him vanquishing a dragon, the symbol of paganism.

Armorique Corniche★. – Between St-Efflam and Locquirec the road picturesquely follows the much indented coast. After Plestin Point there is a view of Locquirec Bay and its Cape. Before reaching the village you will see, on your right and in the distance, the Bretonne Corniche *(p 64)* as far as Trébeurden.

Locquirec. – Pop 1 035. *Facilities p 43.* A small fishing port and seaside resort. The **church★** *(closed on Sunday afternoons),* which was formerly an almonry of the Knights of Malta, is charming, with its little Renaissance belfry turret. Inside, the panelled vaults of the chancel and transept are covered with 18C paintings. At the high altar is an **altarpiece★** illustrating the scenes of the Passion. On the left of the chancel is a niche containing the statue of Our Lady of Succour, flanked by a Tree of Jesse and six panels depicting the life of the Virgin. Against the left-hand pillar in the nave nearest to the chancel is an alabaster *Pietà.*

A walk around **Locquirec Point★** *(½ hour on foot Rtn)* offers fine views of the Bretonne Corniche.

Beyond the mill, Moulin de la Rive, take the road to the right in the direction of Poul Rodou, which follows the corniche overhanging the sea. About 1.5 km - 1 mile before the junction with the D 64 there is a **viewing table**: to the east the Moulin de la Rive, the Sables Blancs beaches and the rocky Corbeau Point; to the north Losquet island stands out from the others by means of the CNET (National Telecommunications Research Organisation) pylon; to the west is Poul Rodou beach (again access 800 m - 2 625 ft below).

ARRÉE MOUNTAINS ★★ (MONTS D'ARRÉE)

Michelin map 🔟230 18, 19

Of all the Breton "mountains", those of Arrée are the most typical. Their picturesqueness is due to the grim and barren face of nature. Several of the peaks afford fine views.

The Arrée Mountains are the highest in Brittany, yet their topmost point is less than 400 m - 1 200 ft. They were perhaps proud peaks in the primary era *(details of Breton formations, p 11),* but erosion has done its work. The sandstone or granite summits have been turned into rounded hills or *menez* (Menez-Bré and Menéz-Hom, *p 120*). The quartz formations, cleared by the action of water on the schist around them, have become sharp crests, fretted into saw-teeth and bristling with *aiguilles* (needles); these are the rocks or *roc'hs* (eg Roc Trévezel). The hills convey the impression of being mountains through their barrenness and solitude, the keen sea winds, the wide views revealed and the mist which often crowns their summits.

The mountain is wooded in parts, especially towards the east, but the summits are usually quite desolate. There is not a tree on them; the heath is pierced by rocky scarps; here and there are clumps of gorse with golden flowers in spring and purple heather in September. A few poor hamlets stand far apart. On the flanks of the hills small streams have dug valleys which are sometimes wild, sometimes full of freshness and verdancy. The whole area of the Arrée Mountains is now affected by the **Armorique Regional Nature Park** set up in 1969. This guarantees, for the greater benefit of tourists, the protection of sites and of fauna and flora.

49

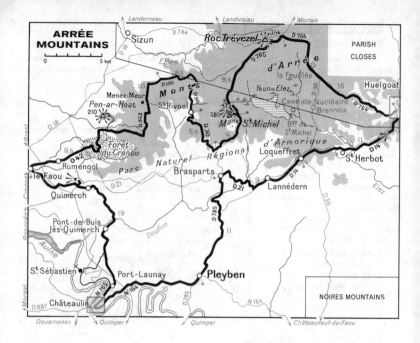

FROM HUELGOAT TO LE FAOU by way of Brasparts

60 km - 38 miles – about 2 hours – Local map above

A little over 2 km - 1 mile from Huelgoat *(p 107)*, the D 14 offers a very extensive view of the Aulne basin and the Noires Mountains.

St-Herbot*. – *Time: ½ hour*. The **church*** with its square tower, stands surrounded by trees in the middle of a desolate, arid countryside. Most of the church is in Flamboyant Gothic style. A small Renaissance ossuary stands against the porch on the right. There is a fine Crucifix in granite from Kersanton in front of the building.

Inside, the chancel is surrounded by a remarkable **screen**** in carved oak, surmounted by a Crucifix. Standing against this screen, on the nave side, are two stone tables for the tufts of hair from the tails of oxen and cows which the peasants offered on the *pardon* to obtain the protection of St. Herbot, the patron saint of horned cattle. Note also fifteen carved stalls (raise the seats), the Saint's tomb, and the stained glass in the main window of the chancel.

Loqueffret and Lannédern. – Pop 511 and 409. Each of these villages has a small parish close. 1.5 km - 1 mile beyond Lannédern leave the D 14 and take the D 21 to Brasparts.

Brasparts*. – Pop 1 189. *Tour: ¼ hour*. An interesting 16C **parish close*** *(details of the closes, p 31)*. On entering the church we see on the right a **Virgin of Pity***. On the left of the chancel is an altarpiece of the Rosary; in the chancel, left of the high altar, a fine 16C stained glass window.

Pleyben**. – *Description p 139*.

Châteaulin. – *Description p 71*.

Take the N 170 to Port-Launay.

Port-Launay. – Pop 549. *Facilities p 44*. This is the port of Châteaulin, on the Aulne.

> **Alternative route via the St-Sébastien Chapel.** – *Extra distance, 5 km - 3 miles – plus ¼ hour sightseeing*. On reaching the village of Port-Launay, 3 km - 2 miles from Châteaulin, take a small road to the left which follows the course of the Aulne before climbing the hillside. In the cemetery beside the chapel are a triumphal arch and a Calvary with 16C figures. Inside the chapel *(ask for the key at the farm on the opposite side of the road)*, 17C **altarpieces*** are to be seen in the chancel and south transept; in the north transept are opening statues with shutters and panels giving story of the Loreto.

Continue on the small road to rejoin N 170, 2 km - 1 mile before Pont-de-Buis.

Pont-de-Buis-lès-Quimerch. – Pop 4 220. The village contains an explosives factory, nearly three centuries old. To its former activities have now been added plastic moulding, ammunition for sport and the industrial application of explosives.

Quimerch. – On the right, half a mile after leaving the town, is a viewing table: the **view*** stretches from the Ménez-Hom to the Cranou Forest taking in the Bay and Peninsula of Plougastel.

The N 170 leads to Le Faou (p 91).

FROM LE FAOU TO HUELGOAT by the heights

62 km - 39 miles – about 2 hours – Local map above

From Le Faou (p 91) take the D 42 towards Rumengol.

Rumengol. – This village is at its most interesting on *pardon* days. People come from all over Brittany to attend these festivals dedicated to Our Lady of all Remedies. The most interesting is on Trinity Sunday *(p 10)*; there is another on 15 August (Assumption Day). Rumengol dates from the time of King Gradlon, who built a chapel there in the 5C. The present church is 16C as is shown by the south porch and the magnificent granite face; there were, however, many fundamental alterations made in the 17 and 18C. Inside, a 15C statue of Our Lady stands at the entrance to the chancel. The altarpieces and organ cases are 17C. In the centre of the village, near the church apse, is a sacred fountain. On a grass lawn surrounded by fir trees stands an oratory where services are held on the two great *pardon* days.

Cranou Forest* (Forêt du Cranou). – The road, hilly and winding, runs through the State Forest of Cranou, which consists mostly of oaks and beeches.

Penn-ar-Hoat*. – Alt 210 m - 687 ft. *1 km - ½ mile from the D 42 – plus ¾ hour walk Rtn.* Leaving Cranou Forest, you reach a gorse covered plateau with a road by a forge; bear right towards St-Rivoal; 800 m - 875 yds farther on, turn left on a surfaced road that goes down to a stream before climbing to a line of heights. At the beginning of a gentle downward slope on the far side, leave your car at the entrance to the village.

Walk along the road branching off on the left at right angles. Bear left around a small village and again left towards the line of heights; after passing between low walls, the climb ends among gorse bushes. The **panorama*** which spreads out before you is a good example of the Breton hill country covered with heath. To the north are hills bordering the left bank of the Élorn, to the east the nearer heights of the Arrée, to the south the Forest of Cranou, and in the distance the Noires Mountains and the Ménez-Hom, and lastly, to the west, the Brest roadstead.

Menez-Meur Estate (Domaine de Menez-Meur). – *Open 10am to noon and 2 to 7pm. Closed Sunday mornings, 1 January, 1 May, 1 November, 25 December. Admission: 2F.*
This heather and gorse covered estate has several rocky ridges which afford good views of the surrounding countryside. The Central Administrative Services of the Armorique Regional Nature Park and a visitors' information bureau are located on the estate.

St-Rivoal. – Pop 225. *Museum open 1 June-30 September from 9am to noon and from 2 to 6.30pm. Closed Sunday, mornings and 1 January, 1 May, 1 November, 25 December. Admission: 2F.*
A house dating from the 18C is one of the many exhibits, dispersed throughout the park, that go to make up the open-air museum showing the different styles of Breton architecture.

Farther on, the road winds through a countryside of hills, and of green and wooded valleys whose freshness contrasts with the bare summits, which are rocky and covered with heath.

St-Michel Mountain* (Montagne St-Michel). – *The way is signposted (1 km - ½ mile) leading off the D 785. It goes to a parking place from which you may reach the summit by a stony road.*

From the top of the rise (alt 380 m - 1 246 ft), where there is a little chapel at an altitude of 391 m - 1 251 ft you will see a **panorama*** of the Arrées and Noires Mountains. From the foot of the hill a great peat bog called the Yeun Elez extends towards the east. In the winter mists, the place is so grim that Breton legend says it contains the "Youdig", a gulf forming the entrance to Hell. Beyond it may be seen the reservoir dam of St-Michel which supplies the Arrée Mountains thermo-nuclear establishment at Brennilis.

There are fine views of the countryside and the mountains from the road.

Trévezel Rock** (Roc Trévezel). – *Description p 179.*

Continue to Huelgoat (p 107).

ASSÉRAC

Michelin map **230** 51, 52 – Pop 1 079

Lying on the western periphery of the **Brière Regional Nature Park** *(p 97),* this village has in the coastal waters a shell-fish breeding centre.

EXCURSIONS

Pen-Bé. – *6.5 km - 4 miles to the west by the D 82 then the D 282.* This vantage point affords a **view** of the bay with its profusion of upstanding poles for mussel rearing, Merquel Point and Dumet island in the distance.

Bile and Scal Points*. – *Round tour of 30 km - 19 miles to the west by the D 82 and the D 201. Turn left at Kerséquin.*

Bile Point. – The **view*** extends over two small offshore islets and the great ochre coloured cliffs.

Take the road leading to Pénestin and turn left in the direction of **Poudrantais.** The road follows the coast for a short distance giving glimpes of the cliff line.

Mine d'Or Beach. – Two strange rocks, one in the shape of a menhir interrupt this long stretch of beach at the foot of tall cliffs.

Once through Pénestin, branch off to the left. The village **Le Haut-Pénestin** has many attractive houses.

Halguen Point. – Heathland and pine trees cover this headland. Walk down to the rocky beaches which are backed by a short line of cliffs.

Return to Pénestin following the south bank of the river Vilaine.

Tréhiguier. – This small fishing port is a mussel breeding centre. Anchored in the estuary are pleasure craft mingling with the many motor and rowing boats used for the mussel fishing. Walk to **Scal point** to see the estuary widen between the Halguen and Pen-Lan headlands.

Return to Assérac by the D 192 and the D 83.

When visiting the Continent

use Michelin Red Guides
Benelux – Deutschland – España Portugal – France – Italia
(hotels and restaurants)

and the Michelin Green Guides
Austria – Germany – Italy – Portugal – Spain – Switzerland
(sights and tourist routes)

AUDIERNE ★

Michelin map **230** 16 – *Local map p 75* – Pop 3 679 – *Facilities p 42*

This fishing port is on the estuary of the Goyen, at the foot of a wooded hill and in a pretty **setting★**. The beach is 1.5 km - 1 mile from the town.

Audierne is engaged chiefly in fishing for lobsters and crawfish along the coast, but there is also tunny fishing between June and October *(details on the fishing industry, p 17)*. The tourist will be interested in the busy port. A *pardon* is held on the last Sunday in August.

Thatched Cottage (La Chaumière). – *To reach the cottage, take the Quai Pelletan, towards the beach. Guided tours from 1 April to 20 September from 8am to 8pm. Admission: 4F.*

The cottage contains 17 and 18C Breton furniture as well as everyday life objects.

EXCURSIONS

Raz Point★★★. – *15 km - 9 miles – about 2 hours. Description p 76.*

Sein Island★. – *Boat services and description p 176.*

AURAY ★

Michelin map **230** 36 – *Local map p 124* – Pop 10 398

This ancient town is built on the banks of the Loc or Auray River near the famous sanctuary of Ste-Anne-d'Auray. For the tourist it has the attraction of its harbour, as seen from the Loch promenade, and its old St-Goustan quarter.

The Battle of Auray (14C). – The town is famous in Breton history for the battle that was fought under its walls in 1364 and ended the War of Succession *(p 20: Historical Facts)*. The troops of Charles of Blois, backed by Du Guesclin, held a bad position on a marshy plain north of Auray. Charles's cousin, Jean de Montfort, Olivier de Clisson, and the English, under Chandos, were in a dominating position.

Against Du Guesclin's advice, Charles attacked and was beaten. His body was picked up on the battlefield. On seeing the corpse of his rival, whom the Bretons made into a saint, Montfort could not master his emotion. But Chandos roused him, saying, "You cannot have your cousin alive and the Duchy too. Thank God and your friends."

Du Guesclin had fought like a desperate man: having broken all his weapons, he felled his opponents with his iron gauntlets. The English leader saw him, pushed through the mêlée and persuaded him to surrender by saying: "The day is not yours, Messire Bertrand; you will be luckier another time." As for Olivier de Clisson, whose action was decisive, he lost an eye in the fight.

Cadoudal, or the last Chouan. – Cadoudal was a farmer's son. He was twenty-two years old when the Chouannerie (Breton royalist revolt) broke out in 1793. He plunged into it body and soul. When the men of the Vendée were beaten he carried on the struggle in Morbihan. He was captured and imprisoned at Brest but escaped, went back to the guerrillas, took part in the action at Quiberon *(p 147: historical notes)*, came away unhurt, submitted to Hoche in 1796 and reopened the campaign in 1799. The mobile columns that hunted him afterwards undertook huge engineering works; the banks and hedges of the country, which the Chouans used as ramparts and hiding-places, were cleared away. Bonaparte offered the rebel a pardon and the rank of general, without success. The struggle ended only in 1804; Cadoudal had gone to Paris to try to kidnap Napoleon; he was arrested, sentenced to death and executed. His body was given to medical students for dissection. The great surgeon Larrey kept the skeleton, mounted on wire. The remains were finally buried in a tomb built within sight of Cadoudal's house on Kerléano Hill, at the gates of Aurey.

■ **MAIN SIGHTS** *time: ¾ hour*

Loch Promenade. – You will find a hillside promenade under trees from which there is a good **view★** over the port, the St-Goustan quarter and the Auray River, crossed by an old stone bridge.

To explore the St-Goustan Quarter on the left bank, go down winding paths to the riverside quay.

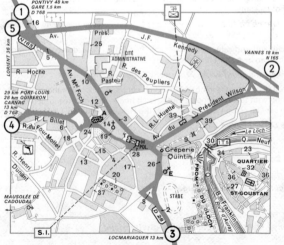

AURAY

0   300 m

St-Goustan Quarter* (Quartier St-Goustan). – From the Place St-Sauveur, a picturesque square with 15C houses, the Rue Neuve, a narrow alley edged with old houses, strikes off to the left. Ahead is the Rue St-René, which is steep and cut by steps. Climb this and turn right into the Rue St-Sauveur, which leads to the Church of St-Goustan. In front of the church turn to the right again along a paved alley which slopes downhill and ends in the Rue du Petit-Port. This street, lined with picturesque dwellings, leads back to the Place St-Sauveur.

The quay to the left of the square is called after Benjamin Franklin. In 1776, during the War of Independence, the famous American sailed from Philadelphia to negotiate a treaty with France and landed at Auray, for head winds prevented his ship from going up the Loire to Nantes. The house where he stayed (150 m from the square) bears a tablet.

■ ADDITIONAL SIGHTS

Eternal Father Chapel (Chapelle du Père-Eternel) (E). – Inside there are carved wooden **stalls***.

St-Gildas (A). – This church was built in the 17C, and contains a very fine **altarpiece*** at the high altar. At the end of the church, on the left, is a baptismal font with a carved canopy.

EXCURSIONS

Ste-Anne-d'Auray*. – *Round tour of 15 km - 9 miles – about 1 hour. Leave Auray by* ① *on the plan, road D 768.*

Carthusian Monastery of Auray (Chartreuse d'Auray). – *Open 10am (10.30am Sundays and holidays) to noon and 2 to 5.30pm. Closed 1 to 12 September.*
On the battlefield where he defeated Charles of Blois *(p 52)*, Jean de Montfort (who became Duke Jean IV) built a chapel and a collegiate church which were afterwards transformed into a Carthusian monastery. In 1968 a fire ravaged this monastery, then an institution for blind and deaf-and-dumb women. The funeral chapel, built in 1829 to hold the bones of exiles and Chouans who were shot on the Champ des Martyrs in 1795, after the unsuccessful Quiberon landing *(p 147)*, was badly damaged. Over the burial vault stands a black and white marble mausoleum bearing the names of 953 exiles, with low reliefs. This is intact.

Champ des Martyrs. – *Apply for a guide at the "Café de Toul-Bahadeu".* The exiles and Chouans were shot in this enclosure. An expiatory chapel was built in 1829.

Shortly after the Champ des Martyrs the road skirts the Kerso bog (on the right) where the Battle of Auray was fought, climbs the leftward slope of the deep Valley of the Loc and leaves on its right the monument erected in 1891 to the memory of the Count of Chambord, the Pretender who narrowly failed to upset the régime at the beginning of the Third Republic.

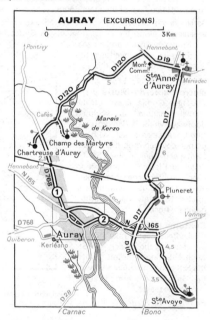

AURAY (EXCURSIONS)

> **Ste-Anne-d'Auray*.** – *Description p 176.*
>
> **Pluneret.** – Pop 1 871. In the cemetery, alongside the central alley, on the right, are the tombs of the Countess of Ségur, the writer of children's books, and of her son, Mgr de Ségur.

Ste-Avoye. – *4 km - 2½ miles – about ¼ hour. Leave Auray by* ② *on the plan, road N 165.* Among picturesque cottages, near a wash-house, stands a pretty Renaissance chapel *(ask for the key)*. According to legend the boat used by Ste Avoye to reach Brittany was a hollowed out stone. The fine oak **rood-screen*** is carved and painted to represent the apostles on the side facing the nave and the virtues on the side towards the chancel.

Boat trip on the Auray River and to the Morbihan Gulf**. – *To arrange a trip – from June to mid September – get in touch with the Vedettes Vertes, Tel 66 10 78 and 66 10 79 at Vannes, at Auray, Quai St-Goustan or the Tourist Information Centre of Auray, Tel 24 09 75.*

BARNÈNEZ Tumulus ★ (Cairn de Barnenez)

Michelin map **230** 5 – 4 km - 2½ miles northwest of Plouézoc'h

Open 1 June to 30 September; closed Tuesdays; apply to the nearby caravans with the following mention "Musée des Affaires culturelles, service des recherches archéologiques".
This megalithic monument (barrow) surmounted by an impressive **tumulus**, in this case a mound of dry stones (**cairn** in Brittany and Scotland), stands on the Kernéléhen peninsula, dominating the Bay of Térénez and the Morlaix estuary. Discovered accidentally it is now possible to see this ancient burial place in cross section. Excavations between 1955 and 1968 revealed eleven burial chambers, two of which were roofed with great horizontal slabs. The entrances all faced south and were preceded by 7-12 m - 23-39 ft long passages. From the colour of the stones, it would appear that there were two distinct periods of construction: the first tumulus in a local green stone is more than 6 000 years old while the second one, nearer the slope is 300 years younger and is composed mainly of the light coloured Stérec granite, from an offshore island.

BATZ-SUR-MER ★

Michelin map 230 51 – 7 km
- 4 miles west of La Baule –
Local map p 101 – Pop
2 236 *– Facilities p 42*

Bordered by the ocean on
one side and the salt marshes on
the other, Batz's tall church belfry
acts as a ready landmark. The
rocky coastline is interrupted by
three sandy beaches: Valentin, La
Govelle and St-Michel, the latter
being protected by a breakwater
beside which stands the Pierre-
Longue menhir.

St-Guénolé★. *– Time: about ½
hour.* Originally belonging to a
priory in the 13C, the church was
rebuilt in the 15 and 16C. Its
belfry, 60 m - 190 ft high, surmounted by a pinnacled turret,
dates from 1667.

In the **interior**, you will notice
at once that the central axis is
off-centre, that massive pillars
support Gothic arches and that
the wooden roof is shaped like
the keel of a boat. The **keystones**
of the arches in the north aisle
are remarkably carved. One of
the windows in the south aisle
commemorates the consecration of the building in 1488. Against the pillar to the right of the
chancel is the 15C Flemish **Statue of the Virgin★** (Our Lady of the Precious Blood). On leaving note
to the right and left of the main doorway, two 17C statues in painted wooden cupboards.

Ascent to the belfry. – *15 June to 15 September. Admission: 2F.* There is an extensive
panorama★★ along the coast from the St-Gildas Point, south of the Loire, to the shores of
the Rhuys Peninsula and, at sea,
to Belle-Ile; you overlook the
chessboard pattern of the salt
marshes *(details p 100).*

Notre-Dame-du-Murié (A). –
The fine Gothic **ruins★** of the
chapel include a sculpted
doorway which is flanked by a
turret staircase intact with its
granite covered roof. It is said to
have been built in the 15C by
Jean de Rieux de Ranrouët to
keep a vow he made when in peril
at sea: legend has it that he was
guided to safety by a burning
mulberry bush.

**Customs Officers' Path (Sen-
tier des Douaniers).** – Take the path
in front of the beach of St-
Michel, turning to the left. It skirts
the cliff edge and offers a view of
the Grande Côte and, later, of
impressive **rocks★**.

Return by the Rue du Golf.

LA BAULE

Albatros (Av. des) _____ CY 2
Améthystes (Allée des) _ EZ 3
Andrieu (Av.) _____ BZ 4
Armorique (Av. d') _____ FZ 6
Baguenaud (Av. d') _____ DZ 7
Berry (Av. du) _____ EZ 8
Chambord (Av. de) _____ EY 10
Champsavin (Av. Guy de) _ AZ 12
Chateaubriand (Av.) ___ EZ 13
Chaumont (Av. de) _____ EZ 15
Chenonceau (Av. de) ___ EY 16
Clemenceau (Av. G.) ___ DY 17
Concorde (Av. de la) ___ CYZ 19
Dr.-M.-Chevrel (Bd) ___ CDY 20
Duruy (Av.) _____ BY 21

BATZ

Gare (R. de la) _____ 2
Gaulle (R. Ch. de) _____ 3
Maupertuis (R.) _____ 4
Parcs (R. des) _____ 5
Plage (R. de la) _____ 6
St-Jean (R.) _____ 7

BAUD

Michelin map 230 36 – Pop 5 137 *– Facilities p 44*

The village overlooks the Evel Valley. The nave of the church (1927) opens off a 16C chapel
of Our Lady of Light; old wooden statues.

EXCURSION

The Venus of Quinipily. *– 2 km - 1 mile to the west.* Leave Baud by the Hennebont road; after
1 500 m - 1 mile, take a narrow road downhill, leaving your car 500 m farther on at a fork. Walk
straight ahead for 20 m then bear left and left again to pass between gateway pillars.

The Venus is on the right, standing over a fountain. The origins of the statue are uncertain. It
has been taken for a Roman idol or an Egyptian Isis. When it was the object of almost pagan
worship, it was twice thrown into the Blavet by order of the ecclesiastical authorities; the people
fished it out. The figure which was recarved in the 18C, bears only a very remote resemblance to
the Goddess of Beauty.

A gourmet ... ?
*If you are, look in the current Michelin Guide France
for the establishments with stars.*

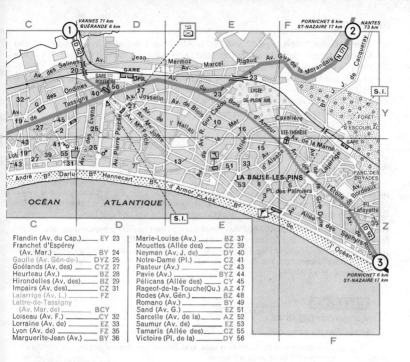

La BAULE ★★★

Michelin map 230 51, 52 – *Local map p 101* – Pop 15 193 – *Facilities p 42*

Started in 1879 La Baule is one of the best known seaside resorts on the Atlantic coast and one of the most fashionable in Brittany. Its splendid beach of fine sand extends for over 5 km - 3 miles.

Now an amenity the sand was in the past responsible for the disappearance of the village of Escoublac. Measures were taken in 1840 to fix the dunes by planting 400 ha - 1 000 acres of maritime pines and the village was then rebuilt farther inland. However, in 1879 the construction of La Baule was started, near the original site of **Escoublac** *(p 100)*. The town was to enjoy a mild climate by the pines to the north and the Points of Ponchâteau and Chémoulin on the west and east.

The attraction of La Baule for the tourist lies in the beautiful bay, the animated and colourful scene on the beach, the promenade beside it, the Casino, the large hotels, pretty villas and fine parks. Added to this is the **pleasure boat harbour** created in the well sheltered channel linking the ocean to the salt marshes.

La Baule is extended eastwards by the resort of **La Baule-les-Pins★★**, which was built in 1930, in an area forested with pine trees. The Allée Cavalière links the **Escoublac Forest** to the Boulevard de l'Océan. To the east of Place des Palmiers, the park, **Parc des Dryades**, is a haven with its shaded alleys and colourful masses of highly scented flowers. Salt-water swimming pools are part of a thalassotherapy institute (salt-water cure).

EXCURSIONS

Guérande Peninsula★ (Presqui'île de Guérande) – *Round tour of 63 km - 39 miles – about 2½ hours. Description p 100.*

St-Nazaire by the coast road★. – *Round tour of 38 km - 24 miles – about 1¼ hours.*
The coast road provides good views of the bay of La Baule and goes through the seaside resorts of Pornichet (*p 146 – take the D 292 as you come out of the town*), Ste-Marguerite and St-Marc.

St-Marc. – *Facilities p 42.* The village is backed by cliffs which afford views of Chemoulin Point to the west and Fort de Lève to the east. Take the path to the left of the beach which climbs to a small wood.

BÉCHEREL

Michelin map 230 25 – Pop 543

From this village, once a wartime vantage point, perched on a hill 176 m - 577 ft high there is an extensive view towards Dol, Dinan and Combourg. Only a few traces of ramparts of the former fortress remain.

Caradeuc Castle. – *1 km - ½ mile to the west. To visit the park, apply to the porter at the entrance gates. Admission: 3F.* This former home of a famous Attorney-General, Louis-René, Marquess of Caradeuc de la Chalotais *(details p 157)*, has a very fine **park★**.

From the north terrace there is an immense view towards Dinan and the Upper Valley of the Rance.

EXCURSION

Couëlan; Rophémel Dam. – *Round tour of 20 km - 12 miles – about ¾ hour. Leave Bécherel by the D 20 which passes in front of Caradeuc Castle. After 4 km - 2½ miles turn right.* By way of Plouasne and the D 25, from which there are views of the dam area of the Rance, you come to a spot, not far from Caulnes, from where you can see Couëlan Castle.

BÉCHEREL

Couëlan Castle. – This large 17 and 18C building has a beautiful, symmetrical and well balanced façade. Outbuildings and terraced gardens may be seen on the right. The whole makes a pleasant and unified group. *No visits allowed.*

Continue towards Caulnes, take the D 766 and then turn right to run along the banks of the Rance. Follow the D 89 and the D 90. From Guenroc you can make for a belvedere (car park) which looks straight down on to the Rophémel Dam.

Return to Bécherel by Le Val and Plouasne.

BEG-MEIL ★

Michelin map **230** 32 – *Facilities p 42*

Beg-Meil is a watering-place at the entrance to the La Forêt Bay, opposite Concarneau, in wooded country. The little sandy beach to the right of the port is framed in rocks among which pines grow; the Grande Plage, backed by dunes, faces the Atlantic. From this side there is a view of the Glénan archipelago. From Beg-Meil Point beyond a large menhir knocked down by the Germans, on the left, there is a fine view of Concarneau and the La Forêt Bay.

Boat trips. – During the season you may reach Concarneau (p 73) by crossing the bay, the St-Nicolas island (Glénan p 97), Quimper (p 149) by the Odet (p 151).

Apply to M. R. Guillou at Beg-Meil, Tel 94 97 94 or Transports Maritimes at Concarneau, Tel 97 11 59. Information from the Tourist Information Centres at Beg-Meil (Tel 94 97 47) and Concarneau (Tel 97 01 44).

BELLE-ILE ★★

Michelin map **230** 48, 49

Access: *See the current Michelin Guide France. Private cars for hire.*

We strongly recommend the following excursion which, besides the sea trip, includes a tour of the island, notably the famous **Côte Sauvage.**

This, the largest of the Breton islands, is a schist plateau measuring about 84 sq km - 32 sq miles – 17 km long and 5 to 10 km wide – 11×3-6 miles. The mean altitude is 40 m - 128 ft (highest point: 63 m - 200 ft). It is crossed by many valleys which cut deeply into the high rocks and end as deep, safe harbours. There is a marked contrast between the middle of the plateau, exposed to wind, sun and rain and covered with wheat fields alternating with patches of gorse, and the small sheltered valleys, with their lush fields and fine trees. The east side, which is well protected, has many creeks with good bathing.

On the slopes the 140 villages of the island form clusters of whitewashed houses surrounded by fields in which wheat, oats, potatoes, maize and green peas are grown. Sheep of a highly valued breed graze on the salty pastures.

HISTORICAL NOTES

Fouquet, Marquis of Belle-Ile. – The Retz family, who owned Belle-Ile after 1572, sold it to Superintendent Fouquet in about 1650. The latter, wishing to make it a safe retreat in case of misfortune, completed the fortifications. His immense wealth even enabled him to keep his own fleet, of which the flagship was the *Grand Écureuil* (Great Squirrel – the Fouquet coat of arms includes a squirrel with the motto: "How high shall I not climb?"). This audacious policy, added to the swindles and slights which he practised on Louis XIV, was his undoing.

The last act was played out at Nantes, which the Court was visiting in 1661. D'Artagnan and the Musketeers seized Fouquet as he came out of the castle and put him in a coach which made all speed for Vincennes. He died in 1680.

A fortified rock. – As an outlying citadel of the French coast, Belle-Ile has been attacked many times by British and Dutch fleets. It was taken twice by the British and occupied until the Treaty of Paris (1763). The island has conserved its defensive system: in addition to Le Palais citadel there are several 18 and 19C isolated outworks (redoubts) around the coast.

Canadians, Bretons. – In 1765 many Canadian families came to live on the island; they brought with them the potato many years before Parmentier introduced it to France. These Canadians were descendants of the French who had lived in Canada since the beginning of the 17C and had refused to submit to the English who had held Nova Scotia from the time of the Treaty of Utrecht, 1713. The Canadian families were moved to New England and then, after the Treaty of Paris, to France and finally to Belle-Ile.

A refuge for artists. – Since the late 19C, numerous are the artists who have been attracted by the beauty and calm of this isle, a haven for inspiration: Claude Monet, Sarah Bernhardt and the musician Albert Roussel.

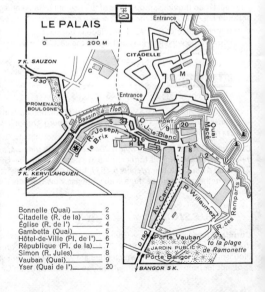

LE PALAIS

Bonnelle (Quai)	2
Citadelle (R. de la)	3
Église (R. de l')	4
Gambetta (Quai)	5
Hôtel-de-Ville (Pl. de l')	6
République (Pl. de la)	7
Simon (R. Jules)	8
Vauban (Quai)	9
Yser (Quai de l')	20

- ## LE PALAIS

Pop 2 649 – Facilities p 42 – Time: 2 hours

This the island's main town is where most of the facilities are to be found. Boat services link it to Quiberon on the main land. Arriving by boat or from the Rue des Remparts there is a good view of the port, with its fishing and pleasure craft, overlooked by the citadel.

Citadel★. – *Free access with 1st rampart. Access beyond 2nd rampart and to museum from 9am to 6.30pm. Closed Wednesdays. Keep or museum: 5F.*

Built in 1549 on the orders of Henri II, the citadel was Fouquet's stronghold. The double ramparts and powerful corner bastions strongly resembles Vauban's military architecture. The citadel was both a prison and barracks till 1961. Note in the southwest corner a three walled round tower, the remains of the first castle. Numerous views of Le Palais and the coast.

The **museum** in the Louis XIII buildings contains interesting documents on the island's history and souvenirs of Fouquet and Albert Roussel.

TOUR STARTING FROM LE PALAIS

47 km - 30 miles – about 4 hours – Local map below

Leave Le Palais by the Portes Vauban and Bangor (south on the plan, the D 190).

The Grand Lighthouse★ (Grand Phare). – *Open 1 July to 15 September 9am to 6pm; the rest of the year by request; time: ½ hour.* The lighthouse, opened in 1835 and itself 46 m - 150 ft high stands perched on a rock so that its light is actually 84 m - 275 ft above the level of the sea. The beam carries 64 km - 40 miles; the equipment also includes a radio beam.

From the balcony there is a fine **view★★** of the island, the sea , the islands and coast round Lorient (where the great crane can be seen in clear weather) as far as Locmariaquer.

Port Goulphar★. – *Facilities p. 42. ¼ hour on foot Rtn. Leave the car near the Goulphar manorhouse and bear left.* You will find the port of Goulphar, a narrow inlet, framed by picturesque cliffs.

The Port-Coton Needles★★ (Aiguilles de Port-Coton). – Leave the car at Port-Coton, so-called because the sea there seems to boil and builds up a great mass of foam like cotton wool.

Turn a sharp right and on to a spur projecting into a cove in which the Aiguilles (Needles) stand; some of these pyramids are pierced by grottoes. Follow the cliff edge to the right (without going too near) for a view over Port-Coton Bay.

Port-Donnant★★. – *¼ hour on foot Rtn.* Leave your car a little before the end of the road and continue on foot until you reach a fine sandy beach dotted with rocks and enclosed between high cliffs. The setting is superb, bathing dangerous.

Apothicairerie Grotto★★★ (Grotte de l'Apothicairerie). – *½ hour on foot Rtn.* Its name is derived from the cormorants' nests which at one time were placed in rows in the rocky cavities, like the jars on the shelves of a chemist's shop. At the end of the point, in front of the Hôtel de l'Apothicairerie, by the signpost, go down a flight of steps cut in the rock *(caution: slippery steps)*. Before reaching the entrance, you will see on your left the Pierced Stone (Roche Percée). The grotto forms a deep cavity into which the sea flows, the water taking on a curious blue-green colour.

Poulains Point★★. – *½ hour on foot Rtn.* At the end of the tarred road and the following road you will find on the left, overlooking a creek framed in rocks, the small fort once owned by Sarah Bernhardt and where she spent several summers.

Leave the car and make your way down the slip to the sandy isthmus which connects the island with Poulains Point. On the point stands a lighthouse from which, looking left, you will see, below, the Dog's Rock (Rocher du Chien). From this same point there is a **panorama★** from left to right of the Vieux-Château Point, the rocks of the Côte Sauvage, Groix Island, the peninsula and bay of Quiberon, the Rhuys peninsula, the islands of Houat and Hœdic and Taillefer Point.

Sauzon★. – Pop 566. This busy little yachting basin lies in a pretty setting on the left bank of the estuary of the Sauzon River.

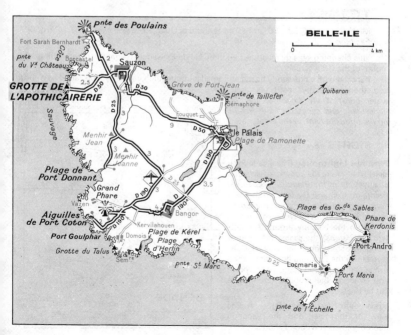

■ **ADDITIONAL SIGHTS**

From the edge of the cliff you will see a very extensive panorama of the coast: the **Taillefer Point** and the **Vieux-Château Point** with traces of Roman entrenchments, the **Le Talus Grottoes** and the **St-Marc Point**, the **Echelle Point**, with its semicircle of jagged rocks.

Locmaria. – Pop 565. In the church are two pictures of the Spanish school attributed to Murillo. The cove of Port-Maria is 500 m away.

Kerdonis Lighthouse (Phare de Kerdonis). – It helps ships to navigate between Hœdic and Belle-Ile.

Beaches. – Among the most beautiful are **Kerel** and **Herlin**, facing south, **Port-Andro**, where the English landed in 1761, and the **Grands Sables** (Great Sands), where the Dutch Admiral van Tromp tried to land in 1696.

BELLE-ISLE-EN-TERRE

Michelin map **230** south of 7 – Pop 1 269

This old township stands in a picturesque piece of country at the meeting of two rivers, the Léguer and the Guic. It is a centre for excursions, shooting and fishing.
The town has a paper mill which uses water power from the Léguer.
Every year, on the third Sunday in July or the following Tuesday, Belle-Isle-en-Terre holds a Breton wrestling championship. This is an original and very ancient sport which may be of interest to tourists *(see p. 24: Pardons)*.

EXCURSIONS

Menez-Bré★. – *9 km - 5½ miles to the northwest – about ½ hour. Description p 120.*
Go out by the N 12, the Guingamp road. 2.5 km - 1½ miles after Louargat, turn left into the Menez-Bré road which goes steeply uphill.

Loc-Envel★. – Pop 104. *4 km - 2½ miles to the south – about ¼ hour.* Leave by the Callac road, the D 33, and turn right fairly soon into the D 33B which is winding and picturesque.
The church of Loc-Envel in Flamboyant Gothic style rises from the top of a mound and dominates the village. One is struck, on entering, by the rich decoration of the wood panelled **vaulting★**. Also interesting are the raising pieces, the two hanging keystones, a Christ in benediction at the entrance to the choir and a Holy Trinity with angels at the transept crossing. The four supporting ribs of the crossing have each at their base a coloured statue of an Evangelist. The 16C furnishings are in keeping with the statuary and carvings: the Flamboyant rood-screen, the screens near the font, the ancient statues, the main window in the chancel and the later 17C altarpiece at the high altar.

Locmaria. – *1 km - ½ mile to the north, follow the Trégrom road, the D 33.*
There is a good view from near the church; inside is a fine 16C rood-screen.

Gurunhuel. – Pop 508. *9 km - 5½ miles to the southeast by the D 22 – about ¼ hour.* Near the 16C church stands a Calvary of the same date. From the base rise three crosses: the central one bears a Crucifixion with Christ between the Virgin Mary and St. John on one side and a Virgin of Pity on the other. The other two crosses show the robbers, their souls in the form of little men leaving their bodies and being received by an angel in the case of the good robber, and a demon in the case of the bad. Standing on the base are a Roman soldier, St. Peter, St. Michael and St. Paul.

BÉNODET ★

Michelin map **230** 32 – 16 km - 10 miles south of Quimper– *Local map p 151* – Pop 2 087 – *Facilities p 42*

This charming seaside resort lies on the Côte de Plaisance in a pretty, green setting at the mouth of the Odet estuary.

Bénodet with a fine sandy beach and small harbour much used by yachts, also has a casino and thalassotherapy institutes (salt-water cure). *Daily boat services for pedestrians and cyclists, to Ste-Marine on the opposite bank of the Odet.*

■ **SIGHTS** *time: 1½ hours*

Pyramid Lighthouse (Phare de la Pyramide) (A). – *Take the coast road, which is one-way, from the Plage du Trez to the Pointe du Coq and the ferry dock. Make your way to the lighthouse-keeper's house. The keeper will show you round.*
From the balcony around the lantern *(192 steps)* the **panorama★** extends along the coast from the Bay of Concarneau to the Eckmühl light, and at sea to the Glénan Archipelago. To the north you overlook the wooded countryside cut by the Odet.

View over the Odet (B). – A fine view of the river and the yachting harbour between wooded shores.

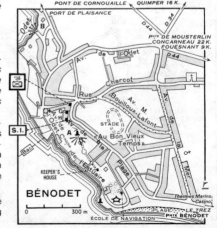

BÉNODET

Bénodet Point. – Take the Corniche de la Plage, then follow the shores along the Corniche de la Mer to reach the Lichaven Dune *(viewing table)*. Extensive view over Loctudy, Moutons Island and the Glénan Archipelago, Mousterlin Point and the Mer Blanche, a lagoon used as headquarters by the Letty sailing school.

Cornouaille Bridge (Pont de Cornouaille). – *1 km - ½ mile to the northwest. Toll: for rates see the current Michelin Guide France.*

This elegant modern structure carries the D 44 across the Odet. The vital statistics of the bridge from which there is a good **view*** of the port, Ste-Marine and the estuary: total length 610 m - 2 001 ft; central span 200 m - 655 ft and height above the water 30 m - 98 ft.

EXCURSION

Mousterlin Point. – *Facilities p 42 – 8 km - 5 miles to the southeast – about ¼ hour. Go out by road D 44, and after 4 km - 2 miles take road D 134.*

From the end of the point there is an extensive view of the coast. The Eckmühl light can be seen on the right after dark.

BOAT TRIPS

For all information apply to Vedettes de l'Odet "Aigrettes", BP no 8 or telephone 91 00 58 at Bénodet.

Up the Odet River**. – *To Quimper (time: ½ hour), departure from Bénodet in July and August at 9.15am, 1.15pm, 2.30pm, 3.15pm, 4pm; in May, June and September at 2.30pm only. Description of the trip down the Odet p 151.*

Loctudy; Glénan Islands. – *Crossing time: ½ hour for Loctudy and 1¾ hours for the Glénan Islands. Description of Loctudy, p 117 and of the Glénan Islands, p 97.*

BERVEN

Michelin map **230** 4 – 1.5 km - 1 mile north of Plouzévédé

The triumphal arch through which you enter the parish close *(details on parish closes p 31)* is a fine specimen of Renaissance art directly inspired by antiquity with its three semicircular arches and its pilasters with capitals.

Church*. – *Apply to Mademoiselle Anna Picart, Place du Champ de Foire.* The church, which is 16C, has a façade surmounted by a square tower crowned with a dome with small lanterns and ornamented by balustrades; it was the first of its kind in Brittany (1573) and served as a model for many others. A wooden rood-screen stands before the very fine chancel **enclosure***, ornamented on the front with small fluted granite columns and at the sides with wood carvings. In the chancel are some 17C stalls with arm-rests in the form of winged caryatids. In the chapel to the left of the chancel is a 16C altarpiece whose panels depict, in low relief, scenes from the life of the Virgin; in the centre is a statue showing the Virgin on a crescent moon.

From the Notre-Dame-de-Berven fountain 50 m to the south there is a good view of the parish close.

BLAIN

Michelin map **230** 54 – Pop 7 208

The Nantes to Brest canal separates this market town in a countryside of orchards, from its castle, whose main building is now occupied by a private school, the Institution N.-D. de la Groulaie.

La Groulaie Castle (Château de la Groulaie). – *Only the outside can be seen.* This fortress which originally belonged to Olivier de Clisson became Rohan family property from 1407 to 1802. Despite the fact that in 1628 Richelieu razed the ramparts there are still impressive **ruins***. The 16C **Drawbridge Tower** (Tour du Pont-Levis) with its pepper-pot roof, overlooks the now dry moats. Beyond the outbuildings and the playground stands the 15C **King's Apartments** (Logis du Roi). The main façade with its tall pinnacled dormer windows, strange gargoyles and its brick patterned chimney stacks, reveals all the charm of the Renaissance. The rather severe looking tower to the right is called the **Constable's Tower** (Tour du Connétable, 1386).

EXCURSION

Gâvre Forest* (Forêt du Gâvre). – *Round tour of 13 km - 8 miles to the north by the D 15.* The road crosses the stands of oak interspersed with beeches and pines, which cover 4 400 ha - 10 900 acres to reach the **Belle Étoile crossroads**, the meeting point of ten converging avenues. Near a picnic site with benches, and tables is a hut displaying a map of the forest.

Follow the D 35 to the east and turn left onto the track at La Maillardais.

La Magdeleine Chapel. – *Apply to Madame Gilles Gautier for the key.* Formerly part of a leper hospital, this modest 12C chapel with a timber roof has a charming 15C polychrome **Virgin***.

Return to La Maillardais and continue straight on to Le Gâvre.

Le Gâvre. – Pop 825. The 12-15C church (restored) has a strange 17C lateral belfry. Inside there is a timber cradle roof. The stained glass windows dating from the 1930s evoke the First World War.

Places to stay

A wide variety of places to stay – pleasure boat harbours and resorts – have been selected to make your holiday more pleasant.
A map on pp 40-41 shows the location of the places listed on pp 41-44.

Michelin map **230** 8 – Pop 553 – *Facilities p 43.*
Access: *See the current Michelin Guide France.*

Bréhat is a much frequented holiday resort which deserves a visit. Seen from the coast, the island is fine and colourful: its pink rocks stand out on a blue or green sea. It is a pleasant place for a ramble. Cars are not allowed.

GEOGRAPHICAL AND HISTORICAL NOTES

Bréhat, which is about 3.5 km - 2 miles long and 1.5 km - 1 mile wide, consists of two islands joined by a narrow tongue of land. The coast, much broken and indented, is formed of pink granite rocks. It is surrounded by many islets and reefs.

The interior is a labyrinth of paths, with low houses turning their backs to the strong west and north winds and tiny fields bounded by dry stone walls. Scattered about the island are many villas and parks. Thanks to the very mild climate (winter average 6 °C - 43 °F) mimosa, oleander, myrtle and fig trees grow in the open. There is little rain, the clouds generally passing over this flat island to condense over the mainland.

Bréhat once enjoyed a certain amount of sea traffic. The Bay of La Corderie, deeply cut into the west coast, was used as a port by many ships. According to local tradition it was a sea-captain from Bréhart, Coatanlen, living in Lisbon, who revealed the existence of the New World to Christopher Columbus in 1484 – eight years before its official discovery – and showed him the course taken by the island's fishermen, who were already familiar with Newfoundland waters.

TOUR OF THE ISLAND *2 to 4 hours*

According to the tides the boats come in at one of three landing points, the nearest **Port-Clos** is used at high tide. The woodland, **Bois de la Citadelle**, overlooks the cliffs and has a camp site within its bounds. The most popular beaches are the **Petit** and **Grand Guerzido** both basically shingle beaches with alternating stretches of sand. The main road crosses both islands and in so doing passes through the capital, **Le Bourg** grouped around its small square and 12-18C church with a strange granite wall-belfry.

St-Michel. – High on a mound this chapel serves as a landmark for shipping. There is an attractive **view★** over the south of the island, the Kerpont sound and the roadstead, Etang de Birlot overlooked by the ruins of a once tide-operated mill.

Maudez Cross (Croix de Maudez). – Isolated amidst the heather the cross evokes the memory of a monk named Maudez who founded a monastery, in the year AD 570, on a neighbouring island. There is a fine **view★** of the islands of Béniguet to the left and Maudez to the right and various other reefs.

Beyond the bridge, Pont ar Prat, the road forks and each one leads to one of the island's two lighthouses. The pleasant route to the west skirts the bay. The **Rosédo lighthouse** dating from 1862 stands in the heart of

BRÉHAT

0   500 M

Paimpol ↓   l'Arcouest – S! Quay-Portrieux

the island. To the north the Paon road passes on the left the salt-water pool, Ar Lenn, before terminating in a footpath.

Paon Lighthouse★ (Phare de Paon). – Built in 1853 it was subsequently destroyed in 1944 to be rebuilt five years later. The paved platform at the foot of the lighthouse affords a remarkable view of the broken coastline, the chasm, the pink rocks and light coloured shingle. This is the wildest part of the island.

BOAT TRIPS

For information apply to the agencies running the Bréhat boat services: Tel 20 00 11 Bréhat; Tel 20 82 30 Paimpol. Departures from Arcouest Point.

Tour of the island★★. – *Time: about 1 hour. Departures from Arcouest and Port-Clos, with possible landings on the island if conditions permit.* The tour allows the visitor to see the changing aspects of the coast: the beauty of the northern rocks and cliffs; the Mediterranean charm of the eastern seaboard and the ever changing colour of the sea, which is so often a deep blue.

Pontrieux. – Pop 1 549. *Time: about 1¾ hours.* Pleasant excursion on the Trieux estuary.

The perfect companion to this guide:

Michelin map 230 *at a scale of 1:200 000*
Sightseeing, principal sights, viewpoints, road conditions.

Michelin map **230** 17 – *Local map p 47* – Pop 172 176

Brest was heavily damaged during the Second World War. However, the capital of western Brittany has completely recovered. As well as being the first French naval port, it is also a commercial and industrial centre.

It has also developed into the second university centre of Brittany. The **Cultural Centre** (Palais des Arts et de la Culture) *(p 63)* has become a focal point for a large variety of activities. Erected on the shore of Ste-Anne-du-Portzic *(p 64)*, the **Oceanographic Centre** offers opportunities for scientific research.

After the war, Brest was rebuilt on a geometric plan with its main artery at the wide Rue de Siam which links the naval base to the Place de la Liberté.

The streets open onto the Penfeld or the Cours Dajot from where there are good views over the magnificent roadstead (*rade*) in which all the fleets of Europe could lie.

HISTORICAL NOTES

The English set foot in Brest (14C). – During the War of Succession which began in 1341, Montfort, ally of the English, was rash enough to let them guard the town. When he became Duke of Brittany, Montfort tried to drive out the intruders by force of arms. He failed. The King of France also failed. At last, in 1397, Charles VI persuaded the King of England, Richard II, who had married Isabella, the French King's eldest daughter, to restore Brest to the Duke.

The "Belle Cordelière". – On 10 August 1513, St. Lawrence's Day, the English fleet of Henry VIII set out to attack Brest. The Breton fleet sailed to meet it. Soon its panic-stricken commander fled back to the sound. The *Belle Cordelière*, the gift of Anne of Brittany to her Duchy and on which 300 guests were dancing when the order came to weigh anchor, covered the commander's retreat and bore the brunt of the attack. Fire broke out on board the *Cordelière* as she was fighting gun to gun with an English ship. The commander, Hervé de Portzmoguer, or as he was known in France: Primauguet, knowing that his ship was lost, exhorted his crew and his guests to die bravely with the words: "We will now celebrate the Day of St. Lawrence who died by fire!" The two ships blew up together.

The Work of Colbert (17C). – Colbert, the greatest Minister the French Navy ever had, completed the task begun by Richelieu, making Brest the maritime capital of the kingdom. To obtain good crews he set up the Inscription Maritime (marine record and administrative office) which still exists today. After completing their military service, fishermen between the ages of eighteen and forty-eight are placed on the French Naval reserve; the Inscription Maritime looks after them and their families all their lives.

Colbert also founded at Brest a school of gunnery, a college of marine guards, a school of hydrography and a school for marine engineers.

From this enormous effort a magnificent fleet emerged. Ships reached a tonnage of 5 000 and carried up to 120 big guns. Artists like Coysevox worked at Brest on carved prows and poops.

Duquesne improved the dockyard, built ramparts round the town and organised the defence of the Sound (Le Goulet). Vauban, the military architect, completed the undertakings. Tourville improved mooring facilities in the roadstead laying down buoys to which ships could moor instead of dropping anchor.

The "Belle Poule". – In 1778, during the American War of Independence, the frigate *La Belle Poule* encountered the British *Arethusa* and forced her to retreat. This success was very popular at court where all the ladies wore a new hair-style *La Belle Poule* which included, perched on their tresses, a model ship in full sail.

The "Surveillante". – In 1779 Brest celebrated the triumphal return of the *Surveillante* frigate, commanded by Du Couëdic, which had taken part in one of the most furious sea duels of all time with the British frigate the *Quebec*, commanded by George Farmer. After a spirited battle, north of Ushant, both ships were dismasted. The sails of the *Quebec* fell across its guns setting the ship on fire. Du Couëdic ordered rescue action. Later the *Quebec* blew up with the wounded Farmer perishing. Du Couëdic had also been wounded in the fight – by two musket balls to the head and another in the stomach from which he later died. He was laid to rest in the Church of St. Louis (destroyed in 1944).

Brest during the War. – As the advanced base of Europe, Brest, with its port, its dockyard and its roadstead, was of first class strategic importance to the Germans, who were shut in on the Continent, and a considerable threat to Allied convoys sailing between America and Britain. The town, therefore, was heavily bombed for four years.

The naval and commercial authorities just managed to clear the port completely in June 1940 before the Germans marched in and began to use it. They also built a concrete shelter for submarines at Laninon. Allied bombings attacked these objectives to the end and in September 1944, when the Americans entered, they found a city in ruins.

■ SIGHTS *time: 3 hours*

Cours Dajot and the view over the Roadstead★★ (BCZ). – This fine promenade which was laid out on the ramparts in 1769 by convicts from the naval prison bears the name of the engineer who drew the plans.

There is an excellent view from the viewing table at the east end of the promenade. You see the Brest roadstead from the mouth of the Élorn, and past the Ménez-Hom and the Roscanvel Point right over to Portzic Point. The anchorage is vast (150 km² - 58 sq miles), deep (12–20 m - 6–10 fathoms – over large areas), framed between heights and connected with many big estuaries. It communicates with the Atlantic through a sound, with steep banks, the Goulet, 5 km - 3 miles long and about 1 800 m - 1 mile wide. This information explains why Brest has had such great military importance for 2 000 years.

To the left the estuary of the Élorn crossed by the great Albert-Louppe Bridge, makes a safe anchorage for yachts. Straight ahead in the foreground is the commercial port which imports coal, wine, hydro-carbons, building materials, and exports farm produce. Originally a naval repair centre, the port is tending more and more to develop into a maritime servicing station. Beyond lies the Plougastel Peninsula, hiding the southeast corner of the roadstead. On the horizon to the right you may see the Crozon Peninsula and the opening of the sound between Portzic Fort and the Espagnols Point.

Before the castle, the inner harbour, protected by its breakwater, serves as anchorage for the fleet. The Naval School is at Lanvéoc on the south side of the roadstead. The building overlooking the roadstead between Brest and Ste-Anne-du-Portzic houses the Midshipmen's and Petty Officers' Schools.

The Commercial Port (Port de Commerce) (CZ). – *As viewed from the cours Dajot.* The port was built in 1860 to take the overflow of military and cargo vessels from the Penfeld basin.

The present trade, mainly agricultural, increases yearly and now exceeds 2 million tons a year.

Imports include cereals for stock feeding, hydro-carbons, cement, exotic wood and citrus fruits while exports are principally potatoes, frozen chickens and livestock for which there are two special quarantine centres. The Atlantic maritime servicing station includes facilities such as 2 dry docks, one for ships up to 250 000 tonnes – a third is under construction for the 500 000 tonne vessels – refueling and tank cleaning (degasification) plants.

Alongside the great cargo vessels are the small fishing boats used to collect the scallops, the speciality of the Brest roadstead.

The Brest Naval Base (Port de Guerre) (AZ). – The base was founded in the Penfeld river valley; the estuary is enclosed and winding, 3 km - 2 miles long, 80–100 m - 262–328 ft wide and 10–12 m - 30–38 ft deep at low tide. For small ships and the simple building methods of other days, this was an ideal situation; work could be carried on in shelter from storms. It is different now with the huge plant of a modern arsenal, handling ships of over 35 000 tons, 250 m - 800 ft long. Huge works have been carried out. Rock was blasted and hills razed to make open spaces and erect buildings; these were built up in storeys to the level of the plateau above, yet the Penfeld dockyard remained cramped and had to be extended farther into the open.

At the end of the 19C a breakwater was built parallel with the Laninon beach to form the boundary of a great inner harbour. The port of Laninon was developed; open spaces were arranged to take some of the arsenal buildings, and two large dry docks are for the separation of large tonnage ships and the other for the assemblage of prefabricated elements.

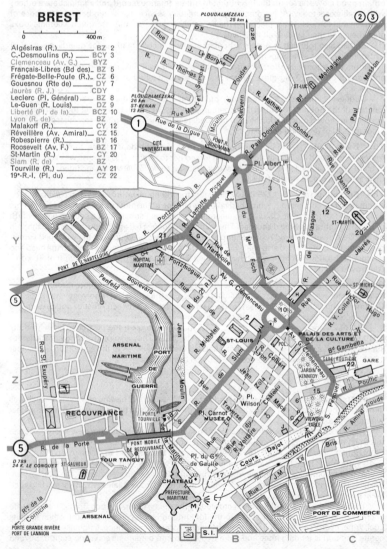

In 1970 two jetties were added to the main breakwater increasing the berthing space for aircraft carriers, battle-cruisers and guided missile destroyers.

Only French nationals are allowed to visit the arsenal and naval base.

Near the entrance to the dockyard the Penfeld is crossed by the **Recouvrance Bridge**, the biggest drawbridge in Europe. The steel pan, about 87 m - 285 ft long and weighing some 530 tons, swings between four concrete pylons (64 m - 209 ft high) over the quays of the dockyard. Farther upstream the **Harteloire Bridge** (634 m - 693 yds long) crosses the dockyard at a height of 40 m - 128 ft.

The Castle (Château) (ABZ). – *Open 9.30am to noon and 2 to 6pm. Closed Tuesdays. Admission: 5F.*

The castle is the last reminder of the history of Brest and enables one to study at close quarters the site that gave the port of Brest its military value. The Penfeld Gate has been fortified since Roman times and the castle itself has often been besieged. The towers and fortifications were built between the 12 and 17C.

From the Madeleine Tower there is a view of the roadstead and the ports of Brest. The whole roadstead from the Albert-Louppe Bridge to the Sound (Le Goulet) can be seen from the Paradise Tower.

Naval Museum (Musée naval). – Five rooms of the Paradise Tower have been turned into a naval museum. Pictures, models and parts of boats evoke the history of the Brest navy.

Tanguy Tower (Tour Tanguy) (AZ). – *Open 9am to noon and 2 to 7pm. Closed 1 May. Admission: 1F.*

Standing opposite the castle on the other bank of the Penfeld, this 16C tower dominates the arsenal and houses the **museum of old Brest**. Dioramas executed by a local painter, Pierre Peron, evoke Brest's main historical events: pre-Revolution *(1st floor)*; Revolution to 1939 *(2nd floor)*; 1939 to present day *(3rd floor)*.

Museum (BZ). – *Open 10am to noon and 2 to 7pm; closed on Tuesdays and public holidays.*

The museum has 17 and 18C paintings from the Italian, French and Dutch schools (Guercino, Recco, Van Loo and Schalcken). The 19C works include the Neo-classicism of Delorme (*Hero and Leander*), the Romanticism of Cibot and the experimentalism of the local Pont-Aven school (Lacombe and Emile Bernard). Note the luminous pastels of Levy-Dhurmer.

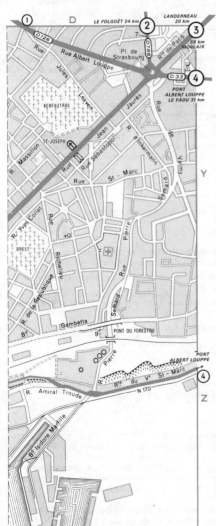

St. Louis (BZ). – This is a large modern building in keeping with the St-Louis Square that it overlooks. The impression of height is increased by the vertical lines of the adjoining bell-tower. The main part of the building is in rough stone, cement being used for the belfry and the narrow areas between the stained glass windows in the south wall.

The interior, which is very high and very plain, again emphasises the vertical theme. Rocher's and P. and J. Bony's stained glass windows are simple and let in a lot of light. Skilful design focuses the light from a window over the nave directly onto a great Crucifix above the high altar both by Kaeppelin. In a chapel on the south side, is a modern tapestry with a yellow background by Olin hanging above a golden altar.

Cultural Centre (CZ). – *Closed Mondays.* A meeting place for the people of Brest, the centre includes an amphitheatre with 1 100 seats, exhibition galleries, a conference hall seating 500, making for a variety of events: drama, cinema, concerts, conferences and exhibitions.

EXCURSIONS

St-Mathieu Point**. – *27 km - 16 miles – about 1½ hours. Leave Brest by ⑤, road D 789. Make first for Le Conquet (p 48), then follow the D 85 along the shore which provides good views until you reach the St-Mathieu Point (p 171). Return by Plougonvelin (facilities p 42) and Le Trez-Hir.*

Round tour* by Ste-Anne-du-Portzic and Petit Minou Point. *15 km - 9½ miles – about ¾ hour. The road is hilly (max. gradient 13% – 1 in 8), winding and sometimes very narrow between Brest and the Ste-Anne-du-Portzic corniche.*

Leave Brest by the Rue de la Porte, turn left into the Rue St-Exupéry to reach the corniche road. Interesting views over the roadstead and the Laninon naval dockyard.

Ste-Anne-du-Portzic. – Leave the car by the seashore. This is the site chosen for the **National Oceanographic Research** Centre. **View★** over the roadstead and the Ménez-Hom; to the right the Espagnols Point and still farther right Le Goulet.

In Cosquer bear left to return to the D 789, go towards Le Conquet and after 4.5 km - 3 miles turn left into the D 38.

Petit Minou Point. – Ruined fort. Leave the car and go to the lighthouse from which there is a fine **view★** over the sound, the Crozon Peninsula and the Raz Point.

Return to Brest by the D 789 and ⑤ on the plan.

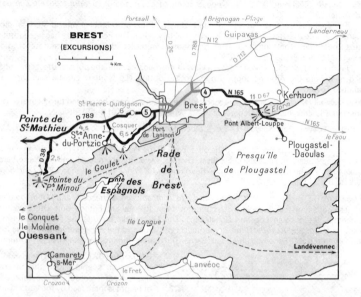

Albert-Louppe Bridge; Plougastel Peninsula★ (Pont Albert-Louppe; presqu'île de Plougastel). – *Round tour of 56 km - 35 miles – about 4 hours. Leave Brest by ④ on the map, the D 33.* You pass successively on the left the D 233 and D 67 which lead to the well situated small resort of **Kerhuon**.

Albert-Louppe Bridge. – Called after the chairman of the General Council of Finistère who promoted it, this bridge crosses the Élorn estuary. It is 880 m - 2 887 ft long and has three 186 m - 610 ft spans.

Four statues by the sculptor Quilivic stand at the ends of the bridge – a man and a woman from the Léon region on the Brest shore and a man and a woman from Plougastel on the opposite shore. The bridge stands over 42 m - 137 ft high and offers a very fine **view★** over the Élorn Valley and the Brest Roadstead.

The D 33A on the right leads to Plougastel-Daoulas.

Plougastel Peninsula★. – *The rest of the drive is described on p 140.*

Tour of the Abers. – *146 km - 91 miles – about 8 hours. Description p 47.*

BOAT TRIPS

Apply to the office of the Vedettes Armoricaines on the first quay in the commercial port of Brest Tel 44 44 04, or to the Tourist Information Centre, Place de la Liberté, Tel 44 54 04.

On the Roadstead. – *June to September. Time: 1½ hours.* It includes the visit *(guided)* of the naval port and the sound.

Across the Roadstead★★. – *The Le Fret Trip: daily. Time: ¾ hour. Coach connections to Morgat, Camaret and Crozon on each trip.*

Ushant★★ (Ile d'Ouessant). – *Description p 180.*

BRETONNE CORNICHE ★★
Michelin map **230** 6, 7

The Bretonne Corniche, the coast road which joins Perros-Guirec and Trébeurden following the "pink granite coast", is one of the most interesting runs in north Brittany.

GEOLOGICAL NOTES

The strange forms of the enormous pink granite rocks which are the attraction of the Brittany Corniche are due to erosion. Granite is composed of quartz, mica and feldspar. The feldspar turns into kaolin (china clay), which is washed away by the water, and the residue of quartz grains makes sand, which is carried away by rain or waves. Little by little the stone changes shape and presents various surprising forms: almost perfect spheres, chiselled and fretted masses, boldly balanced piles and swaying stones. Erosion here has been very severe because the rocks are coarse grained and easily broken up.

Local imagination has given names to the most typical rocks: Napoleon's Hat, St. Yves, the Gnome, the Witch, the Death's Head, the Elephant, the Whale, the Ram, the Rabbit, the Tortoise *(illustration p 12)*, the Horse, the Thimble, the Torpedo, the Armchair, the Umbrella, the Sentinel, the Corkscrew, etc.

FROM PERROS-GUIREC TO TRÉBEURDEN
22 km - 13 miles – about 1½ hours – Local map below

The interest of this tour is in the visits to the seaside resorts with their beaches, points and rocks. Tourists who like to stroll in picturesque surroundings and to take short walks will find a suggested route under each town heading.

After the town of Perros-Guirec *(p 138)*, the road skirts the small hill on which the signal station stands and opens up a **view*** straight ahead of the rocks of Ploumanach, seaward of the Seven Islands, looking back of the beaches of Perros-Guirec and, in the distance, of the Port-Blanc coast.

    Ploumanach**. – *Description p 142.*

    Trégastel-Plage**. – *Description p 177.*

As you come out of the village, at the end of a short rise, you get a view looking backwards, of the Seven Islands.

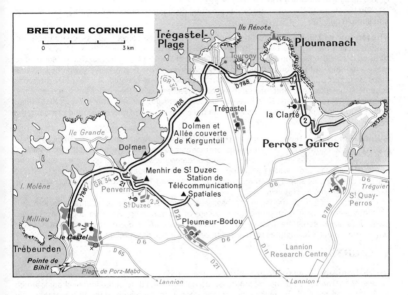

    Dolmen and covered alley of Kerguntuil. – *1 km - ½ mile from the crossroads between the D 788 and a path leading to the dolmen.*
    From this crossroads extends a fine view of the coast and its rocks. From the dolmen can be seen at the end of a field the covered alley which can be reached by walking behind the farm building.

Then the road runs close to the sea, at high tide this wild shore is rather picturesque. You can see a strange coast, dotted with islands and reefs; in the background is the **Grande Island** (Ile Grande) *(facilities p 43)*, with its heaths and rows of houses. Soon after the Café Paccata, at the top of a slight rise (700 m before arriving to the Penvern crossroads), a dolmen hidden amidst the foliage looks down onto the Kerivon shore.

Turn left into the D 21.

    St-Duzec Menhir. – *800 m further on from the crossroads with the D 788, at Pont de Penvern.*
    After the Café du Menhir in the hamlet of Penvern, a path on the left leads to the giant menhir surrounded by a Crucifixion. Roughly carved instruments of the Passion, surround the figure of a praying woman.

Turn back to the D 21 towards Pleumeur-Bodou Station.

    Space Telecommunications Station of Pleumeur-Bodou*. – *Description p 139.*

Return to the coast road and turn left for Trébeurden (p 177).

BRIGNOGAN-PLAGE

Michelin map **230** 4 – *Local map p 47* – Pop 1 039 – *Facilities p 43*

    A family seaside resort lying at the end of the Bay of Pontsuval, and possessing a magnificent sandy beach.
    On either side of Brignogan piles of rocks, sometimes curiously shaped, separate small beaches agreeable for those who like to be alone.

Pontusval Point. – This walk crosses a countryside dotted with blocks of granite. The Men Marz, which stands halfway, is a fine menhir, 8 m - 25 ft high, surmounted by a Cross.

The times indicated in this guide

when given with the distance allow one to enjoy the scenery
when given for sightseeing are intended to give an idea of
the possible brevity or length of a visit.

BULAT-PESTIVIEN

Michelin map 230 north of 21 – 17 km - 11 miles southwest of Bourbriac – Pop 678

Church*. – This fine building was put up in the 15 and 16C. The Renaissance tower, which is the oldest of this period in Brittany, had a spire added in the 19C. There are remarkable porches. Inside is a monumental sacristy with a loggia which projects into the church. There is a curious lectern in the chancel representing a young peasant in the local Vannes costume.

A *pardon* takes place on the Sunday after 8 September.

Bulat possesses three sacred fountains: the fountain to the Virgin (1718) in the cemetery and, on either side of the Callac road out of the town, the fountain of the Seven Saints (1683) and the Cock fountain (16C).

There is a fine Calvary at **Pestivien** *(1 km - ½ mile north of Bulat)*.

CAMARET-SUR-MER

Michelin map 230 16, 17 – *Local map p 80* – Pop 3 272 – *Facilities ρ 42*

An important lobster port in France *(details about lobster fishing , p 17)*, Camaret is also a quiet and simple seaside resort.

On the shore, to the left of the *Sillon,* a natural dyke which protects the port, is a small sand and shingle beach.

The landing of 1694. – The Crozon Peninsula, which forms an advanced bastion for Brest, has been attacked many times by the British, Spanish and Dutch. Vauban, the military architect, fortified it in 1689. Five years later, during the reign of William III, an Anglo-Dutch fleet tried to make a landing, but the fort and hidden batteries covering the port were very effective; several ships were put out of action, and the landing troops were decimated. A charge by dragoons scattered the attackers, and the coastguard militiamen, with their pitchforks and scythes, completed the rout. The encounter, which caused a sensation at the court of Louis XIV, ended with 1 200 killed and 450 taken prisoner from the enemy side and only 45 wounded among the French.

Submarine trials. – It was in Camaret bay in 1801 that the American engineer **Fulton**, who had settled in France in 1797, carried out an underwater experiment. He had built a small vessel which, with a crew of five, could be propelled under water with jointed oars at a speed of two knots. It could stay under water for six hours. This rudimentary submarine was intended to affix to the hull of an enemy ship a bomb or "torpedo" containing 100 lb of powder, which was to be exploded by a time mechanism.

A British frigate, at anchor in the bay, was to serve as the target. Fulton attacked, but unfortunately for him the ship, though unaware of his approach, weighed anchor and sailed away. This failure spoilt the inventor's chances and he returned to America. It was not until the last quarter of the 19C that this bold concept became a practical project.

■ **SIGHTS** *time: ¾ hour*

Notre-Dame-de-Rocamadour. – This chapel stands at the end of the dyke. It was built between 1610 and 1683 using the building materials from the third of the former chapels which once stood on the site. Originally a pilgrimage chapel on the pilgrim route to Rocamadour in Quercy. The pilgrims from the north who came by sea used to disembark at Camaret to continue the journey by land. A *pardon* is held on the first Sunday in September: benediction of the sea.

Naval Museum (Musée de la Marine). – *Open 1 June to 3pm September 10am to noon and 1 to 7pm and 1 October to 30 May on Wednesdays, Saturdays and Sundays 1.30 to 5.30pm. Admission: 4F.*

In the "castle" built by Vauban, engravings, models, statues and paintings to do with the navy are all exhibited.

EXCURSIONS

Penhir Point***. – *3.5 km - 2 miles to the southwest by the D 8 – about 1 hour. Description p 79.*

Espagnols Point**. – *Round tour of 36 km - 23 miles to the north – about ½ hour. Leave Camaret by the D 8, going towards Crozon; turn left into the D 355 at the top of a hill after passing the last houses. The remainder of the drive is described on p 80.*

CANCALE *

Michelin map 230 12 – *Local map p 91* – Pop 4 846 – *Facilities p 43*

Fishing port and seaside resort. The **setting*** of the port is picturesque.

The town has derived its gastronomic reputation for centuries from the oysters which flourish in the beds in the bay and which oyster-lovers come to eat in the hotels and bars around the port. Sales reached their highest level in the First Empire with 48 million oysters in one season.

For the the last twenty years only young oysters bought from Auray have been cultivated in the bay, for a mysterious disease decimated the native spat. Since then spat has begun to flourish in the immense beds in the open sea and an oyster with a particular flavour is developing due to the richness of the plankton of Mont-St-Michel Bay *(for details about oysters see p 18)*.

■ **SIGHTS** *time: 2 hours*

The Port* (AZ). – A fine scene at high tide. Go to the Fenêtre jetty for a view of the bay and, at low tide, of the oyster-beds.

St-Méen (BY A). – *To climb the tower – 189 steps – take a ticket at the kiosk of the Tourist Information Centre, Place de La République. Price: 2F.*

From the upper platform, where there is a viewing table, you can enjoy a wide **panorama*** of Mont-St-Michel Bay, Granville and forty belfries. In clear weather you can see the Chausey Isles and Jersey.

Wood carvings* (Bois Sculptés) (BY). – *The museum is open from Easter to 1 October from 9am to noon and 2 to 7pm. Apply to Photos Quémerais, Place de la République.*

All the wood carvings are by Father Quémerais who was born in Cancale. The principal pieces are: *National Deliverance, The Cross of Sacrifice, To the Glory of Sport* and *The Poem of the Apple,* which depicts the toils and the pleasures derived from this favourite fruit of the Bretons.

Hock Point* and the **Sentier des Douaniers** (BYZ). – From the point you get a **view*** over Cancale Rock, the Bay of Mont-St-Michel and the mount itself; below on the right, at the foot of the cliff, are the oyster-beds. On either side of the Hock Point you may take the Sentier des Douaniers (Customs Officers' path) and enjoy a walk overlooking the shore. If you follow the coastline as far as Port-Mer you will get a splendid view of the Chaîne Point opposite Cancale Rock.

War Memorial (Monument aux Morts) (AZ B). – Extensive view of the Bay of Mont-St-Michel, with the port below.

Jeanne Jugan's House (Maison de Jeanne Jugan). – Coming out of Cancale on the St-Malo road, ② on the plan, the house stands at a place called "Les Petites Croix". The house is the birthplace of Jeanne Jugan (1792-1879), the founder of the order known as the Little Sisters of the Poor *(details p 170).*

Chaîne Point. – *1.5 km - 1 mile – plus ¼ hour on foot Rtn. Leave Cancale by a narrow road* (BY). *Leave your car after about a mile and go on foot to a high platform facing Rimains Island and Cancale Rock.*

The view extends from Landes and to Mont-St-Michel.

EXCURSION

Grouin Point**. – *4.5 km - 2½ miles to the north by the D 201 – about ½ hour. Leave Cancale by ② on the plan; after 300 m turn right into the road which leads straight to the Grouin Point (p 99).*

Administrateur-chef-Thomas (Quai)	AZ 2
Dinan (R. de)	AY 3
Fenêtre (Jetée de la)	AZ 6
Gambetta (Quai)	AZ 8
Hock (R. du)	BZ 9
H.-de-Ville (R. de l')	BY 20
Port (R. du)	AZ
République (Pl. de la)	BY 23
Roulette (R. de la)	AZ 24
Victoire (Pl. de la)	BY 26

CARANTEC *

Michelin map **230** 5 – Pop 2 588 – *Facilities p 43*

Carantec, which lies on a peninsula between the estuary of the Penzé and the Morlaix River, is a family seaside resort. There are several bathing beaches; the most important are the Grève Blanche and the Grève du Kélenn, the latter being the larger. Two *pardons* are held at Carantec, on Whit Monday and the third Sunday in July and the blessing of the sea the first Sunday after 15 August.

■ SIGHTS *time: 3 hours*

Church. – *Closed Sunday afternoons.* This modern church contains, in the chapel to the left of the chancel, a 17C silver **processional cross***.

The Priest's chair (La Chaise du Curé). – View of the coast, Callot Island and Taureau Castle.

Pen-Lan Point*. – *1.5 km - 1 mile to the south. Turn left on leaving Carantec. 200 m beyond the tennis courts on the left leave your car at a wooden fence. Go on foot to a rocky height on your left (about 100 m).*

The **view*** extends along the coast from the Bloscon Point crowned by Ste-Barbe Chapel, near Roscoff, to the point at Primel; opposite you can see the castle on Taureau Island, which guarded the mouth of Morlaix River *(see Historical Notes, p 126).*

Callot Island. – *To the north 2 hours on foot Rtn.* From the point between the port and the Grève Blanche you can reach the island at mid-tide.

The Chapel of Our Lady *(ask for the key in the house nearby, Mme L'Hour)* on the island was founded in the 16C and rebuilt in the 17 and 19C. Inside is a 16C statue of the Virgin. A great many pilgrims come to the *pardon* on the first Sunday after 15 August.
The island is excellent for fishing.

Guarded beaches
Many beaches along the Brittany coast are entirely safe for bathing – many are guarded.
If flags are hoisted – green for safe bathing, red for too dangerous to bathe – obey them; if the beach is unguarded take local advice in case there are currents, hidden rocks or shelving.

CARHAIX-PLOUGUER

Michelin map 📖 20 – *Local map p 134* – *Pop 8 949* – *Facilities p 44* – *Town plan in the Michelin Guide France*

In the Roman era Carhaix was an important town commanding seven main roads. It is still a road junction but now in the middle of a cattle-raising district, making it the milk production centre for the area.

La Tour d'Auvergne (1743-1800). – The great man of Carhaix is Théophile-Malo Corret, known as La Tour d'Auvergne. When still very young he became keenly interested in the Breton language. But he also had a taste for the profession of arms, and he became a soldier but was still only a junior captain at forty-six. Then he became fired with revolutionary ardour. His exploits were such that he was offered the most exalted rank, but he refused it to remain with his troops.

Whenever this hero could pause in his campaigns, he would bring his faithful Celtic grammar out from under his shirt. At last he retired and gave all his time to his favourite study, making most serious researches to discover whether Adam and Eve did not converse in Breton.

Then the son of his Celtic master was called up for the army. La Tour, moved by the old teacher's grief, took the young man's place and enlisted, at fifty-four years of age, as a private soldier in the 46th half-brigade. New exploits followed. Bonaparte offered La Tour a seat on the Legislative Council, but failed to overcome the Breton's modesty. He was awarded a sword of honour and the title of "First Grenadier of the Republic".

He was killed in 1800, during the Rhine campaign. All the army wore mourning for him. Every year, the last Sunday in June, Carhaix celebrates the name-day of La Tour d'Auvergne.

■ **SIGHTS** *time: ½ hour*

Plouguer Church. – Rebuilt on Romanesque foundations in the 16C, the church was burnt down in 1923 and was rebuilt in red sandstone soon afterwards. A solid 16C tower rises at the opening to the nave.

St-Trémeur. – A porch opens from the lower part of the tower (16C); the tympanum over the doorway is adorned with the statue of St. Trémeur whose legend dates from the 6C *(p 153)*.

House of the Seneschal (Maison du Sénéchal). – This fine Renaissance building houses the Tourist Information Centre.

EXCURSION

Bulat-Pestivien; Corong Gorges★. – *Round tour of 79 km - 49 miles – about 4 hours – local map below. Leave Carhaix by the D 54 to the north of the map. After 11 km - 7 miles – take the D 154.*
The Carnoët road is on the right of the hamlet of Lesquern; follow this until you come to a signposted road going up to the **St-Gildas Chapel** *(500 m Rtn)*, a 16C building with grotesques at the east end. It is possible to get up to the **St-Gildas beacon** *(¼ hour on foot Rtn)*, where there was once a Roman encampment and from which there is an immense panorama.

Return to Lesquern; after 4 km - 2½ miles bear left into the Plourac'h road.

Plourac'h. – The Renaissance church in the form of a T was built largely in the 15 and 16C. The south face is the most ornate. The porch, which is Gothic in character, contains statues of the Apostles surmounted by canopies. A beautiful doorway with windows on either side is crowned by three gables adorned with coats of arms. Near the font is a 17C altarpiece depicting the mysteries of the rosary. Among the many statues ornamenting the church should be noted those of St. Guénolé, St. Maudez, St. Adrian and St. Margaret. Also a *Pietà* in which the Virgin wears a Breton cloak of mourning.

In the presbytery is a magnificent reliquary, a chalice and a paten in fretted and chased silver.

Go back to the D 54 which provides fine views of the countryside, then turn off right along the D 28 to Callac.

Callac. – Pop 3 225. This town is dominated by the ruins of Botmel Church. In front of the horse-stud stands a bronze statue of the stallion Naous. The town is also the home of the Breton spaniel.

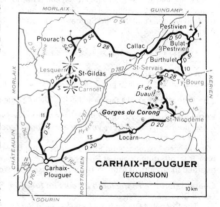

Take the N 787 on the left, then the D 50, the Bulat road, on the right.

Bulat-Pestivien. – *Description p 66.*

Reach Burthulet by the D 31.

Burthulet. – The chapel stands in melancholy surroundings; one does not doubt the truth of the legend that there "the devil died of cold". Inside are many old statues.

At Ty-Bourg turn right to St-Servias and, after crossing the Duault Forest, right again, into the road marked with arrows to the Corong Gorges.

Corong Gorges★. – *1 hour on foot Rtn.* Follow the path along the river bank and into the Duault Forest. The river disappears beneath a **mass of rocks** to reappear as a series of cascades.

Take the road to St-Nicodème and there turn right into the D 20 from which there are views over undulating country.

Locarn. – Pop 695. Locarn, perched on a hillside and overlooking a little tributary of the Hyères, is worth stopping at. Its church has a remarkable 16C stained glass window, a finely carved pulpit and, above all, a **treasury★** *(which can be seen in the presbytery next to the smithy)* with a reliquary in the form of an arm and, even more noteworthy, a reliquary in the form of a head of St. Hernin made in silver in the 16C.

At a time when sea bathing did not yet draw crowds of holiday makers, Carnac was known as a prehistoric capital. Many, even today, associate the name of Carnac with menhirs and rows of stones rather than a resort *(details p 27)*. The museum is an excellent introduction to the lives of the people of ancient Brittany. Another interesting feature is the church.

More recently, Carnac-Plage has grown up in the shelter of the Quiberon Peninsula; it is gently sloping and one of the finest beaches on the south coast of Brittany. Villas and hotels are scattered among the pines beside a beach over a mile long from which there is a pretty view of the coast, Houat, Belle-Ile and the Quiberon peninsula.

■ SIGHTS *time: 2 hours*

Ménec Lines★★ **(Alignements du Ménec).** – *North of Carnac by the D 196.*
The Ménec Lines, 1 km - ¾ mile long and 100 m - 330 ft wide, are on the left of the road. They include 1 009 menhirs, of which the tallest is 4 m - 12 ft high. They begin with a semicircle of seventy stones partly surrounding the hamlet of Ménec.

Kermario Lines★ **(Alignements de Kermario).** – *Illustration p 27.* The D 196 follows these lines for more than 1 km - ½ mile.

J. Miln and Z. Le Rouzic Prehistorical Museum★★ **(M).** – *Open Easter to 30 September, 10am to noon and 2 to 5pm (in July and August, 9am to noon and 2 to 6pm). Admission: 2F.*

Founded by a Scotsman, J. Miln, and added to by Zacharie Le Rouzic, this museum contains prehistoric specimens found during excavations among historic buildings and deposits in the area. To see them in chronological order, it is best to go round clockwise. Note: polished axes made of rare stones, necklaces and pendants made of *callais* (a blue stone like turquoise), decorated vases, bronze and gold-leaf arms and ornaments and casts of carvings on the local megalithic monuments.

St-Michel Tumulus★. – *Guided tours from end of March to end of September. Admission: 2F.*

The tumulus, which is 120 m long and 12 m – 395×38 ft high, is a mound of earth and stones covering several burial chambers. Most of the

CARNAC
CARNAC PLAGE

Atlantique (Av. de l')	2
Courdiec (R. de)	8
Druides (Av. des)	12
Dunes (Av. des)	13
Emigrés (Av. des)	15
Goémons (Allée des)	16
Kerlois (Av. de)	17
Kermario (Av. de)	18
Korrigans (R. des)	19
Légénèse (Bd de)	20
Ménec (R. du)	23
Orient (Av. d')	27
Palud (Av. du)	28
Pô (R. du)	31
Pointe (Av. de la)	32
Port en Dro (Av. de)	33
Poste (Av. de la)	34
Rahic (Av. du)	35
Roer (Av. du)	36
St-Colomban (Av.)	37
St-Cornely (R. de)	38
Salines (Av. des)	39

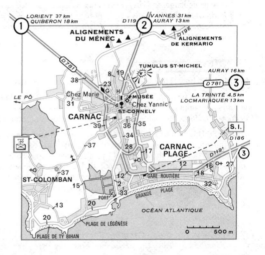

things found there are now in the Carnac museum. From the top of the mound, where there stands a Chapel to St. Michael, with walls covered with recent (1960) paintings, a small Calvary with sculptured figures and the Touring Club de France viewing table, there is a **view**★ of the megalith country, the coast and the islands.

St-Michel Tumulus. — Section of internal chambers and galleries.

Church★. – This is dedicated to **St. Cornély**, the patron saint of horned cattle; his statue stands on the façade between two oxen. The saint's *pardon* is held on the 2nd Sunday in September.

The church dates from the 17C. The porch on the left side is surmounted by a canopy in the form of a crown which is unique in Brittany. Inside, the wooden vaults are covered with curious paintings. The pulpit and chancel grille are of wrought iron (18C).

EXCURSIONS

Megalithic Monuments★★. – *Round tour of 13 km - 8 miles – about ½ hour – Local map below. Leave Carnac by the D 196 which follow the Ménec and Kermario lines (p 69).* Several thousand great stones, or megaliths, cover the Carnac district.
Leave the car at the entrance to the Castle of Kercado.

Kercado Tumulus★. – *Open 9am to noon and 2 to 7pm. Time: ½ hour. Apply to the keeper (tip).* This tumulus is 30 m - 98 ft across and 3.50 m - 11 ft high and covers a fine dolmen. A menhir stands on the summit.

Kerlescan Lines★. – A great semicircle of thirty-nine menhirs.

Moustoir Tumulus★. – A great tumulus with a central underground chamber, like the St-Michel Tumulus.

Return by the D 119.

Other Megaliths. – Tourists who are interested will see, between Plouharnel and Erdeven, the following megaliths: **Rondossec Dolmens★**; **Ste-Barbe Lines**; **Crucuno Dolmen★**; **Kerzerho Lines★**.

MEGALITHIC MONUMENTS

St-Michel and Ste-Anne-de-Kergonan Abbeys. – Gregorian chants.

St-Michel-de-Kergonan Abbey (Benedictine nuns). – *3 km - 2 miles by ① on the plan. The approach leaves the road 2 km - 1 mile from Carnac, on the right. Services: 10am, 4pm (5pm in winter).*

Ste-Anne-de-Kergonan Abbey (Benedictine monks). – *3.5 km - 2 miles by ① on the plan and, from Plouharnel, D 768 (towards Auray). The approach leaves D 768, to the right, after Plouharnel cemetery. Services: 10am, 11.30am and 6pm weekdays (Thursdays 3.15pm May to October).*

CHAMPEAUX ★

Michelin map 🔢 27, 28 – 9 km - 6 miles northwest of Vitré – Pop 311

The **village square★** is the type of charming surprise which awaits tourists who appreciate picturesque simplicity. It offers no spectacular features, but the harmony of a church, a small *mairie* with a large four-sided roof, and a few houses standing around an old well.

Church. – This 14 and 15C church has some fine Renaissance canopied **stalls★**. To the left of the high altar and in a chapel on the left of the chancel are two mausolea belonging to the d'Espinay family, who founded the church. (The d'Espinays were cousins of François I; their 16C castle stands to the south of Champeaux.) In the apse is a Renaissance **stained glass window★** of Calvary. Another **window★** in the sacristy shows Abraham's sacrifice *(to see this, enter the chancel and look above the woodwork on the right).*

Campers...

*The Michelin Guide **Camping Caravaning France***
describes in detail the resources and amenities of selected sites.
Use the current edition.

CHÂTEAUBRIANT

Michelin map 🔢 41 – Pop 13 826

On the borders of Brittany and Anjou, surrounded by woods with many pools, stands this old fortified town with its fine castle.
A modern historical association can be seen at the town gates, on the road to Pouancé, where there is a memorial to the twenty-seven hostages executed by the Nazis on 22 October 1941

Françoise of Foix and François I (16C). – Among the ladies of Châteaubriant were two whose memory has survived the centuries. One, Sybille, gave a rare example of conjugal fidelity; when her husband returned from a Crusade in 1250, she died of joy as she embraced him. The story of the second, Françoise de Foix, is less edifying.
At the age of eleven she was married to Jean de Laval, Count of Châteaubriant. He was terribly jealous, tried to keep his child-wife away from the dangers of the world and sulked in his castle like an owl. None the less, Françoise grew in beauty, wit and culture. She aroused great curiosity. François I sent word to the Count that he would like to make her acquaintance. Laval took no notice. When the King insisted, he went to Court, but alone; his wife, he said, liked only to be alone, and moreover she was weak minded. The Count had arranged with his wife that she should join him only at a certain signal. A servant came upon the secret and sold it to the King. One fine day Laval saw Françoise alighting from her coach and being royally received. Mad with rage, he left the Court, leaving his wife unprotected. Dazzled by this new life, she yielded and became the King's mistress. But royal loves are not eternal and she was superseded. Laval returned, took his wife away to Châteaubriant and shut her up, with her daughter, aged seven, in a room hung with black. The child sickened and died. The mother stayed there for ten years, when, it has been said her husband hastened her end with a thrust of his sword.

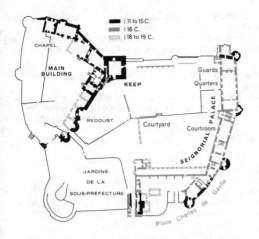

Legend:
- ▬ : 11 to 15 C.
- ▦ : 16 C.
- ▨ : 18 to 19 C.

CHAPEL

MAIN BUILDING

KEEP

Guards Quarters

REDOUBT

Courtyard

Courtroom

SEIGNORIAL PALACE

JARDINS DE LA SOUS-PRÉFECTURE

Place Charles de Gaulle

SIGHTS time: ½ hour

The Castle★ (Château). – During the school holidays guides show the courtyard, the oratory and Françoise de Foix's room.

A part of the castle which has been remodelled several times is feudal and another part, dating from the Renaissance, was built by Jean de Laval. You can stroll round it along the esplanade and the gardens which go right down to the Chère.

Enter through the Place des Terrasses. All that remains of the feudal castle is a large keep on a height, connected with the entrance tower and the chapel by walls against which the two wings of the (Tribunal d'Instance), a fine

main building stand. Opposite is the Seignorial Palace building with ornamented dormer windows.

The south wing houses the public library.

Of the colonnade which used to surround the Court of Honour there are only two sections left: one abutting on a charming staircase-pavilion, the other enclosing the main courtyard.

St-Jean-de-Béré. – The oldest parts, the chancel and the transept crossing, built of fine red sandstone, date from the end of the 11C, the nave is 12C. Outside, near the picturesque south porch (15C), is a rustic pulpit from which sermons were preached at the time of the plague. Over it are two low reliefs depicting the Annunciation (13C) and the Visitation (15C).

Inside you will see the elaborate altarpiece at the high altar (1665), those of the two side altars, of the same period, a 17C panel representing the Eternal Father, a Virgin of the 15C and other 17C statues (a St. Elizabeth represents Maria Theresa, Louis XIV's wife).

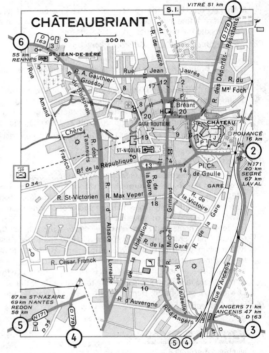

CHÂTEAUBRIANT

Belêtre (R. de)	2	Môquet (R. Guy)	12
Béré (Fg de)	3	Motte (Pl. de la)	13
Briand (R. A.)	4	Pasteur (R.)	14
Champ-de-Foire (R. du)	5	St-Michel (R. du Fg)	16
Château (R. du)	6	Vernisserie (R. de la)	17
Couéré (R. de)	7	Viaud (R. Marcel)	18
Denieul-et-Gatineau (R.)	8	Victor-Hugo (Bd)	19
Grande-Rue	9	11-Novembre-1918 (R. du)	20
Kléber (R.)	10	27-Otages (R. des)	21

CHÂTEAULIN

Michelin map 230 18 –
Local map p 50 –
Pop 5 668

This little town stands on a bend of the Aulne, in the green and deep valley through which the canalised river flows. Two lines of shady quays are its most decorative features.

The tide does not reach Châteaulin. It dies out a little way downstream, at Port-Launay, where small seagoing ships can tie up to the quay.

Salmon fishing. – Châteaulin shares with Châteauneuf-du-Faou the distinction of being the chief salmon fishing centre in the Aulne Valley; the salmon has always appeared on the coat of arms of the town. Hundreds of these fish come up the river to spawn, trying to leap

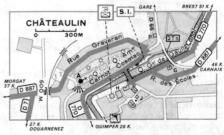

CHÂTEAULIN

the small waterfalls formed by the overflows from the locks. Some pass in a flash; others miss their jump, are washed down and try again.

Fishing is done 10 or 15 m - 33 or 50 ft below the lock, with fly or spinner. Salmon fishing here is one of the chief attractions for sportsmen who like to stay in Châteaulin, generally in the early months of the year.

Notre-Dame (A). – *Take the steeply rising path which starts opposite the cemetery. Apply for the key at the house near the chapel.*

The chapel with its Renaissance belfry, stands against a background of trees and old houses. In the former cemetery, a 15C cross evokes a rather curious scene of the Last Judgment. Inside are, under the organ, a group of St. Anne and the Virgin and Child; an altarpiece on the right of the altar, and a few healer saints.

There is a fine view of the Aulne Valley from the precincts of the chapel which overlooks the town.

EXCURSION

Ménez-Hom*. – *Round tour of 52 km - 32 miles – about 2 hours. Leave Châteaulin by the D 887 going west. After 3.5 km - 2 miles turn right into the D 60 which crosses Dinéault.* You pass the massif of the Ménez-Hom on your left and come in sight of the Aulne threading its way between mountains often covered with woodlands, until it reaches Argol.

Argol. – Pop 773. Go into the parish close by a monumental doorway built in the Classical style in 1659. The equestrian statue of King Gradlon is part of an old Calvary.

By way of the D 163 rejoin the D 887 and turn off to the left. After 1 800 m - a little more than a mile take the D 63 to the right.

St-Nic. – Pop 813. In the 16C church with its pierced belfry you may see, if you ask at the presbytery, a fine silver shrine in the form of a chapel which came from the Chapel of St-Côme as did the old statues.

Continue to follow the D 63 and after 1 km - ½ mile turn right.

St-Côme. – *Ask for the key at the farm.* This little chapel with its unified construction and typically Breton character possesses a rare harmony in its totality. An elegantly decorated façade is surmounted by a well proportioned belfry.

Inside, the 17C **woodwork*** testifies to the skill of Breton craftsmen. The roof-trees rest on beams that are carved with motifs taken from flora and fauna together with many inscriptions; the corbels in the aisles depict strange figures and also worthy of note are a fine wooden Christ and the elegant group formed by the altarpiece and the front of the high altar.

Return to St-Nic and there take the D 108 on the right; go up to Ménez-Hom by the D 83.

Ménez-Hom*. – *Description p 120.*

Return to the D 887 and turn left.

Ste-Marie du Ménez-Hom. – *Ask for the key in the café opposite.* The west face has two gables. To get into the chapel go through the close which has a very plain rounded doorway dated 1739. The Calvary has three crosses rising from separate bases. The chapel is entered by a doorway beneath the belfry which has well proportioned galleries and a cupola that give an upward sweep to the massive building.

Inside, the ornamented **altarpieces*** *(illustration p 30)* catch the eye as a group right along the east wall, combining well with the window apertures. While both the central altarpiece with the family and life of the Virgin as its theme and the north altarpiece depicting the saints, have figures that are somewhat heavy and expressionless, the figures of the Apostles on the south altarpiece show life and elegance. The skill with which they were carved, marks a great leap forward in Breton sculpture. The lovely beams in the north transept, a remarkable St. Lawrence, a graceful St. Barbara in wood should also be noted.

Return to Châteaulin by the D 887.

CHÂTELAUDREN

Michelin map **230** 8 – Pop 1 047

The town, an important commercial centre, stands at the head of the Leff Valley, a river known for its trout.

Notre-Dame-du-Tertre. – *½ hour walking and sightseeing.*

The chapel is perched on a mound; to reach it, take the Notre-Dame *venelle* (alley) or the Rue Aribart-Notre-Dame.

Ninety-six panels dating from the 15C on the roof of the chancel, forming a group of unusual size in France, depict scenes from the Old and New Testaments; those in the chapel to the south of the chancel, the lives of St. Margaret and St. Fiacre. Over the altar is a very fine gilded wooden **altarpiece***; in the chapel on the north is an alabaster statue of Our Lady. A *pardon* takes place on 15 August.

COMBOURG

Michelin map **230** 26 – Pop 4 719

This small old town, standing at the edge of a great pool and dominated by an imposing feudal castle, is picturesque. On the Place Albert-Parent, the 16C restored Maison de la Lanterne houses the Tourist Information Centre.

Tourists who only want to take a quick look at the castle from the outside, should walk along the local road which branches off the Rennes road and goes along beside the pool facing the castle and the village.

Chateaubriand at Combourg. – The castle was built in the 11C and enlarged in the 14 and 15C. It belonged first to the Du Guesclin family, and then in the 18C to the Count of Chateaubriand, father of François-René.

In his *Memoirs*, Chateaubriand *(details of his life p 168)* recalled the two years he spent at Combourg in his youth, adding still more to their romantic nature. The Count, a sombre and moody man, lived very much in retirement; when the family met he would walk up and down for hours in the drawing-room, in silence, while no one dared to speak. The Countess, who was unwell, only kept a distant eye on the children. Months passed without a visitor. Left to themselves, the boy and his sister Lucile grew close, sharing their boredom, their dreams and their fears.

The old castle, almost deserted, was gloomy; the pool, the woods and the surrounding heath breathed sadness. The Cat Tower (Tour du Chat), in which François-René had his lonely room, was haunted; a former Lord of Combourg was said to return there at night in the form of a black cat, for which the boy watched anxiously. The owls fluttering against the window and the wind rattling the door and howling in the corridors made him shiver. It was there that the dreamy and melancholy soul of the writer was formed, or perhaps confirmed.

(After L. Genty photo, Combourg)

Combourg. — The castle.

■ THE CASTLE ★ ½ hour

Open Easter to end September, 2 to 6pm. Closed Tuesdays. Admission: 5F. Park: open Easter to end September, 9am to noon and 2 to 6pm. Admission: 2.50F.

Chateaubriand's room and the former archive room have been made into a museum containing various souvenirs: autographs, furniture and the bed in which the writer died in Paris.

There is a very fine view from the top of the Cat Tower.

EXCURSION

Lanrigan Château. – *5 km - 3 miles to the east – about ¼ hour. Leave Combourg by the road that runs along the south bank of the lake.*

The little château of Lanrigan *(tour of the exterior from 1 June to 31 August 1 to 7pm on Wednesdays, Thursdays and Fridays)* with its well balanced proportions would recall the smaller châteaux of the Loire if it were not built of granite.

The charming Renaissance front can be seen perfectly from the road. In the angle formed by the main building and its flanking tower, with canted walls, an original note is added by a gracefully constructed gallery.

Don't use yesterday's maps for today's journey.

CONCARNEAU ★★

Michelin map **230** 31, 32 – Pop 19 040 – *Facilities p 42*

Concarneau, France's third largest fishing port and one of the biggest markets for tunny *(details of fishing and maritime life p 17),* also possesses many fish canneries.

Apart from the amusing and interesting scene of its seagoing life, the port has the picturesque attraction of a walled town enclosed in granite ramparts. It is also a popular seaside resort.

There is an attractive **general view★** of Concarneau and the inner harbour *(p 74)* from road D 783 where it crosses the Moros Bridge (Pont du Moros) on entering the town by ② on the plan.

The **Filets Bleus Festival** (Blue Nets) includes various folk events (dances and processions in local costumes). First held in 1905, it was originally organised in aid of sardine fishermen and their families.

(After Yvon photo)

Concarneau. — Entrance to the Walled Town.

CONCARNEAU★★

■ **SIGHTS** *time: about 1 hour*

Leave from the Place Jean-Jaurès.

Walled Town★★ (Ville Close). – Narrow alleys cover the islet of irregular shape (350×100 m - 1150×330 ft) linked to the mainland by two small bridges between which stands a fortified building. Massive ramparts, built in the 14C and completed in the 17C, surround the town.

Cross two small bridges and pass under a gateway leading to a fortified inside courtyard.

Tickets for the walk round the ramparts may be obtained at the top of the staircase on the left of the doorway. Open Easter to 30 September, 8am to 7.30pm (the rest of the year, 9am to noon and 1.30 to 6pm). Admission: 1.20F.

Follow the signs. For the first part of the tour, go up a few steps on the left and follow the path going round the walls. Glimpses of the inner harbour and the fishing fleet can be caught through the loopholes. You also get an overall impression of the tower known as the Gunpowder Tower (Moulin à Poudre).

Return by the same path and descend the steps for the second part of the tour.

After skirting the Little Castle esplanade you overlook the channel between the two harbours. When you reach a big tower turn sharp left and go down a ramp to a walk beneath the ramparts.

Return to the town by the Porte du Passage. By the corner of the Hospice take the Rue St-Guénolé, which bears left towards the Place St-Guénolé.

From this square a short alley leads to the Porte au Vin through the ramparts. As you go through the gate you will get a typical view of the trawlers moored in the harbour. The Rue Vauban goes in front of the fishing museum and brings you back to the way out of the Walled Town.

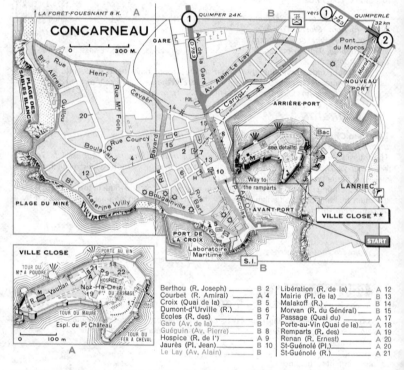

Berthou (R. Joseph)	B 2	Libération (R. de la)	A 12
Courbet (R. Amiral)	A 4	Mairie (Pl. de la)	B 13
Croix (Quai de la)	B 5	Malakoff (R.)	B 14
Dumont-d'Urville (R.)	B 6	Morvan (R. du Général)	B 15
Écoles (R. des)	B 7	Passage (Quai du)	A 17
Gare (Av. de la)	B	Porte-au-Vin (Quai de la)	A 18
Guéguin (Av. Pierre)	B 8	Remparts (R. des)	A 19
Hospice (R. de l')	A 9	Renan (R. Ernest)	A 20
Jaurès (Pl. Jean)	B 10	St-Guénolé (Pl.)	A 20
Le Lay (Av. Alain)	B	St-Guénolé (R.)	A 21

Fishing Museum (Musée de la Pêche) **(M)**. – *Open Easter to 30 September, 10am to 12.30pm and 2.30 to 7pm (in July and August, 9.30am to 8.30pm). Admission: 3F.*

This museum is located in the former arsenal which also served as barracks and a fishing school. Accompanying notices, models, photos, dioramas explain the history of Concarneau, its evolution as a port, its fishing boats, its canning industry and the marine vocabulary. A large hall is devoted to fishing: an Azores whaleboat and other boats, a harpoon gun, a giant Japanese crab, a coelacanthe (a fish whose origins date back 300 million years).

Shellwork Display Centre (A) – *Admission: 2F.*

Scenes, bouquets and people are made out of shells and shell-fish. The imagination of the artist is shown throughout – note especially the landscape scene of the Walled Town with waves of mussels beating its sides, a bristling cat and an impressive Louis XV vessel with sails made of mother-of-pearl from the region.

The Harbours. – By way of the Avenue Pierre-Guéguin and the Quai Carnot, go and take a quick look at the inner harbour, particularly the new harbour, where the main fishing fleet (trawlers and cargo boats) is moored. Then follow the route marked on the plan and walk round the outer harbour, alive with pleasure craft. The embarkation point for excursions is at the end of this quay, on the left.

On the left of the Quai de la Croix is the marine laboratory of the Collège de France. Inside visit the Marinarium *(open 10am to noon and 2 to 6pm; admission: 3F)*. After passing the old fish-market where fish used to be sold by auction, the Chapel of Our Lady of Succour (N.-D.-de-Bon-Secours, 15C) and a small lighthouse, you may skirt the Port de la Croix (Boulevard

Bougainville), which is sheltered by a jetty. Here the arrivals and sailings of the fishing fleet are interesting. Looking back, there is a good view of the Cabellou Point and, farther on, of the Beg-Meil Point. Out at sea are the Glénan Islands.

Follow the shore line.

The Beaches. – Go along the Boulevard Katerine-Wily which runs beside the Plage du Miné, then take the Boulevard Alfred-Guillou which leads to the Plage des Petits Sables Blancs and the Plage des Grands Sables Blancs.

Return by the Rue Henri-Cevaër, the Rue Bayard, Rue Joseph-Berthou and the Rue des Écoles.

EXCURSIONS

Cabellou Point*. – *7 km – 4½ miles to the south – about ½ hour. Leave Concarneau by ② on the plan, road D 783. 3.5 km - 2 miles from the town, turn right.* The road, running round the point, offers pretty **views*** of Concarneau, the Forêt Bay and the coast. It passes through **Le Cabellou** *(facilities p 42).*

After going round the point, return by the same way.

La Forêt-Fouesnant, by the coast road. – *7 km - 4½ miles to the northwest – about ½ hour. The road is hilly (max. 15% – 1 in 7), winding and narrow. Leave Concarneau by the Boulevard Alfred-Guillou and continue on the by-road which skirts the seashore.*
The **coves*** along the shore are very pretty, especially at high tide.

Return from La Forêt-Fouesnant (p 93) by the D 44 which joins the D 783.

CORNOUAILLE **

Michelin map **230** 16, 17, 18, 31, 32

Historic Cornouaille, the Kingdom and then the Duchy of mediaeval Brittany, extended far to the north and east of its capital, Quimper, reaching Landerneau, the neighbourhood of Morlaix and Quimperlé. The area included in our tour is much smaller and is limited to the coastal districts of Cornouaille, west of Quimper and south of Douarnenez. This very extensive coastline is marked by two rocky peninsulas, Cape Sizun, "Le Cap" and the Penmarch Peninsula which are its main attractions for tourists. This is a maritime country in which fishing plays an important part; the ports of Guilvinec, Audierne and Douarnenez specialise in sardines and crayfish.

The interior is densely cultivated (potatoes and early vegetables), and the countryside with its quiet horizons is covered with small hamlets of whitewashed houses.

FROM QUIMPER TO PLOZÉVET by the Raz Point
91 km - 57 miles – allow a whole day – Local map below

Leave Quimper *(p 149)* by the D 63 to the northwest, which goes up the rural valley of the Stëir with its wooded slopes and crosses an undulating countryside.

Plogonnec. – Pop 2 708. The 16C church has a fine Renaissance tower; it also has 16C stained glass windows depicting the Transfiguration, the Passion, etc. There is a Gothic triumphal arch to the cemetery.

Locronan**. – *Description p 117.*

The D 7, with the extensive Forest of Nevet on its left, leads to the sea.

Kerlaz. – Pop 582. *Time: ¼ hour.* Parish close as it was in 16 and 17C *(details on parish closes, p 31).* There is a good view of Douarnenez, which is reached after skirting the fine Plage du Ris.

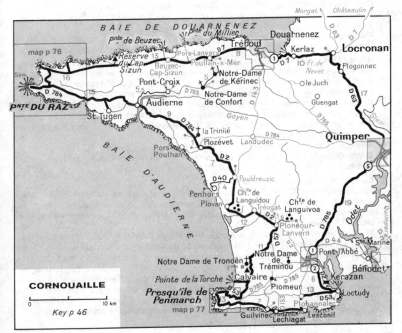

CORNOUAILLE

0   10 km

Key p 46

Douarnenez★. – *Description p 87.*

Leave Douarnenez, go through Tréboul and make for the D 7.

Notre-Dame-de-Kérinec and Confort. – *5 km - 3 miles from Poullan-sur Mer.*

Notre-Dame-de-Kérinec Chapel *(ask for the key at the house next door)* which stands surrounded by trees, dates from the 13 and 15C: the elegant 17C belfry was struck by lightning in 1957 but has now been rebuilt to the original pattern. Note the east end. Inside, look at the massive pillars of the transept crossing.

Notre-Dame-de-Confort Church (16C) has old stained glass windows in the chancel. Over the last arch in the nave, on the north side, hangs a carillon wheel with twelve little bells. The chimes are rung to beg the Virgin for the gift of speech for children who are backward in learning to speak and for other favours.

Alongside the chapel is a Calvary with triangular base dating from the 16C; the statues were renewed in 1870.

Cape Sizun Bird Sanctuary★ (Réserve du Cap Sizun). – *Guided tours 15 March to 31 August 10am to noon and 2 to 6pm. Time: ½ hour. Admission: 2F. Binoculars are recommended.*

Make for Beuzec Cape Sizun and then turn left into the signposted road. Leave the car in the car park at the sanctuary entrance.

The dates when visitors are allowed are arranged at a time of maximum interest – namely at nesting time in the spring and when there are young. Starting in March most birds finish nesting by mid-July. The adults and chicks then leave the sanctuary until the end of August.

In the magnificent and wild setting of the Castel-ar-Roc'h, more than 70 m - 230 ft above sea-level, can be seen, sitting on their nests and feeding their young, such sea birds as auks and guillemots, crested cormorants, common herring gulls, lesser black-headed gulls, great black-backed gulls which are the rarest of all, tridactylous sea-gulls, puffins, petrels, ravens and red-beaked choughs, etc.

Brézellec Point★. – Leave the car at the roundabout beyond Kermeur and continue on foot to the rock platforms nearby. There is a magnificent **view★** along the longest stretch of coast in Brittany of saw-tooth rocks and sheer cliffs.

Turn back and turn right towards the Van Point.

Van Point★★. – *Leave the car in the car park about 800 m - ½ mile beyond Trouguer.*

The 15C St-They chapel stands on the left of the path. On the point itself follow the half-hidden path, bearing always to the left, which goes right round the headland. Van Point, which is too big to be seen all in one glance, is nevertheless less spectacular than the Raz Point, but it has the advantage of being off the beaten track of tourists. There is a **view★★** of Castelmeur Point, Brézellec Point, the Chèvre Headland, St-Mathieu Point and the Tas de Pois Islands on the right; Sein Island, the Vieille Lighthouse and Raz Point on the left. Tourists who climb down the cliffs should take care.

The landscape becomes ever harsher: no trees grow; stone walls surround small fields of sparse crops which are finally replaced by the barren moss which covers the final headland.

Trépassés Bay. – It was once thought that the drowned bodies of those who had been shipwrecked, and which the currents brought to the bay, gave the bay its name of Bay of the Dead. Another, less macabre explanation, based on the existence of a stream that flowed in the marshes, was that the original Breton name for the bay was "boé an aon" (bay of the stream), which became "boé an anaon" (bay of the troubled souls). Now it is believed that the bay was the embarkation point from the mainland for Druids' remains which were taken over to Sein Island for burial. According to local legend the town of Is *(details p 22)* once stood in the little valley which is now covered in marshes.

A splendid swell runs freely and powerfully into the bay.

By the Relais de l'Ile de Sein Restaurant a road on the left leads to the tiny fishing port of **Bestrée.**

Raz Point★★★. – *Supervised car park: 2F.*

To tour the point (1¼ hours Rtn) ask for the guides. It is wise to wear shoes with soles that do not slip. The path follows the edges of deep chasms *(do not leave the safety rope)*, the deepest of which is the Plogoff Inferno (the Enfer de Plogoff) with its sheer walls against which the waves beat deafeningly.

The long, narrow spur, cut away by the sea, towers more than 70 m - 220 ft above the waves. It reaches out into the ocean by a chain of reefs on the very last of which is perched the Vieille Lighthouse. The setting is particularly impressive in stormy weather. As you walk round the semaphore, past the statue of Our Lady of the Shipwrecked (Notre-Dame-des-Naufragés), a wide **panorama** of the horizon unfolds; you see, straight ahead, Sein Island and beyond, in clear weather, the Ar Men Lighthouse. Between the Sein Island and the mainland is the fearful Raz de Sein or tide race, which, so the old saying has it, "no one passes without fear or sorrow"; to the northwest can be seen the Tévennec Lighthouse standing on an islet.

Leave the D 784 a moment to get to St-Tugen.

St-Tugen*. – The nave and the tower of the St-Tugen Chapel *(open in July and August)* are in the Flamboyant Gothic style of the 16C, the transept and the east end in the Renaissance style of the 17C. There is a fine south porch. Inside may be seen interesting 17 and 18C furnishings including several altarpieces and a curious catafalque for coffins. The baptismal chapel is surrounded with balustrades and painted panels. The statue of St. Tugen *(p 22)* stands to the right of the high altar. A *pardon* is held every year *(p 10)*.

Audierne*. – *Description p 51.*

Pont-Croix*. – Pop 1 961. *5.5 km - 3½ miles from Audierne. Time: ½ hour.* A small town built up in terraces on the right bank of the Goyen. Its narrow streets, hemmed between old houses, slope picturesquely down to the bridge. The **Church of Notre-Dame-de-Roscudon*** is interesting. The nave is Romanesque, the rest of the building is Gothic (15-16C). It has a very fine **belfry***, with a steeple 67 m - 223 ft high which served as a model for those of Quimper Cathedral. There is a pretty porch on the south side. Inside, under the altar of the apsidal chapel, is a sculptured Last Supper (17C). Fine **stained glass*** in the chapel on the right of the chancel. A *pardon* is held on 15 August.

Chapel of the Holy Trinity. – *1 km - ½ mile from the D 784.* The chapel is shaped like a T; the nave was built in the 14C and the remainder added in the 16C. This is the most interesting part outside; note the charming Louis XII decoration on the south transept face.

Inside, the chancel arches come down on to groups of thin columns with florally decorated capitals.

Plozévet. – Pop 3 443. There is a Gothic porch to the 15C church, of which some parts are Romanesque and date from the 13C. To the right of the building flows a sacred fountain *(details on fountains).* A menhir has been placed here as a 1914-18 war memorial.

FROM PLOZÉVET TO QUIMPER by the Penmarch Peninsula
87 km - 54 miles – allow the day – Local map p 75

The journey is made through the "bigouden country" which has become known through the local costume of the women and especially the unique coiffe *in the shape of a little lace menhir.*

From Plozévet *(see above)* to the tip of the Penmarch Peninsula the sea breaks against a great sweep of shingle, continually rolling and knocking the stones of the 20 km - 12 mile arc. The even coastline, altogether inhospitable and desolate, does not possess a single cove where a ship could shelter. The little villages with their white houses, which lie back from the coast, turn, for their livelihood, entirely to the hinterland.

Penhors. – *4 km - 2½ miles from Pouldreuzic.* In September the great *pardon* of Notre-Dame-de-Penhors, one of the largest of Cornouaille *(p 10)* takes place. After the service the procession *(illustration p 24)* walks through the countryside until it comes to the shore line where the benediction of the sea takes place.

Plovan. – Pop 783. Little 16C church with beautifully coloured modern stained glass windows.

Languidou Chapel. – The 15C chapel, though now in ruins, still has some interesting points, particularly the fine rose window.

Languivoa Chapel. – *1.5 km - 1 mile to the east of Plonéour-Lanvern.* The ruins of this 14 and 17C chapel form an imposing ensemble adorned by rose windows and Gothic arcading. The dismantled belfry porch still dominates the devastated nave and Classical style entrance with its engaged Doric columns. The adjoining presbytery, rebuilt in 1971, enshrines the Virgin of Notre-Dame-de Languivoa suckling her child *(the public is admitted during the Easter holidays and in July and August).*

Notre-Dame-de-Tronoën. – *Open in season 2 to 6pm.* The 15C chapel, in the bare and wild country of the dunes, has a small pierced belfry, flanked by two turrets. Beneath the vaulted roof are old statues and a beautiful Flamboyant piscina. Standing in front of the south face, which is pleasantly ornate, is a 15C **Calvary****, the oldest in Brittany *(details about Calvaries, p 32).* It depicts scenes from the Passion in the round or in high relief and is a composite work, for the most part in coarse granite, with three scenes on the north face carved in Kersanton granite; the hundred figures are sorely weather-beaten. A *pardon* is held every year *(p 10).*

Torche Point. – The name is a corruption of the Breton "Beg an Dorchenn": flat stone point. Fine **view*** of the St-Guénolé rocks and the Audierne Bay. There is a tumulus with a big dolmen.

Penmarch*. – Pop 6 921. The parish includes several villages: St-Guénolé, Kérity, Tréoultré, St-Pierre.

The **St-Nonna Church*** was built in the 16C in Flamboyant Gothic style. On either side of the doorway, the buttresses are carved into low reliefs of ships and caravels, recalling that the church was built with moneys from the ship-owners and fitters. A gable tower stands above the roof *(details on belfries and towers and illustration, p 28).* Inside, old statues stand against the pillars and walls. Note St. Michael and St. Anne with the Virgin and Child.

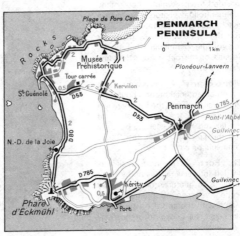

CORNOUAILLE★★

The **Penmarch Peninsula** was one of the richest regions in Brittany up to the end of the 16C: cod-fishing (the "lenten meat") brought wealth to the 15 000 inhabitants. Then firstly the cod deserted the coastal waters, and next a tidal wave brought devastation. Final disaster came with the brigand La Fontenelle *(p 87)*. The houses and built up areas were too widely separated to be able to be protected by an encircling wall and each house put up its own defences. La Fontenelle took each by surprise. He killed 5 000 peasants, burned down 2 000 houses and loaded 300 ships with booty which he then took back to his stronghold on Tristan Island.

The Penmarch Peninsula with its low-lying rocks, bears no resemblance to the great headlands of the Raz or Penhir. The tourist is in much closer touch with the sea, the pounding of the waves on the rocks is more impressive.

St-Guénolé. – *Description p 165.*

Notre-Dame-de-la-Joie – A *Bigoudens' pardon* (pretty costumes) in which tourists join, is held on 15 August.

Eckmühl Lighthouse★ (Phare d'Eckmühl). – *Open 10am to noon and 2 to 7pm, 1 May to 15 September.* The Eckmühl Lighthouse stands at the very end of the Penmarch headland. Leave the car in front of the lighthouse.

The lighthouse is 65 m - 213 ft tall and its light of 2 million candle-power has a range of 54 km - 33½ miles. It was inaugurated in 1897, having been built with money given by the Marquess of Blocqueville, daughter of Davout (1770-1823), Marshal of France and Prince of Eckmühl. From the gallery at the top of the tower *(307 steps)* there is a **view★★** of Audierne Bay, Raz Point, the lighthouse on Sein Island, the coast of Concarneau and Beg-Meil and the Glénan archipelago.

Passing to the left of the lighthouse, you will reach the very tip of the headland on which stand the old lighthouse – it now serves as a sea-mark – a little fortified chapel and a signal station. The sea is studded with reefs covered in seaweed. Farther east, as at Penmarch the coast shows a succession of rocky points and dunes.

Kérity. – Little port devoted to sardine and tunny fishing. Ste-Thumette Church (1675) has an elegant front flanked by a turret.

A tarred road leads to Guilvinec.

Guilvinec. – Pop 4 612. *Facilities p 42.* Trawler fishing port with many sardine and tunny boats as well as four fish canneries which handle the fish as it is unloaded. With **Lechiagat**, where numerous pleasure boats anchor, it forms a well sheltered harbour.

Lesconil. – *Facilities p 42.* Small trawler fishing port.

Loctudy. – *Description p 117.*

Kerazan-en-Loctudy Manor★. – *Open 15 June to 15 September, 10am to noon and 2 to 6pm. Closed Tuesdays. Time: ½ hour. Admission: park 2F; museum 2F.*
The castle was bequeathed to the Institut de France in 1929 by Mr. Joseph Astor, the son of the U.S. Senator. It consists of two wings, one of which dates from the 16C, the other one from the 18C.
Mr. Astor, wishing to help the young women of the countryside, left his fortune to the Institut to endow courses in embroidery and needlework at the castle.
The furnished rooms contain collections of pictures and drawings from the 15C to the present: Flemish, Dutch and French schools. Auguste Goy, one of Ingres's followers, evokes the Breton life of the past.

Pont-l'Abbé. – *Description p 145.*

Leave Pont-l'Abbé by ② on the plan and return to Quimper (p 149).

Le CROISIC ★

Michelin map **230** 51 – Pop 4 305 – *Facilities p 42*

This is a port for sardine and crustacea fishing, coastal traffic and pleasure craft and an important centre for the cultivation of shell-fish. Le Croisic overlooks the Grand Traict lagoon and is an agreeable small seaside town which has many summer holiday visitors. The **Port-Lin** beach, facing the Atlantic, is 800 m from the centre of the town on the far side of the peninsula; that of **St-Goustan**, on the roadstead, is the same distance away.

Mont-Esprit★. – This is a drive laid out on an artificial mound built from ships' ballast. From the top there is a fine **view★** of the salt-marshes, of Hœdic and Houat Islands, Belle-Ile and the coast as far as the Rhuys Peninsula on a clear day.

The Port. – The port, which is divided into several basins by three islets, is a picturesque and busy scene between September and March with the arrival of the prawn catchers. The quays are flanked by 17C houses.

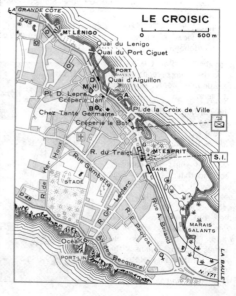

LE CROISIC

Fish Market (Poissonnerie) (A). – This is where the fish is sold by auction at 3 and 7am (6am on Saturdays) and 3pm.

Town Hall (Hôtel de ville) (H). – The 17C building includes a naval museum *(open in July and August. Admission: 3F).*

Notre-Dame-de-Pitié (B). – Chapel in Flamboyant Gothic style (early 16C).

Côte d'Amour Aquarium★ (D). – *Open 1 July to 31 August from 10am to 10pm; the rest of the year 10am to noon and 2 to 7pm. Closed on Tuesdays from October to March. Admission: 7F; children: 4F.*

In addition to a collection of local species visitors can see pink lobsters from the Canaries, giant spiders from the deep-sea beds; penguins; tropical tortoises. On display on the 1st floor are multicoloured coral fish, Polynesian shell-fish and fossils.

Mont-Lénigo. – **View★** over the Le Croisic roadstead of Castelli Point, and in the distance, the Rhuys Peninsula.

At the foot of Mont-Lénigo is the memorial erected to Hervé Rielle. During the Battle of La Hougue in 1692, when Tourville was defeated by a much stronger Anglo-Dutch fleet under the command of Admiral Russell, this pilot saved twenty French ships by leading them at night through the dangerous Raz Blanchard channel.

Follow the quay to the jetty at the end; from there you get a view of the roadstead and the *corniche* road.

EXCURSION

The Grande Côte★. – *Round tour of 26 km - 16 miles – about 2 hours – Local map p 101. Leave Le Croisic by D 45, northwest of the plan.*

After the canning factory and the cure centre, the road follows the coast. At **Croisic Point** begins the wild coastline; the road overlooks the sea, passing the beaches of Por-Lin, Valentin and its sailing school, and Batz-sur-Mer. Farther on the view opens out over Le Pornichet, the estuary of the Loire and the coast.

After **Le Pouliguen★** *(p 146)*, return to Le Croisic by the N 771, via the charming village of **Kervalet** *(p 100)* and **Batz-sur-Mer★** *(p 54).*

CROZON Peninsula ★★★

Michelin **230** 16, 17

This magnificent excursion is one of the most typical you can make in Brittany. Nowhere else, except perhaps at the Raz Point, do the sea and coast reach such heights of grim beauty, with the giddy steepness of the cliffs, the colouring of the rocks and the fury of the sea breaking on the reefs. Another attraction is the variety of views over the indentations and estuaries of the Brest roadstead, the Goulet, the broken coast of Toulinguet, Penhir, Dinan Castle, Cape Chèvre and Douarnenez Bay. From the summit of the Ménez-Hom all these features can be seen arrayed in an immense panorama.

1 ★★★ROUND TOUR OF THE PENHIR POINT
43 km - 27 miles – about 2 hours – Local map p 80

Crozon. – Pop 7 993. *Facilities p 42*. This little town has given its name to the peninsula in the middle of which it stands. The church is modern. The altar to the right of the high altar is ornamented with a large 17C **altarpiece★** coloured to depict the martyrdom of the Theban Legion, in which 10 000 Christian soldiers died for their faith during the reign of the Emperor Hadrian. Below are two 16C panels: the Flagellation, on the left, and the Bearing of the Cross, on the right.

Leave Crozon by the D 8, west of the town and make for Camaret. To the left, by Kerloc'h, there is a fine view of Dinan Bay and the vast beaches of Kerloc'h and Goulien.

Camaret-sur-Mer. – *Description p 42*.

You will leave on your right the roads leading to the Chapel of Notre-Dame-de-Rocamadour and Toulinguet Point, as well as the **Lagatjar Lines**, which contain about 100 menhirs *(details on prehistoric monuments p 27)*.

Penhir Point★★★. – *Time: ¾ hour*. A memorial to the Bretons of the Free French forces has been erected on the cliff 150 m from the road, on the right. *Leave the car at the end of the surfaced road.* Go on to the platform that stands at the end of the promontory and look straight down 70 m - 229 ft to the sea below.

The setting is magnificent as is the panorama. Below are the formidable single rocks called the **Tas de Pois**; on the left is Dinan Point; on the right the St-Mathieu and Toulinguet Points, the second with its little lighthouse, and at the back the Ménez-Hom. In the distance can be seen the Raz Point with Sein Island to its left, and on clear days, the Isle of Ushant over to the right. Tourists who enjoy scrambling over rocks should take a path going down on the left between the platform at the end of the road and the monument. Halfway up the sheer drop of the cliff there is a view of a little cove. Here take the path on the left which climbs towards a cavity covered with a rock beyond which you will reach the **Chambre Verte**, a grassy horizontal strip. From here there is a most unusual view of the Tas de Pois and Penhir Point.

Return to the car and take the Camaret road again. Turn right after 1.5 km - 1 mile into the D 8. As you come out of Camaret leave the D 8 at the top of a climb and turn left into the D 355, once a strategic road. The view opens out to show Camaret Bay on the left and, on the right, the Brest Roadstead. The road enters the walls which enclose the Roscanvel Peninsula before Quélern. These fortifications date from the time of Vauban and the Second Empire. This road, the D 355, running alongside the roadstead is picturesque, particularly in the evening. The curious contrast between the slopes on either side of the peninsula is striking: the western slope, facing the west wind and the sea is moorland and lacks vegetation: the eastern slope is covered with trees and meadows.

CROZON Peninsula ★★★

The D 355 affords views of the Atlantic, Toulinguet Point, Grand Gouin Point, Camaret Bay, the Brest Channel and in the far distance, St-Mathieu Point.

Espagnols Point★★. – From here one can see a remarkable **panorama**★★ which includes the Goulet (Sound), the town and harbour of Brest, the Élorn Estuary, the Albert-Louppe Bridge, Plougastel Peninsula with the Armorique Point at its tip, and the end of the roadstead.

Then the road skirts the eastern coast of the peninsula affording a good view on the left of the Brest roadstead, the Plougastel Peninsula and, the, Longue, Morts and Trébéron Islands.

Roscanvel. – Pop 653. The church was rebuilt after a fire in 1956 and now possesses fine dark stained glass windows by Labouret in which very dark blue panes predominate, and a coloured terracotta Stations of the Cross by Claude Gruer.

The D 355, which to the south of Roscanvel goes round the end of the roadstead, affords fine views of Longue Island, and in the foreground, of the two smaller islands, Trébéron and Morts. You leave the peninsular territory once more by the ruined fortifications.

About 500 m beyond St-Fiacre, turn left into D 55 to Le Fret.

Le Fret. – *Facilities p 42.* A small port with regular boat service to and from Brest (*p 64*).

The road runs along the jetty bordering Le Fret Bay. When you come to a fork, take the D 155 to Crozon, leaving the Lanvéoc road on your left. Take a last, backward look at the roadstead.

CROZON PENINSULA

0 — 3 Kn.

Key p 46

② ★★DINAN POINT

12 km - 8 miles Rtn –
– about 2 hours –
Local map adjoining

Leave Crozon (p 79) by the D 308 to the west.

Dinan Point★★. – *Time: 1 hour. Leave your car at an open space used as a car park at the end of the road. Continue on foot, climbing for about 500 m to the path on the left that leads to the point.* A fine **panorama** can be seen from the edge of the cliff; on the left are Cape Chèvre, the coast of Cornouaille and the Raz Point; on the right, Penhir Point and the Tas de Pois. Skirting the cliff to the right you will see the rock or Dinan Castle, where the point ends. A natural arch joins this enormous rocky mass to the mainland (it looks like a ruined stronghold).

Dinan "Castle". – ½ *hour on foot Rtn, over rocky ground; wear non-slip soles.* On the right-hand slope of the little "castle" peninsula, take a path over the natural arch.

Continue along the path, and after a half-hour's walk when level with a shingle beach, bear right across the heath to get back to the car. Return to Crozon by the same route.

③ ★CAPE CHÈVRE

21 km - 13 miles Rtn – about 1 hour – Local map above

Leave Crozon (p 79) by the D 887 to the southwest.

Morgat★. – *Description p 126.*

From Morgat to Cape Chèvre the road runs through an austere landscape of rocks and stunted heath, open to the ocean winds, with little hamlets of houses huddled together which seem to hide in the folds of the ground. To the left, the view gradually opens out over Douarnenez Bay, with the massive outline of the Ménez-Hom in the distance.

Cape Chèvre★. – *Time: ½ hour. Leave your car on an open space at the entrance to the army training ground and walk inland, bearing slightly to the right.* Make for a former German observation post, from which there is an extensive **view**★ over the Atlantic and the advanced points of Finistère; from right to left, you will see Penhir Point and the Tas de Pois, Sein Island, Cape Sizun and its *finistères* (world's ends), the Van and Raz Points which enclose Douarnenez Bay on the south side.

Return to your car and take the direct road to Morgat.

La Palud Beach (Plage de la Palud). – *2 km - 1 mile – plus ½ hour on foot Rtn. You are not advised to bathe here: the waves are very strong.* About 5 km - 3 miles from Cape Chèvre, turn left at St-Hernot (picturesque chapel), go through the hamlet of Brégoulou; 500 m farther on, leave the car. Another 500 m on foot will take you to the shore, from which there is a remarkable view of the sea.

Return to Crozon by the Morgat road.

DAOULAS ★

Michelin map **230** 18 – *Local map p 137* – Pop 1 083

This little town lies on both banks of the Daoulas River, whose estuary forms one end of the many inlets in the Brest roadstead.

■ SIGHTS *time: ½ hour*

Parish Close★. – On leaving the N 170 where it crosses the Irvillac road and following the signposts you will come to the close from the west. On the left stands the abbey; ahead and slightly to the right, is a 16C **porch★** with the usual Breton decoration of figures of the Apostles. Go through the porch which serves as a belfry. The church, which has been restored, still has its 12C west door. The 17C ossuary at the east end has been turned into a sacristy. At the end of the main pathway in the cemetery stands a very old Calvary. Outside the close there is a chapel to St. Anne with a 17C doorway ornamented with statues of the Virgin and St. Anne.

The Abbey. – *Bell on the right of the door. Admission: 2F.* Although the 12C **cloisters★** lack one side, and the roof has not been rebuilt, they remain a very elegant specimen of Romanesque architecture. In the middle of the close is a basin decorated with twelve heads and Romanesque ornaments. After this, in an agreeably green and fresh setting, you may visit a small oratory dedicated to Our Lady of the Fountain (Notre-Dame-des-Fontaines), beside which is a fountain restored in 1532.

EXCURSIONS

Plougastel Peninsula★ (Presqu'île de Plougastel). – *Round tour of 54 km - 34 miles – about 3 hours.*
Make for Plougastel-Daoulas by the Brest road, the D 33. Turn left at Lesquivit into the D 29. Description p 140.

Dirinon. – Pop 1 218. *5.5 km - 3½ miles – about ¼ hour.*
Turn right to Dirinon about 2.5 km - 1½ miles beyond Daoulas on the Brest road.
The church which stands in a delightful setting surrounded by trees is crowned by a remarkable Renaissance belfry: above the square tower, two sets of bells and two storeys of balustraded balconies are surmounted by a slender, stone spire. Above the doorway with its pointed Gothic arch, stands a statue of St. Nonna in a niche with pilasters. St. Nonna is patroness of the parish and her 16C tomb lies in the neighbouring chapel.

(After Le Doaré photo, Châteaulin)

Dirinon. — The church.

DIABLE Rocks ★ (ROCHES DU DIABLE)

Michelin map **230** 34 – 12 km - 8 miles northeast of Quimperlé

The approach downhill to the Ellé River from Locunolé is beautiful. Soon after the river bridge there is a shady path leading off to the left along the Ellé; follow it until you come to a mass of rocks dominated by the Diable Rocks (½ hour on foot Rtn).
Go back to the car and at the nearby crossroads take the steeply climbing road on the left to the terrace about 400 m on the left farther on (notice-board prohibiting smoking). An overgrown path brings you to the highest point of the rocks, from which you look down in a sheer drop of the rushing waters on the Ellé below.

DINAN ★★

Michelin map **230** 25 – *Local map p 155* – Pop 16 367 – *Facilities p 44*

The town and surroundings of Dinan will give great pleasure to tourists. The old town, with its old houses and old streets, is gay with trees and gardens; it is surrounded by ramparts and guarded by an imposing castle, and it stands on a plateau overlooking the Rance from a height of 75 m - 240 ft. The port begins at the foot of a viaduct which bestrides the valley, but the only vessels to be seen there now are those of the St-Malo and Dinard motorboat services and a few pleasure craft.

HISTORICAL NOTES

Du Guesclin against Canterbury. – In 1359 the Duke of Lancaster besieged Dinan, which was defended by Bertrand du Guesclin *(details p 156)* and his brother Olivier. After several encounters with the superior English forces, Bertrand asked for a forty days' truce, after which, he promised, the town would surrender if it were not relieved.
Olivier, who had gone out of the town unarmed, was made prisoner, in violation of the truce, by an English knight, Canterbury, who demanded a ransom of 1 000 florins. Bertrand challenged the Englishman to single combat. The encounter took place at a spot now called the Champ-Clos (enclosed field). Lancaster presided. Canterbury lost and had to pay Olivier the 1 000 florins he had demanded and surrender his arms to Bertrand. He was also discharged from the English army.
This success won Du Guesclin the admiration of a pretty girl of Dinan, Tiphaine Raguenel. The union of this cultivated and even scholarly young woman with the rough warrior, who was later to be Constable, was very happy.

Du Guesclin's Tombs. – After more than twenty years' campaigning for the King of France *(p 21)* Bertrand du Guesclin died on 14 July 1380, before Châteauneuf-de-Randon, to which he had laid siege.

He had asked to be buried at Dinan. The funeral convoy, therefore, set out for that town. At Le Puy the body was embalmed and the entrails buried in the Jacobins' church (now the Church of St. Lawrence). As the embalming was inadequate, the remains were boiled at Montferrand and the flesh was removed from the skeleton and buried in the Franciscans' church (destroyed in 1793). At Le Mans an officer of the King brought an order to bring the body to St-Denis; the skeleton was then handed over to him. Only the heart arrived at Dinan, where it was deposited in the Jacobins' church. It has since been transferred to St. Saviour's.

So it was that while the kings of France had only three tombs (for the heart, entrails and body), Du Guesclin had four.

Royal good humour. – During the League, Dinan was surprised and taken by partisans of Henry IV. One of the attackers, a worthy burgher of St-Malo named Pépin, went off at a gallop to take the good news to the King. In Paris he hurried to the Louvre. "Sire, I've taken Dinan," he cried. As Marshal de Biron seemed incredulous, Pépin turned maliciously to Henri: "He knows better than I do, yet I was there!" But Pépin was all in and asked boldly: "Is this the house of God, where no one eats or drinks?" The King, amused by the scene, gave him a meal. The next day he asked him if he would like a title. "No, Sire," answered the proud citizen of St-Malo, "at home I drive the nobles out of our town with a stick. But give me a horse, for mine's dropped dead!"

■ MAIN SIGHTS *time: 1 hour*

Leave your car in the Place St-Sauveur and follow the route marked on the plan.

English Garden (Jardin Anglais) (BYZ). – The terraced garden on the site of the former St-Sauveur Cemetery affords a **view★★** of the Rance, crossed by a Gothic bridge (rebuilt since the war), the port and the viaduct, 250 m - 820 ft long and 40 m - 128 ft high.

Follow the fine Duchesse-Anne promenade along the ramparts; 20 m before the entrance to the garden in front of the castle, go down a staircase on the left, pass under a gateway flanked on the outside by two semi-cylindrical towers, and turn right.

Petits-Fossés Promenade (AZ). – The promenade skirts the 13-15C ramparts on the outside and is overlooked, on the right, by the castle.

The Constable's statue by Frémiet stands at the end of the Place Du-Guesclin.

Old Town★ (Viéille Ville). – Go along the Rue Ste-Claire to the Rue de l'Horloge (old houses); turn left.

Clock Tower (Tour de l'Horloge) (BZ). – *Open in summer 10am to noon and 2 to 6pm.* This 15C belfry houses a small museum and the clock offered by the Duchess Anne.

At a crossroads turn left and cross the **Place des Merciers★** (ABYZ – *illustration p 34*) with its old, triangular-gabled houses with wooden porches. In the Place des Cordeliers, turn right into the Rue de la Lainerie, which is prolonged by the **Rue du Jerzual★** (BY). This slopes down steeply between 15 and 16C shops with overhanging upper storeys before ending at the Jerzual Gate.

Turn into the first alley (Rue Croix-Quart) on the right, right again in the Rue Haute-Voie and immediately left into the Rue du Coignet. This street leads back to the Place St-Sauveur.

(After CAP photo, Paris)

Dinan. — The Rue du Jerzual.

■ ADDITIONAL SIGHTS

The Castle★ (AZ **A**). – *Open 1 May to 30 September, 9.30am to noon and 1 to 7pm; in October 9am to noon and 2 to 5pm, except on Mondays; December to February, 2 to 4pm; in March and April, 10am to noon and 2 to 5pm. Closed November. Admission: 3F.*

You may visit the 14C Coëtquen Tower, the keep and the gallery between them. The enormous 14C tower, known as the Dungeon of Duchess Anne, over 34 m - 100 ft high, has bold machicolations. It contains a museum of local history and ethnography. Exhibits include old measures, a reconstruction of a room and displays of costumes and *coiffes* of the Rance area, farm implements, pottery, wickerwork, etc. There is also a collection of popular woodcarvings of Upper Brittany.

There is a fine **panorama★** from the top of the castle.

St. Saviour's Basilica★ (St-Sauveur) (BZ **B**). – A Romanesque porch surmounted by a Flamboyant Gothic gable opens the façade; the right-hand wall is 12C, all except the outside chapel which was added in the 15C. The rest of the church is 15 or 16C. The dome of the tower, which was destroyed by lightning, was replaced in the 18C by a timber steeple covered with slates.

Inside, the lack of symmetry of the building is noticeable: the south side is Romanesque, while the north side, chancel and transept are Flamboyant. In the north arm a 15C cenotaph, restored in the 19C, contains the heart of Du Guesclin. Note the 18C high altar, a granite baptismal font of the 12C and a 15C stained glass window representing the four Evangelists. The modern windows are by Louis and Jean Barillet.

As you leave the basilica you may see on the left the house where the explorer of French Indo-China, Auguste Pavie, was born in 1847.

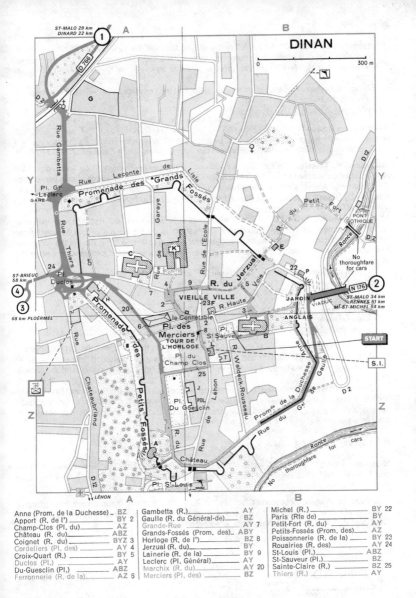

St-Malo (AY C). – This church, in the Flamboyant Gothic style, was begun in the 15C and finished in the 18C. The chancel and apse, which are all that is left of the early work, are worth seeing.

You can get a good general view of the apse *(holidays only)* from the college which now occupies the former Franciscan monastery *(see below)*.

Governor's House (BY E). – The house is in the Rue du Petit-Fort, which is a continuation of the Rue du Jerzual and looks rather like it. It is a fine 15C house in which a hand-weaving workshop has been installed.

Grands-Fossés Promenade (ABY). – This magnificent avenue follows the north ramparts with a garden laid out between the trees and the rampart walls.

Former Beaumanoir Mansion (BY F). – Notice, in the courtyard, the window decoration and a 16C turret.

Former Franciscan Monastery (AY K). – *Open in July and August only.*

The monastery is now a college. From the entrance there is a good view of the east end of St. Malo Church on the left. Of the former monastery the 15C Gothic cloisters and the main courtyard with its turrets with pepper-pot roofs of the same period can still be seen. The whole is much restored. It is worth looking at the chapterhouse, which now serves as a refectory, for the fine timberwork and ogive vaulting.

Hôtel Kératry (BZ L). – This attractive mansion with three granite pillars houses the Tourist Information Centre.

EXCURSIONS

Banks of the Rance*; Léhon. – *2 hours on foot Rtn, plus ½ hour sightseeing.* Go down to the Rance and cross the Gothic bridge. On the right, take a path *(no cars allowed)* which passes under the viaduct and follows the river in a green and sheltered setting, where it is pleasant to stroll.

Cross the Rance to reach Léhon.

83

Léhon. – Pop 2 684. Of the former priory of St-Magloire, the 12C church (Anjou vaulting, beautiful monolithic stoup, Beaumanoir tombs), the cloister ruins (17C) and the monks' refectory, remain. *To visit go through the gateway on the left of the church and turn right (tip).*

From the castle ruins perched on top of a hillock at the entrance to the village there is a good view of the Rance Valley.

The D 12 brings you back to Dinan.

Tour of the Rance★. – *79 km - 50 miles – about 4 hours. Description p 154.*
In the season the Rance can be descended by boat, but if you wish to return the same day you will have to take a bus or train back *(details from the Tourist Information Centre, Tel 39 03 61).*

Bourbansais Castle. – *15 km - 9 miles – about ½ hour. Leave Dinan by ② on the map and the N 794. After just under 11 km - 7 miles turn right into the D 137. At Pleugueneuc turn left into the D 75 from which, after 400 m you will see the long drive to the castle branch off. Garden and zoo open 9am (10am 1 October to 31 March) to noon and 2 to 7pm (6pm 1 October to 31 March). Admission: 9F.*

The castle is an impressive 16C building which was enlarged in the 18C. It stands in an immense park. Three generations of the Huart family, counsellors to the Breton parliament, rejoiced in the French garden that you see today, ornamenting and adding to it. You can go round the outside of the castle; the main building is flanked by bell-turrets and gable-roofed pavilions, characteristic of the 18C.

One of the castle faces looks on to the garden, which has a low wall at its edge; this does not, however, cut the view. Great urns stand on the lawns.

DINARD ★★★

Michelin map **230** 11 – *Local maps pp 91 and 155 – Pop 9 588 – Facilities p 43*

This smart resort, which lies in a magnificent setting on the estuary of the Rance, opposite St-Malo, is frequented by British and Americans. The place was "launched" about 1850 by an American and developed by the British. Before that it was a small fishing village and an offshoot of St-Énogat.

The tourist will be interested by the extraordinary contrast between Dinard and St-Malo: the former, a town born yesterday and luxurious resort with modern installations, intense social activity, princely villas and splendid gardens and parks; the latter an old city, surrounded by ramparts, possessing a family beach, a commercial port.

■ **MAIN SIGHTS** *time: 1 hour*

Moulinet Point★★ (CX). – A walk to this point offers a series of magnificent **views★★** of the coast from Cape Fréhel, on the left, to St-Malo and beyond on the right, and, farther on, of the Rance estuary.

The Grande Plage or Plage de l'Écluse★ (CX). – This is where the casino is. Following the promenade along the beach to the left you will reach a terrace from which you can see St-Malo. The Great Beach is an astonishing sight at bathing time.

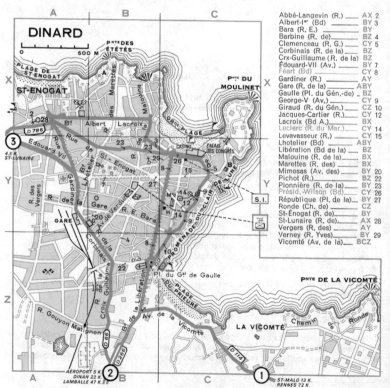

Abbé-Langevin (R.)	AX 2
Albert-I⁽ᵉʳ⁾ (Bd)	BY 3
Bara (R. E.)	BY
Barbine (R. de)	BZ 4
Clemenceau (R. G.)	CY 5
Corbinais (R. de la)	BZ
Crx-Guillaume (R. de la)	BZ
Édouard-VII (Av.)	BY 7
Féart (Bd)	CY 8
Gardiner (R.)	AY
Gare (R. de la)	ABY
Gaulle (Pl. du Gén.-de)	BZ
George-V (Av.)	CY 9
Giraud (R. du Gén.)	CZ 10
Jacques-Cartier (R.)	CY 12
Lacroix (Bd A.)	BX
Leclerc (R. du Mar.)	CY 14
Levavasseur (R.)	CY 15
Lhotelier (Bd)	ABY
Libération (Bd de la)	BZ
Malouine (R. de la)	BX
Marettes (R. des)	BX
Mimosas (Av. des)	BY 20
Pichot (R.)	BZ 22
Pionnière (R. de la)	BY 23
Présid.-Wilson (Bd)	CY 26
République (Pl. de la)	BY 27
Ronde (Ch. de)	CZ
St-Énogat (R. de)	BY
St-Lunaire (R. de)	AX 28
Vergers (R. des)	AY
Verney (R. Yves)	BY 29
Vicomté (Av. de la)	BCZ

■ ADDITIONAL SIGHTS

The Clair de Lune Promenade★ and the **Prieuré Beach** (CYZ). – This walk lies along a sea wall which follows the water's edge and offers pretty views over the Rance estuary. *Open-air concerts of recorded music are held on Tuesdays and Thursdays from 15 June to 25 September from 9.30 to 10.30pm on the floodlit promenade.*
   The Prieuré Beach is at the end of the promenade. It owes its name to a priory founded in 1324, of which a few romantic-looking ruins remain.

Étêtés Point (BX). – View of the islands and the coast beyond St-Malo.

Port-Riou Garden (BX A). – A fine view as far as Cape Fréhel.

St-Énogat Beach (AX). – The beach lies in a picturesque setting under steep cliffs.

Aquarium and Marine Museum (CY B). – *Open Whitsun to 15 September, 10am to 1pm and 2 to 7pm. Admission: 3F.*
   Marine exhibits; souvenirs of Commander Charcot's expeditions.

EXCURSIONS

Vicomté Point★★ (CZ). – *2 km - 1 mile – plus 1 hour on foot Rtn.*
   The Vicomté, a fine estate divided into lots, is becoming one of the most fashionable quarters of Dinard. The circular road (walk it) offers splendid **vistas★★** towards the harbour, the Rance estuary and the Rance tidal power scheme.

Tour of the Rance★. – *79 km - 50 miles – about 4 hours. Description p 154.*

BOAT TRIPS

   For all additional information apply at the landing stage or at the Tourist Information Centre, Tel 46 12 54.

St-Malo★★★. – *Crossing: 10 minutes. Description of St-Malo p 167.*

Cruise to Cape Fréhel★★★. – *Daily service in the season. Time taken: 3 hours. Description of Cape Fréhel p 96.*
   On the way out the boat skirts the coast as far as Cape Fréhel, and goes round the Island of Cézembre on the way back.

Dinan, by the Rance★★. – *Information and description p 154.*

Cézembre Island. – *Time: 40 minutes Rtn, plus 2½ hours on the island*. A fine sea trip.

Chausey Islands. – *See Michelin Green Guide Normandy*. A wild granite rock archipelago.

AIR TRIPS

   Regular daily flights leave for the Channel Islands of Jersey and Guernsey.

DOL-DE-BRETAGNE ★

Michelin map **230** 12 – Pop 5 042

   Dol, a former bishopric and proud of its fine cathedral, is now the little capital of the "Marais", marsh, district *(p 86)*. It stands on the edge of a cliff about 20 m - 64 ft high which was washed by the sea until the 12C.

St. Samson's Cathedral★★ (A). – *Time: ½ hour*. The cathedral is a vast structure, built of granite in the 13C and re-modelled during the next three centuries. It gives an idea of the importance that the bishopric of Dol then enjoyed.
   On the outside, the most interesting part is the south wall, which includes two porches. The **Great Porch★** (14C) is very fine. Seen from the north, the cathedral looks like a fortress, its crenellated parapet was linked to the old fortifications of the town.
   The interior, 100 m - 328 ft long, is impressive. Notice in the chancel: the medallion-glass **window★★** (13C restored), the eighty stalls (14C) and the Bishop's throne (16C carved wood). In the north arm of the transept, is the tomb of Thomas James Bishop of Dol from 1482 to 1504. The 14C wooden statue of the Virgin was coloured in 1859. In the St-Magloire Chapel, in the south aisle note the Christ.

DOL
DE-BRETAGNE

0   200M

24 K. ST-MALO (by D 4)
23 K. CANCALE
4 K. MONT DOL

26 K. DINAN

Carmes (R. des)	2
Cathédrale (Pl. de la)	3
Ceinte (R.)	4
Chateauoriand (Pl.)	5
Gaulle (Pl, Gén.-de)	6
Grande-Rue-des-Stuarts	7
Le-Jamptel (R.)	8
Nominoë (Square)	10
Paris (R. de)	12
Ponts (R. des)	13
Résistance (Square de la)	14
Toullier (Pl.)	15

CHÂTEAU DE LANDAL 12 K.

LE MONT ST-MICHEL 28 K.
FOUGÈRES 51 K.

MENHIR DE CHAMP-DOLENT RENNES 54 K.

Promenade des Douves★. – *Cars not allowed.* Fine **view★** of the Dol Mound and Don Marsh (Marais).

Trésorerie Museum (M). – *Open Easter to All Saints' Day, 9.30am to 7pm. Admission: 2F.*

The museum is installed in the 16C house of the Trésorerie and is devoted to the history of Dol: dioramas, 17-19C arms. The treasure gallery contains a fine collection of wooden statues (13-18C) of old Breton saints as well as 16-19C faience statues of virgins.

Grande-Rue-des-Stuarts. – This busy street has several interesting old houses. No 17, a florist, dates from the 11 and 12C and has Romanesque arcading; no 27, antique-dealer; no 33 a 1617 dwelling with fine dormer windows; no 18 a former Templars' inn with a 12C vaulted cellar now transformed into a bar; no 32 has a charming 16C courtyard.

EXCURSIONS

Champ-Dolent Menhir. – *2 km - 1 mile. Leave Dol by ②, the D 795. After 600 m, leaving D 4 on your left, turn left into a tarred road and leave your car at the road leading to the menhir.* The dolmen, one of the finest in Brittany, stands over 9 m - 30 ft high. The name Champ-Dolent (Field of Pain) refers to a legendary struggle which is supposed to have taken place here.

Landal Castle. – *12 km - 7½ miles – about ¾ hour. Leave Dol by ① on the plan, the D 155. At La Boussac take the D 285 going uphill; turn right one mile farther on opposite the Calvary. Leave the car by a lake.*

The approach on foot, starting along the lake bank and then up an avenue of great trees, makes a pleasant walk. The sudden appearance of the feudal castle, standing surrounded by trees at the end of rolling lawns, is striking.

The courtyard may be visited and the ramparts climbed.

The courtyard, with the castle at one corner, is partly walled by 15C ramparts flanked with round towers. The four sides of the courtyard are completed by the outhouses facing the castle and a lake on the near side.

A little chapel was built to stand outside the walls.

DOL Mound ★ (MONT DOL)

Michelin map **230** 12

This granite mound, though only 65 m - 208 ft high, overlooks a great plain and resembles a small mountain. The remains of many prehistoric animals – mammoth, elephant, rhinoceros, reindeer, etc. – and flint implements have been unearthed on its slopes.

It is possible to go round the mound by car by way of the surfaced patrol road.

The summit is reached from Mont-Dol church by a narrow but practicable road (hardly large enough for two cars), a hairpin bend and, at first, an average gradient of 1 in 6 – 16%.

DOL MOUND

Ascent to the tower from Easter to All Saints' Day, 10am to noon and 2 to 6.30pm.

With a little imagination and the help of the plan you can reconstruct the legendary struggle which took place here between **St. Michael** and Satan. Satan was thrown down so violently that he made a depression in the rock and scratched it with his claw. With one blow of his sword, the Archangel made a hole in the mountain into which he hurled his enemy. But the Devil reappeared on Mont-St-Michel and mocked him. As he made one bound from Dol to Mont-St-Michel, St. Michael left the imprint of his foot on the rock.

A signal tower put up in 1802 serves today as a belfry for the Chapel of Notre-Dame-de-l'Espérance *(open Easter to All Saints' Day, 8am to 8pm)*, which is the goal of a popular pilgrimage. Note a gigantic chestnut tree planted in the 17C.

Panorama★. – To the north can be seen, the Chausey Islands and Cancale Point; to the northeast, Mont-St-Michel, Avranches and Granville; to the south, on the edge of the Marais, Dol and its fine cathedral with the Hédé heights in the background; to the southwest, Dinan; to the west St-Malo and St-Servan; and below, the Dol Marsh fields with their bordering hedges and trees.

The Dol Marsh. – This is the name given to land reclaimed from the marshes and the sea in Mont-St-Michel Bay. Seen from the mound the countryside looks strange and monotonous; it extends for about 15 000 ha - 40 000 acres from the mouth of the Couesnon River to near Cancale. The old shore line ran through Cancale, Châteauneuf, Dol and St-Broladre and along D 797.

Until some time between the 4 and 8C the marshland and the Bay of Mont-St-Michel were covered by a great forest; Mont-St-Michel and the Dol Mound were just hills. When the sea invaded the area they became islands. Later, the water-level fell, leaving many marshes which were still flooded by the spring tides. From the 12C onwards the local people began to drain the area – a work that has gone on until the present day. The Marsh proper is today a fertile wooded district of 12 000 ha - 32 000 acres where cereals, vegetables and forage are grown. Apple trees dot the fields, and long lines of poplars or willows divide the country into a chessboard pattern.

The establishment of large-scale mussel-beds in the Vivier area has somewhat modified its appearance and given Vivier a new impetus.

The polders. – When the marshes had been reclaimed, work was started on areas that had always been part of the sea-bed; these lay beyond the marsh and to the west of the Couesnon canal. They have been transformed by polders used in the same way as in Holland. The areas now appear as an empty plain cut across by canals and dykes; only some parts are under cultivation with new buildings and modern farms. The main roads branch off the D 797 and are built on dykes, extending with the polders and crossing the lines of poplars that mark each new stretch of land reclaimed from the sea.

Only exceptionally high tides reach the top of the banks along the bay. Grass grows on them, forming the famous salt pastures; the sheep which graze there yield very good meat.

DONGES

Michelin map **230** 52, 53 – 17 km - 11 miles east of St-Nazaire – Pop 6 285

The oil port of Donges, which is an annexe of the port of Nantes-St-Nazaire, has constructed two berths for large oil tankers. The town is also an important refining centre.

The village, at some distance from the refinery complex, was built after the Second World War and is now dominated by the slender, copper-covered steeple of its unusual church.

Church*. – This is built of concrete and granite. A huge Calvary set in a parabolic arc, with a stained glass window as background, dominates the front façade. Standing back and to the right is the square bell-tower. Inside there is the same feeling of simplicity and upwards sweep as when standing before the façade. Twin arches, as sharply pointed as they are pure in line, divide the side chapels. These like the nave and chancel are lit by stained glass windows by Max Ingrand.

(After Les Artistes paysagistes photo, Aigueperse)

Donges. — The church.

DOUARNENEZ ★

Michelin map **230** 17 – *Local map p 75* – Pop 19 311 – *Facilities p 42*

Douarnenez, Ploaré, Pouldavid and Tréboul were amalgamated to form the community of Douarnenez. This community, lying on either side of the Pouldavid estuary, is engaged in contrasting activities. Douarnenez is the great centre for fishing and canning. Tréboul is joined to the rest of the community by a big steel bridge across the Port-Rhu estuary and is a much frequented seaside resort.

The site of the town, deep in a great bay with gracefully curving shores, the lively and colourful picture of its quays, and the streets of the old quarter, zigzagging down to the sea, are Douarnenez's chief attractions.

The port is one of the busiest on the Breton coast. It handles mackerel, sardines, tunny and large sea fish and crustaceans.

La Fontenelle (16C). – According to local tradition the palace of King Mark was at Douarnenez and the island at the mouth of the Pouldavid estuary was, therefore, given the name of his nephew, Tristan *(details about Tristan and Iseult p 22)*.

In the 16C this island was the lair of one La Fontenelle, the most dangerous of the guerrilla leaders who devastated the country during the troubles of the League. Political and religious questions meant little to him; he "plucked the goose where it was fat".

La Fontenelle seized Tristan's Island. To obtain materials for fortifications he demolished those of Douarnenez. His cruelties are legendary. In 1598 he agreed to lay down his arms on condition that he was allowed to keep this island; this was granted by Henri IV. But in 1602 the King took his revenge: involved in a plot, La Fontenelle was sentenced to be broken on the wheel. He was bound to a St. Andrew's cross, and the executioner broke his bones with an iron bar. His shattered body was then fixed on the wheel and publicly exposed until he died.

■ **SIGHTS** *time: 1 hour*

Leave your car in the Place Gabriel-Péri and follow the plan.

This route brings the visitor to the "Guet" where the Pouldavid River runs into the bay.

Pouldavid River and the Plage des Dames (DY). – A coast road runs along the shore and affords picturesque views of the Island of Tristan (now the property of the J. Richepin family), Tréboul, the narrow streets clustering round the port, and the estuary, which is spanned by a bridge 24 m - 78 ft high. There lies Port-Rhu, the commercial port of Douarnenez. The path then skirts the Plage des Dames and ends on an esplanade beside the sea.

Boulevard Jean-Richpin* and the New Harbour (DEY). – Follow this boulevard, which offers superb **views*** of Douarnenez Bay. You will see the new fishing port, which is developing in the shelter of a jetty some 741 m - 800 yds long. Do not fail to go on to this new jetty, from which there is a still wider **view*** of the bay, dominated by the Ménez-Hom.

DOUARNENEZ★

Rosmeur Harbour★ (EYZ).
– Here the tourist will get interesting and amusing glimpses of local life, especially when the fish is sold by auction. A walk along the Rosmeur jetty also gives a good view of the harbour quarter *(illustration p 18)*.

Ste-Hélène (EZ A). – *Go in by the small door on the south side*. This chapel, in the Flamboyant Gothic style, was remodelled in the 17 and 18C. Over the side altars there are some 18C pictures and at the end of the nave, two 16C stained glass windows.

Return to the Place Gabriel-Péri by way of the covered market. In the morning a multitude of coiffes may be seen at the open-air market.

Boat trips. – *Landing stage at Rosmeur harbour. Boat trips in the afternoon and sea fishing in the morning from July to August. Apply to the Tourist Information Centre, Tel 92 13 35.*

PLOARÉ

Church (EZ C). – *Closed Sunday afternoons.* The church has a nave and four aisles and dates from the 16 and 17C. It is crowned by a fine Flamboyant and Renaissance **tower★**, 55 m - 180 ft high, with a crocketed steeple with four pinnacles at the corners.

The façade is flanked with Gothic buttresses surmounted by pinnacles, while the buttresses of the nave and transept are crowned with small Renaissance lanterns. Inside is a 17C painted wooden group representing the Holy Trinity.

Cemetery (EZ). – Laënnec (1781–1826), the inventor of the stethoscope, is buried in the cemetery. Kerlouarnec, the country house *(not open)* where this eminent physician died, can be seen at the end of a fine avenue leading to the church.

DOUARNENEZ

Anatole-France (R.)	EZ 2	Jean-Bart (R.)	DZ 12
Duguay-Trouin (R.)	DZ	Port (R. du)	EY 39
Grivart (R.)	EZ 15	Résistance (Pl. de la)	DZ 42
Guet (R. du)	DY 16	Vaillant (Pl. Ed.)	DZ 48
Jaurès (R. J.)	DEZ	Voltaire (R.)	EZ 59

TRÉBOUL

The much frequented resort of Tréboul *(facilities p 42)* lies at the foot of a wooded hill *(plan p 89)* on the left bank of the Pouldavid River. It is an important sailing centre with a pleasure boat harbour and a sailing school. It also has a salt-water cure centre. Coming from Douarnenez, you will find its little harbour very picturesque at high tide.

A pleasant path along the rocky ridge between the Biron pier and the Sables Blancs beach affords fine views of Douarnenez Bay and the Ménez-Hom.

EXCURSIONS

Sentier des Plomarc'hs★ and the Plage du Ris. – 2½ *hours on foot Rtn.* The Plomarc'hs path begins at the port of Douarnenez *(plan p 90)* and runs along the side of a slope affording some very picturesque **views★** of Douarnenez. It leads to the Plage du Ris, a great beach of fine sand. *Return by the same way or by the D 7.*

Le Juch; Guengat. – *15 km - 9½ miles – about ½ hour.* Leave Douarnenez by ②, the D 765. 1.5 km - 1 mile farther on, turn left opposite **Pouldavid** (art-lovers will see the painted panels in the choir of the 16C church).
4.5 km - 3 miles on, turn left for Le Juch.

Le Juch. – Pop 725. Inside the church, the old 17C stained glass window at the east end shows scenes from the Passion: to the left and right of the chancel are statues depicting the Annunciation, placed in niches with 16C painted shutters. At the top of the north aisle is St. Michael overcoming a dragon known as the Devil of Le Juch. *Pardon on 15 August.*

Guengat. – Pop 1 273. The Gothic church has a few 15 and 16C **stained glass windows★** in the choir. In the middle of the church, to the left, is a Flemish statue of St. Barbara.
The treasure *(apply to the parish priest)* contains some fine 16C enamelled chalices and a processional cross dating from 1584. On the left as you enter the church is a 15C tomb damaged during the Revolution. In the cemetery stands a fine Calvary.

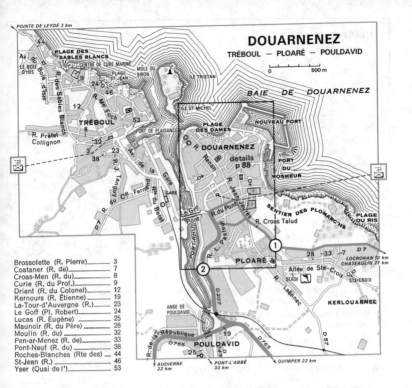

DOUARNENEZ

TRÉBOUL — PLOARÉ — POULDAVID

Leydé Point★. – *Round tour of 6 km - 4 miles to the northwest.*
From the Sables Blancs beach follow the road no 9. The road, running through woods and across heath, overlooks the coast, giving fine views of Douarnenez Bay. After the village of Leydé, turn right in the direction of the holiday centre of the "Caisse d'Allocations Familiales". **View★** from the point. *Go down to a road which, bearing left, brings you back to Tréboul.*

ELVEN Towers ★ (TOURS D'ELVEN)

Michelin map **230** 37 – 15 km - 9 miles northeast of Vannes

These imposing feudal ruins stand in the middle of a park. In the last century, during the great vogue for Octave Feuillet, all France knew of the Elven Towers which are the scene of several episodes in his famous *Roman d'un jeune homme pauvre.*

The road to the towers branches off from N 166 between two pillars, at the Tours d'Elven bus-stop. *700 m from N 166, at the entrance to the estate, apply at the keeper's lodge on the left for admission: 2F. Park the car at the end of the road, 800 m farther on. Time: ½ hour.*

The Castle of Largoët belonged to Marshal de Rieux, who was first a councillor of Duke François II and then tutor to his daughter, Anne of Brittany. When the troops of the King of France, Charles VIII, invaded Brittany in 1488, all the Marshal's strongholds, including Largoët, were burnt down or razed to the ground.

You will pass first under two successive fortified gateways. Of the castle there remains an impressive 14C keep, 44 m - 144 ft high, with walls 6 to 9 m - 19 to 29 ft thick. Near the keep is a smaller tower, remodelled as a hunting lodge.

EMERALD COAST ★★★ (CÔTE D'ÉMERAUDE)

Michelin map **230** 9, 10, 11

The name, given to this part of the coast between the Grouin Point and Le Val-André, includes some famous beaches: Dinard, St-Lunaire, Paramé, etc., and the famous city of the privateers: St-Malo. The Emerald Coast is broken, rocky and picturesque. From it a series of points, from which fine panoramas can be seen, project into the sea: Cape Fréhel being the best example. The coast is bisected by the estuary of the Rance, on which an enjoyable and well-known boat excursion between Dinan and St-Malo can be made.

TOUR

The road by which you can tour the Emerald Coast is one of the most frequented by tourists on the north coast of Brittany. Though it does not skirt the sea everywhere, it offers a remarkable choice of local excursions to imposing coastal scenes, where views and panoramas reveal the nature of the coast with its bays, creeks, capes and points. Cape Fréhel, with its extensive panorama, is an unforgettable place.

FROM CANCALE TO ST-SERVAN

23 km - 14 miles – about 4 hours – Local map p 91

Leave Cancale (p 66) by ② on the map, turn right towards the Grouin Point, 300 m farther on.

Grouin Point★★. – *Description p 99.*

After Le Verger, the road follows the coast and offers lovely views.

La Guimorais. – A quiet and simple seaside resort. Its fine beach stretches between the Meinga Point and the peninsula which encloses the harbour of Rothéneuf on the east.

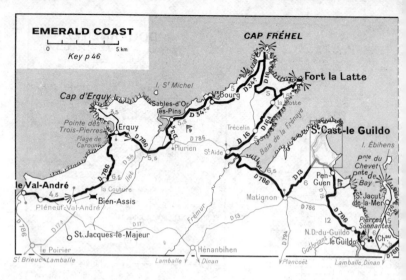

The road skirts the harbour of Rothéneuf which is closed by narrows. This stretch of water almost empties itself at low tide; the flow of the tides was once used to work a mill.

Rothéneuf and Le Minihic. – *Description p 171.*

From D 201 there are fine glimpses of the Bay of St-Malo.

Paramé**. – *Description p 171.*

St-Malo***. – *Description p 167*

St-Malo extends southwards to St-Servan *(p 170).*

FROM ST-SERVAN TO DINARD

Here the tourist has a choice of excursions:

The crossing of the Rance estuary by the D 168, which goes over the crown of the Rance tide-powered factory and affords glimpses of the estuary. It is the quickest way to get to Dinard.

The Rance Valley by boat** *(4 hours, not counting a stop at Dinan).* This is particularly recommended. *Information and description p 154.*

The Rance Valley by car* *(79 km - 50 miles – about 4 hours).* A quicker but less interesting excursion than the previous one. The visit to Dinan is worth the detour. *Description p 154.*

FROM DINARD TO CAPE FRÉHEL
56 km - 35 miles – about 4 hours – Local map below

Unfortunately, the road does not follow all the indentations of the coast between Dinard *(p 84)* and Cape Fréhel. However, it has interesting coastal sections and opens up fine panoramas and remarkable scenes. Many fashionable and family resorts lie along the shore.

St-Lunaire**. – *Description p 166.*

Garde Guérin Point*. – *0.5 km - ½ mile, plus ¼ hour on foot Rtn.* After crossing the point at its base, turn right at the $\frac{1}{10}$ km stone no 8 along a road, barely fit for driving, to the foot of the hill, which is honeycombed with casemates. Climb on foot to the top of the promontory, from which a fine **panorama**** extends from Cape Fréhel to the Varde Point.

St-Briac-sur-Mer. – Pop 1 619. *Facilities p 43.* This agreeable and picturesque resort has a fishing and yachting harbour and several beaches. It shares with Dinard an excellent golf course covering more than 60 ha - 170 acres. There are good views of the coast from the Emerald Balcony (Balcon d'Émeraude) and the Sailors' Cross (Croix des Marins). As you come out of St-Briac you cross the Frémur River on a bridge 330 m long, to reach Lancieux; fine view.

Lancieux. – Pop 1 084. *Facilities p 43.* This quiet and simple resort has a very extensive beach of fine sand, from which there is a good view of the Hébihens Island and the advanced points of the coast, St-Jacut-de-la-Mer, St-Cast and Cape Fréhel.

Ploubalay. – Pop 2 217. *Water tower: 1.5 km - 1 mile from the crossroads of the D 786 and the D 168. Take the St-Servan road and after 800 m turn left.* The water tower *(open 1 April to 30 September, 9am to midnight; 1 October to 30 November, on Saturday afternoons, Sundays and public holidays only; the rest of the year by arrangement, Tel 27 80 03; lift: 1 F)* has a circular terrace 104 m - 341 ft up which offers a good vantage point for Ploubalay, the Frémur River, St-Jacut, St-Cast Point and in clear weather Cape Fréhel and Jersey.

Alternative* route via St-Jacut-de-la-Mer and the Chevet Point. – *Extra distance: 11 km - 6 miles.* (Pop 957 - *Facilities p 43).* The road follows a long peninsula and goes through St-Jacut, a small fishing port and seaside resort. After skirting the beach of Le Rougeret, you will reach the high and picturesque cliff at the **Chevet Point**; there is a fine **view*** of the Island of Hébihens, opposite, and its tower; also, to the left, of the Bay of Arguenon and St-Cast, and to the right of the Bay of Lancieux.

Le Guildo. – *Description p 104.*

Bay Point. – *1 km - ½ mile from the D 786.* The road leads to a large car park. The view includes the Arguenon estuary with its four lines of mussel poles and St-Jacut.

Pen-Guen. – Fashionable beach.

St-Cast-le-Guildo**. – *Description p 164*

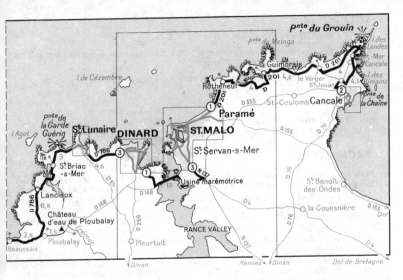

Leaving St-Cast the road makes a big loop round the Bay of La Frênaye, and skirts the head. After Petit-Trécelin, leave the D 16 on the left and follow the D 16A through La Motte to the village of La Latte. *Leave the car in the car park.*

La Latte Fort★★. – *Description p 116.*

On the return journey, turn right 200 m before La Motte, to pick up the Cape Fréhel road (p 96).

FROM CAPE FRÉHEL TO LE VAL-ANDRÉ
28 km - 17 miles – about 1 hour – Local map p 90

Turn back and then bear right into the tourist road, D 34A which twists and turns on the moor affording striking **views**★★ of the sea and cliffs.

Vieux-Bourg. – Pop 759. The beach of Le Vieux-Bourg lies on the right. Ahead, there is a fine view over the sea.

Sables-d'Or-les-Pins. – *Facilities p 43*. This resort gets its name from the immense beach of fine sand. Pleasant walks can be taken in the pine woods.

After Plurien, at the top of a downward slope, you will see the coast at St-Quay, on the other side of St-Brieuc Bay.

Erquy. – Pop 3 347. *Facilities p 43*. This busy scallop fishing port is growing rapidly. The finest of its numerous beaches, Caroual, is noted for its view of the bay and the cape.

Cape Erquy★. – *3.5 km - 3 miles from the D 786 plus ½ hour Rtn on foot.* From the point where the road ends there is an extensive view of grey-pink shingle beaches lapped by transparent waters, opposite Caroual beach and the Vallées seashore. Pléneuf Point and Verdelet Islet. Pleasant footpaths bordered by bracken cross the heath dotted with patches of yellow and mauve, and afford glimpses of the reefs.

Le FAOU

Michelin map **230** 18 – *Local map p 50* – Pop 1 611

The town occupies a **site**★ at the head of the Faou estuary which has a lot of character at high tide.

Main Street. – This is flanked by old houses with overhanging upper storeys and slate-covered façades.

Church. – 16C. The church stands on a terrace overlooking the river.

EXCURSION

Térénez coast road★; **Térénez Bridge.** – *Round tour of 25 km - 16 miles – about ½ hour. Leave Le Faou by the N 791.*

Térénez coast road★. – At first the road affords views over the estuary of the Le Faou river and, in the distance, the Plougastel Peninsula. Farther on, after the Aulne estuary, you will see Landévennec ahead, on the right *(p 113)* and, soon afterwards, the whole of the Landévennec Peninsula and the course of the Aulne. At the end of a short rise you will overlook the narrow part of the Aulne Valley, crossed by the new Térénez Bridge.

Térénez Bridge. – This elegant structure has a central span of 272 m - 893 ft. Leaving the main road on your right, take the road on the left that leaves the river, reaches the plateau (belvedere) and runs through Rosnoën. *At Quimerch take N 170 on the left.* On the right as you leave the town is a viewing table from which there is a **view**★ extending from the Ménez-Hom to the Cranou Forest.

The companion guides in English in this series on France are
**Châteaux of the Loire, Dordogne,
French Riviera, Normandy, Paris, Provence**

Other Michelin Green Guides available in English
**Austria, Germany, Italy
Portugal, Spain, Switzerland
London, New York City**

Le FAOUËT

Michelin map 230 20 – Pop 3 245

This village is the centre of a very picturesque district extending between the Inam and the Ellé, two rivers flowing from the Noires Mountains.

Church. – The restored church dates from the 16C. The former ossuary is on the right of the porch-belfry.

Market. – Very fine 16C timberwork.

Monument to Corentin Carré. – The youngest soldier of France. In 1915 he enlisted at the age of fifteen, and died in aerial combat in 1918. He was then a sergeant-major.

EXCURSIONS

St-Fiacre*. – 2.5 km - 1½ miles – about ½ hour – Local map below. Leave Le Faouët by the Rue de Quimper (D 782), then turn left on the D 790, which leads to the hamlet of St-Fiacre.

To visit the chapel (½ hour) ask for the key. The chapel is a fine 15C building. The façade shows one of the best Breton specimens of a gable-belfry (details p 29).

Inside, the **rood-screen****, an example of lace-like woodcarving, is a Flamboyant work of 1480 (illustration p 30). On the nave side it is adorned with statues of the Archangel Gabriel, the Virgin, St. John, Adam and Eve. The most curious figures are on the chancel side; they picture theft (a man picking fruit from a tree), drunkenness (a man vomiting a fox), lust (a man and a woman) and laziness (a Breton peasant playing bagpipes and a bombard). The decoration of the panels on the tribune is remarkably varied. The partition is made of elaborately carved panels.

The stone altarpiece against the left-hand pillar shows the martyrdom of St. Sebastian.

There are 16C stained glass windows in the chancel and transepts; also old statues.

Ste-Barbe; St-Nicolas; Langonnet Abbey; Ellé Valley. – Round tour of 28 km - 17 miles – about 3 hours – Local map below. Leave Le Faouët by the D 132. The road runs down into the Ellé Valley. At the hamlet of Grand Pont, after passing a road signposted to the Chapel of St. Barbara but before coming to the Ellé Bridge, park the car. By the Café de l'Ellé take the path on the left that goes along the bank. Just before a group of houses, turn left. Continue a few yards beyond the path leading off to the chapel on the left and bear right so as to see the fountain.

Return and go up to the chapel.

Ste-Barbe. – Open mid-June to mid-September all day long; Easter holidays, Sundays and holidays Easter to mid-June only in the afternoon. Ask for the key in the keeper's house on the terrace. This chapel in Flamboyant Gothic is built in a rocky depression on the side of a hill. The **site*** is very pretty: from a height of 100 m - 300 ft it overlooks the little Valley of the Ellé. Owing to its position, the chapel has only a single aisle and an apse. Inside are statues, carved panels and Renaissance stained glass. Pardons take place on the last Sunday in June and on 4 December (p 10).

The great Renaissance stairway to the terrace is linked by an arch to the St. Michael Oratory, built on a rock spur. Nearby, in a little building, is the bell tolled by pilgrims to call down blessings from heaven. From there there is a steep descent to the Grand Pont.

Take the D 132 on the left to return to the car. Follow the road for 5 km - 3 miles, then turn right for 1 km - ½ mile, and then right again.

St-Nicolas. – The little chapel stands alone in a beautiful setting of young pines and fine trees. The style of the building is Gothic strongly influenced by Renaissance design. Ask for the key M. Robic at Kerviguen, a hamlet beyond the chapel.

The Renaissance **rood-screen***, which it is interesting to compare with the Gothic one to be found at St-Fiacre, is a fine piece of Breton sculpture.

Above an attractive screen, the legend of St. Nicholas is shown in nine panels, while on the other side, caryatids separate niches containing figures of the Apostles.

Return to the D 132 and turn right. After 500 m leaving on your immediate left the road to Langonnet, bear left towards the abbey. Good view of Bel-Air Lake.

Langonnet Abbey. – The abbey was rebuilt in the 17 and 18C but has kept its 13C chapterhouse. There is a museum of African missions.

Return to Le Faouët by the D 790.

LE FAOUËT
(EXCURSIONS)

Le FOLGOËT ★★

Michelin map 230 3, 4 – Local map p 47 – Pop 2 253

You should see this little village and its magnificent Church of Our Lady (Notre-Dame) during the great pardon (p 10) which takes place in September. It is the best known in the Léon region and one of the biggest in Brittany. The ceremonies begin at 4pm the day before and continue the day after. Other pardons, less frequented, take place every Sunday in May and on 15 August. The pardon of St. Christopher with the blessing of cars is on the 4th Sunday in July.

Legend. – The name of Folgoët (Fool's Wood) recalls the legend attached to the foundation of the church. In the middle of the 14C a poor half-wit named Salaün lived in a hollow oak in a wood, near a spring not far from Lesneven. He knew only a few words, and he constantly repeated them: "O Itroun Guerhez Mari" (O Lady Virgin Mary). After his death a lily grew on his grave; the pistil made the words "Ave Maria" in letters of gold. Men dug up the earth and found that the lily sprang from Salaün's mouth. News of the miracle spread in Brittany. The War of Succession was then raging. The Pretender Montfort vowed, if he won, to build a sumptuous chapel for the Virgin. After his victory at Auray *(details p 52)* he gave orders for the building to begin. The altar was to stand over the spring where the simpleton used to drink. The work was completed by Montfort's son in 1423.

The church was pillaged in the Revolution. To save it from being demolished, twelve farmers subscribed to buy it. It was returned to the cult at the Restoration, and has been gradually repaired since.

Church★★. – *Time: ½ hour*. A great esplanade with inns on each side leads up to the church, but is not even wide enough to hold the crowd on *pardon* days. The **north tower★** of the façade *(illustration p 28)* supports one of the finest belfries in Brittany.

The church is square, which is unusual; the Chapel of the Cross forms a branch like a transept at the end of the chancel, its east wall prolonging this part of the building. This chapel has a fine **porch★**. Salaün's fountain *(illustration p 29)*, where pilgrims come to drink, stands outside, against the apse wall. The water comes from the spring under the altar.

Inside is a masterpiece of Breton art of the 15C, the admirably carved granite **rood-screen★★**. Five 15C Kersanton granite altars stand in the apse, which is adorned, as is the Chapel of the Cross, by fine rose windows. There is a 15C statue of Our Lady of Folgoët.

In the presbytery close, a small museum contains a collection of stone statues and the remains of a Calvary of 1543.

South of the church, the little 16C manorhouse of Le Doyenné, though much restored, forms an attractive group with the pilgrims' inn and the church.

FOUESNANT

Michelin map **230** 32 – Pop 5 041 – *Facilities p 42*

This town is in the middle of one of the most fertile areas in Brittany; the villages stand among cherry and apple orchards. This is also where the best Breton cider is produced.

The costumes and *coiffes* of Fouesnant are a very pretty sight at the feast of the apple trees, at the *pardon* of St. Anne *(p 10)* and at the exit from Mass.

Church. – This 12C church was partly rebuilt in the 17C. On the square stands a 17C Calvary; the monument to the dead, left of the porch, is the work of the Breton sculptor Quillivic, remarkable for the stately yet serious expression of the peasant woman wearing a local *coiffe*. An unusual stoup is built into an engaged pillar. A triumphal arch separates the nave from the transept where stands the altar.

EXCURSIONS

Beg-Meil★. – *5 km - 3 miles to the south. Description p 56*.

Ste-Anne. – *1.7 km - 1 mile to the north*. A chapel in a pretty setting. Picturesque *pardons* on 26 July and the following Sunday.

La Forêt-Fouesnant. – Pop 2 060. *Facilities p 42. 3.5 km - 2 miles to the east*.
This quiet village lies buried in greenery at the head of La Forêt Bay.
It possesses a small parish close and 16C Calvary.
The church porch, dating from 1538, is adorned with two old and somewhat rough statues of St. Rock and King St. Melar.
Inside at the high altar are an altarpiece and, on either side, two angel musicians in plaster. The chapels at the end of the church contain a statue in wood of St. Alan and a font carved in 1628 and that on the south side of the chancel, an ancient entombment.
A 16C silver-gilt chalice is kept in the presbytery.

Port-la-Forêt. – This port for pleasure craft has been built near La Forêt-Fouesnant. Departures leave for the Glénan Islands *(p 97)* and excursions go up the Odet River *(p 152)*.

FOUGÈRES ★★

Michelin map **230** 28 – Pop 27 653

Fougères, though industrial, will be very interesting to tourists. This former stronghold is built in a picturesque setting on a promontory overlooking the winding valley of the Nançon. Below it, on a rocky height almost entirely encircled by the river, stands a magnificent feudal castle whose walls, with their thirteen big towers, are among the most massive in Europe.

HISTORICAL NOTES

A frontier post. – Standing on the border of Brittany and France, Fougères acquired great military importance in the early Middle Ages, when its barons were very powerful. The most famous is Raoul II. He lived in the middle of the 12C under Conan IV, known as "the Little", Duke of Brittany. This weak sovereign submitted to Henry II Plantagenet, King of England and Duke of Normandy, but the proud Raoul rebelled against the English yoke. He formed a league with some of the Breton nobles and opened the struggle against Plantagenet. In 1166 Henry II invested Fougères, which capitulated after three months' siege. The castle was completely demolished, Raoul immediately began to rebuild it, and part of his work still stands. In the 13C the fief passed to some Poitou noblemen, the Lusignans. They claimed to be descendants of the fairy Mélusine and gave her name to the finest of the towers that they added to the walls.

Fougères is an example of a formidable fortress which was often taken. Among those who fought their way into it between the 12 and late 18C were St. Louis, Du Guesclin, Surienne, a leader from Aragon in the service of the English (at night without striking a blow), La Trémoille, the Duke of Mercœur and the men of the Vendée.

After the union of Brittany and France, there were a succession of governors at Fougères; ten of its towers bear their names. The castle was then mainly used as a prison. In the 18C it became private property. The town bought it in 1892 for 80 000 F, half of which was given by the State.

FOUGÈRES★★

In the Chouan country. – Victor Hugo, in *Quatre-vingt-treize* (Ninety-three), and Balzac in *Les Chouans* have introduced Fougères and its inhabitants into their stories of the royalist rebellion. They gleaned their information on the spot. In 1836 the poet, accompanied by Juliette Drouet (who was born at Fougères), gave a glowing account of the town and castle. "I should like to ask everyone," he wrote, "have you seen Fougères?" Balzac stayed with friends at Fougères, explored the neighbourhood with survivors of the adventure and wrote his novel there in 1828.

The Breton and Vendéen revolt continued, with a few pauses, from 1793 to 1804. Its supporters were named after their call imitating the hoot of an owl *(chat-huant)*. The instigator of the movement was the Marquis of La Rouërie, who was born at Fougères. His life was a real adventure film. A turbulent youth resulted in a warrant for his arrest; to avoid the Bastille, he fled to Switzerland. Thinking he had a religious vocation, La Rouërie shut himself in a Trappist monastery. But he then felt the call to arms. Discarding the habit, he went to America, where the War of Independence was being fought, and became a general in the American Army. He returned to France on the eve of the Revolution. When it broke out the Marquis refused to emigrate and prepared for resistance by a war of surprise and ambuscade, well suited to the Breton country. He organised stores of hidden arms and provisions and recruited a secret army which would rise at a sign. But the plotter was betrayed and obliged to flee. He went into hiding and died, worn out, in January 1793. The following month the Assembly decreed the mass levy: Brittany rebelled, and the war foreseen by La Rouërie broke out.

The shoe town. – In the 13C and for 300 years Fougères made a lot of money by manufacturing cloth first of wool then of hemp when the sailcloth of Fougères flapped on the yards of the French fleet until the triumph of steam.

In 1832 woollen slippers came in; leather shoes followed in 1852, the workers sewing them by hand at home.

1870 saw the introduction of sewing-machines, and mechanical techniques gained ground every day. In 1890 about thirty factories were mass-producing cheap shoes, chiefly for women. After the First World War the eighty factories in the town felt the effects of foreign competition and the world crisis.

The six remaining ones now manufacture 1 million pairs of shoes, mostly for women.

■ THE CASTLE★★

time: 1 hour

The castle, a fine example of military architecture of the Middle Ages, has made the tourist reputation of Fougères. A general view before the visit in detail will give you a better understanding of the difficulties of siege warfare.

General view of the Castle★ (Place aux Arbres★ – AZ). – The Place aux Arbres is a very well-kept **public garden★**, partly terraced on the former ramparts of the town, partly on the slopes of the Couesnon Valley. By following the low wall by the balustrade to the entrance, you will get a view of the hedge-bordered

(After Arthaud photo, Nantes)

Fougères. — The castle.

fields which are characteristic of the district. From the part of the terrace within the balustrade there is an interesting general **view★** of the castle *(compare it with the plan p 95)*.

The site is curious. Most of the town, once encircled by ramparts remains of which can be seen on the right, is perched on a promontory overlooking the Nançon Valley, while the castle stands below, on the valley floor.

A loop in the river, washing a rocky eminence, a very narrow peninsula in shape, formed an excellent defensive position. Military architects took advantage of this site to build ramparts and towers and turn the peninsula into an island by a short diversion of the Nançon at the base of the loop. As the castle was connected with the upper town by the city ramparts, the garrison could take part in its defence; they also had the advantage of being able to retire into the fortress and hold it, should the town fall, as a frontier post for the Duchy of Brittany.

The fortress as we see it has suffered much in the course of centuries. The wall is complete, with its curtains closely following the lie of the land and its thirteen towers. Unfortunately we can no longer see the high keep that commanded all the defences; it was razed in 1166 by King Henry II of England and there are now only traces which can be seen when visiting the inside of the castle. The main buildings which occupied part of the inner court were also demolished down to their foundations at the beginning of the 19C. History tells us that the defenders often succumbed and that attackers were able to seize these high walls, either by surprise attack or after long sieges.

An outer tour of the castle shows the attackers' point of view; an inner tour, that of the defenders.

Outer tour★. – *Park your car in the Place Raoul II and walk along the Boulevard de Rennes and then, left, along the Rue Le-Bouteiller. Skirt the fortifications.*

As you circle the walls you will see the splendid towers in all their variety of appearance and structure. At the start you will also see in the middle of the north rampart, the 14C Guibé Turret, a corbelled sentry-post built on to the wall.

Going round the spur formed by the ramparts towards the west, you will see how massive the defences are concentrated at this point. The whole forms a triangle with two towers at the base and a postern at the apex. The 15C postern today looks out on empty space, but it was once connected with a double ar-cade that crossed the moat to communicate with an outwork. The 13 and 14C Gobelin Tower, to the left of the postern, and the 14C Mélusine, to the right, are round and overlook the walls from a height. Stripped of their machicolations and with their upper parts probably re-built they have lost much of their proud aspect. The Mélu-sine is regarded as a master-piece of military architecture of the period; it is over 13 m - 41½ ft in diameter, with walls 3.50 m - 11 ft thick and rising 31 m - 99 ft above the rock.

Farther on are two squat, horseshoe-shaped towers, the Surienne and the Raoul, which mark the last stage in the building of the castle (15C). Built to serve as platforms for artillery, they contain several storeys of very strong and well-preserved gun platforms. To re-

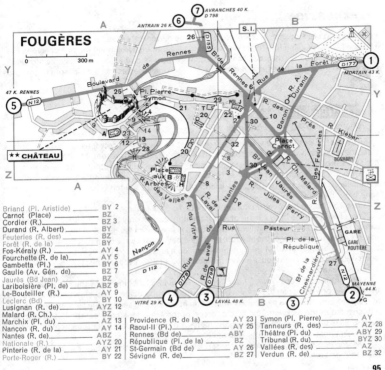

TOUR OF THE CASTLE

FORMER COURSE OF THE NANÇON

sist enemy artillery fire, their walls are 7 m - 22 ft thick. At the end of the 15C, artillery had been in use for nearly a century and a half, and siege warfare often took the form of an artillery duel at short range. The design of the machicolations shows that military art at that time was not indifferent to decoration.

Opposite the two towers stands the Church of St-Sulpice. On the right is the Place du Marchix Quarter (p 96).

Still following the walls, you will see the 13C Sundial Tower, two centuries older than the others. It is small, square and badly damaged, not nearly as strong as its neighbours and recalling the time when fire-arms had not yet taken the place of bows and arrows.

Farther on, Our Lady's Gate is the only one left of the four rampart gateways preceding the four gates in the walls which encircled the town. The left-hand tower, which is the higher and is pierced with narrow loopholes, dates from the 14C; that on the right, with very ornamental machicolations, dates from the 15C, as do the Surienne and Raoul towers. In the middle, over the carriage gateway, are vertical slits to receive the arms of the drawbridge. *Go under the gate and follow the Rue de la Fourchette, then turn a sharp right into the Rue de la Pinterie.* Fifty metres farther on cross the gardens that have been laid out along the former parapet-walk which has been reconstructed. From there you get a good view of the Nançon Valley and the mass of the castle. *To leave the garden, go under the ruins of a beautiful chapel doorway and go once more into the Rue de la Pinterie on the left. This leads to the castle entrance.*

FOUGÈRES

FOUGÈRES★★

Inner tour★★. – *Guided tours at 10am, 11am, 2pm, 3pm and according to the time of year also at 9am, 4pm, 5pm, and 6pm; in February, Sundays only; in November, Saturdays and Sundays. Closed in December and January. Admission: 5F.*

The entrance *(plan p 95)*, preceded by a moat filled from a diversion of the Nançon, is through the square tower of La Haye-St-Hilaire. To reach it, you first had to go through a town gate and the wall before it. The castle has three walls in succession. The *Avancée* (advanced wall) was the first obstacle; it was guarded by three 13C towers with many loopholes. When this line of resistance had been crossed, attackers would enter a small courtyard on the island formed by a second diversion of the river, and would come under the converging fire of defenders posted on the four sides. Thus exposed, the attackers had to cross a second moat before reaching the main ring of fortifications, guarded by four towers dating from 12 and 15C. When both lines had been stormed they would burst into the main inside courtyard, where stood the overlord's house, the chapel and the well; but the defenders still had a chance to rally. A third position, the redoubt, standing on the highest eminence and girt with a wall and two towers, and the keep (demolished in the 12C), made a long resistance possible, and when driven from these positions the garrison could still seek safety in flight through the postern. Once they had mastered the successive hurdles of the castle, the attackers had only to crush the last nests of resistance in the towers.

Entering the great courtyard, go round the walls on the wall walk. This enables one to appreciate the might of such a fortress and also to enjoy some good views of Fougères. At the end of the highest wall of the castle is the Mélusine Tower which commands a fine view of the castle and the town. Farther on are the remains of the keep and north wall, and beyond the Guibé Turret and the Coigny Tower (13 and 14C), whose second and third storeys were turned into a chapel in the 17C. The summit was disfigured by the addition of a loggia during its first restoration in the 19C. In the courtyard an open-air theatre has been arranged in a pleasant setting.

■ ADDITIONAL SIGHTS

St-Sulpice★ (AY A). – A Gothic building in the Flamboyant style, erected between the 15 and the 18C. It has a 15C slate covered steeple, very slender and of original design. Inside, in the north aisle is a traditionally miraculous 12C statue of the Virgin suckling her Infant. The altars in the aisles have 15C granite **altarpieces★**. The woodwork in the chancel is 18C.

Place du Marchix (AZ 13). – This Place du Marchix quarter, with its picturesque old houses, has always been of interest to painters.

Take a walk along the Rue du Nançon with its 16C houses.

There are other interesting houses at the corner of the Rue de la Providence and the Rue de Lusignan.

On the Place du Marchix are two fine 16C houses, nos 13 and 15. Take the Rue des Tanneurs to cross the bridge over the Nançon; looking back, you will see a picturesque group formed by the backs of the houses of the Place du Marchix.

St-Léonard (AZ B). – The church, built in the 15 and 16C, has a richly decorated 16C north façade and a 17C tower. Inside two diptychs by the Devéria brothers adorn the organ loft, the *Adoration of the Magi* and *Jesus amid the Rabbis* on the right, and the *Crucifixion* and the *Resurrection* on the left. In the sacristy there is an Italian painting depicting the *Crowning of Thorns*. The modern stained glass windows are by Lorin. In the chapel of the Cross, on the left as you go in, are two scenes of the life of St. Benedict, and in the 12C baptismal chapel 16C stained glass windows.

Town Hall (AZ H). – A 16C building with a Renaissance doorway.

EXCURSION

Fougères State Forest★. – *3 km - 2 miles to the northeast. Leave Fougères by* ①, *D 177.*
Those who like walking in a forest will spend pleasant hours strolling in the fine beech woods, along the forest roads. They can see two dolmens in ruins and a line of megalithic stones. At Landéan, at the edge of the forest, are the 12C cellars once used as a secret hide-out by the lords of Fougères.

FRÉHEL Cape ★★★

Michelin map ⧉ 10 – *Local map p 90*

The **site★★★** of this cape is one of the grandest on the Breton coast. Its red, grey and black cliffs stand vertically above the sea to a height of 70 m - 229 ft and are fringed with reefs on which the swell breaks heavily. The coastal **panorama★★★** (especially beautiful towards evening) is immense in clear weather; it stretches from the Grouin Point, on the right (with the Cotentin Peninsula in the background), to the Island of Bréhat, on the left. The Channel Islands can sometimes be seen.

The lighthouse can be visited from Easter to 15 September from 9.30am to noon and 2 to 6.30pm. The lantern is lit by a lamp of 3 kW; the light carries only 200 m in foggy weather but it can be seen from 110 km - 70 miles away when it is fine. From the gallery at the top of the tower there is an immense view of the horizon: on a clear day you may see Bréhat to the west, Jersey to the north, Granville, a part of the Cotentin Peninsula and Chausey Island to the northeast. At a point 400 m from the lighthouse a siren mounted in a shelter gives two blasts once every minute in foggy weather.

Walk round the cape *(tour: ½ hour from the restaurant)*, beginning by the left. After passing the extreme point you can look down on the curious Fauconnière rocks, crowded with seagulls and cormorants; these are particularly interesting in the nesting season; the contrast between the mauvish red of the rocks and the blue or green of the sea is striking. Near the Restaurant de la Fauconnière take a steep path on the right; halfway down, it reaches a platform from which there is another remarkable view of the Fauconnière rocks, detached from the point.

Motor-boats from Dinard bring tourists near Cape Fréhel by sea (p 85). It is most impressive from this viewpoint.

GAVRINIS Tumulus ★★

Michelin map 230 50 – *Local map p 124.*

The Gavrinis Tumulus is the most interesting megalithic monument in Brittany and perhaps in the world *(details on prehistoric monuments p 27)*. It is situated on the Island of Gavrinis, at the mouth of the Morbihan Gulf, south of Larmor-Baden, from which it can be reached.

Crossing and tour. – *Daily from 15 March to 15 September; the rest of the year, Saturdays, Sundays and holidays by previous request: write to M. Guillemot, Route de Vannes, 56790 Lamor-Baden. Leave your car at the port opposite the embarking point. Boats run to the Island of Gavrinis (crossing: ¼ hour; admission: 5F).*

Eight metres high and 100 m round (25 ft - 328 ft) – the tumulus is made of stones piled on a hillock. It was discovered in 1832, and it contains: (1) a covered gallery 13 m - 43 ft long with twenty-three supports, on which lie nine tables. The supports are covered with carvings; (2) the funeral chamber, probably a royal tomb, with a ceiling made of a single granite stone, 4 m by 3 m (12×9 ft), resting on eight supports placed in a rectangle.

From the top of the tumulus there is a wide view of the Morbihan Gulf.

On the tiny island of **Er Lanic**, a little south of Gavrinis, are two tangent circles of menhirs *(cromlechs)* in the form of a figure eight of which half is submerged. This gives evidence of the subsidence of the soil in prehistoric times which created the gulf.

GLÉNAN Islands

Michelin map 230 32

The archipelago consists of nine islets surrounded by reefs and lies off Concarneau.

Access. – *There are boat services to the islands:*

Leaving Concarneau: for information apply to the Tourist Information Centre of Concarneau, Tel 97 01 44.

Leaving Quimper, Bénodet or Loctudy: for information, apply to Vedettes de l'Odet "Aigrettes", Tel 91 00 53 at Bénodet.

Leaving Beg-Meil, La Forêt-Fouesnant (Port-la-Forêt), apply to M. R. Guillou, Tel 94 97 94 at Beg-Meil.

Tour. – The chief islands are St-Nicolas, from which the view of the coast extends from Penmarch to Pouldu, the Cigogne (the Stork), on which an extension of the marine laboratory of Concarneau is housed in an 18C fort, and Penfret Island with its lighthouse.

The chief interest of the islands lies, however, in the sailing instruction school, the Centre Nautique des Glénans. It is a training school where youngsters learn how to handle sailing craft at sea and the rules governing coastal and high seas navigation. On the St-Nicholas island is the Centre International de Plongée, a skin diving school.

The uninhabited islands are kept as bird sanctuaries; terns especially nest there.

GOULVEN

Michelin map 230 west of 4 – 6.5 km - 4 miles north of Lesneven – Pop 444

This little place has a restored Gothic church. The Renaissance **belfry★**, a high tower crowned by a pointed steeple, is one of the finest in Brittany. To the right of the porch, which opens under the belfry, is a Gothic doorway with twin doors and a carved stoup on the pier between them.

Inside the church are a monumental Renaissance stoup, a high altar in Kersanton stone and an altar with decorative woodwork. The 16C organ loft has been built on to a former rood-screen. Two fine 17C embroidered banners are displayed in the chancel during the summer.

GRANDE BRIÈRE ★★

Michelin map 230 52

Also known by the name of **Grande Brière Mottière**, this region covers 6 700 ha - 16 550 acres of the total 40 000 ha - 98 840 acres belonging to the **Brière Regional Nature Park**. Marshland constitutes 38 per cent of the park which was designated in 1970. Lying to the north of St-Nazaire the area is renowned for its wildfowling and fishing. The world at large was to discover this region in 1923, through the pages of Alphonse de Chateaubriant's novel, *La Brière.* Although the factory now plays a part in the livelihood of these people, their way of life remains unique.

The Brière in the past. – In early geological times the area was a forested, undulating basin which reached to the hills of Sillon de Bretagne *(p 11)*. Neolithic man was expelled from the area when there was a momentary maritime incursion. Marshes formed behind the alluvial banks deposited by the Loire. The trees died and were submerged and vegetable matter decomposed to form **peat bogs**, often entrapping fossilised tree trunks over 5 000 years old.

The Brière from the 15 to 20C. – This swampy area was subdivided, water pumped and the drainage improved. The area was to remain the common property of all Brièrons, a fact which was to be confirmed by several royal edicts. For centuries the Briérons have cut the peat, gathered the reeds and rushes for thatching, woven baskets with the buckthorn, tended their gardens and kept poultry. They have trapped leeches, harpooned eels, placed eel-pots in the open stretches of water and wickerwork traps to catch pike, tench and roach, and with his dog in a boat patiently awaited the arrival of wildfowl, hidden by a clump of willow trees. For ages the Briéron has propelled with a pole his **blin**, a flat-bottomed boat, loaded with cows or sheep going to pasture.

The Briéron of the 20C has remained closely attached to the land, but by force of circumstance he is turning more to local industries: metallurgy in Trignac, dockyards and aeronautics at St-Nazaire. Nevertheless, he continues to fish, shoot, graze animals or cut reeds, and pay his annual fee. Change is inevitable, roads now link the islets, locks have been built, marsh has become pastureland but despite it all La Grande Brière has retained its charm and when the Briéron returns home he fishes and shoots for his own pleasure. Many who have boats are willing to take visitors on trips on the network of canals and smaller channels beautiful with yellow irises *(mid-May to mid-June)* and pearly water lilies *(mid-June to late July)*.

GRANDE BRIÈRE★★

ROUND TOUR STARTING FROM ST-NAZAIRE
84 km - 52 miles – about 4 hours – Local map below

Leave St-Nazaire (p 172) by ①.

Trignac. – Pop 7 254. This rural community has seen the implantation of new industries. A road to the left leads to the **Pont de Paille** which affords a **view** of the Trignac canal.

At **Montoir-de-Bretagne** turn left onto the D 50.

St-Malo-de-Guersac. – Pop 2 466. The largest of the islets, it offers a viewpoint from Guérands in the west to the hilly region, Sillon de Bretagne, to the east.

The road passes near the slate roofed houses before reaching the small port of **Rosé**, a former departure point for the barges plying upstream to Nantes or Vannes. Turn left before entering St-Joachim.

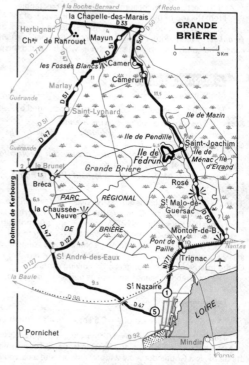

Fédrun Islet ★. – Linked to the St-Joachim road by two bridges, this, the most attractive of the islets is entirely surrounded by marshland. At no 180 of the main street are the **Administrative Services** of the Regional Nature Park. At no 308 on the circular street stands the **Chaumière briéronne** *(open 1 July to 15 September, from 10am to 6pm; admission: 2F)* which shows a typical interior of a Brière cottage. The low, flower bedecked houses retain the traditional thatched roof. The cottages on the islet's periphery are backed by a **dyke**, often planted with vegetables and fruit trees, which itself borders the canal **curée** where the residents tie up their boats. On the local holiday, **Fête de la Brière** *(15 August)* there is a boat race.

Boat trips★★. – *Numerous boatmen are willing to take visitors; price: 5F per person; about ½ hour.* Larger canals are linked by smaller bulrush bordered channels, great pools open up vast horizons broken only by the steeples of the surrounding villages. In winter the flooded marshes, with reeds the colour of ripe grain, are bathed in colours reflecting an ever-changing sky. The Brière has its charm in all seasons: the mass of flowers in spring; the summer cloak of green slashed by the black banks and the russet tints of autumn with the cries of wildfowl overhead.

St Joachim. – Pop 4 165. The village extends along the two islets of **Brécun** and **Pendille** (alt 8 m - 26 ft) dominated by the tall white spire of its 19C **church** with very low aisles. The altar is adorned by a stone Calvary and the ambulatory has fine Romanesque arcading.

The D 50 traverses the islets of **Camerun** and **Camer**.

La Chapelle-des-Marais. – Pop 2 767. In the **church** where the granite pillars stand out against the white stone, there is a polychrome statue of St Corneille, protector of the flocks. In the town hall *(daily 9am to noon and Mondays to Wednesdays 2 to 6pm)* a 7 m - 23 ft fossilised tree trunk is on view.

Take the road in the direction of Herbignac, the D 33 and turn left 1.5 km - 1 mile before the village. A track to the left leads to a farm, go beyond the buildings.

Château de Ranrouët. – This 12-13C fortress *(under restoration)* dismantled in 1616 by Richelieu, burnt under the Revolution, is still a spectacular ruin with six round towers and encircled by a moat. Cannon balls embedded in the walls, recall that the castle once belonged to the Rieux family whose coat of arms includes ten gold cannon balls.

Return to the D 33 and turn right. At **Mayun**, a wickerwork centre, take the D 51.

Les Fossés-Blancs. – From a landing stage on the Canal du Nord, there is a fine **view** of the Brière.

At Brunet turn right towards Kerbourg.

Kerbourg Dolmen★. – On a mound near a windmill stands this gallery grave covered by four massive blocks.

Return to Brunet and continue to Bréca.

Bréca. – Good view over the Brière and the Bréca canal.

Return to the D 47. At St-André-des-Eaux turn left into the D 127.

La Chaussée-Neuve. – It was from this former port that the boats loaded with peat used to leave. Stocks of cut reeds stand out to dry. From here there is a wide **view**★ over the Brière.

Boat trips *(20 F an hour for the hire of a small boat)* to the heart of the marshland.

Return to the D 47 which leads back to St-Nazaire by ⑤.

GRAND-FOUGERAY

Michelin map 230 40 – Pop 2 020

This small town has the ruins of a castle, a church, partly Romanesque and a 13C cemetery cross standing near the church. Of the old castle there remains the restored keep.

During the War of Succession Du Guesclin captured the castle by a ruse. Having learnt that firewood was to be delivered to the castle, he and his men disguised themselves as woodcutters carrying sticks. When they got into the place they brought out their weapons and slew the garrison. *Details about Du Guesclin, pp 21, 52, 81, 106, 156.*

GROIX Island

Michelin map 230 34 – *Facilities p 42*

Groix is smaller than its neighbour, Belle-Ile, but has the same geological form – a mass of schist rock worn away by the sea.

Access: *see the current Michelin Guide France.*

The coast to the north and west is wild and deeply indented: there you will see cliffs and giant rocks, valleys and fjords in which fishing boats shelter. **Port-Tudy**, which was formerly a tunny fishing port, is today a safe harbour for trawlers and pleasure boats. On the west side of the island one may visit Pen-Men with its cliffs and new lighthouse, the Trou de Tonneurre and the Trou de l'Enfer caves.

The east and south sides of the island are flatter and along the coast there are many sheltered sandy creeks, among these is the fine beach known as the **Grands Sables** and the Nosterven with its silicate sands. Also in the south is the picturesque **Locmaria** Bay surrounded by an area rich in mica schist and such rare minerals as glauconite, epidote and garnet.

Groix is the birthplace of the Breton poet J. P. Calloch who wrote in Celtic and is known under the name of Bleimor.

GROUIN Point ★★

Michelin map 230 12 – *Local map p 91*

At the end of the road, after the Hôtel de la Pointe du Grouin, leave your car on a broad terrace and take a path to the right of the signal station which leads directly to the point.

In a fine **setting★★**, this wild, rocky headland *(illustration p 12)* overlooks the sea from a height of 40 m - 131 ft and affords a **panorama★★** which stretches from Cape Fréhel to Mont-St-Michel. At low tide one can take a path to a cave in the cliffside (height 10 m - 32 ft – depth 30 m-98 ft).

The Landes Island opposite is a bird sanctuary and nature reserve.

GUÉHENNO ★

Michelin map 230 37 – 11 km - 7 miles southwest of Josselin – Pop 849

The **Calvary★** stands in the cemetery near the church *(details on Calvaries p 32)*. It dates from 1550 and was restored in the last century. All its beauty lies in its perfect composition. A column stands before it on which a cock is perched in allusion to the denial of St. Peter.

Behind this monument is a small ossuary whose entrance is protected by the figures of two guards on duty. A low relief framed in the gable depicts the Passion.

GUÉRANDE ★

Michelin map 230 51 – *Local map p 101* – Pop 8 001 – *Facilities p 44*

The town stands on a plateau which overlooks the salt marshes from a height of 50 m - 160 ft. It has kept the appearance of the Middle Ages; its ramparts are almost intact.

The first Sundays in July and August are the occasions for folk dancing at the foot of the ramparts. The colourful costumes of the salt-marsh workers and the more sombre ones of the farm tenants intermingle with other local Breton costumes to make a lively picture.

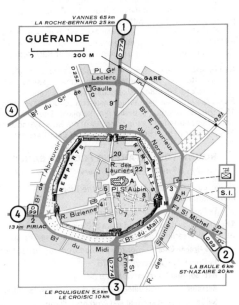

GUÉRANDE

■ **SIGHTS** *time: 1 hour*

Walk round the ramparts★. – The ramparts, in which there is still no breach, were built in the 15C. They are flanked by eight towers and pierced by four fortified gateways. In the 18C the Duke of Aiguillon, Governor of Brittany, had the moats filled in and arranged the present circular promenade, which the tourist can follow by car.

Bizienne (Fg)	2	St-Jean (Pl.)	7
Marché-au-Bois (Pl. du)	3	St-Michel (R.)	
Pilori (Pl. du)	4	Ste-Anne (Fg)	9
Pilori (R. du)	5	Vannetaise (R.)	20
Saillé (R. de)	6	Vieux-Marché (Pl. du)	22

GUÉRANDE*

The St-Michel or Castle Gate (M). – *Open Easter to 30 September, 9am to noon and 2 to 7pm. To visit, go through the gateway and up the tower on the right, where you apply to the keeper. Admission: 3F.*

The gatehouse, formerly the governor's house, is now a museum. The galleries (look at the woodwork) contain old furniture, a weaving loom, pictures and a large collection of old salt-marsh workers' costumes on life-size figures.

The relief plan of a salt-pan shows how it is equipped and worked.

St-Aubin* (A). – *Organ concerts at 9.30pm on Fridays in July and August. Admission: 20F.*

This collegiate church, built from the 12 to the 16C, presents a granite façade decorated with bell-turrets and crocketed pinnacles. The **interior** is imposing with vast pillars in the transept. The Romanesque columns of the nave support Gothic arches whose **capitals** portray grotesque and floral decoration. The 15C chancel with aisles opening onto four 16C chapels is lit by a magnificent 18C **stained glass window** showing the Coronation of the Virgin. The small 13C window on the left shows the Martyrdom of St. Peter. The **crypt** to the right contains a Merovingian sarcophagus discovered under the chancel and a 16C recumbent figure.

GUÉRANDE Peninsula *

Michelin map **230** 51, 52

This is a very interesting district in which you may see, besides the curious salt-marsh country, several breaches of which La Baule is the finest; the picturesque Grande Côte; busy fishing ports; Guérande and its ramparts; and Batz and its church.

The former gulf. – Between the rocky Batz Island and the Guérande ridge a great sea gulf stretched in the Roman era. According to some writers this was the scene of the naval battle in which the fleet of the Veneti was destroyed *(details p 124)*. A change of level of 16 m - 50 ft turned the gulf into marshes.

Sand brought down by the currents linked the Batz Island with the mainland through the strip on which La Baule and Le Pouliguen stand. To the west the sandy Pen Bron Point has not quite reached the island; a channel remains open opposite Le Croisic through which the sea flows at high tide into the Grand and Petit Traict, vestiges of the former gulf. At low tide it retreats, exposing mud-flats on which the coast dwellers raise oysters and mussels, clams and winkles. The rest of the marsh is used for salt-pans.

Salt-pans. – These form a great chessboard bounded by low banks of clay soil. The sea water, brought in by the high tides through canals or *étiers*, spreads and is caught in a series of reservoirs which get shallower and shallower; in the *œillets*, which it reaches last, the depth is only two inches. It is here that the salt crystallises as the water evaporates.

From the beginning of June to mid-August men collect the grey salt formed at the bottom with large rakes, while women skim the white salt off the surface with flat spades. The salt is put to dry on little platforms built on the banks, then piled in large heaps or *mulons* at the edge of the salt marsh before being stored in sheds.

Though some have been abandoned there are now about 10 000 *œillets* on the peninsula, including Guérande and Mesquer.

Each *œillet* measures 70-80 sq m - 853-861 sq ft and gives 1 200 kg - 2 650 lb of grey salt and 80 kg - 176 lb of white salt, each year. In a very dry summer it may amount to 3 000 kg - 6 600 lb *per œillet*.

A hard struggle. – The salt-pans of Guérande were very prosperous until the time of the Revolution, for, thanks to a relic of the former rights of the province, the salt could be sent all over Brittany without paying the *gabelle* or salt tax. Dealers or salt makers could exchange it in neighbouring provinces for cereals. Trafficking by "false salt makers" or smugglers was on a great scale.

Today the competition of salt marshes in the south, favoured by hotter sunshine and of the salt mines in the east is getting severe. The drying, refining and testing of locally gathered salt is now being undertaken in a modern factory at Batz with good results.

Cliffs and Dunes. – The cliffs and rocks of the Grande Côte, between Penchâteau Point and Le Croisic, offer a striking contrast to the immense sandy beach at La Baule.

In 1527 a violent wind spread the sand accumulated in the Loire estuary over the village of **Escoublac**. After this gale, which lasted for several days, sand continued to accumulate, and in the 18C the last inhabitants finally left the place. The village was rebuilt several miles farther back. The pines planted to fix the dunes form the Bois d'Amour of La Baule. The coast which became very popular in the 19C, took the name of **Côte d'Amour**.

ROUND TOUR STARTING FROM LA BAULE

63 km - 39 miles – about 2½ hours – Local map p 101

Leave La Baule (p 55) by ④ on the map, the N 771. On reaching Le Pouliguen turn left immediately after the bridge.

Le Pouliguen*. – *Description p 146.*

The road hugs the coast and there is soon a fine view of the shore south of the Loire as far as the St. Gildas Headland and the Blanche Lighthouse.

The Grande Côte*. – *For trip by road from opposite direction see p 79.*

Le Croisic*. – *Description p 78.*

Batz-sur-Mer*. – *Description p 54.*

Kervalet. – A small village of salt-marsh workers with a chapel dedicated to St. Mark.

Saillé. – A typical small salt workers' village.

Turn left into D 92.

Pen Bron Point. – *4.5 km - 3 miles from the D 92 after Toulan.* From the jetty there is a fine view of Le Croisic, the belfry of Batz and Le Trait.

La Turballe. – Pop 3 127. *Facilities p 42.* The modern buildings of the town stretch along the seafront. The busy artificial port receives both pleasure craft and sardine boats. The modern granite Church of St-André has a low belfry adjoining the apse; small 1907 stained glass windows light the chancel.

The **view** is beautiful along the coast after Lerar. After Penhareng, turn left twice.

Castelli Point★. *Make for the signal station.* Wide panorama: to the right lies the low shore of the Rhuys Peninsula where Dumet Island is distinctly visible. On the left are the roadstead and peninsula of Le Croisic with the church towers of Batz and Le Croisic.

Piriac-sur-Mer. – Pop 1 110. *Facilities p 42.* A small resort and fishing village. In the square, before the church, there is a fine group of 17C houses.

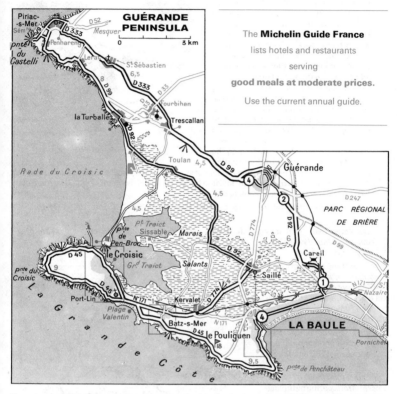

The **Michelin Guide France**

lists hotels and restaurants

serving

good meals at moderate prices.

Use the current annual guide.

To get out of Piriac take the road that runs beside the harbour towards **Mesquer** (Pop 1 015 – *Facilities p 42*), turn right after the canning factory and take D 333 to the left after the cemetery. Go through St-Sébastien. From the D 99 as it runs along the Guérande ridge there is a fine view of the salt marshes and the harbour of Le Croisic. In the evening the light effects on the marshes are surprising.

Trescallan. – The main square is dominated by a small Calvary. The church with buttresses has fine columns with capitals and a statue of St. Bridget.

Guérande★. – *Description p 99.*

Careil Château. – *Guided tours 25 March to 30 September, 10.30am to 12.30pm and 2.30 to 7.30pm. Admission 5F. 15 June to 30 August, Wednesdays and Saturdays, tour by candlelight at 9.30pm. Admission: 4F.*
Still inhabited, this former 14C stronghold was altered in the 15 and 16C. Of the two wings one is Renaissance with gracious dormer windows, the second is ornamented at roof level with armorial decorated pediments. The stone flagged guardroom and the adjoining salon have fine timbered ceilings. The captain's has a salt-marsh worker's bed and the chimney surround is decorated with a Maltese cross. It is said that the priest's room, downstairs, once served as hiding place for the Prince of Condé.

Return to La Baule by the D 92.

La GUERCHE-DE-BRETAGNE

Michelin map **230** 41, 42 – Pop 3 810

This little town, once a manorial estate with Du Guesclin as its overlord, still retains some old houses besides an interesting church. The local cider is famous.

Church. – Only the chancel remains of the original building erected in 1206. The nave and the interesting south aisle were rebuilt in the 15 and 16C; the north aisle and the belfry are modern. The riches of this church lie in its stalls with their amusing Gothic misericords – the carved decoration of the woodwork is clearly of the time of Henri II (1547-59), a more advanced period – and the remains of the 15C stained glass windows. The fine Annunciation should also be noted.

Old Houses. – Houses with porches may be seen in the Place de la Mairie, near the church and in the neighbouring streets.

EXCURSIONS

The Fairies' Rock★ (La Roche-aux-Fées); Les Mottes Lake. – *Round tour of 45 km - 28 miles – about 2 hours – Local map below. Leave La Guerche by the Rennes road, D 463.*
At Visseiche turn left into the D 48 which soon reaches an arm of the Marcillé Lake formed by the junction of the Seiche and Ardenne Valleys; this is the reason for its curved shape. On leaving Marcillé-Robert, cross the Seiche and then follow the banks of the other arm of the lake. Turn right after 1 km - ½ mile and then right again 3 km - 2 miles farther on. On the right, 800 m from the road, stands the Fairies' Rock.

The Fairies' Rock★. – *Time: ½ hour.* This is one of the finest megalithic monuments in Brittany.

To judge from its appearance it was not intended as a funeral monument, it is, therefore, neither a dolmen nor a covered alleyway. Built in purple palaeozoic schist, it consists of forty-two stones, of which half a dozen weigh between 40 and 45 tons each. There is a massive portico entrance and then a low ceiling-ed corridor leading to a large, very high room which is divided. Since, according to legend, it was built by the fairies, young couples wishing to get married came there to get the fairies' counsel on the night of the new moon. The man walked round the rock in a clockwise direction, the girl anticlockwise; if, by the time they had returned to their starting

(After P. Mesny photo, Rennes)

La Roche-aux-Fées.

point, each had counted the same number of stones all was well; if the difference in number was not more than two, they might still find happiness, but if the number varied by more than two it was best to separate immediately.

Turn round for Le Theil, where in front of the station you turn left into the D 94 for Ste-Colombe.

Les Mottes Lake. – Charming artificial lake towered over by magnificent trees *(fishing permitted: Thursdays, Sundays and holidays).*

When within sight of Ste-Colombe, turn left into the D 47. By way of Coësmes and the edge of Le Theil Forest you come to Retiers.

Retiers. – Pop 3 358. Proud little town where the church contains paintings and several 18C altarpieces in carved wood.

Continue along the D 47 which crosses Arbrissel, the birthplace of Robert d'Arbrissel who founded the famous abbey of Fontevrault (near Saumur) where he was buried. *From Rannée, the D 178 takes you to La Guerche.*

Louvigné-de-Bais. – *16 km - 10 miles to the northwest – about 1 hour.*

Take the D 95 going northwest from La Guerche. After Carcraon, which is at the end of a lake, you come to Bais.

Bais. – Pop 2 022. The town is built on the side of a hill and overlooks the little valley of the Quincampoix. The porch of the Gothic church was for local lepers. It stands over a fine Renaissance doorway consisting of twin doors beneath a triangular pediment; the doors also have individual pediments. The rich and fantastic ornament juxtaposes skulls, salamanders, the bust of François I and Aphrodite triumphant.

Continue along the D 95 which passes near Lake Daniel and leads to Louvigné-de-Bais.

Louvigné-de-Bais. – Pop 1 122. The chapel north of the chancel is the only remnant of an earlier church (11C). This 16C building has Gothic arcades with short pillars. The reredos of the high altar is 17C.
What makes the church at Louvigné outstanding are its superb stained glass windows produced during the great period of Breton art: there are windows of the Resurrection and the Transfiguration designed by a painter from Vitré in 1542 and 1544; Christ's descent to Hell made in 1567 and very well repaired in 1607; a window of 1568 of the life of St. John and, in the north aisle, a window of the life of the Virgin (1543 or 1548).

Join us in our never ending task
of keeping up to date.
Send us your comments
and suggestions, please.
Michelin Tyre Co Ltd
Tourism Department
81 Fulham Road, LONDON SW3 6RD

In the midst of a highly picturesque region the waters of the Blavet River form a winding reservoir known as Lake Guerlédan – a magnificent stretch of water. It is one of the finest sights of inland Brittany and a lovely place to sail.

TOUR OF THE LAKE

Round tour of 44 km - 27 miles starting from Mur-de-Bretagne – about 1½ hours – Local maps below and p 144

Mur-de-Bretagne. – Pop 2 259. *Facilities p 44.* This is one of the liveliest towns in the interior of Brittany.
The 17C St. Suzanne Chapel stands on the north side of the town as you enter it. It is set in picturesque green surroundings; the great oaks often inspired the painter Corot (1796-1875).

Leave Mur-de-Bretagne by the D 18, going west. Leave the car at the roundabout at the end of the road. From there you get a good **view★** of the artificial lake, a stretch of water some 350 ha - 865 acres in area, lying in the Blavet Gorges and contained by a big dam (206 m - 240 yds long along the top and 45 m - 147 ft high). Below the dam is the canal linking Nantes to Brest (not used for the moment between Guerlédan and Pontivy).

Return to Mur-de-Bretagne.

South of the town, take the D 35 on the right and, after the canal, turn right into the D 31.

St-Aignan. – Pop 706. In the charming little church is a fine woodcarving of the Tree of Jesse. The winding road turns to the right after 1 km - ½ mile to go down to the lake where there is a roundabout with a belvedere looking over the dam.

Come back by the same road for 1 km - ½ mile and bear right. You will cross a countryside of fields and pastureland until you come to the Quénécan Forest.

Quénécan Forest. – The forest of 2 500 ha - 6 175 acres stands on an uneven plateau overlooking the Blavet Valley. Apart from beech and spruce around Lake Fourneau and Les Forges des Salles the forest consists of pine, scrubland and heath.

Sordan Bay (Anse de Sordan). – Pleasant site on the edge of the Guerlédan Lake. *Boat trips on the lake from 15 June to 15 September. Time: 1 hour. Fare: 10F, children 6F.*

Les Forges des Salles. – This is a charming place. The hamlet of Les Forges and its castle lie in the valley to the right; entirely surrounded by greenery and overtopped by a fine group of trees.

Les Salles Lake and Castle. – *2 km - 1 mile – plus ¾ hour on foot Rtn. Return to the entrance to Les Forges then turn right into the D 15A from which you will see Lake Fourneau. At a crossroads leave the car and take a path to the right. At a further crossroads 800 m on follow the road to the left which forks soon after; bear right.* Of Les Salles Castle there remain only a few ruins and the main building, which has become a farmhouse. Near it there is a pretty view over the lake.

Return to Les Forges. Its name recalls the furnaces where Breton iron ore was smelted with wood fuel until the beginning of the 19C.

The road runs down the valley of the Forges stream, then enters the Blavet Valley, which it crosses. 200 m after the bridge an avenue opens on the right, leading between walls towards the ruins of the Abbey of Bon Repos.

Daoulas Gorges★. – *Go up the gorges by the D 44.* The fast flowing waters of the Daoulas run in a narrow, winding valley with steep sides covered with gorse, broom and heather.

To join the Blavet, the river hs made a deep cut through a belt of schist and quartzite. The slabs of rock rise almost vertically; some end in curious needles, with sharp edges.

2 km - 1 mile farther on turn your car in a lane before two houses.

The N 164 *bis* which you take to the left, crosses undulating country and provides views of the lake.

After 5 km - 3 miles turn into the little road to Keriven on your right. After dropping down into a small pine wood it provides a beautiful **view★** of Lake Guerlédan as it follows the lakeside banks before rejoining the N 164 *bis* at Caurel.

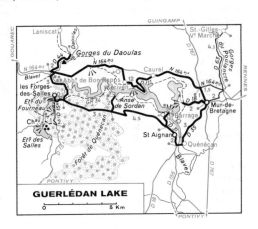

GUERLÉDAN LAKE

Tourists who do not wish to make the further excursion to the Poulancre Valley, should make straight for Mur-de-Bretagne by way of the D 167.

Poulancre Valley. – *6.5 km - 4 miles. Go straight on by the N 164 bis; 2 km - 1 mile after this crosses the D 167 take the D 63 on the left.*
The valley is deeply sunk between rocky or wooded slopes and forms narrow and very picturesque gorges.

At the entrance to St-Gilles-Vieux-Marché, turn round and take the D 63 again to bring you back to Mur-de-Bretagne.

Le GUILDO

Michelin map 📖230📖 10, 11 – 10 km - 6 miles south of St-Cast – *Local map p 90.*

This village lies in a picturesque setting on the shore of the Arguenon estuary. From the bridge across it you will see, on the right bank, the ruins of the Castle of Le Guildo. In the 15C this was the seat of Gilles de Bretagne a carefree and gallant poet, who led a gay life at Le Guildo and among his friends in the neighbourhood. But Gilles was suspected of plotting by his brother, the reigning duke, and thrown into prison. As he did not die fast enough he was smothered. Before he died he summoned his brother to the judgment of God within forty days. Only forty-five days later the Duke, prostrated with remorse, expired.

EXCURSION

The Ringing Stones (Les Pierres Sonnantes). – *3 km - 2 miles to the west by the D 786 – about ¾ hour.* West of the bridge, level with the Hotel Gilles de Bretagne, leave your car and take a lane along the Arguenon.

Opposite the ruins of the castle *(to the right, on the far bank)* you will find a pile of rocks which emit a metallic note when you strike them with a stone of the same type. This resonance is due to the perfectly even grain of the rocks.

GUIMILIAU ★★

Michelin map 📖230📖 4, 5 – *Local map p 137* – Pop 700

The fame of the little village of Guimiliau is due to its very remarkable parish close *(details of closes p 31).* The Calvary and the church, with its magnificently ornamented furniture, are the most interesting features of this charming group.

■ **PARISH CLOSE**★★ *time: ¾ hour*

Calvary★★. – The Calvary, the most curious and one of the largest in the region, dates from 1581 to 1588 and includes over 200 figures.

On the upper part stands a large cross with a thorny shaft bearing four statues grouped in pairs: the Virgin and St. John, St. Peter and St. Yves. On the platform are scenes from the Passion and a composition representing the story of Catell-Gollet *(details p 32).* The figures on the frieze are numerous and depict, in no chronological order, several scenes from the life of Jesus. The four Evangelists stand at the corners of the buttresses.

Church★. – This 16C building was rebuilt in the Flamboyant Renaissance style at the beginning of the 17C. *Closed from November to March.*

Go round the south of the church to see the triple-panelled apse, which is charming. Continue round the building, passing the foot of the belfry in the west gable, all that remains of the original church.

The **south porch**★★ is remarkable. The arching adorned with statuettes gives an interesting picture of the Bible and the Gospels. Above the triangular pediment over the porch is the statue of St. Miliau, King of Cornouaille. To the left of the porch is a small ossuary with low reliefs depicting scenes from the life of Christ. The inside of the porch is a fine example of a form of decoration frequent in Brittany *(details on porches, p 29).* Under the usual statues of the Apostles is a frieze ornamented with rose medallions, tresses and scenes from the Old Testament. You will notice on the left side, to the left of the date 1606, the Creation of Woman. In the end wall are two round arched doorways surmounted by a statue of Christ.

(After Nédelec photo, Morlaix)

Guimiliau. — The baptistry.

Inside, the church is roofed with panelled vaulting. At the end of the south aisle is a fine carved oak **baptistry**★★ dating from 1675. Eight spiral columns support an elaborately carved canopy, surmounted by a dome which shelters a group representing the baptism of Our Lord.

In the **organ loft** are three 17C **low reliefs**★; on the nave side, David playing the harp, and St. Cecilia at the organ; opposite the baptistry, the Triumph of Alexander.

The **pulpit**★, dating from 1677, is ornamented at the corners with statues of the four Sibyls. The panels carry medallions representing the Cardinal Virtues.

The chancel with its central stained glass window (1599) is closed by a 17C altar rail. Note from right to left: the **altarpiece of St. Joseph**, on which can be seen, St. Yves, the patron saint of barristers between a rich man and a payer, and the blind St. Hervé with his wolf; the **altarpiece of St. Miliau**, representing scenes from the Saint's life; the **altarpiece of the Rosary**, surmounted by a Trinity.

Ossuary chapel. – The chapel in the Renaissance style, dating from 1648, has an outdoor pulpit set in one of the windows. Two fine embroidered 17C banners and a superbly decorated gold cross may also be seen.

Sacristy. – Built in 1683 beside the funerary chapel it carries a statue of St. Miliau on its conical roof.

Michelin map **230** 7, 8 – Pop 10 752

This quiet little town is an important agricultural market which is rapidly expanding industrially.

Of the original feudal city odd ramparts and a ruined castle remain.

■ **SIGHTS** *time: ¾ hour*

Basilica of Notre-Dame-de-Bon-Secours*. – This church was built in the Gothic style in the 14C (a Romanesque part remains at the transept crossing); but two centuries later the south tower collapsed, demolishing the south side of the nave. The town asked several architects to plan its reconstruction. One old master presented a purely traditional Gothic design; but a young man named Le Moal submitted plans in which the Renaissance style, almost unknown in Brittany at that time, appeared. Quite unexpectedly the people of Guingamp awarded the prize to the "revolutionary". Since then the church has had the unusual feature of being Gothic on the left and Renaissance on the right, with a very fine round arched doorway with delicate decorations, half sacred and half profane. The patroness of Notre-Dame-de-Bon-Secours is the Black Virgin. She stands in a chapel formed by the doorway which opens on the left of the church, into the Rue Notre-Dame.

A great *pardon (p 10)* draws thousands of pilgrims on the Saturday night before the first Sunday in July. The procession is held by candlelight. After the procession three bonfires are lit by the bishop who presides over the ceremony.

Place du Centre. – Here are a few old houses and the popular fountain called "la Plomée", with three lead and stone basins dating from the Renaissance.

Former Hospital (Ancien Hôtel-Dieu). – The façade of the 17C chapel is the most interesting part.

EXCURSIONS

Menez-Bré*. – *13 km - 8 miles to the west – about 1¼ hours. Leave Guingamp by 7, N 12 to Morlaix. 11.5 km - 7 miles from Guingamp, after a house on the right, turn right into a steep uphill road (max. 16% - 1 in 6) which leads to the summit of the Menez-Bré. Description p 120.*

Grâces. – *Pop 1 769. Round tour of 7 km - 4 miles. Leave Guingamp by the D 54, west on the plan.* Turn right after

Bourbriac (Rte de)	2	Marne (Bd de la)	7	Rustang (R.)	13
Carmélites (R. des)	3	Notre-Dame (R.)	8	St-Michel (R., Pts)	14
Champ-au-Roy (Pl.)	4	Pompe (R. de la)	9	St-Yves (R.)	15
Corlay (Rte de)	5	Riou (R. Yves)	10	Vally (Pl., R. du)	16
Clemenceau (Bd)	6	Ruello (R.)	12	Verdun (Pl. de)	17

2 km - 1 mile; shortly after you will see the large Church of Grâces standing beside the road in the centre of the village.

Notre-Dame. – Originally the Church of Our Lady would appear to have been a pilgrims' chapel, probably founded by Queen Anne. Built in the 16C, it was slightly altered in the 17C and restored in the 19C. The four gables of the single aisle give it a saw-tooth silhouette from the south.

Inside, the barrel roof timbers of the nave and aisles stand on magnificent, carved beams. Mockery of drunkenness is the main theme; but there are also hunting scenes, monsters, and a poignant Holy Face surrounded by little angels.

Note also the tie beams of the nave. A wooden shrine contains the relics of Charles of Blois, killed at the Battle of Auray *(p 52)*.

Continue along the D 100 to rejoin the N 12 which will bring you back to Guingamp by ⑦ on the plan.

Bourbriac; Avaugour Chapel. – *Round tour of 30 km – 19 miles – about ½ hour.*

Leave Guingamp by ⑤ on the plan. The D 8 follows the Trieux Valley and then, for a short while, goes into the Kerauffret Wood which lies over on the left. The countryside is almost flat.

Bourbriac. – Pop 2 903. Rising in the centre of the town and surrounded by gardens, is the church with its towering belfry 66 m - 216 ft high. There have been several buildings erected on the site: of the first there remains a crypt probably of the 10 or 11C; of the Romanesque church which followed, there is the very high transept crossing – the tower above it was burnt down in the fire of 1765 and has been replaced by a turret belfry. In 1535 building on the west tower began; it is a remarkable example of the style that was to come: while the big ogival arched porch and all the lower floor are in the Flamboyant style, the remainder of the tower is definitely Renaissance. The spire was added in 1867.

Inside, the tomb of St. Briac is invoked as a cure for epilepsy. Behind the tomb is the sarcophagus of St. Briac dating from Merovingian times.

The D 24 going towards St-Péver, crosses the heath to the D 167 which you take on the left. You are once more in the Trieux Valley. After 800 m bear right.

Avaugour Chapel. – The chapel stands in an attractive setting and contains a finely carved wood sacrarium (shrine) of the 16C and an interesting collection of statues of the Apostles.

Return to Guingamp by the D 167 and ④ on the plan.

HÉDÉ

Michelin map 26 – Pop 524

The village stands on a hill between the Ille-Rance Canal, and a pool. Houses and hanging gardens, the ruins of a feudal castle on a rocky promontory all give it an air.

There is a wide **panorama★** from the tower of the Romanesque church.

EXCURSION

Les Iffs★; Montmuran★. – *7 km - 4 miles to the west – about 1 hour.*

Church of Les Iffs★. – *Time: ¼ hour.* The church is an attractive Gothic building with an entrance porch and belfry, as well as fine Flamboyant style windows in the south wall. Inside are nine good 16C **stained glass windows★**, low reliefs representing the Apostles and a 15C font carved with a hare playing a musical instrument. There are also a strange 15C high altar that was discovered beneath the wooden altarpiece and a Stations of the Cross carved in wood by Colette Rodenfuser.

Montmuran Castle★. – *800 m north of Les Iffs, at the end of a fine avenue. Guided tours 2 to 7pm. Time ½ hour. Admission: 3F.* Of the 12-14C castle, standing on a picturesque site, there remain imposing **towers★** and a Flamboyant style chapel built on the site where Du Guesclin *(details p 156)* was knighted in 1354 after a skirmish with the English in the neighbourhood. Later he married, as his second wife, a Montmuran, Jeanne de Laval. The main building which dates from the 17C, was remodelled in the 18C.

From the top of the towers *(mind the machicolations)* there is a view of Hédé and Dinan.

HENNEBONT

Michelin map 35 – Pop 12 461 – *Facilities p 44 – Town plan in the Michelin Guide France*

Hennebont is a former fortified town on the steep banks of the Blavet. a *pardon* takes place at Hennebont on the last Sunday in September.

During the last war the town was used by the Germans as an annex to the naval base at Lorient.

The siege of 1341. – During the War of Succession *(p 20)* one of the Pretenders, Jean de Montfort, was held a prisoner in the Louvre. In 1341 his wife, Jeanne of Flanders, was besieged in Hennebont by Charles of Blois and French forces. The Countess fought like a true knight, but the attackers opened a breach in the walls. The garrison, demoralised, compelled her to negotiate. She obtained permission to march out with the honours of war if her reinforcements did not arrive in three days. Before the date fixed, the English fleet sailed up the Blavet and saved the town.

■ **SIGHTS** *time: 1 hour*

Notre-Dame-du-Paradis. – On the huge Place du Maréchal-Foch, made still larger by the destruction of the old quarter, stands the 16C Gothic church of Our Lady of Paradise. Its very big belfry is surmounted by a steeple over 72 m - 230 ft high. At the base of the tower is a fine Flamboyant porch, shapely and ornamented with niches.

Iron well. – Old well, with fine wrought iron work.

Broërec Gate and ramparts. – This gateway, a vestige of the 13C fortifications, was once used as a prison. It was badly damaged by bombardment and lost its roof and its interesting local museum.

The 15C ramparts of the old fortified town are worth looking over.

Gardens are laid out along the walls.

Stud. – *Open 10am to 6pm. Go there by the Rue Nationale, the Rue Gabriel-Péri and the Rue Victor-Hugo.*

The Hennebont stud farm numbers about 140 stallions. It supplies breeding animals (draught horses, Breton post-horses and some bloodstock) to stations in South Finistère, Morbihan and Ille-et-Vilaine. The stud houses the premises of a national riding club.

You may visit the ruins of the Abbaye de la Joie within the grounds. The 17C gateway is interesting.

EXCURSION

Kervignac; Merlevenez; St-Cado. – *18km - 11 miles – about ¾ hour. Leave Hennebont by the D 781. After 1 km - ½ mile turn left into the D 9.*

Kervignac. – The new houses, built after the town was burnt down in 1944, stand on the left of the road. Skilfully reconstructed the little city encircles a modern church which has an attractive simplicity.

The Church of Our Lady of Pity (Notre-Dame-de-Pitié) is planned in the form of a Greek cross. The four sides consist of a lower part in granite which supports the clerestory containing stained glass windows. Above rises a triangular gable. In one of the re-entrant angles is a square tower surmounted by a small belfry with a pierced spire.

Inside, the lovely polished pinewood panelling goes well with the glowing stained glass windows depicting the life of the Virgin Mary and with the sober wooden Stations of the Cross outlined in charcoal and chalk and varnished.

Merlevenez. – Pop 1 223. This little town also suffered during the war, but its church escaped total destruction. It is one of the few Romanesque churches in Brittany which has kept complete its elegant doorways with chevron and saw-tooth mouldings, its tiers-point arches in the nave, its storiated capitals and dome on squinches rising above the transept crossing.

6 km - 4 miles from Merlevenez you come to the D 781 which crosses the River Étel at **Pont-Lorois.** This short and pretty run gives one a glimpse of the immense estuary which on the left opens out into a gulf and on the right pours itself into a deep channel which winds down to the sea. *Turn almost immediately into the D 16; follow this for 1 km - ½ mile and then turn left into the St-Cado road. Leave the car on the level ground beside the sea wall.*

St-Cado. – ¼ *hour on foot Rtn*. This is a former Templars' chapel and, with the church at Merlevenez, is one of the few Romanesque buildings in Morbihan. Its general simplicity, with unornamented rounded arches, rare capitals with very plain decoration as well as its dim lighting (since most of the windows have been walled up), contrasts with the fine Flamboyant style gallery that ornaments the inside of the façade, built in 16C. It is in this chapel that the deaf seek help from St. Cado.

The chapel, the Calvary and the little fishermen's houses make a charming Breton picture that is at its best at high tide.

Return to Hennebont by the same route.

HUELGOAT ★

Michelin map **230** 19 – *Local maps pp 50 and 137* – Pop 2 334 – *Facilities p 44*

The forest, the pool, the running water and the rocks make Huelgoat one of the finest **sites**★★ in inner Brittany. You must visit the rocks. Huelgoat is not only a good excursion centre but a favourite place for anglers (especially for carp and perch in the lake and trout in the river).

■ **THE ROCKS**★★ *time: 1½ hours on foot*

The beauty of Huelgoat is in its hilly forest (alt 180-210 m - 590-688 ft), cut by deeply sunken watercourses and scattered with great blocks of granite and sandstone. There are fine specimens of beech, oak, Norway spruce and forest pine.

Leave your car in the Place Aristide-Briand and follow the Rue des Cendres and the route indicated on the plan. When you reach the pool, take a path to the right which follows the right bank of the Argent River.

Mill Rock Chaos (Chaos du Moulin). – This pile of rounded granite rocks, surrounded by greenery, is very picturesque.

Devil's Grotto (Grotte du Diable). – *To reach this, climb down an iron ladder between the rocks, under which a brook babbles.*

In front of the green amphitheatre the path turns to the left, goes in loops down to the river which runs underground here, and is prolonged on the left bank by a walk from which an uphill path branches off. This is known as the Lovers' Walk (Sentier des Amoureux) and leads to Artus' Camp and the Boars' Pool (Mare aux Sangliers).

Trembling Rock (Roche Tremblante). – You can make this 100-ton block sway on its base. *Return to the river by a path.*

The Virgin's Kitchen Pots (Ménage de la Vierge). – An enormous pile of rocks shaped rather like kitchen utensils.

Violette Alley★ (Allée Violette). – An agreeable path in the woods on the left bank of the stream. *Follow the Allée Violette to D 164, which will lead you back to the Place Aristide-Briand.*

■ **ADDITIONAL SIGHTS AND WALKS**

Notre-Dame-des-Cieux (A). – This Renaissance chapel, whose belfry was built in the 18C, has curious painted low reliefs depicting scenes from the life of the Virgin and the Passion around the chancel and the side altars. A *pardon* takes place on the first Sunday in August.

Church (B). – A 16C church with a modern tower. At the top of the south aisle is a statue of St. Yves, the patron of the parish, between a rich man and a pauper *(illustration p 23)*.

The Cintrée Rock★ (La Roche Cintrée). – From the top of the rock *(¼ hour on foot Rtn)* there is a **view**★ of Huelgoat; to the north are the Arrée Mountains and to the south the Noires Mountains.

The Chasm★ (Le Gouffre). – *1 hour on foot Rtn*. The Argent River, flowing from the Huelgoat Pool, falls into a deep cavity, to reappear 150 m away.

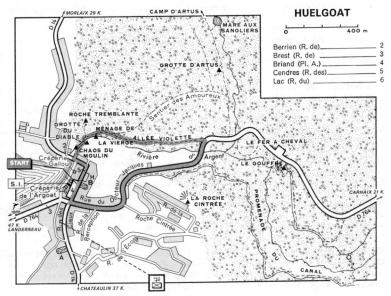

HUELGOAT

0 _____ 400 m

Berrien (R. de)	2
Brest (R. de)	3
Briand (Pl. A.)	4
Cendres (R. des)	5
Lac (R. du)	6

The path, beginning at the steps, skirts the river and, a few yards from the chasm, passes a footpath leading off to the right to a point *(¼ hour on foot Rtn)* commanding a view of the chasm. The original path continues for a further 1 km. A forest path brings you to the N 164.

Canal Walk★ (Promenade du Canal). – *2 hours on foot Rtn by the Rue du Docteur-Jacq and by the road on the right that runs along the canal.* A pool and canals were dug in the 18C to work the silver-bearing lead mines of Huelgoat, already known to the Romans. The waters were used to wash the ore and drive a crusher. From the 15C until 1914 the mines were under German management; young engineers from Germany, just leaving school, came there for training. The canal now serves a hydro-electric power station.
Return by the same road.

Artus' Cave, Boars' Pool and Artus' Camp (Grotte d'Artus, Mare aux Sangliers et Camp d'Artus). – *2 hours on foot Rtn by the Rue du Docteur-Jacq and 150 m after a bridge over the Argent River, by a path in the woods. Pass the Sentier des Amoureux on your left and continue on the path. Artus' Cave is above, on the left.* Continue along the path and, after some large boulders on the left, turn right along a path which goes down to the Boars' Pool (Mare aux Sangliers), in a pretty setting. Return to the path and continue along it. After about 800 m turn off to the left towards the important Graeco-Roman Camp of Artus, bordered by two enclosures. Turn round the camp by a path which follows the second enclosure.

Horseshoe Walk (Promenade du Fer à Cheval). – *1 hour on foot Rtn by the Rue du Docteur-Jacq and a path on your right.* A pleasant walk through the woods.

HUNAUDAIE Castle

Michelin map 🔟🔟🔟 north of 24

The castle ruins of La Hunaudaie rise in a lonely, wooded spot. Still impressive and severe, they reflect the power of the great barons, equals of the Rohans, who built the castle.

The castle, built in 1220 by Olivier de Tournemire, was partly destroyed during the War of Succession *(p 20)*. Rebuilt and enlarged by Pierre de Tournemire in the 14C, enriched in the 17C by Sébastien de Rosmadec, husband of one of the Tournemire heiresses, it was dismantled and then burnt by the Republicans at the time of the Revolution. The pillage of the castle stones was only stopped when the castle was bought by the Nation in 1930.
Open 1 July to 31 August, 10am to noon and 2 to 4pm. Admission: 3F.

The shape is that of an irregular pentagon with a tower at each corner. The two smallest derive from the first building, the other three were built in the 15C. The moat, once fed by two lakes, now only contains water on the east side. A wooden staircase gives access on the south side to a little postern gate opening between the keep and a large rounded doorway surmounted by a coat of arms. This leads to the courtyard.

The east tower, at the back on the right, is the best preserved. One can still see its circular staircase and its chimneys. The baronial living quarters partially conceal the north tower. The little that still remains nevertheless gives one some idea of its former elegant construction in contrast to the military austerity of the earlier buildings.

JOSSELIN ★★

Michelin map 🔟🔟🔟 37 – Pop 2 995 – *Facilities p 44*

This little town stands in a picturesque setting. Its river, the Oust, reflects the famous castle of the Rohan family *(illustration p 33)*. Behind the fortress-mansion, on the sides and the summit of a steep ridge, old houses with slate roofs are scattered around the venerable basilica of Our Lady of the Rosebush (Notre-Dame-du-Roncier).

The prosperity of the region depends on tourism and local industries such as meat canning and cardboard manufacturing.

HISTORICAL NOTES

Low Sunday dive (Middle Ages). – In the Middle Ages Lenten restrictions were strictly observed at Josselin, as elsewhere in Brittany. The butchers closed their shops and the fishmongers made fortunes. But a curious ceremony, which took place on Low Sunday (Quasimodo), reminded the happy fishmongers that every rose has thorns. That day the judges, followed by a great crowd of people, went to the bridge and summoned the fishmongers to appear. A special tax was demanded from each of them. Any who refused it were sentenced to dive into the Oust in their shirts only, amid the jeers of the crowd.

The Battle of the Thirty (14C). – By the middle of the 14C the Castle of Josselin had already been razed and rebuilt. It belonged to the Royal House of France; Beaumanoir was its Captain; the War of Succession was raging *(p 20)*. Josselin supported the cause of Blois; the Montfort party held Ploërmel, where an Englishman, Bembro, was in command. At first the two garrisons had frequent encounters as they ravaged the countryside; then the two leaders arranged a fight between thirty knights from either camp: they would fight on foot, using sword, dagger, battle-axe and pike. After taking Communion and praying all night at Our Lady of the Rosebush, Beaumanoir's men repaired, on 27 March 1351, to the rendezvous on the heath at Mi-Voie, between Josselin and Ploërmel (a stone pyramid marks the spot today). In the opposite camp were twenty Englishmen, six Germans and four Bretons. The day was spent in fierce hand-to-hand fighting until the combatants were completely exhausted. Josselin won; the English captain was killed with eight of his men, and the rest were made prisoner. During the struggle, which has remained famous as the Battle of the Thirty, the Breton leader, wounded, asked for a drink. "Drink your blood, Beaumanoir, your thirst will pass!" replied one of his rough companions.

Constable de Clisson (14C). – Among owners of Josselin the greatest figure is that of the Olivier de Clisson who married Marguerite de Rohan, the widow of Beaumanoir. He acquired the castle in 1370. He had a tragic childhood; for when he was only seven his father was accused of betraying the French party in the War of Succession and beheaded in Paris.

The widow, Jeanne de Belleville, who had been quiet and inconspicuous hitherto, became a fury. She hurried to Nantes with her children and, on the bloody head of their father nailed to the ramparts, made them swear to avenge him. Then she took the field with 400 men and put to the sword the garrisons of six castles which favoured the French cause. When the royal troops forced her to flee, she put to sea and sank every ship of the opposite party that she met.

In this school Olivier became a hardened warrior and his career, first with the English and then in the army of Charles V, was particularly brilliant. He was a comrade in arms of Du Guesclin and succeeded him as Constable. All-powerful under Charles VI, he was banished when the King went mad, and he died in 1407 at Josselin, of which he greatly strengthened the defences. At this time the castle, entirely rebuilt and guarded by nine towers, was a very important stronghold. It then passed to the Rohan family, who still own it.

The de Rohans at Josselin (15 and 17C). – In 1488, to punish Jean II de Rohan for having sided with the King of France, the Duke of Brittany, François II, seized Josselin and had it dismantled. When his daughter Anne became Queen of France she compensated Jean II, who was able in the rebuilding of the castle, to create a masterpiece worthy of the proud motto of his family: "Roi ne puis, Prince ne daigne, Rohan suis" (I cannot be king, I scorn to be a prince, I am a Rohan). The owner of Josselin showed his gratitude in the decoration of the palace; in many places, carved in the stone, is the letter A, crowned and surmounted by the girdle which was Anne's emblem, and accompanied by the royal *fleurs-de-lys*. In 1629 Henri de Rohan, the leader of the Huguenots, the sworn enemies of Richelieu, met the Cardinal in the King's ante-room where the cleric, who had just had the keep and five of the nine towers of Josselin razed, announced with cruel irony: "I have just thrown a fine ball among your skittles, Monsieur."

■ **MAIN SIGHTS** *time: 1 hour*

The Castle (Château). – To get a good **view** of the castle stand at the turning after the D 4 and 126 cross-roads, coming from Malestroit.

From this point the building has the appearance of a fortress, with high towers, curtain walls and battlements. The windows and dormer windows appearing above the walls belong to the palace built by Jean II.

The castle is built on a terrace of irregular shape, surrounded by walls of which only the bases remain, except on the side which is seen from the bridge. The isolated "prison tower" marked the northeast corner of the enclosure.

Open daily 1 June to 14 September 2 to 6pm; Wednesdays, Sundays and holidays only from 19 March to 31 May. Admission: 6F.

The delightful **façade** of the dwelling house (restored in the 19C) makes an extraordinary contrast with the fortifications of the outer façade. Nowhere else in Brittany has the art of the sculptor been carried further in that hard material, granite: brackets, florets, pinnacles, gables, crowns and

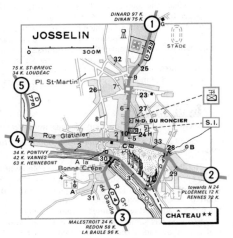

Beaumanoir (R.)	2	Rohan (Pl. A.-de)	24
Canal (R. du)	3	St-Jacques (R.)	25
Chapelle (R. de la)	4	St-Martin (R.)	26
Château (R. du)	5	St-Michel (R.)	27
Clisson (R. Olivier de)	6	St-Nicolas (Pl.)	28
Devins (R. des)	7	St-Nicolas (R.)	29
Douves (R. des)	8	Ste-Croix (Pont)	30
Duchesse-Anne (Pl.)	9	Ste-Croix (R.)	31
Notre-Dame (Pl.)	10	Sorciers (R. des)	32
Rohan (Cours J.-de)	23	Trente (R. des)	33

curled leaves in profusion adorn the high dormer windows and balustrades.

Notre-Dame-du-Roncier*. – Founded in the 11C and several times restored and remodelled – the transept spire was erected in 1949 – the basilica is, generally speaking, in the Flamboyant style. It is famous in the country round for its great *pardon (p 10)*. This has been called the "barker's pardon" since 1728, when three children were cured of epilepsy at the festival.

The name, Notre-Dame-du-Roncier, which dates only from the 15C, is based on a very old legend. About the year 800 a peasant, cutting brambles in his field, discovered a statue of the Virgin. He picked it up and carried it home, but the statue returned to its place. This was repeated until the man understood that the Virgin wanted a sanctuary, which became Our Lady of the Rosebush, to be built on the spot. The miraculous statue was burnt in 1793. Only a fragment of it remains which is kept in a reliquary and displayed in the basilica.

Inside, in the chapel to the right of the chancel, is the **mausoleum*** of Olivier de Clisson and his wife Marguerite de Rohan (15C). The chapel of the Virgin of the Rosebush is on the left of the chancel (modern statue). In the nave is a fine wrought iron pulpit of the 18C.

The organ case is 16C. The modern stained glass window in the north transept was designed by Gruber.

Ascent of the tower. – *Open daily in season 9 to 11.30am (except Sundays and holidays) and 2 to 6pm.* The tower commands a view of the northeast façade and inner court of the castle, and far over the whole countryside.

■ **ADDITIONAL SIGHTS**

Ste-Croix (A). – The St. Cross Chapel still has an 11C nave. From the surrounding cemetery, which is ornamented with a Calvary, there is a pretty view of the Oust and the castle.

After a visit to the chapel, stroll in the picturesque Ste-Croix quarter.

Fountain of Notre-Dame-du-Roncier (B). – Built in the 17C. A place of pilgrimage.

Old House (C). – The old house is very picturesque; it dates from 1624.

KERJEAN Castle *

Michelin map 230 4 – 5 km - 3 miles southwest of Plouzévédé

Kerjean Castle, half fortress, half Renaissance mansion, rises in the midst of a huge park.

The Ladies of Kerjean. – Towards the middle of the 16C Louis Barbier inherited a fortune from his uncle, a rich abbot of St-Mathieu, and decided to devote his money to building a castle which would be the finest residence in Léon.

One of his descendants, René Barbier, who married Françoise de Quélen, went to the court of Maria dei' Medici and boasted, before several gentlemen, of the close affection between his wife and himself. Four courtiers proposed a bet, rather in the spirit of the 17C: they would go to Kerjean, and the one who won the favours of Françoise would send to Barbier, in proof of his success, the engagement ring, a brooch, a ribbon and a lock of hair of the young woman. The bet was accepted. By a trick the gallants obtained the four tokens and sent them to the husband. But Françoise, who was both virtuous and shrewd, detected their game and managed to shut them all up in a room. When the anxious Barbier hurried home she led him to the four seducers, who were engaged in making coarse cloth with a spinning-wheel and a loom.

The last lady of the castle, Suzanne de Coatanscour, was seventy when the Revolution broke out. As the National Guard at Lesneven came too often to the castle she withdrew to St-Pol-de-Léon where she was arrested with her sister. They were sentenced to death on 13 June 1794, and executed the same day. The following October the Committee of Public Safety ordered them to be released!

TOUR *about ½ hour*

Guided tours 9 to 11.15am and 2 to 5pm. Closed Tuesdays. Admission: 4F.
The castle has belonged to the State since 1911. The buildings are guarded by a moat and a rampart with walls up to 12 m - 40 ft thick. A dwelling house with two wings and a large portico enclose the main courtyard, which is adorned with a fine Renaissance well.

The chapel has a wooden vault with carved beams and cornices. The kitchens have monumental chimneys; part of the house forms a small museum of Breton art containing very fine old furniture (box beds, chests, etc.). The keeper shows the room where Françoise de Quélen locked up the four gentlemen, and the hiding place of Suzanne de Coatanscour.

At the end of the north park, a Renaissance fountain overlooks a pool.

KERMARIA *

Michelin map 230 8 – 3.5 km - 2 miles northwest of Plouha

Open 1 June to 30 September 8am to noon and 2 to 7pm. The rest of the year apply to Mme Chancerel, in the house near the chapel.

The **Chapel of Kermaria-an-Iskuit** * (House of Mary who preserves and restores health) is a popular scene of pilgrimage (3rd Sunday in September). This former baronial chapel, in which a few of the bays of the nave are 13C, was enlarged in the 15 and 18C. Over the south porch is the former court room, with a small balcony from which the sentences were read to the people. The inside of the porch is adorned with statues of saints *(details of porches p 29)*

Kermaria has some 16C **frescoes** * which are known to archaeologists. They decorate the walls over the arcades. The best preserved, in the nave, depict a striking dance macabre. Death, in the shape of jumping and dancing skeletons and corpses, drags the living into a dance; those depicted include pope, emperor, cardinal, king, constable, *bourgeois*, usurer, lover, lord, ploughman, monk, etc.

Above the high altar is a great 14C Christ. In the right transept are five alabaster **low reliefs** * *(removed temporarily)* of scenes from the life of the Virgin. In the chancel and transept are numerous wooden statues, including a curious figure of the Virgin suckling her unwilling Child.

KERNASCLÉDEN **

Michelin map 230 21, 35

Tourists coming to Kernascléden from the south should take D 769 at Plouay, then D 110 which runs through the narrow Valley of the Scorff, skirting the **Forest of Pont-Calleck**.

On the northern edge of the forest they will be able to admire the site of the institution Notre-Dame-de-Joie – formerly Pont-Calleck Castle, now a children's home – and its lake by turning *(¼ mile by car Rtn)* into a very steeply falling road that branches off from D 110 towards the east, 500 m south of the Chapel of Ste-Anne-des-Bois. *(It is possible to walk along the left shore of the lake.)*

■ **THE CHURCH** ** *time: ½ hour*

Though the church at Kernascléden was consecrated in 1453, thirty years before the Chapel of St-Fiacre (p 92), there is a legend that they were built at the same time and by the same workmen. Every day, angels carried the men and their tools from one site to the other.

A characteristic feature of this church, which earns it a special place among the innumerable religious buildings in Brittany, is the rare striving for perfection that appears in every detail. The very slender tower, the foliated pinnacles, rose carvings and delicate tracery help to adorn the church without

(After Le Marigny photo, La Seyne)

Kernascléden. — Detail from a fresco.

overloading it. Two porches open on the south side. The left **porch** *, which is the larger, is ornamented with statues of the twelve Apostles *(details of porches p 29)*.

Inside, instead of being roofed in wood, the church has ogival stone vaulting. The vaults and walls surmounting the main arches are decorated with restored 15C **frescoes**** representing episodes in the lives of the Virgin and Christ. The finest, on the north side, are the Virgin's Marriage, Annunciation and Burial. In the north transept are eight angel-musicians; over the triumphal arch (on the chancel side), the Resurrection of Christ. On the walls of the south arm are fragments of a death dance and a picture of Hell (facing the altar) which is remarkable for the variety of tortures it depicts.

LAMBADER *

Michelin map **230** 4 - 8 km - 5 miles northeast of Landivisiau

The church is usually open after 10am, if not obtain the key at the Stéphan's house, on the road to Plouvorn.

The **church*** has a belfry 58 m - 190 ft high which was rebuilt in the 19C. Inside is a very fine carved wood **rood-screen*** in the Flamboyant style (1841), bearing statues of the Virgin and the Apostles.

A sacred fountain with a *Pietà* stands on the south side of the chapel.

LAMBALLE

Michelin map **230** 23, 24 – Pop 5 538

Lamballe is a commercial and picturesque town built on the slope of a hill crowned by the Church of Notre-Dame-de-Grande-Puissance. It is an important market centre (pigs and cattle).

Horse lovers should not fail to visit the stud (horse shows).

HISTORICAL NOTES

Bras-de-Fer before Lamballe (1591). – The town, which was the capital of the County of Penthièvre from 1134 to 1420, suffered a great deal in the War of Succession *(p 20: Historical Facts)*. During the League it was one of the strongholds of Mercœur, Duke of Penthièvre (Charles IX made the County a Duchy). In 1591 Lamballe was besieged by the famous Calvinist captain, La Nouë, nicknamed "Bras-de-Fer" because he wore a metal hook in place of the arm he had lost. He was killed during the siege of the town. Henri IV keenly felt his loss. "What a pity," he exclaimed, "that such a little fortress destroyed so great a man; he alone was worth an army!"

In 1626 César de Vendôme, Lord of Penthièvre, the son of Henri IV and Gabrielle d'Estrées, conspired against Richelieu and the castle was razed by order of the Cardinal. Only the chapel remains.

The Princess of Lamballe (Revolution). – In 1767, at the age of twenty, the Prince of Lamballe (this was the title given to the heir to the Duchy of Penthièvre) led such a dissolute life that his father, the Duke, in an effort to reform him, married him to a gentle Piedmontese princess of seventeen; but the heir did not mend his ways, and he died, worn out with debauchery, three months later.

In 1770, when Marie-Antoinette married the future Louis XVI, she made friends with the young widow, who remained faithfully attached to her for twenty years. When the tragedy of the Revolution took place, the Princess of Lamballe bravely stood by the Queen. She died a year before her. In the massacres of September 1792 the rioters cut off her head and paraded it on a pike.

LAMBALLE

0 — 500 m

Augustins (R. des)	Z	2
Cartel (R. Ch.)	Z	3
Champ de Foire	Y	4
Dr-A.-Calmette (R. du)	Y	5
Marché (Pl. du)	Z	6
Martrai (Pl. du)	Z	7
Palitré (Pl. du)	Z	8
St-Jean (R.)	Z	9
St-Lazare (R. de)	Z	10
St-Martin (R.)	Y	13
Val (R. du)	Z	15

■ **SIGHTS**

time: 1 hour

Collegiate Church of Notre-Dame (Y A). – *Open daily from Easter to All Saints' Day.* The Gothic church has Romanesque features. It is built on a terrace which overlooks the Gouessant Valley and from which there is a fine view of the lower town and its surroundings.

At the entrance to the south aisle in the chancel is a fine carved wood rood-screen in the Flamboyant style.

Place du Martrai (Z 7). – This square reveals interesting old houses. The former executioner's house, which dates from the 15C, contains the Tourist Information Centre and a small **museum** (M) dedicated to Mathurin Meheut (1882-1958), a local book illustrator *(open 15 June to 15 September, 10am to noon – except Sundays – and 2.30 to 6pm; the rest of the year, Tuesdays and Fridays, 2 to 5pm; closed 16 September to 15 October; admission: 3F).*

Stud (Haras) (Y). – *Open daily noon to 4pm and also Sundays and holidays 9am to noon. Apply to the porter. No visits during the covering season (15 February to 20 July).*

Founded in 1828, the stud contains 142 stallions (mostly post-horses and Breton draught horses). The horses go out every day, either ridden or harnessed in tandem, in pairs or in fours. From mid-February to mid-July all the stallions are sent out to breeding stands in the Côtes-du-Nord and the north of Finistère. The stud houses the premises of a school of dressage (40 horses) and a riding club (35 horses).

A horse show is held the weekend after 15 August.

St-Martin (Y B). – The church was remodelled in the 15 and 16C. On the right is an unusual little porch with a wooden canopy (11-12C).

LAMPAUL-GUIMILIAU

Michelin map **230** 4 – 4 km - 2 miles southeast of Landivisiau – *Local map p 137* – Pop 1 540

This place has a complete parish close *(details on closes p 31)*. The church is especially noteworthy for its rich decoration and furnishing.

■ PARISH CLOSE★ *time: ½ hour*

Triumphal arch. – The round arched gateway to the cemetery is surmounted by three crosses (1669).

Mortuary chapel. – The former ossuary (1667) abuts on the arch and has grooved buttresses crowned with small lantern turrets. Inside is the altar of the Trinity, with statues of St. Rock, St. Sebastian and St. Paul and his dragon.

Calvary. – Very plain 17C.

Church★. – The church is dominated by a 16C bell tower whose steeple was struck by lightning. The lower part of the tower includes a porch under which you must pass to make a complete tour of the church. The apse, with a sacristy added in 1679, forms a harmonious whole in which the Gothic and Classical styles are blended. The porch on the south side dates from 1533 *(details of porches p 29)*. Under it are statues of the twelve Apostles and, between the two doors, a statue of the Virgin and Child.

Inside★★, a 16C **rood-beam** *(p 31)* crosses the nave, bearing a Crucifix between statues of the Virgin and St. John. Both its faces are adorned with sculptures representing, on the nave side, scenes from the Passion and, on the chancel side, the twelve Sibyls separated by a group of the Annunciation. The pulpit dates from 1759.

At the end of the right aisle is a **font** surmounted by a very fine canopy dating from 1651. Higher up, on the right of the St. Lawrence altarpiece, is a curious stoup representing two devils writhing in the holy water; above, the Baptism of Christ.

In the chancel are 17C stalls, and on each side of the high altar, carved woodwork illustrating, on the left, St. Paul on the road to Damascus and the Saint's escape; on the right, St. Peter's martyrdom and divine virtues. The high altar and side altars have 17C altarpieces.

The altar of St. John the Baptist, on the right of the chancel, is adorned with low reliefs of which the most interesting (on the left) represents the Fall of the Angels. The altar of the Passion, on the left of the chancel, has an altarpiece in eight compartments depicting scenes of the Passion in high relief and, on the top, the Resurrection. On either side are two panels showing the Birth of the Virgin (left) and the Martyrdom of St. Miliau (right).

In the north aisle is a 16C *Pietà* with six figures carved out of a single piece of wood and also 17C banners, embroidered in silver on a velvet ground. The impressive **Entombment** was carved by the naval sculptor, Anthoine. Note Christ's head which is in white stone whereas all the other figures are coloured (1676). The organ case *(being restored)* is 17C. The sacristy contains a 17C chest *(apply to the guide)*.

LANDERNEAU

Michelin map **230** 4 – *Local map p 137* – Pop 15 660

The ancient town of Landerneau, once the capital of Léon, is built in a pretty setting. It is an excellent centre from which to make excursions including the tour of the parish closes.

Landerneau is the port of the Élorn estuary where salmon and trout are fished. The town is also the market for the locally grown spring vegetables and later market garden produce and fruit.

The saying "That'll make a din in Landerneau" (Il y aura du bruit dans Landerneau) arose from the practice of the local inhabitants of serenading and mocking any widow should she decide to marry again.

LANDERNEAU

Audibert (R. du Gén.)	Y 2
Brest (R. de)	YZ
Cartier (R. Jacques)	Y 3
Champ-de-Bataille	Z 4
Champ-de-Foire	Z 5
Cornouaille (Quai de)	Z
Daniel (R. Alain)	Z 6

Donnart (Av. Mathieu)	Y 7
Fontaine-Blanche (R. de la)	Y 8
Léon (Quai de)	Z 9
Libération (R. de la)	Z 10
Marché (Pl. du)	Y 12
Pont (R. du)	Z 13
Port (Quai du)	Z 14
Quimper (Rte de)	Z 23
St-Julien (Pl.)	Y 24
St-Thomas (R.)	Z 26
Tour-d'Auvergne (R. de la)	Y 29
4-Pompes (Pl. des)	Z 30

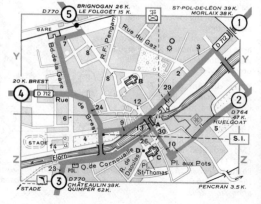

■ **SIGHTS** *time: 1 hour*

Old Bridge over the Élorn (Z A). – Picturesque, with old, overhanging houses. Go to the Hôtel de Ville (Town Hall) for a good view of the bridge.

St-Houardon (Y B). – The Renaissance domed tower and the porch (1604) on the south side of this church remain *(illustration p 29)*.

Church of St. Thomas of Canterbury (Z C). – Belfry tower with three superimposed balconies.

Former ossuary (Z D). – The building was erected as an annexe to the church of St. Thomas in 1635.

Market Place (Y 12). – Old houses.

EXCURSIONS

Parish Closes★★. – *Round tour of 130 km - 81 miles. Description p 137.*

Pencran★. – *3.5 km - 2 miles – plus ½ hour visit. Leave Landerneau by a small road to the southeast of the plan. This turns right into the Rue de la Libération. One mile farther on turn right (signpost).*

The 16C church has a belfry with a double balcony. A gateway with three small lantern-turrets leads to the parish close; farther to the right, in front of the church, is a **Calvary★** dating from 1521. On the other side of the church is the 16C ossuary.

On the right side of the church is an interesting, though weather beaten **porch★** (1553) with vaultings adorned with statuettes illustrating scenes from the Old Testament – Noah's Ark is on the right; on the tympanum, the Nativity, and under the porch, statues of the Apostles which were decapitated at the time of the Revolution.

Inside the church, old statues stand against the pillars of the nave, including a *Pietà* and the Annunciation. In the chancel, to the left of the high altar is a fine Descent from the Cross (1517) in relief and painted wood.

Return to Landerneau by the same route.

LANDÉVENNEC ★

Michelin map **230** 18 – Pop 423 – *Facilities p 42*

The approach road (D 60) is picturesque. It branches off the D 791 between Térénez Bridge and Tal-ar-Groas. At a crossroads 2 km - 1 mile before Landévennec turn right on to the V 1 running downhill.

Site★. – On the way down there are gaps in the hedge on your right through which you can reach vantage points from which there are fine **views★** of the site of Landévennec. Below is the course of the Aulne River, with the Island of Térénez; beyond, the Landévennec Peninsula and the Faou River. A steep descent leads to the settlement, a little summer resort surrounded by woods and water and Mediterranean vegetation.

The Abbey. – The Benedictine Abbey, rebuilt in 1965, and the ruins of the former abbey are approached from different roads.

Benedictine Abbey. – *To get to the abbey turn right halfway downhill and follow the road signs.*

Services are held at 11.15am during the week and 10.30am on Sundays and festivals; vespers are at 6.15pm during the week and 6pm on Sundays.

Ruins of the former abbey. – *The path to the ruins begins to the right of the centre of the town.*

The ruins are open from 15 June to 15 September, 10am to noon and 2.30pm (3pm Sundays) to 6pm. The rest of the year, only Sunday afternoons. Closed from All Saints' Day to Easter.

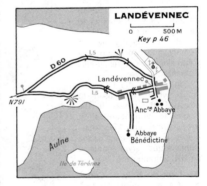

Of the monastery founded by St. Guénolé in the 5C, only the ruins of the Romanesque church remain.

A diorama illustrates the outstanding events in the history of the monastery.

As you go uphill on the D 60 you will see Bindy Point on the far bank, and in the background the Daoulas River estuary.

LANDIVISIAU

Michelin map **230** 4 – *Local map p 137* – Pop 7 775

Landivisiau is a busy town. Its cattle fairs are among the biggest in France.

■ **SIGHTS** *time: ½ hour*

St-Thivisiau. – A modern church in the Gothic style. It still has the belfry and the fine porch of a former 16C church *(illustration p 29)*.

St-Thivisiau Fountain. – This fountain is built of fragments of 15C sculptures.

St-Anne. – The chapel was an ossuary in the 17C. The façade is adorned with caryatids.

LANMEUR

Michelin map 📖 230 5, 6 – Pop 2 113

The modern church contains a curious statue of St. Melard. To the left as you go in is a 15C *Ecce Homo* in coloured wood.

Panels with photographic enlargements, retrace the life of St. Melard; each picture is taken from a chapel dedicated to the Saint, who had his right hand and left foot amputated simultaneously. An angel is shown bringing him a new silver hand and foot.

The pre-Romanesque **crypt★** is ascribed to the 6C and is one of the oldest religious buildings in Brittany.

300 m northwest, in the cemetery close, stands the large **Chapel of Kernitron**, with a 12C nave and transept and 16C chancel. Look at the outside of the Romanesque doorway of the south transept. Inside, at the entrance to the chancel, a rood-beam carries Christ on the Cross between the Virgin and St. John.

Pardon on 15 August.

LANNION ★

Michelin map 📖 230 6 – Pop 18 296

Lannion, a port on the Léguer River, will attract the tourist by its typical "Old Brittany" character.

The Centre de Recherches de Lannion and the Centre National d'Etudes des Communications where research is undertaken in telecommunications and electronics have been built 3 km - 2 miles north of Lannion at the crossroads of the D 11 and the D 788.

Place Général-Leclerc★. – Houses of the 15 and 16C border the square. At the corner of the Rue Geoffroy-de-Pontblanc and the Rue Cie-Roger-Barbé, on the left, a granite cross has been sealed in the wall at the spot where the Chevalier de Pontblanc, a defender of the town, distinguished himself during the War of Succession *(p 20).*

Brélévenez Church★. – The church was built on a hill by the Templars in the 12C and remodelled in the Gothic period. The tower is 15C.

It is approached by a staircase of 142 steps.

When you reach the terrace, however, there is an attractive view of Lannion and the Léguer Valley.

Before entering by the Romanesque doorway on the south side, look at the curious Romanesque apse.

Inside, on the left, is a stoup which was used to measure tithe wheat. In the chapels to the right and left of the chancel are 17C altarpieces. Under the chancel the Romanesque crypt contains an 18C Entombment.

St-Jean-du-Baly. – *Closed Sunday afternoons.* 16-17C. Over the door of the sacristy is a fine portrait of St. John the Evangelist.

LANNION

0   400 m

Aiguillon (Quai d')	2
Augustins (R. des)	3
Buzulzo (R. de)	4
Capucines (R. des)	5
Cie-Roger-Barbé (R. de la)	6
Donval (R. Noël)	7
Duguesclin (R.)	8
Foch (Quai du Mar.)	9
Gaulle (Av. Gén.-de)	10
Halles (Pl. des)	13
Jeanne-d'Arc (R.)	5
Joffre (Quai du Mar.)	04
Kérivaily (R. de)	16
Kermaria (Pont et R.)	18
Leclerc (Pl. Gén.)	20
Letaillandier (R. E.)	22
Mairie (R. de la)	23
Morlaix (Rte de)	24
Palais-de-Justice (Allée du)	25
Ploubezre (Rte de)	27
Pont-Blanc (R. Geoffroy-de)	28
Renan (Av. Ernest)	29
St-Nicolas (R.)	30
St-Yves (R.)	32
Savidan (R. Jean)	33
Viarmes (Quai de)	36

The statue by Jean Boucher, to the northeast of this church is a monument to the novelist. Charles Le Goffic *(p 35),* who was born and died at Lannion (1863-1932).

The Bridge. – From the bridge there is a good view of the port at high tide.

EXCURSIONS

Kergrist Castle; Kerfons Chapel★; Tonquédec Castle★. – *Round tour of 27 km - 17 miles – about 1¾ hours.* Leave Lannion by ④, the D 11; 1.5 km - 1 mile after Ploubezre you will see five granite crosses standing at a fork 2.5 km - 1½ miles farther on, turn left into the avenue leading to Kergrist Castle.

Kergrist Castle. – *Closed interior and west façade; open gardens with an itinerary marked out.* One of the principal attractions of the castle lies in the variety of its façades. The north side is Gothic with dormer windows set in tall Flamboyant gables; the main building, which belongs to the early part of the 16C, nevertheless presents an 18C façade on the opposite side, while the wings running at right angles and which were built at an earlier date, have Classical fronts overlooking the gardens.

The tall conical roofs of the great towers which flank the main buildings to the south and stand at the end of the wings, the turrets with their canted sides which enclose the narrow north face and have each an overhanging pepper-pot roof, add a light touch to the general design.

Return to the D 11 and take it bearing right. After 500 m turn right then 1 km - ¾ mile farther on turn left. 1 km - ¾ mile farther on again the V 12 leads off to the right to the Kerfons Chapel.

Kerfons Chapel★. – In front of the chapel is an old Calvary, surrounded by chestnut trees; it makes a good setting. *Open spring and summer school holidays, 9am to noon and 1.30 to 7pm. Apply to the little house on the left of the Calvary. Admission: 2F.*
The chapel was built in the 15 and 16C and contains a very fine carved **rood-screen★** (1520). Some fragments of old stained glass remain in the windows of the chancel and north transept.

Turn back and take the road to Tonquédec on the left. After 1 km - ¾ mile turn left. Soon the path starts to wind downhill providing good views over the ruins of Tonquédec in the Léguer Valley. Cross the swiftly flowing river. Level with the Restaurant des Ruines take the path on the left and walk up to the castle.

Tonquédec Castle★. – *Open spring school holidays to 30 September. Admission: 3F.* The ruins, which are still impressive, stand in very fine surroundings on a height overlooking the valley. The castle, which was built at the start of the 13C, was dismantled by order of Richelieu in 1622. The entrance gate is opposite a pool now run dry.
You enter an outer fortified courtyard. On the right, two towers connected by a curtain wall frame the main entrance to the second enclosure.
You enter the second courtyard by a postern. Opposite, standing alone, is the keep, with walls over 4 m - 13 ft thick. If you go up *(76 steps)* you will get a good idea of the local countryside: a wide, fertile and populous plateau is intersected by deep and wooded picturesque valleys running north and south. They are now almost uninhabited – the old mills that gave them some life are nearly all abandoned.

Continue towards Tonquédec, where you take D 31 to the left.

From Buhulien – on the D 767 – two further visits can be made:

Caouënnec. – Pop 472. *Apply to the Sacristan.* The church contains an excessively ornamented altarpiece which is nevertheless beautiful.

Coatfrec Castle. – *1.5 km - 1 mile by the Ploubezre road. Apply to the farm.* Beautiful ruins.

Return to Lannion by the D 167.

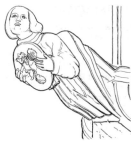

Le Yaudet; Locquémeau and Séhar Point★; Trédrez. –
Round tour of 34 km - 21 miles –
about 1 hour. *Leave Lannion by ⑤, the D 786. After 3 km - 2 miles turn right into the D 88 which crosses Ploulec'h.*

Le Yaudet. – *Facilities p 43.* This hamlet in its beautiful setting was the episcopal seat in the early centuries of our era; it has an interesting chapel overlooking the bay. Inside *(recorded commentary)* you will see, above the high altar, a curious sculptured panel: a recumbent figure of the Virgin with the Infant Jesus at her side; God the Father is sitting in an alcove at the foot of the bed over which hovers a dove, symbolising the third Person of the Trinity.
A *pardon* is held on the 3rd Sunday in May.

Turn back and after Yaudet turn right. In Christ, turn right towards Locquémeau.

Locquémeau. – The village overlooks the little resort and the fishing harbour. It has a pretty little 15C church with interesting 18C altarpieces *(apply to Mme Quesseveur).*

Séhar Point★. – Leave your car near the port of Locquémeau and make for the point, from which the **view★** extends westward as far as the Primel Point and eastward to the seaside resort of Trébeurden.

Leave Locquémeau by the D 88. After 2.5 km - 1½ miles turn right into the D 88ᴮ.

Trédrez. – St. Yves was Rector of Trédrez in the 13C. His church *(apply at the presbytery)* was built at the start of the 16C and is particularly remarkable for its furnishings. Among these are a 14C granite font with a 17C baldachin in which is a fine example of woodcarving; 17C panels to the altars in the side chapels; an altarpiece in the south chapel of a beautiful Virgin and Child in a Tree of Jesse, while in every corner, at the end of every beam and strut, angels in flight have been carved. Facing the pulpit is a fine Crucifix of the 13C.

Leave Trédrez by the road going towards Kerbiviou and follow the road that leads to the headland, Beg an Fourm, where, shortly before a large house, you will discover a magnificent view of the bay and the Lieue de Grève.
Return to Trédrez and turn right towards St-Michel-en-Grève; the road runs beside the sea to the town and affords a good view.

St-Michel-en-Grève. – *Description p 49.*

(After Dr Le Thomas photo)

Trédrez. — End of a beam.

LANNION*

From there go back directly to Lannion, by the D 786 or, if you have time, make a detour, take the D 30 to **Ploumilliau** whose church *(ask for the key at the presbytery)* contains thirteen wooden panels, carved and painted in many colours and serving as a Communion table and a curious portrayal of Ankou (Death), so often mentioned in Breton legend.

Rejoin the D 786 by the D 88ᴬ.

Loguivy-lès-Lannion. – *2.5 km - 1½ miles to the west. Leave Lannion by the Quai du Maréchal-Foch.* For 2 km - 1 mile you will have a picturesque drive, especially at high tide, along the left bank of the Léguer.

The 13C **church** at Loguivy is interesting and stands in pleasant surroundings. A curious outdoor stairway leads to the tower which was built in 1570.

Inside the church, in the chapel off the south aisle, there is a 16C wooden panel depicting the Nativity with bagpipers in Breton costume. There is also a fine wooden balustrade by the same sculptor, and a few old statues.

A Renaissance fountain made of granite stands in the cemetery.

LANRIVAIN

Michelin map **230** 21 – 7 km - 4 miles northwest of St-Nicolas-du-Pélem – Pop 761

In the cemetery you will see a 15C ossuary with trefoil arches. To the right of the church stands a 16C Calvary with figures of great size.

Near Lanrivain, in the hamlet of Guiaudet, is the **Chapel of Notre-Dame-du-Guiaudet**; inside, over the high altar, is a curious sculptured scene representing a recumbent Virgin holding the Infant in her arms. *Automatic peal of sixteen bells from 1 May to 30 September.*

La LATTE Fort **

Michelin map **230** 10 – southeast of Cape Fréhel – *Local map p 90*

At the village of La Motte, take D 16ᴬ towards the fort. After 150 m turn right, and a km - 1 mile farther on leave your car at the car park. A gate marks the entrance to the park which is private property. Turn right after 80 m and pass a menhir known as Gargantua's Finger, before turning sharp left to reach the entrance to the stronghold.

Guided tours at Easter, Whitsun and from 1 June to 25 September from 9am to noon and 2 to 6.30pm. Admission: 4 F.

This castle, which was built by the Goyon-Matignons in the 13 and 14C and restored in the 17C, has kept its feudal appearance. It stands on a picturesque **site**★★, separated from the mainland by two crevasses which are crossed on drawbridges.

Guided by the keeper, you will visit in succession: the two fortified enclosures, the inner courtyard, the chapel, the cannon ball foundry, the Échauguette tower and a look-out post from which you will see a **panorama**★★ of the Bay of La Frênaye, St-Cast Point, the Hébihens archipelago, the resorts of St-Briac and St-Lunaire, Décollé Point, St-Malo, Paramé and Rothéneuf, the Island of Cézembre and Meinga Point. You will then reach the keep; from its wall walk there is a fine view of the walls, the Sévignés Cove and Cape Fréhel.

LOCMARIAQUER **

Michelin map **230** 50 – *Local map p 124* – Pop 1 289 – *Facilities p 42*

Within the bounds of this village, where the church still possesses its original 11-12C chancel and Romanesque capitals in the transept cross, there are also several megaliths, including some of the best known in Brittany.

Dolmen of Mané Lud.* – *Time: ¼ hour. Take the D 781 out of Locmariaquer.* Park the car after 500 m and walk left; 50 m beyond a large white house (on the right) you will find on the left, behind a cottage, the dolmen of Mané Lud, the flat top of which is level with the ground. The stones which remain standing inside the chamber are carved.

Great Menhir ** **and Merchants' Table** ** **(dolmen).** – *Time: ¼ hour. Leave Locmariaquer by the D 781 and turn left before the cemetery.*

The Great Menhir is 200 m away, on the right. It is broken into five pieces. Four of them remain lying on the spot; they are over 20.30 m - 64 ft long, and their weight is estimated at about 347 tons. This is the biggest menhir known.

Behind the menhir, to the right, is the Merchants' Table. This dolmen, planted in the remains of a tumulus 36 m across, consists of three flat tables with seventeen pointed supports. A gallery leads under the great table which rests at one end on an ornamented support (ears of wheat ripened by the sun, etc.). Under the table is a plough in the form of an axe, connected by a shaft bearing traces of harness with an animal of which the two hind legs can be distinguished.

EXCURSIONS

Kerpenhir Point*. – *Round tour of 5 km - 3 miles.* On the Place Évariste-Frick, take the Rue Wilson. 2.5 km - 1½ miles farther on you reach Kerpenhir Point from which there is a **view**★ of the Morbihan channel. Continue along the road which runs beside the beach giving views of the horizon; return to Locmariaquer by the country road no 7.

Morbihan Bay and the Auray River by boat★★. – A motor-boat service from Locmariaquer makes it possible to tour the Morbihan Bay and the Auray River. *For all information apply to the Vedettes Vertes, Place de la Mairie at Locmariaquer and Gare Maritime at Vannes, Tel 66 10 78.*

You will find a selection of touring programmes on pp 36-39.

Plan your route with the help of the map of principal sights and tourist regions on pp 4-7.

LOCRONAN **

Michelin map **230** 18 – *Local map p 75* – *Pop 686* – *Facilities p 44*

The little town once prospered from the manufacture of sailcloth. Traces of its golden age are to be found in its fine **square****, with its granite houses built at the Renaissance, and in its old well, large church and pretty chapel.

The Troménies. – The hill or Mountain of Locronan, which overlooks the town, presents a very original spectacle on days devoted to *pardons*, which are known here as *Troménies*. There are **Petites Troménies** when the procession makes its way to the top of the hill, repeating the walk that St. Ronan, according to tradition, took every day, fasting and barefooted.

The **Grande Troménie**** takes place every sixth year. (The next will be in 1983.) This *pardon*, which attracts many people from Cornouaille, goes round the hill, halting at twelve points. At the resting places each parish displays its saints and relics on the local altar. The circuit follows the boundary of the former Benedictine priory, founded in the 11C, which was a place of retreat. Hence the name of the *pardon*: Tro Minihy or Tour of the Retreat, gallicised as Troménie.

■ **SIGHTS** *time: 1½ hours*

Church and Chapel of Le Pénity**. – 15-16C. The chapel is attached to the church. Enter by the main porch. The nave communicates with the chapel, which contains the tomb of St. Ronan. His early 15C statue was one of the first works to be executed in Kersanton, a kind of granite in which most of the Breton Calvaries are carved. There is also a 16C Entombment in stone with six figures, and, on the base, two fine **low reliefs***. The decoration of the **pulpit*** (1707) depicts the life of St. Ronan. In the apse are a fine **stained glass window*** and old statues. The cemetery behind the church contains an ornate cross.

(After Le Doaré photo, Châteaulin)

Locronan. — The square.

Notre-Dame-de-Bonne-Nouvelle. – The 16C church is reached by an alley which starts from the square and leads down the slope of the ridge. With the Calvary and the fountain it forms a typically Breton scene.

St-Ronan Workshop. – The workshop is on the way out of Locronan, where the roads to Douarnenez and to Quimper cross. It includes looms, warp beams and a spinning table for hand weaving flax, linen or wool. There is also a shop.

Weaving mill of the former India Company. – *Place de l'Église.* You may visit the workshop to see the linen weaving that is done by hand and the Ronan-Pré workshop on the first floor: sculpture in wood and in stone.

Tour Carrée Workshop. – *Rue Lann.* The different stages of the weaving of wool, linen and silk are demonstrated in this workshop.

Museum. – *Open May to end of September, 9am to noon and 3 to 7pm. Admission: 3F.* The museum contains pictures, sculptures and engravings by contemporary artists depicting scenes of Breton life and Breton furniture, costumes and faience.

EXCURSIONS

Locronan Mountain*. – *2 km - 1 mile to the east. Leave Locronan by the Châteaulin road, D 7; after 700 m go straight along an uphill road – which is in poor repair (max. 10% - 1 in 10).* This goes along the side of the hill providing views of the bay, Ménez-Hom and the Porsay hollow. From the top you will see a fine **panorama*** of Douarnenez Bay. On the left are Douarnenez and the Leydé Point; on the right Cape Chèvre, the Crozon Peninsula, the Ménez-Hom and the Arrée Mountains. To the right of the chapel is a pulpit surmounted by the statue of St. Ronan.

Kergoat Chapel. – The Gothic chapel is dominated by its domed belfry; it has a fine 17C east end. The **stained glass windows*** are old and one shows the Last Judgment. A popular pilgrimage takes place on the Sunday following 15 August.

Ste-Anne-la-Palud. – *8 km - 4 miles to the northwest. Leave Locronan by D 63. After Plonévez-Porzay, turn left.* The 19C chapel *(open Easter to October, 8am to 7pm; the rest of the year only Saturdays and Sundays)* contains a much venerated painted granite statue of St. Anne dating from 1548 *(legend p 23).* The *pardon* on the last Sunday in August is one of the finest and most picturesque in Brittany. After the candlelight procession on the Saturdays, High Mass is celebrated at 9pm. On the Sunday Pontifical Mass, vespers and a great procession.

LOCTUDY

Michelin map **230** 32 – *Local map p 75* – *Pop 3 544* – *Facilities p 42*

Loctudy is a quiet little seaport at the mouth of the Pont-l'Abbé River and a resort from which you can visit the interesting Kérazan-en-Loctudy Manor *(p 78).*

Port. – A pretty view of the wooded Island of Garo and, in the distance, the Chevalier Island in the Pont-l'Abbé estuary and Tudy Island and its beach.

Church*. – Dating from the beginning of the 12C (except its façade, which was rebuilt in the 18C), this is the best preserved Romanesque building in Brittany. The inside is elegant and well proportioned. In the cemetery to the left of the church, near the road, is the 15C Chapel of Pors-Bihan. Behind is a Gallic stele 2 m - 6 ft high surmounted by a Cross.

BOAT TRIPS

For all information apply, during the season, to the Vedettes Aigrettes at the harbour office, Tel Bénodet 91 00 58 (in season) or 56 08 10 (out of season).

Quimper along the River Odet**. – *2 hours by boat (departure at 2.30pm in July and August). Description of Quimper p 149.*

Ile-Tudy. – Pop 541. *A pretty fishing port accessible from Loctudy by boat (passengers only).*

Glénan Islands. – *Departure at 10.30am and 2pm in July and August. Description p 97.*

LORIENT

Michelin map **230** 34, 35 – Pop 71 923

Lorient is at the same time a naval base and a dockyard, a commercial port and one of the few Breton fishing ports to be organised on an industrial basis. The new city bears no comparison with the old one of which 85% was destroyed by wartime bombing and shelling. The fishing harbour is a constant source of entertainment to strollers.

HISTORICAL NOTES

The India Company. – After the first India Company, founded by Richelieu at Port-Louis, failed, Colbert revived the project in 1664 at Le Havre. But as the Company's ships were too easily captured in the Channel by the British, it was decided to move its headquarters to the Atlantic coast. The choice fell on an extensive tract of free land on the right bank of the Scorff. The port, building slips, warehouses and dwellings erected on this site, took the name of ''l'Orient'', for the Company's activities were confined to India and China.

In the 18C, under the stimulus of the well known Scots financier Law, business grew rapidly; sixty years after its foundation the town already had 14 000 inhabitants. The loss of India caused the ruin of the Company, and in 1770 the State took over the port and its equipment.

The war years. – Lorient was occupied by the Germans on 25 June 1940, and had its first taste of air warfare on 27 September and was destroyed in August 1944. The fighting between the entrenched German garrison and the Americans and locally based Free French Forces which encircled the Lorient pocket devastated the surrounding area so that when the townspeople returned on 8 May 1945, all that greeted them was desolation.

Today it is a fine modern town, bustling with life and activity due to the naval dockyards, the commercial port and, especially, the fishing port which, after Boulogne-sur-Mer is the largest in France.

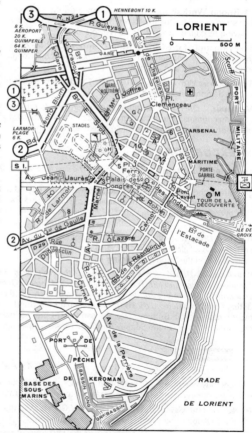

■ **SIGHTS** *time: 1 hour*

The *Ingénieur-Général Stosskopf Submarine Base (Base sous-marine) and the Dockyard (Arsenal) are not open to foreigners.*

Keroman fishing port. – *Best seen in the morning at its busiest.* Partly reclaimed from the sea, the port of Keroman is the only French harbour designed and equipped for fishing from its inception in 1920. It has two basins set at right angles: the Grand Bassin and the Bassin Long, dug in such a way that they are accessible to all fishing boats at any time.

The Grand Bassin is sheltered by a jetty 250 m - 265 yds long which is used as a loading and unloading quay for cargo steamers and trawlers. The basin has two other quays, one with refrigerating and cold-storage plant for the trawlers and fish dealers, the other at the east end of the Bassin Long where trawlers unload their catch. In front of the quays is the 600 m - 650 yds long auction market, and, close behind it, the fish dealers' warehouses which open on a railway platform and lorry loading bay. The fish thus passes straight from the market to the dealers and is immediately packed and loaded into refrigerated trucks or lorries.

Alsace-Lorraine (Pl.) 2	Foch (R. Mar.)	6	Liège (R. de)	9
Anatole-France (Av.) 3	Leclerc (Bd Gén.)	7	Patrie (R. de la)	10
Faouédic (Av. du) 5	Lefort (R. Cap.)	8	Port (R. du)	12

In five bays of the slipway, trawlers can be dry-docked or repaired. A large area round the basins, available for the industries and commerce connected with fishing, completes the zone.

The port of Keroman sends out ships all the year round for all kinds of fishing. The largest vessels go to sea for a week to a fortnight and carry their own store of ice to the fishing grounds; the freezing plant produces 360 tons of ice a day, or enough to fill thirty-six ordinary goods trucks.

Notre-Dame-de-Victoire★ (A). – *Closed Sunday afternoons.* The church stands in the Place Alsace-Lorraine which is itself a most successful example of modern town planning. The church is built in reinforced concrete and has very plain lines. It is square with a flattened cupola roof and a square tower flanking the façade.

The whole beauty of the church lies in its **interior★**. Little panes of glass, yellow and plain, reflect the outside light into the building from the top of the rotunda. The bays lower down contain windows, glazed in warm coloured glass with red predominating. Covering the wall at the back of the high altar and well lit by tall narrow side windows is a mural in pastel tones, while in the nave a masterly Entombment in monochrome faces a delicate Annunciation. The Stations of the Cross are shown, drawn in outline only, each at its most dramatic moment.

EXCURSION

The coast between Scorff and Laïta. – *Round tour of 40 km - 25 miles – about 1¼ hours. Leave Lorient by ② on the plan, D 29, passing the Kernével road on the left.*

Larmor-Plage. – Pop 5 408. *Time: ¼ hour.* A seaside resort for the people of Lorient.
In the 14-17C church there are interesting altarpieces at the high altar and, on the left, on the Jews' altar. There are also multicoloured 16C statues including a *Pietà* with twelve Apostles. Every year, on the Sunday before or after 24 June, there is a blessing of the Coureaux (the channel between the Groix Island and the coast). The procession of boats draws a large crowd. By tradition, warships leaving Lorient salute the Church of Our Lady of Larmor with three guns, while the priest blesses the ship, has the church bells rung and hoists the flag.

Leave Larmor by D 152, which follows the coast fairly closely, passing many little seaside resorts.

Kerpape. – *Facilities p 42.*
After Kerpape the run affords extensive views of the coast of Finistère, beyond the cove of Le Pouldu and over the Groix Island. In the foreground are the coastal inlets in which lie the little ports of Lomener, Perello, Kerroch and Le Courégant and the great beach of **Fort-Bloqué**.

Guidel-Plage. – *Facilities p 42.*
At the mouth of the Laïta, follow the D 306. From Guidel you can make a trip to the St-Maurice Bridge *(3 km - 2 miles)* over the Laïta. The **view★** up the enclosed valley is magnificent.
From Guidel return to the N 165 which brings you directly to Lorient.

BOAT TRIPS

For all further information apply at Port-Louis, at the grocer's, Mme Pézennec (Tel 65 36 49) or at the waiting room, except Saturdays and Sundays (Tel 65 47 50).

Belle-Ile★★. – *Description p 56.*

Port-Louis. – *Crossing time: ½ hour. Description p 146.*

Groix Island. – *Description p 99.*

LOUDÉAC
Michelin map **230** 22, 23 – Pop 10 135

This little agricultural town has big fairs. Some of the most interesting horse races in Brittany are held on the racecourse on the road to Pontivy on Easter Sunday and Monday, the following Sunday and the third Sunday in September.

MALESTROIT
Michelin map **230** 38 – Pop 2 539

This old place still has Gothic and Renaissance houses. Near the Church of St-Gilles the façade of one of these dwellings carries humorous sculptures: on the first floor Malestroit, a *bourgeois* in his nightgown, canes his wife.

St-Gilles. – This 12 and 16C church is curious for the juxtaposition of styles and the double nave. Notice the south doorway, with its two doors with 17C carved panels, flanked by massive buttresses adorned with the symbolic attributes of the four Evangelists. The lion of St. Mark is mounted by the youth for St. Matthew, and St. Luke's ox rests on a pedestal adorned with the eagle of St. John. About 3pm the shadows of the ox and the eagle between them suggest the well known profile of Voltaire. The pulpit is unusual in that the staircase cannot be seen.

La MEILLERAYE-DE-BRETAGNE
Michelin map **230** 55 – Pop 1 045

The presence of a nearby abbey did much to stimulate the growth of this town which stands on an eminence near the **Vioreau Forest** (800 ha - 1 977 acres).

EXCURSIONS

Melleray Abbey. – *2.5 km - 2 miles by the D 18. The church only is open to the public during services on Sundays and public holidays: 10.30am and 3pm in winter; 11am and 4pm in summer. Apply at the porter's lodge.*
Founded in 1142 near a great pool surrounded by trees, that one can admire from the road, this Cistercian abbey has buildings which date from the 18C.

La MEILLERAYE-DE-BRETAGNE

The **Church of Notre-Dame-de-Melleray**, completed in 1183, has been restored to its Cistercian severity, including a series of grisaille windows. The white stone pointed arches are supported by square pillars of pink granite. In the flat east ended chevet, the high altar is dominated by a gracious 17C wood polychrome **statue of a Virgin**.

Opposite the entrance avenue there is a curious 15C granite calvary.

Vioreau Reservoir. – *5 km - 3 miles to the south by the D 178 and then forest tracks.* The great stretch of water, pounded back by a dam, has green sandy banks and is suitable for sailing. It is linked to other pools in the region and feeds the Nantes to Brest canal.

MÉNEZ-BRÉ ★

Michelin map **230** 7 – 9 km - 6 miles east of Belle-Ile-en-Terre

The road (1 km - ½ mile – max. 18% - 1 in 6) climbs steeply.

The Ménez-Bré, a lonely hill with an altitude of 302 m - 991 ft appears considerably less tall since it rises out of the Trégorrois Plateau which lies at an altitude half the height of the Ménez-Bré. The Chapel to St-Hervé, which crowns the hill summit, commands a wide **panorama★** to the north where the plateau slopes gently towards the sea, cut by the deep Valleys of the Trieux, the Jaudy, the Guindy and the Léguer, to the south over the maze of hills and valleys of Cornouaille and to the southwest towards the Arrée Mountains.

MÉNEZ-HOM ★★★

Michelin map **230** 18

The Ménez-Hom (alt 330 m - 1 082 ft), a detached peak at the west end of the Noires Mountains, is one of the great Breton viewpoints and a key position commanding the approach to the Crozon Peninsula.

On 15 August a folklore festival is held at the summit.

Access. – *It is reached 2 km - 1 mile by D 83, which branches off D 887, 1 km - ½ mile after the Chapel of Ste-Marie (p 72), going towards Crozon. Leave your car in the car park and walk for 150 m.*

Panorama★★★. – *Viewing table.* In clear weather there is a vast panorama. You will see Douarnenez Bay, bounded on the left by the Cornouaille coast as far as Van Point, and on the right by the coast of the Crozon Peninsula as far as Cape Chèvre. To the right the view extends to St-Mathieu Point, the Tas de Pois Islands, Penhir Point, Brest and the Brest Roadstead, in front of which you will see the Longue Island on the left, the Ronde Island and the Armorican Point on the right, with the common estuary of the Faou and Aulne Rivers. The nearer valley – that of the Aulne – follows a fine, winding course, spanned by the suspension bridge at Térénez. In the distance are the Arrée Mountains, the Mountain of St-Michel crowned by its little chapel, the Châteaulin Basin, the Noires Mountains, the Mountains of Locronan and its chapel, Douarnenez and Tréboul.

Go as far as the bench mark of the Geographical Institute to get a complete view of the horizon on all sides. You will then see, in the Doufine Valley, the village of Pont-de-Buis, where there is a powder mill nearly three centuries old.

MONCONTOUR

Michelin map **230** 23 – Pop 1 149

Moncontour is an old fortified town built on a spur at the meeting of two valleys.

The Granges Castle (18C) stands on the top of a hill north of the town. Place de Penthièvre, in the town centre, is bordered by the Church of St-Mathurin. This church, built in the 16 and 18C, has six Renaissance **stained glass windows★**. A *pardon* is held at Whitsun *(p 10)*. Narrow alleys and picturesque stairways descend from the church to the foot of the ramparts.

EXCURSION

Notre-Dame-du-Haut; Touche-Trébry Castle. – *5.5km - 3½ miles to the north. Leave Moncontour by the D 768 going towards Lamballe.* At the crossroads, after the filtering plant, turn right into the D 6 towards Collinée, then right again into the D 6A, cross Trédaniel and continue until you reach the chapel 600 m farther on.

Notre-Dame-du-Haut. – *Ask for the key from M. Hesran at the nearest farm.* You will see the wooden statues of seven healer-saints: St. Mamertus, who is invoked against colic, St. Livertin *(illustration p 22)* and St. Eugenia for headaches, St. Leobinus for rheumatism, St. Méen for madness, St. Hubert for sores and dog bites and St. Houarniaule for fear. A *pardon* is held on 15 August.

Return by the same road as far as Trédaniel where you turn right and cross the D 6. Continue along the D 25. About 2 km - 1½ miles on, near a pond on the left of the road, La Touche-Trébry Castle stands alone, surrounded by trees.

Touche-Trébry Castle. – *Open in July and August, 2 to 7pm; on written request the rest of the year. Closed on Sundays and public holidays. Admission: 3.50F.*

Although built at the end of the 16C La Touche-Trébry looks like a mediaeval castle. It stands protected by its defensive walls forming a homogeneous whole, unaltered in character by the restorations that have taken place. Two lodges, standing up against two huge towers, watch over the entrance which consists of a great gate and a small postern with wall walk above. The courtyard is regular in shape with the main building, with its symmetrical façade, at the far end. On either side, at right angles, are the two wings with pointed roofs; next to them are the outhouses, not so tall but extending all the way to the two lodges at the entrance. In the corners between the main building and the side wings stand two turrets. Towers and turrets all have domed roofs.

MONT-ST-MICHEL ★★★

Michelin map 230 13 – Pop 114

Mont-St-Michel, that "wonder of the western world", leaves an indelible memory on every visitor, so individual is its setting, so rich its history and so perfect is its architecture.

Visitors able to do so should try to attend the Feast of the Archangel Michael, which is both religious and popular, held in early autumn *(p 10)*. Another spectacle is the flooding in of the particularly high tides round the island twice a month at the new and full moon and, in even greater force, at the spring and autumn equinox. *That day, boat trip round the Mount. Apply to the Tourist Information Centre.*

HISTORICAL NOTES

A Masterpiece. – The abbey's origin goes back to the beginning of the 8C when the Archangel Michael appeared before Aubert, Bishop of Avranches, who founded an oratory on the island, then known as Mount Tombe. This was replaced, on what had been renamed Mont-St-Michel, first by a Carolingian abbey and then, until the 16C, by a series of Romanesque and Gothic churches, each more splendid than its predecessor. The abbey was fortified but never captured.

The construction is a masterpiece of skill: granite blocks had to be brought from either the Chausey Islands or Brittany and hauled up to the site which at its crest was so narrow that supports had to be built up from the rocks below.

Pilgrimages. – Pilgrims flocked to the Mont even during the Hundred Years War, the English, who held the surrounding region, granted safe conduct, on payment, to the faithful. Nobles, rich merchants and beggars, who were given free shelter by the monks.

Hoteliers and souvenir craftsmen prospered even then: pilgrims bought emblems bearing the effigy of St. Michael and lead caskets which they filled with sand from the beach. Crossing the bay has its perils and there were deaths among the pilgrims by drowning and sinking into the quicksands so that the mound became known as St. Michael in Peril from the Sea.

Decadence. – The abbey declined into a commandery and discipline among the monks became lax – under this system abbots were not necessarily churchmen and did not always supervise the abbey although they took the stipends. In the 17C, the Maurists were charged with reforming the monastery but in fact only made superficial architectural changes.

The conversion of the abbey into a prison in the late 18 and early 19C brought it even lower – the museums listed on p 123 evoke complacently scenes of horror from this period.

In 1874 the abbey and ramparts passed into the care of the State, which has restored them. In 1977 with a total of 550 000 sightseers, the Mont-St-Michel is one of the major tourist attractions of France.

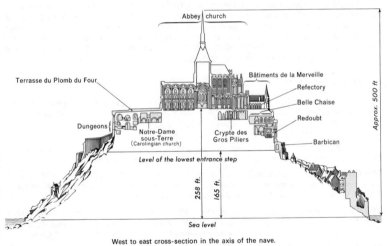

West to east cross-section in the axis of the nave.

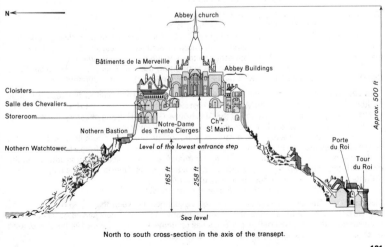

North to south cross-section in the axis of the transept.

Stages in the abbey's construction. – The abbey was built from the 11 to the 16C.

The Romanesque Abbey. – 11-12C. Between 1017 and 1144 a church was built on the mount's summit utilising the earlier Carolingian building as a crypt (Our Lady Below Ground – Notre-Dame-sous-Terre) and as support for the platform on which to stand the three final bays of the Romanesque nave. Additional crypts were built on which to support the transepts and the chancel which extended beyond the rock crest. The conventual buildings were constructed on the mount's west slope and on either side of the nave.

The Gothic Abbey. – 13-16C. In these four centuries there were constructed:
– the magnificent Merveille buildings (1211-28), to the north, for the monks, pilgrims and the reception of notable guests;
– the abbatical buildings (13-15C), to the south, including administrative offices, the abbot's lodging, and the garrison's quarters;
– the redoubt and the advanced defences to the east defending the entrance (14C);
– the church's Romanesque chancel which had collapsed was rebuilt (1446-1521) even more magnificently in Flamboyant over a new crypt.

Alterations. – 18-19C. In 1780 the final three bays of the nave were demolished together with the Romanesque façade. The present belfry, surmounted by a beautiful spire crowned with a statue of St. Michael, dates from 1897.

■ THE ASCENT TO THE ABBEY

Leave the car in one of the official car parks (3F).

The Town's Outer Defences. – The outer gate, which is the only breach in the ramparts, opens on to a fortified courtyard. On the left is the 16C burgesses' guardroom, on the right the Michelettes, English mortars captured in a sortie during the Hundred Years War. A second door leads to a second court and a third door dating from the 15C, complete with machicolations and portcullis and known as the King's Gate since above it was lodged the token contingent maintained on the mount by the King in assertion of his rights. You come out finally into the Grande-Rue where the abbots' soldiers lived in the fine arcaded house on the right.

Grande-Rue★. – This narrow uphill main street, lined with 15 and 16C houses and ending in steps, is picturesque and, in the summer, full and bustling with visitors crowding past the souvenir shops even as it was in the Middle Ages.

The Abbey's Outer Defences. – The Grande-Rue leads to the Grand Degré, a stairway to the abbey which formerly could be obstructed by a swing door. To the right is the entrance to the gardens and from there a stairway to the ramparts. Go beneath an old doorway arch to a fortified court overlooked by the redoubt or châtelet. This consists of two high towers, each shaped like a mortar standing on its breech and linked by battlements – even this military fortification shows the constructor's desire for artistry with alternating courses in the wall of rose and grey granite. The Stairs down to the Pit (L'Escalier du Gouffre), a low roofed staircase, ill lit and steep, starts from this point to the fine Guardroom or Porterie.

■ THE ABBEY★★★

Guided tours from 9 to 11.30am and 1.30 to 4pm (6pm 16 May to 30 September). Closed 1 January and 25 December. Admission: 5F; 2.50F Sundays and holidays. Time: ¾ hour.
When the Mount is crowded (as many as 6 000 are admitted daily), visitors are directed from the Guardroom to the Saut Gautier.
The tour takes you floor by floor through a maze of passages and stairways and not by building or period – the effect is confusing, we therefore suggest you read on.

The Guardroom or Porterie. – This hall was the focal point of the abbey: indigent pilgrims were directed there before being passed on by way of the Merveille Court to the almshouse; modern visitors pass through on their way to the starting point of the tour.

The Abbey Steps. – This impressive stairway, which was defended by a 15C fortified bridge, leads from the abbey buildings to a terrace in front of the south wall of the church, known as Gautier's Leap (Saut Gautier) after a prisoner is said to have hurled himself over its edge.

The West Platform (Plate-forme de l'Ouest). – The view from this vast terrace which occupies the site of the former last three bays of the church extends over Mont-St-Michel Bay.

The Church★★. – The east end with its buttresses, flying buttresses, turrets and balustrades is a masterpiece of delicacy and grace. Inside there is a contrast between the simplicity of the Romanesque nave and the elegance and light of the Gothic chancel. One of the flying buttresses forms a staircase with a carved balustrade, the **Lacework Staircase★★** (Escalier de Dentelle) which leads to a gallery 120 m - 394 ft above the sea from which there is a **panorama★★**.
The most impressive of the three crypts supporting the transepts is the 15C **Great Pillars Crypt★** (Crypte des Gros Piliers) with ten columns each 5 m - 16 ft in circumference.

The Merveille★★★. – The name, literally the Marvel, has been given to the superb Gothic buildings on the north side of the Mount. The east side of the group, the first to be built from 1211 to 1218, consists from bottom to top of the Almshouse, Guests' Hall and refectory; the west side, dating from 1218 to 1228, of the storeroom, Knights' Hall and cloister.
From outside the Merveille is a fortress although its pure and noble lines also give it a religious appearance. Inside, the evolution of the Gothic style is obvious from a simplicity which is almost Romanesque in the lower halls to the total mastery of grace, lightness and line in the cloister. Intermediary stages can be seen in the elegance of the Guests' Hall, the majesty of the Knights' Hall and the mysterious luminosity of the refectory.
The second floor consists of the cloister and refectory.

Cloister★★★. – The cloister appears as though suspended between the sky and the sea. The colours of the stone add variety to the overall harmony of the intricately carved gallery arcades, each supported on a cluster of five, perfect, small columns. Near the entrance is the laver or long washbasin which was used by the monks before meals.

Refectory★. – The first impression is one of disbelief for there is a diffused light throughout although light appears to come only from the two end windows. On entering farther you discover that the architect, without lessening the strength of the walls cut narrow windows at the top of the embrasures, so adding an upper, secondary light.

The first floor consists of the Guests' and Knights' Halls.

Guests' Hall★ (Salle des Hôtes). – It was in this elegant and graceful hall 35 m - 115 ft long divided by slender columns into two aisles and roofed with Gothic style vaulting, that abbots received kings come in pilgrimage – St. Louis, Louis XI and François I.

Knights' Hall★ (Salle des Chevaliers). – The hall's name certainly goes back to the chivalric Order of St. Michael founded in 1469 by Louis XI with the abbey as its seat. This vast and even majestic hall, 26×18 m - 85×58 ft, divided by three rows of stout columns was the monks' workroom. The lower chambers include the Storeroom and the Alms Hall.

Storeroom (Cellier). – It has two lines of square pillars supporting groined vaulting.

Alms Hall (Aumônerie). – The alms hall – now the waiting room (small museum) – is divided into two by a line of pillars which still support the Early Romanesque groined vaulting.

Abbey buildings. – Only the guardroom is open.

Old Romanesque Abbey. – The Monks' Walk (Promenoir des Moines) and the dormitory remains are visited on the tour.

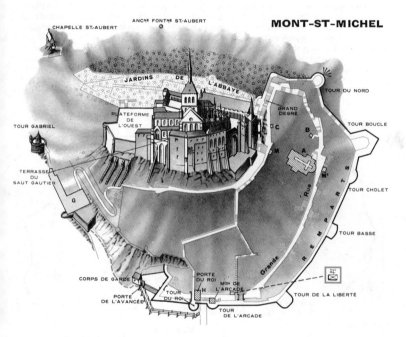

MONT-ST-MICHEL

■ ADDITIONAL SIGHTS

The Ramparts★★. – After seeing the abbey, walk round the 13-15C ramparts by bearing left to the steps leading to the Grand Degré Stairway. The watchpath commands good views of the bay, particularly from the North Tower. Take the stairway before the King's Tower (Tour du Roi) to come out just before the King's Gate (Porte du Roi) on the Grande-Rue.

Abbey Gardens★. – *Admission: 1F*. The gate is on the left going down the Grand Degré. Pleasant walk.

Historical Museum (M). – *Guided tours 1 March to 30 September, 8am to 7pm. Admission: 5F, also valid for the Mont-St-Michel Historical Museum.*

Waxwork dioramas of the Mount's history and outstanding collection of 25 000 clock balance cocks (the incised pieces supporting old clock mechanisms). In the garden, a periscope allows you to see the bay up to 30 km - 19 miles.

Mont-St-Michel Historical Museum (Musée historial du Mont) (M¹). – *Open 1 March to 30 November, 8am to noon and 1 to 6.30pm. Admission: 5F, also valid for the Historical Museum.*

Historical dioramas and clock balance cocks.

Parish Church (A). – Much restored 11C church with the apse spanning a narrow street.

Tiphaine's House (B). – *Admission: 3F*. Du Guesclin, who was commander of the Mont, is said to have lodged his wife, Tiphaine, in this house while he went off to the wars in Spain *(see table p 21 giving the Principal Campaigns of Du Guesclin)*.

The Truie-qui-File House (C). – Literally, the House of the Spinning Sow, where the ground floor consists only of a series of arcades.

ST MICHAEL'S MOUNT, CORNWALL
St Michael's Mount, off the Cornish coast, was originally the site of a priory established by Edward the Confessor in 1044. He granted its administration to the abbot of the Mont-St-Michel.
Following the Dissolution, the buildings were fortified and it became a military stronghold and has been the seat of the same family since the 17C.

The Morbihan Gulf, an inland sea dotted with islands, offers some of the most unusual scenery in Brittany.

It has the most delicate light effects, and its sunsets are unforgettable. A visit, especially by boat, is essential for the tourist who appreciates natural beauty. On its shores are several interesting towns like Vannes and Auray.

HISTORICAL NOTES

In the first century BC the Veneti – after whom Vannes is named – lived around the Gulf of Morbihan. They were the most powerful tribe in Armor and when Caesar decided to conquer the peninsula he aimed his main effort at them. It was a stiff task, for the Veneti were fine sailors and had a fleet which made it useless to attack them by land. The decisive struggle, therefore, had to be waged afloat. The Roman leader had a large number of galleys, built and assembled at the mouth of the Loire which were led to battle by his lieutenant, Brutus.

The encounter, which took place before Port-Navalo, is said to have been watched by Caesar from the top of the Tumiac hill *(p 125)*. On the other hand, geologists declare that the gulf did not exist at the time of the Gallic War. At all events, it is certain that the battle took place off the southeast coast of Brittany.

The Gauls put to sea with 220 large sailing ships, with high, strong hulls. To them the Romans opposed their large flat barges, propelled by oarsmen. The total and unexpected victory of Brutus was due to several causes: the sea was smooth and this favoured the galleys, which could not face bad weather; moreover, the wind dropped completely during the battle, becalming the Veneti in their sailing ships. Finally the Romans had sickles tied to ropes. When a galley drew alongside an enemy sailing ship, a smart sailor heaved the sickle into its rigging. The galley rowed on at full speed, the rope drew taut and the blade cut the rigging; mast and sails came tumbling down. Two or three galleys then attacked the ship and boarded it. After this victory Caesar occupied the country of the Veneti and made them pay dearly for their resistance. All the members of their Senate were put to death, and the people were sold into slavery.

GEOGRAPHICAL NOTES

Mor-bihan means "little sea", while *Mor-braz* means "great sea" or ocean. This gulf, which is about 21 km - 12 miles wide and 16 km - 10 miles deep from the sea to the inner shore, was made by a comparatively recent settling of the land. The sea spread widely over land already despoiled by river erosion leaving, however, inlets and estuaries which run far into the interior, and innumerable islands which give the Morbihan its special character. The Rivers of Vannes and Auray form the two largest estuaries. About forty islands are inhabited; the largest are Arz and Moines Island.

The gulf is tidal; at high tide the sea sparkles everywhere around the low, flat and often wooded islands; at low tide, great mud-banks lie between the remaining channels. A narrow channel, 800 m - ½ mile long, before Port-Navalo gives passage both at high and at low tide. A current of up to 8 or 10 knots prevents the gulf from being blocked by silt from the Loire and the Vilaine.

Morbihan is thronged with boats fishing between the islands, as well as with pleasure boats and trading pinnaces using Auray and the port of Vannes. There are many oyster-beds in the rivers and along the islands *(p 18)*.

THE GULF BY BOAT★★

The best way to see the gulf is by boat. We recommend the excursion which usually starts from Vannes, but can also be made from Locmariaquer, Port-Navalo or Auray or can be combined with a bus trip (either coming or going).

For all information, ask at the Vedettes Vertes kiosk on the Promenade de la Rabine, Tel Vannes 66 10 78 and 66 10 79, at the port in Auray, on the jetty in Port-Navalo or at the Vedettes Vertes office, Place de la Mairie, Locmariaquer.

Quick Tour: *Vannes – Arz Island – Arradon Point – Moines Island and return to Vannes. Minimum time: 2 hours without landing.*

Complete tour as far as Port-Navalo and Locmariaquer: *Minimum time: 3½ hours.*

Day Tour: *Leave from Vannes. Passengers can land at any point and pick up the next boat to continue the trip.* The boat runs down the Vannes River and enters the gulf through the steep sided Conleau Channel. Stops are as follows:

Arz Island. – Pop 332. *Facilities p 42.* The island 3 km - 2 miles long has several megalithic monuments.

Arradon Point★. – *Description below.*

Moines Island★. – Pop 588. *Facilities p 42.* This former monastic fief is the largest of the Morbihan Islands (6 km - 4 miles long). It is a particularly quiet and restful seaside resort where mimosas and camellias grow. Its woods have poetic names: Bois des Soupirs (Wood of Sighs), Bois d'Amour (Wood of Love), Bois des Regrets (Wood of Regrets). The beauty of the island women, often sung by Breton poets, is no doubt responsible for these gallantries.

Port-Navalo. – *Description p 126.*

Locmariaquer★★. – *Description p 116.*

Visit to Moines Island only. – *See below.*

Excursion to Gavrinis Island. – *Access (from Larmor-Baden) and description p 97.*

THE SHORES OF THE GULF BY CAR★

From Vannes to Locmariaquer
46 km - 29 miles – about 1½ hours – Local map p 124

Leave Vannes (p 81) by D 101.

Bridge over the Vincin. – From the bridge over the Vincin River there is a good view all round, especially at high tide.

Arradon. – Pop 2 911. *Facilities p 42.*

Arradon Point★. – Go part-way through the village of Arradon *(one-way traffic)* and then follow D 127; at the post saying, "No through road" *(Voie sans issue)* turn left towards the Quarry dock (Cale de la Carrière – *free car park*). From here there is a very typical **view★** of the Morbihan Gulf in which you can distinguish, from left to right: the Logoden Islands; in the distance, Arz Island; then Holavre Island, which is rocky and quite near and Moines Island.

Return to Arradon. Level with the church, take a road to the left. After the village of Le Moustier, the D 101 becomes the D 316. Turn left on D 316ᴬ towards Port-Blanc *(car parks)* where you will embark for Moines Island *(continual service every ½ hour from 7am to 10pm during the season, 8am to 7pm out of season; crossing time: 5 minutes).*

Moines Island★. – *2.5 km - 1½ miles – plus ¼ hour by boat. Description above.*

The road nest skirts the Kerdelan creek (on the left there is a good view of the gulf and, in the distance, of Moines Island), then the Pen-en-Toul marshes on its right.

Larmor-Baden. – Pop 751. A little fishing port and large oyster cultivation centre. From the port there is a fine view of the other islands and the entrance to the gulf.

Gavrinis Tumulus★★. – *Excursion of ¼ hour by boat from Larmor-Baden. Description p 97.*

Bono. – Pop 1 561. From the suspension bridge there is a picturesque view of the river and the port. You will notice piles of whitewashed tiles used to collect oyster spat *(p 18).*

Auray★. – *Description p 52.* Lovers of old houses should visit the St-Goustan quarter before going into the town.

Leave Auray by ③ on the plan, D 28, the road to Locmariaquer (p 116) which follows megalithic monuments.

From Vannes to Port-Navalo and back
73 km - 45 miles Rtn – about 4 hours – Local map p 124

Leave Vannes by ③, the N 165. After St-Léonard, turn right into the D 780. The road skirts the east bank of the bay.

At St-Colombier you enter the **Rhuys Peninsula★**, which encloses the Morbihan Gulf to the south. Its flora is reminiscent of that of the south of France.

Kerlévenan Château. – The château stands on the left of the road some 500 m beyond St-Colombier. It is quite easy to see the Classical façade, well designed, symmetrical and ornamented with columns and a balustrade.

Sarzeau. – Pop 4 088. *Facilities p 42.* Birthplace of the author Le Sage (1668-1747).

Alternative route by Brillac. – *Extra distance 2.5 km - 1½ miles.* Between Sarzeau and Le Net, the road follows the coast for some distance.

Tumiac Tumulus★ (Caesar's Mound). – *¼ hour on foot Rtn. 400 m beyond the hamlet of Tumiac, leave your car and take a dirt road to the right.* From the top of the tumulus there is an extensive **view★** of the gulf, Quiberon Bay and the islands. This was the observatory from which Caesar is supposed to have watched the naval battle against the Veneti *(p 124: Historical Notes).*

Arzon. – Pop 1 368. *Facilities p 42*. In obedience to a vow made to St. Anne in 1673, during the war with Holland, the sailors of Arzon march in the procession of Ste-Anne-d'Auray every year on Whit Monday.

Port-Navalo. – *Facilities p 42*. A small port and seaside resort. The roadstead is enclosed on the south by a promontory on which stands a lighthouse, and on the north by Bilgroix Point. From the point there is a good **view*** of the Morbihan Gulf *(car park)*. The beach faces the open sea.

During the tourist season there is a motor-boat service leaving Port-Navalo and going round the Morbihan Bay as far as Vannes or up the River Auray as far as the town of Auray (p 52).

St-Gildas-de-Rhuys. – *Description p 165*.

Suscinio Castle*. – *Open 1 April to 30 September 8.30am to 12.30pm and 1.30 to 6.30pm; the rest of the year 8.30am to 1pm and 2 to 5pm. Time: ¾ hour. Admission: 2F.*

The grandiose ruins of Suscinio stand by the seashore on a very wild site swept by the winds from the sea; at one time the high tide used to fill the moat. The castle was built in the 13C and became the summer residence of the Dukes of Brittany. It was confiscated by François I and used as a grace and favour residence. It was greatly damaged in the Revolution so that now only six of its eight towers remain; the large buildings on the inner court have lost their roofs and their floors and only enormous chimneys are left.

Cross the court diagonally to reach a staircase at the far end, on the right, leading to the north wall, along which you can walk.

From St-Colombier return to Vannes by the road by which you came.

MORGAT *
Michelin map **230** 17 – *Local map p 80* – *Facilities p 42*

Morgat is a much frequented seaside resort. The great sandy beach is well sheltered and one of the finest in Brittany. It is enclosed to the south by a point covered with pine woods, the Beg ar Gador, on which stands a lighthouse and which ends in a natural beach. On the north side, a rocky spur separates the Morgat beach from that of Le Portzic. Tunny fishing boats go out from the harbour sheltering behind a jetty. About 400 boats can anchor in the pleasure boat harbour.

Lighthouse. – *Open 10am to noon and 2 to 5pm. Apply to the keeper.* An attractive hillside path leads to the lighthouse from which there is a **view*** over the bay, Ménez-Hom, Douarnenez and the Cornouaille coast; in the distance are the Arrée Mountains.

Small caves. – Small caves at the foot of the spur between Morgat and Le Portzic beaches can be reached at low tide.

EXCURSION

Big caves*. – *Time: ¾ hour. You should go in clear weather, in the morning or early afternoon. You will find motor boats in the port.*

The first group of big caves, situated beyond Beg ar Gador, includes Ste-Marine and the Devil's Chamber (Chambre du Diable) which communicates through a chimney with the top of the cliff. The second group is at the other end of the bay. The finest grotto is that of the Altar (l'Autel), which is 80 m - 256 ft deep and 15 m - 48 ft high. One of its attractions is the colouring of the roofs and walls.

MORLAIX *
Michelin map **230** 5 – *Local map p 137* – Pop 20 532

The first thing the tourist will notice at Morlaix is its colossal viaduct. This structure bestrides the deep valley in which lies the estuary of the Dossen, commonly called the Morlaix River. The town is busy but the port, though it receives in summer an increasing number of yachts, has only limited commercial activity (sand, wood, coal, manure).

HISTORICAL NOTES

Queen Anne's Visit. – In 1505, on King Louis XII's recovery from a serious illness, Queen Anne of Brittany decided to make a pilgrimage to the saints of her duchy. She stayed at Morlaix; as the city then drew great riches from its port, its shipyards and its trade, it received the Queen sumptuously. She was presented with a little golden ship studded with jewels and a tame ermine wearing a diamond-studded collar (the ermine is the emblem of Anne of Brittany). The show-piece of the festival was a live Tree of Jesse representing all the sovereign's ancestors. *Details about Anne of Brittany pp 156 and 181.*

If they bite you, bite them! – In 1522 an English fleet of sixty sail came up the river on the tide. It anchored below the town and landed troops. A spy had told the English that the nobles and citizens of Morlaix would be away in the country on that day, being invited to various festivals. Pillage followed. But the English troops lingered in the cellars and the citizens had time to come back from the country. They fell on the intoxicated intruders and a hard fight ensued. It was then that the town added to its coat of arms a lion facing the English leopard with the motto: "S'ils te mordent, mords les!"

To guard against another attack the people of Morlaix built, in 1542, the Bull's Castle at the entrance to their harbour. Louis XIV took it over and made it a state prison in 1660.

Cornic, the "blue" officer (18C). – Cornic was the great Morlaix seaman of the 18C. He began as a privateer; his exploits were such that the King made him commander of a vessel in his Grand Corps. But Cornic was never more than a "blue" officer. Among the officers, those who had been through the Marine Guard school, nearly all noblemen, wore a red and blue uniform: they were the "red" officers. Those who had risen from the ranks wore a blue coat; they were the "blue" officers. He never rose above the rank of lieutenant.

The Revolution did him justice, but too late for him to resume active service.

The Tobacco farm (18C).

– There was a tobacco factory founded by the India Company and also a "farm" which had a monopoly of sales. Prices were exorbitant and smuggling thrived. Ships loaded in England with smoking and chewing tobacco and snuff were landed on the coast at night. Battles were fought between the smugglers and the farm men.

Morlaix is still a tobacco market. It has a large factory where cigars, cigarillos and snuff are made. *To visit, apply to the Secrétariat de Direction de la Manufacture de Cigares, 39 Quai de Léon, 29 205 Morlaix.*

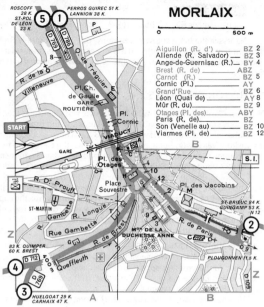

MORLAIX

Aiguillon (R. d')		BZ 2
Allende (R. Salvador)		BZ 3
Ange-de-Guernisac (R.)		BY 4
Brest (R. de)		ABZ
Carnot (R.)		BZ 5
Cornic (Pl.)		AY
Grand'Rue		BZ 6
Léon (Quai de)		AY 8
Mûr (R. du)		BZ 9
Otages (Pl. des)		ABY
Paris (R. de)		BZ
Son (Venelle au)		BZ 10
Viarmes (Pl. de)		BZ 12

■ MAIN SIGHTS

time: ¾ hour

Leave your car in the Place Cornic and follow the route marked on the plan.

Pass the **Viaduct★** (ABY) and make for the Place des Otages from where there is an impressive view of the viaduct. The structure has two storeys and is 58 m - 190 ft high and 285 m - 935 ft long.

Go up the stairs to the right of the viaduct. On the left is an old house with dormer windows dating back to the early part of the 17C. Turn right into the Rue Ange-de-Guernisac which is lined with old houses (Hôtel du Relais de France at no 13) as is the Venelle au Son nearby.

Grand' Rue★ (BZ 5). – Here you will see some very picturesque old houses and low fronted shops with wide windows *(étal)*, especially at nos 8 and 10.

Go round the market building and up a few steps leading to the Rue du Mûr.

Duchess Anne's House★ (Maison de la Duchesse Anne) (BZ). – This corbelled 16C mansion is three storeys tall. The façade is adorned with statues of saints and grotesques.

■ ADDITIONAL SIGHTS

Museum★ (BZ M). – *Open 9am to noon and 2 to 6pm. Closed Tuesdays except in August and some holidays. Admission: 2F.*

The museum of art and folklore of Léon has been installed in the former Church of the Jacobins, which has a fine 15C **rose window★**. There is also a collection of **modern paintings★**.

St-Melaine (BY A). – The church is in the Flamboyant style with an interesting porch on the south side. Inside are altarpieces, a baptistry and a group: *Descent from the Cross.*

St-Mathieu (BZ C). – The church was rebuilt in 1824, the tower is 16C. Inside, over the altar to the left of the high altar, is a 15C statue of the Virgin which opens *(illustration p 83)*.

Hôtel de Kergos (AY E). – A mansion in the Renaissance style.

EXCURSION

Plougonven★; Pleyber-Christ. – *Round tour of 56 km - 35 miles – about 2 hours. Leave Morlaix by the Rue de Paris and D 9 (southeast on the plan).*

Plougonven★. – This village at the foot of the Arrée Mountains has an interesting parish close *(details on closes p 31).*

The **Calvary★★**, built in 1554, is one of the oldest in Brittany. The cross in two tiers, carries, above, the statues of the Virgin and St. John, and, below, two guards; the thieves' crosses stand on either side. At the foot of the main cross is a Descent from the Cross. On the platform and around the base are scenes depicting various episodes in the life of Christ: the Temptation in the Desert, Christ's Arrest, the Entombment, etc.

The church is dominated by a graceful belfry with a balcony and a turret staircase. In front is an ossuary with a trefoil window.

Continue along the D 9 as far as Lannéanou and then turn right into the D 111, a very picturesque road along the Arrée ridge. It crosses a bare but impressive landscape.

Le Relecq. – A 12-13C church and convent buildings are all that remain of the former Cistercian abbey. The façade of the church was rebuilt in the 18C. Two *pardons* with Celtic music concerts are held every year, Ste-Anne *(second last Sunday in July)*, Notre-Dame-du-Relecq *(14 and 15 August)*.

At the crossing of N 785, turn right.

Pleyber-Christ. – Pop 2 525. A small parish close. The Gothic and Renaissance church is preceded by a triumphal arch dedicated to the dead of the First World War. Inside the building, which has fine carved chests and remarkable beams, are some old stalls and a large low relief at the high altar. The treasury contains a fine 16C silver-gilt processional cross, a sanctuary lamp in beaten silver and a 16C statue of St. Anne teaching the Virgin to read. A fine gilt processional cross is kept in the presbytery. Ossuary to the left of the church.

Return to Morlaix by the D 785 and N 12.

NANTES ★★★

Michelin maps 230 54, 55 and 67 3 – Pop 263 689

Nantes is the biggest town in Brittany, but it is not purely Breton, for the Loire has always brought French influence with it. It is a city of art, a great industrial centre, a university city and a busy port. Each year, a carnival enlivens the town *(fourth Thursday and third Sunday before Easter)*.

HISTORICAL NOTES

Nantes, Capital of Brittany. – Nantes was first Gallic and then Roman and was involved in the bloody struggle between the Frankish kings and the Breton counts and dukes. But it was the Normans who did the most damage. In 843 the pirates landed, rushed into the cathedral, where the Bishop was saying Mass, and put the prelate, the clergy and the congregation to the sword. From Nantes they spread all over Brittany and devastated it for nearly a century.

In 937 young Alain Barbe-Torte (Crookbeard), a descendant of great Breton chiefs, who had taken refuge in England, returned to the country, rallied the remaining inhabitants, slaughtered the pirates below Nantes and drove them out of Brittany. Having become duke, he chose Nantes as his capital and rebuilt its ruins. Nantes was the capital of the Duchy of Brittany several times during the Middle Ages, in rivalry with Rennes. The dukes of the House of Montfort *(p 20)*, especially **François II** and Duchess Anne, governed as undisputed sovereigns and restored the prestige of the town and its title of capital.

Edict of Nantes (13 August 1598). – In 1597, Brittany, tired of disorder and suffering caused by the League and also of the separatist ambitions of its Governor, Philip of Lorraine, Duke of Mercœur, sent a pressing appeal on 31 December 1597 to Henri IV, asking him to come and restore order. Before the castle he whistled with admiration. "God's teeth," he exclaimed, "the Dukes of Brittany were no small beer!"

The royal visit was marked by a great historic event: on 13 August 1598, Henry IV signed the Edict of Nantes, which, in ninety-two articles, settled the religious question – or so he thought.

Twenty-eight years later, the son of Henri IV and Gabrielle d'Estrées, César de Vendôme, who was then Duke of Brittany, became involved in the conspiracy of the Comte de Chalais against Richelieu. The Duke was stripped of his title and Chalais executed.

Sugar and "ebony". – From the 16 to the 18C, Nantes had two main sources of revenue: sugar and the slave trade, known discreetly as the "ebony trade". In the Antilles, the slaver would sell the slaves bought on the Guinea coast and buy cane sugar, to be refined at Nantes and sent up the Loire.

The "ebony" made an average profit of 200%. Philosophers inveighed against this inhuman traffic, but Voltaire, whose business acumen is well known, had a 5 000 *livre* share in a slave ship from Nantes.

At the end of the 18C the prosperity of Nantes was at its height: it was the first port of France; its fleet included 2 500 ships and barques. The big shipowners and traders founded regular dynasties which yielded nothing to the nobility in class spirit while they built the fine mansions on the Quai de la Fosse and the former Ile Feydeau.

It was said of the Nantais **Cassard** (1672-1740) that he was France's "greatest seaman". The daring, skill and luck with which he passed convoys of supplies through the strictest blockade have remained legendary.

All Drowned. – In June 1793, Nantes numbered many royalists. The Convention sent Carrier, the Deputy of the Cantal, there as its representative at the beginning of October. Carrier had already spent some time at Rennes *(p 157)*. His mission was "to purge the body politic of all the rotten matter it contained".

The revolutionary tribunal had filled the prisons with Vendéens, priests and suspects, and a problem arose: how to make room for new arrivals. Carrier chose drowning. Condemned people were put into barges which were scuttled in the Loire, opposite Chantenay. The Convention when informed, immediately recalled its delegate. He was put on trial and was sent before the Nantes Revolutionary court, sentenced to death and guillotined in December.

In 1832 tragedy gave way to farce. The **Duchesse de Berry**, a mortal enemy of Louis-Philippe, was convinced that Brittany was still legitimist and scoured the countryside about Nantes. Her failure was complete. She took refuge at Nantes but was betrayed. The police invaded the house and found it empty, but remained on the watch. Feeling cold, they lit a fire in one of the rooms.

Their surprise was great when the chimney-shutter fell open and out on all fours came the duchess and three of her followers, black as sweeps and half suffocated. They had spent sixteen hours in the thickness of the wall.

Development. – The abolition of the slave trade by the Revolution, the substitution of French beet for Antilles sugar cane under the Empire, and finally the increase in tonnage and draught of ships making them unable to reach Nantes were great blows to the town. Nantes abandoned its maritime ambitions and turned to metallurgy and the making of foodstuffs. A manufacturer named Collin developed a method of preserving food which was patented by Appert in 1809.

In 1856 Nantes, again with an eye to the sea, founded an outer port at St-Nazaire; the city then dug a lateral canal. After 1911, when dredging techniques had improved, the canal was abandoned and shipping returned to the estuary. Merchant ships of 7 to 8 m - 22 to 25 ft draught can now come up to Nantes when tides are high.

Nantes today. – Nantes has been completely reconstructed and transformed since the war. An effort was made to preserve the 18C character of its old quarters and the many new buildings have been well incorporated into the town as exemplified by Le Corbusier's living unit *(unité d'habitation*, 1955) at **Rezé**. The east of **Beaulieu Islet** forms a striking contrast with the western section of the harbour populated with cranes, warehouses and popular quarters. Sprouting out of the former meadows are tall white buildings.

Located on the former **Gloriette Islet** are the Faculty of Medicine and Pharmacy and at the west two swimming pools. Built on the former **Feydeau Islet**, which has preserved its 18C houses is the large complex *Centre Neptune* with its conference rooms, stores and post office.

The **Place de Bretagne** (CX 18 *on the plan p 134*) in the centre of town, is witness to this change: a new twenty-four storey building rises opposite the 1954 Social Security and 1961 Post Office buildings. In the northern outskirts of Nantes, to the west of the Erdre, the University

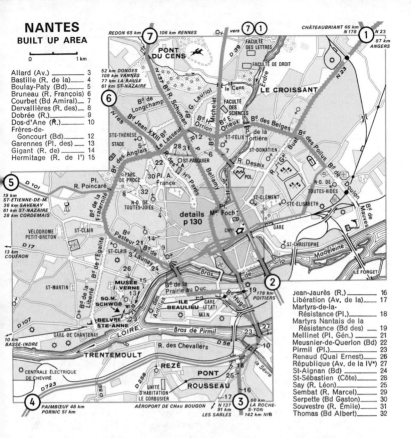

NANTES
BUILT UP AREA

0 ——— 1 km

campus groups the Arts, Science and Law faculties as well as the schools of Architecture and Commerce. New residential quarters have been created to the south of Procé Park, the **Cité des Dervallières** and along the banks of the Loire, near the St-Félix canal, the **Malakoff Quarter**.

A pedestrian zone has been delimited which includes the Place du Change, Rue des Halles, Rue des Carmes, Rue du Moulin, Rue Ste-Croix and Rue de la Juiverie.

The port. – The port installations in Nantes are managed by the Autonomous Port Authority of Nantes-St-Nazaire. The equipment of the port of Nantes and its subsidiaries – Basse-Indre, Coueron and Paimbœuf – includes ninety electric cranes, refrigerated depots, wine warehouses, grain silos, three floating docks and 5 km - 3 miles of public quays.

The total traffic of the port of Nantes with its subsidiaries was 16 168 351 tons in 1977.

Imports consist chiefly of hydrocarbons, metallurgical products, phosphates, chemicals, sugar, timber, soya, crabs, citrus fruits, early vegetables and wine. Exports include cereals, fertilisers and manufactured goods.

Recent improvement to the channel now allows the coming and going of 20 000 ton ships according to the tide.

The visit to Beaulieu Islet will give you a good overall impression of the port's main activities.

Beaulieu Islet. – Arrive on the island by the bridge, Pont Anne de Bretagne, an integral part of the port this is the domain of great cranes and dredging companies. Boulevard Léon-Bureau leads to the État railway station and the street, Prairie au Duc to the Antilles quay where the banana cargoes are unloaded. At the western end of the island there are great piles of wood – whole tree trunks and planks – heaps of coal and sand, great reservoirs, the fruit and vegetable market, the refrigerated depots and attendant lorries of the firm, Loire-Atlantique, the premises of the General Maritime Company and finally to the south of the station, the great market hall of national importance.

Industrial activity. – The industry of Nantes is very considerable: foundries, boiler making and mechanical engineering. As regards foodstuffs, there are sugar refineries, canneries and biscuit factories. The importance of wine growing in the region has brought about the commercial exploitation of the local wines, *Muscadet* and *Gros Plant*. Nantes is also one of the world buying centres for angora wool.

The Nantes shipyards form, together with those of St-Nazaire, the greatest shipbuilding area in France, working partly for the Navy and partly for the merchant marine (especially dredgers, mineral ships, factory ships for the fishing industry and submarines).

The basis of the Nantes metallurgical industry consists of works producing machinery and equipment for oil boring and refining, for industrial refrigeration equipment for aeronatuics, telephone and electronics.

On the left bank. – Located in the new industrial area of 200 ha - 500 acres, is a power station as well as a paper mill and timber manufacturing.

In the industrial corridor of the Basse-Loire, the Indret workshops specialise in the production of ships' boilers and produced the first engines using nuclear energy for ship propulsion. Paimbœuf turns out chemical products and structural steel.

On the right bank. – The **Basse-Indre** works make tinplate for the canneries; the **Couëron** works handle lead and copper ore.

At **Cordemais**, another power station can be found.

Crude oil is treated at Elf's refinery in **Donges** *(p 87)*.

NANTES
CENTRE

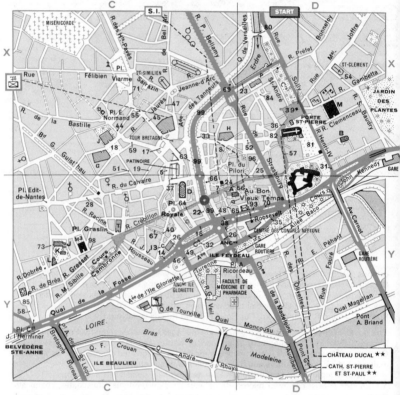

■ **MAIN SIGHTS** time: 3 hours

Cathedral St. Peter and Paul* (Cathédrale St-Pierre et St-Paul). – *Restoration in Progress. Only the nave, the aisles and the transept can be visited.*

This imposing building, begun in 1434 and completed in 1893, astounds the tourist by its austere façade restored in 1930: two plain towers frame a Flamboyant window; note the 15C canopied niches which decorate the pillars supporting the towers. The three portals reveal finely sculpted recessed arches and on the central portal stands a statue of St. Peter. From the north side one can see the chevet with its ring of fine apsidal chapels.

Interior**. – Here, at Nantes, white stone replaces the granite used in purely Breton cathedrals. Being less heavy, this stone has made it possible to build vaults 37.50 m - 123 ft high (the vaulting of Notre-Dame-de-Paris is 33.50 m - 110 ft high, and that of Westminster Abbey 30.50 m - 100 ft).

As you enter you will be struck by the nave's pure, soaring lines, a fine example of Flamboyant work. Stand under the organ loft to appreciate the effect; you will see a double row of vertical lines springing from the ground and shooting up to the keystones of the vaults, where they cross; not a single discordant note will check your eye.

Everything is based on elevation and the dimension of 37.50 m - 120 ft loses significance. Seen from this angle, the slender ribs of the pillars, in very high relief, mask not only the flat wall surfaces that separate them but all the lines, curved or horizontal, of the arcades, the triforium or the upper windows which could break the harmony of this vista, composed entirely of parallel elements. It is rather paradoxical that the Flamboyant style, reputedly complicated and over elaborate, should have succeeded in producing a group of perfect linear purity by the systematic use of verticals. Even the vaults themselves, so often of complicated design, are here quite plain, resting on a network of ogive arches.

Before going round the cathedral look at the niches with 15C carved canopies adorning the pillars which support the towers. A few still contain their statues, among which, on each side of the main doorway, are those of St. Rogatian and St. Donatian, the "children of Nantes", two young Gallo-Roman nobles who were martyred about 290.

Go round the building to the right.

In the south transept is the decorative masterpiece of the cathedral and a very great Renaissance work: the **tomb of François II****. This tomb was carved between 1502 and 1507 by Michel Colombe, a sculptor who was born in Brittany but settled in Touraine. It was

130

commissioned by Anne of Brittany to receive the remains of her father, François II, and her mother, Marguerite of Foix, and it was placed in the Church of the Carmelites. The Revolutionary Tribunal ordered it to be demolished, but the courageous town architect of the time, instead of obeying the order, hid various pieces of the tomb in the homes of his friends. It was reconstructed after the Revolution and transferred to the cathedral in 1817.

The Duke and Duchess recline on a black marble slab. The statues grouped round them are symbolic: the angels supporting their heads represent their welcome to Heaven; the lion couching at the feet of François stands for power, and Marguerite's greyhound for fidelity. The four large angle statues personify the four Cardinal Virtues: for the Duke, Justice (crowned and holding a sword) and Strength (helmed and armed and expelling a dragon from a tower); Prudence and Temperance guard the Duchess. Prudence has two faces: in front, a young girl with a looking glass, symbolising the future, and behind, an old man representing the past. (Prudence consults the past to foresee the future.) Temperance holds a bridle to signify control over passions, and a clock symbolising steadiness.

Below the recumbent figures are sixteen niches containing the statues of saints interceding for the deceased, notably St. Francis of Assisi and St. Margaret, their patrons. Below these again, sixteen mourners represent the sorrow of their people.

This magnificent group is lit by a superb modern **stained glass window**, 25 m - 80 ft tall and 5.30 m - 14 ft wide devoted to Breton and Nantes saints.

You should pause at the transept crossing, where the impression of height is astonishing.

In the north arm of the transept is the **Cenotaph of Lamoricière**★, the work of the sculptor Paul Dubois (1879). The General is shown reclining, under a shroud. Four bronze statues represent Meditation and Charity (at his head) and Military Courage and Faith (at his feet).

Lamoricière (1806-65), a great African campaigner who came from Nantes, captured the Arabian Emir Abd-el-Kader in 1847 during the wars in Algeria.

He later fell into disgrace and when exiled by Napoleon III commanded Papal troops against the Italians. It is the Catholic paladin who is honoured here.

Ducal Castle★★ **(Château Ducal).** – *Museum and Horseshoe Tower open from 10am to noon and 2 to 6pm - Closed on Tuesdays and public holidays. Admission: 1F, free at the weekend.*

The golden age of the castle was the time of Duke François II, when life at the castle was truly royal; five ministers attended the Duke; seventeen chamberlains and a host of secretaries, equerries and footmen served him. Life was luxurious, brilliant and very free as to morals. For a time it was thought great fun to rush through all the rooms in a band just after waking time: sleepers were hauled out of bed and thrown into the moat, to be roused by the cold water. Even the Duke himself was surprised in this way and had to pay a fine to avoid ducking.

The present building was begun by Duke François II in 1466 and continued by his daughter, Anne of Brittany. Defence works were added during the League by the Duke of Mercœur. From the 18C onwards the military took possession, destroyed some buildings and erected others lacking in style. The Spaniards' Tower (Tour des Espagnols), which had been used as a magazine, blew up in 1800. The north part of the castle was destroyed – *the sites of the destroyed buildings are indicated by a red dotted line on the plan below*.

From Charles VIII to Louis XIV, nearly all the Kings of France spent some time at the castle: in its chapel Louis XII married Anne of Brittany; it was here that Henri IV signed the Edict of Nantes. Chalais, Cardinal de Retz, Fouquet, Gilles de Rais (Bluebeard) and the Duchesse de Berry were imprisoned in its towers.

An arm of the Loire washed the south, east and northeast walls until the building of quays and the filling up in 1809 of this branch of the Loire greatly changed the site of the fortress.

The Fortress. – Today the moat has been re-established; the ditches which guarded the north and west sides have been turned into gardens and the old ditches have been restored on the other sides. An 18C bridge leads to the former drawbridge which is flanked by two massive round towers dating from the time of Duke François.

The Palace. – The court was used for jousting and tournaments, also for the performance of mystery plays and farces.

The **Golden Crown Tower**★★ (Tour de la Couronne d'Or) (2), a tower with fine Italian style loggias, contains two staircases leading to the Main Building on the left and the Governor's Major Palace on the right.

The **Main Building** (Grand Logis) (3) built by Anne of Brittany has a bare façade surmounted by five carved dormer windows. It was used as a dwelling house for men-at-arms.

The **Governor's Major Palace** (Grand Gouvernement) (4) is the ducal palace proper. It was rebuilt after the fire of 1684. The basement contained the prisons; on the ground floor were the guardrooms and kitchens; on the first and second floors, the apartments; and in the attics the servants' dormitories.

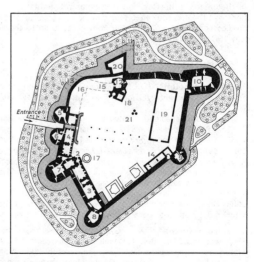

2. Golden Crown Tower. 3. Main Building. 4. Governor's Major Palace. 5. Hind's Foot Tower. 6. Bakery Tower. 7. Jacobins' Tower. 8. Port Tower. 9. River Tower. 10. Horseshoe Tower. 11. Dyke's Tower. 12. Old Keep. 13. Spaniard's Tower. 14. Governor's Lesser Palace. 15. Old Building. 16. Chapel. 17. Well. 18. Porter's Lodge. 19. Harness Building. 20. Mercœur Bastion. 21. Remains of former castle.

Over the **well**★★ (17) there is a wrought iron framework, once gilded, which represents the ducal crown. The curb of the well has seven sides; there are seven pulleys and seven gargoyles for the overflow.

The Romanesque **Governor's Lesser Palace** (Petit Gouvernement) (14) was built under François I, the military **Harness Building** (Harnachement) (19) dates back to 1784.

In the courtyard, near Roman excavations, are traces of the 13-14C castle; the Old Keep (12) forms part with an 18C mansion which houses the porter's lodge.

The **Horseshoe Tower** (la Tour du Fer à cheval) (10) is 16C. In the restored rooms, a special lighting enhances the vaulting with armorial decorated keystones. One of the rooms contains contemporary woven works of art.

Museum of Local Popular Art★. – The museum is located on the first floor of the Governor's Major Palace. The collections include a traditional Breton house, with map and models; *coiffes* and costumes of all the Breton districts, since the end of the 19C; reconstructions of interiors from Vendée and Guérande; furniture from the Morbihan and Quimper regions (a 1731 wardrobe, box beds, cradles, spinning-wheels).

Maritime Museum★ (Musée des Salorges). – This is on the first floor of the large buildings, called Le Harnachement. Among the varied exhibits are three 18-19C figureheads; models of 17 and 18C vessels, in particular slave trade boats; fishing boats of many varieties; and 17-19C navigational instruments, as well as relief plans of Nantes through the ages. Documents and small-scale boats recall navigation on the Loire. The traditional trades and industries of Nantes are evoked: posters and labels represent canning and biscuit making alongside examples of printed materials and 16C Croisic pottery.

The Town Centre. – *Follow the itinerary marked on the plan p 130.*

Place Maréchal-Foch (DX 39). – Two fine 18C hotels flank the Louis XVI Column which was erected in 1790.

From the square you can readily appreciate the dimensions of the cathedral, in particular its soaring height.

Porte St-Pierre (DX). – This 15C gateway is built on the remains of a 3C Gallo-Roman wall. The gateway is built into an elegant turreted building which was formerly part of the episcopal residence.

Skirt the west front to reach **La Psalette** on the south side. This 15C building with a polygonal turret formerly contained the chapterhouse but is now part of the sacristy.

On leaving the Place St-Pierre turn left into Rue Mathelin-Rodier, whose name recalls the architect of the cathedral and part of the castle. It was in the house at no 3 that the Duchess of Berry was arrested *(p 128)*.

Pass the Ducal Castle on the left *(p 131)*.

Ste-Croix (CDY A). – The 17C church stands in a quarter where one still finds 15C (Rue Bossuet) and 16C (Place du Centre, Tourist Information Centre) half-timbered houses. The church is surmounted by the former town belfry crowned by trumpeting angels. The palm tree decoration of the chancel vaulting contrasts with the round vaulting of the nave. Large Flamboyant windows open onto the aisles. The furnishings are 18C.

The 19C town★. – It was the financier Graslin, Receiver General for Farmlands at Nantes, who was responsible for the creation of this area. By way of the Place du Pilori, surrounded by 18C houses, make for the **Place Royale** (CY), which was built by Crucy, the architect of the Palais de la Bourse. This as adorned by a fountain representing Nantes, the Loire and its tributaries (1865).

The **Rue Crébillon** is narrow, commercial and very busy: the people who stroll through it are said to *crébillonner*. Opening onto the Rue Santeuil on the left, is a curious stepped shopping arcade, the **Passage Pommeraye★** which goes down the Palais de la Bourse. Great fluted columns support a terrace, giving access to the upper level shops and statue adorned pedestals serve as bases for lamps. A humorous note is added by the processions of mice and snails carved on the stair risers.

Return to the Rue Crébillon, passing on your right the fine **Place Graslin** (CY) dominated by the Grand Théâtre. The café on the corner, La Cigale, still has a turn of the century air and fine mosaics. Leading off from the same corner is the **Cours Cambronne★** (CY) lined with late 18C and early 19C pillared houses.

■ ADDITIONAL SIGHTS

Fine Arts Museum★★ (DX M). – *Open 9am (10am on Sundays) to noon and 2 to 5pm (6pm 1 April to 30 September). Closed Tuesdays and holidays. Admission: 1F (free Saturdays and Sundays).*

This museum has particularly rich collections of Renaissance and 20C paintings.

Salle Pérugin: three works by the Italian artist Perugino, *Saint Sebastian* and *Saint Bernard*, the *Prophet Isaiah* and *King David*; **salle Tintoret**: striking *Portrait of a man* by Tintoretto; **salle Georges de la Tour**: *Saint Peter's Denial*, *The Angel appearing to Joseph in his dream*, *The Hurdy-gurdy Player*; **salle Lancret**: *La Camargo*; **salle Greuze**: *Bird Catcher* and *Charles Etienne de Saint-Morges as a Child*, in his white suit by Greuze; **salle Ingres**: *Madame de Senonnes*; **salle Courbet**: *The Winnowers*; **salle Boudin**: Impressionists.

The contemporary art galleries include sculptures by the Cubist sculptor Julio Gonzalez, Esther Gentle Rattner and Abstract works by Kandinsky, Poliakoff, Georgio di Giorgi. The Maurice Denis and Manessier galleries group a variety of works from the 19C to the present day.

Botanical Gardens★ (DX). – Opposite the mosaic decorated station is this very fine garden which was created in 1805. This well landscaped garden includes, in addition to the masses of white, pink, purple, yellow camellias, magnolias, rhododendrons and splendid trees, several fine ponds and wooden sculpture. A statue of Jules Verne is a reminder that Nantes was the writer's native town.

Immaculée-Conception (DX B). – The former chapter of the Minimes in an older area of Nantes where 17C porches adorn the houses and streets narrow to alleys. It was built in the 15C Flamboyant style. The aisles are 17C and the 19C pulpit has small columns intertwined with a vine and snake.

St-Nicolas (CY D). – The church was built in the 19C in the Gothic style. There are fine views of the church and its tall spire from Place Royale and of the east end from Rue Cacault.

Natural History Museum★★ (CY M³). – *Open 2 to 6pm and also 10am to noon on Wednesdays. Closed Mondays, Fridays and holidays. Admission: 1F; free on Sundays.*
Formerly the Mint, this building houses important natural history collections. One section deals with all aspects of shell-fish (variety, beauty of the shells and interesting cross sections), a second has a rich variety of skeletons. A vivarium presents numerous reptiles and amphibians from all parts of the world.

Palais Dobrée★ (CY). – *Open 10am to noon and 2 to 6pm. Closed Tuesdays and holidays.*
This Romanesque mansion was built in the 19C by the collector Thomas Dobrée.
On the ground floor Romanesque and Gothic sculptures and *objets d'art* are presented in a modern setting: with statues from the cathedral belfry, carved beams and 13C champlevé enamels from Limoges. On the first floor a gallery shows by rotation selections of 16 to 19C engravings and watercolours. Some miniatures and jewels are exhibited in the library. In addition there are numerous Flemish, Dutch, 15-17C Italian and 19C French paintings, 16C Flemish tapestries and Breton pottery.
The second floor evokes the Vendéen War (1793-5) between the Royalists (Whites) and the Republicans (Blues). Letters, arms, etc., recall this bitter civil war as well as souvenirs of the Duchess of Berry, who attempted to rally the insurrection in its dying stages.
An underground passage housing temporary exhibitions, gives access to the Archaeological Museum *(see below)*.

Manoir de la Touche (CY K). – *Same opening times as for the Palais Dobrée.*
This the manor of Jean de la Touche or Jean V, a member of the Montfort family, stands alongside the Palais Dobrée. He died here in 1442 in the house which served as a country house for the bishops of Nantes. Built in the early 15C the manor contains sections on ethnography, South America (jewels, statuettes and vases), Egypt (sculptures, sarcophagi, Coptic materials), Greek and Etruscan pottery.

Regional Archaeological Museum★ (CY L). – *Enter from the Rue Voltaire. Same opening times as for the Palais Dobrée.*
A modern building in the Palais Dobrée gardens houses a local prehistory collection. On the first floor the Palaeolithic, Neolithic, Bronze and Iron Ages are described while an exhibition of tools, axes, jewellery and arms demonstrates the relatively slow technical evolution of those times. The second floor has an exhibition on art in the Gallo-Roman period, illustrated by sculptures both funerary and mythological, everyday utensils (dishes, glass and ceramic ware) and the typical decorative themes of the times. Several display cases contain Merovingian exhibits: bricks from the earliest local basilicas: jewellery and swords.

Notre-Dame-de-Bon-Port (CY F). – *Closed on Sunday afternoons.* Also known as the Church of St. Louis, this unusual building overlooks the Place Sanitat. This great cubic mass is adorned by a fresco and a triangular pediment and topped by a majestic dome. Built in 1846, massive hexagonal pillars support the dome decorated alternatively with panels of stained glass and frescoes.

Place Général-Mellinet. – *Northwest of Place Sanitat* (CY 85). Eight Charles X (1924-30) hôtels border this splendid square.

Jules Verne Museum. – *3 Rue de l'Hermitage. Guided tours at 10am, 11am, 2pm, 3pm and 4pm. Closed on Tuesdays. Admission: 1F; free on Sundays and public holidays.*
A 19C mansion houses the museum devoted to the Nantais author Jules Verne (1828-1905), one of the first to write science fiction novels such as *Five Weeks in a Balloon*; *A Journey to the Centre of the Earth* and *Around the World in Eighty Days*. His life is retraced with the help of memorabilia: autographs, furniture, personal objects, portraits, busts and a collection of his works.

Former Feydeau Islet★ (CY). – At the beginning of the century, the islet was linked to the mainland and a second island, Ile Gloriette, by infilling several arms of the Loire. The islet has retained its 18C aspect, especially between Place de la Petite Hollande and the more recent, Rue Olivier-de-Clisson (no 4 was the birthplace of Jules Verne). It was here that rich shipowners used to build their vast mansions which stretch from the central street, Rue Kervégan right back to one of the outer avenues, allées Turenne or Duguay-Trouin. Curved wrought iron balconies and grotesque masks, probably the work of seafaring craftsmen, adorn the façades. The inner courtyards have staircases with remarkable vaulting (eg 21 Rue Kervégan, 9 Allée Turenne, 15 and 16 Allée Duguay-Trouin and 1 Place de la Petite Hollande).
Opposite on the northern bank, there are also some fine 18C houses on **Place de la Bourse** (nos 7 and 11) and its continuation, **Quai de la Fosse** (nos 54, 72 and 86).
The bridges crossing to the Beaulieu Islet *(pp 128 and 129)* to the south, afford a fine view of the river and its traffic.

Ste-Anne Belvedere. – *Plan p 129.* Access is by the climbing Rue de l'Hermitage. From the belvedere there is a good **view**★ of the port installations. Beyond the many cranes one can make out the dockyards and the Beaulieu Islet. A viewing table helps the visitor to pinpoint Nantes' main sights.
Steps lead up to the **statue of Ste-Anne**, blessing the port, which stands in a small garden. The view of the town from here is more restricted, from the spire of St-Nicolas to Le Corbusier's new town.
Cross the shaded Place des Garennes which is overlooked by the west front of the Church of Ste-Anne and take the Rue des Garennes to reach the Square Maurice-Schwob.

Square Maurice Schwob. – This garden is dominated by an expressive statue of a Breton cursing the sea. Through the trees and bushes one can make out part of the port, in the far distance the dome of St-Louis and all the belfries of Nantes and Rezé.

Erdre Valley. – *Plan p 129.* By car one can drive along the right bank of the river as far as La Tortière Bridge.

NANTES***

Boat trip. – *Landing stage: 24 Quai de Versailles, all enquires to the Lebert-Buisson Shipping Company Tel 71 08 76; running commentary; departure time: 2.30pm on Sundays and public holidays from March to November, in addition on Wednesdays and Saturdays in April, May and October and every day from June to September.*

Boat trip with lunch aboard: 12.30pm (return at 5.30pm) on Sundays and public holidays from March to November; in addition on Saturdays in September and Mondays and Thursdays from June to September. Boat trip with dinner aboard: 8.15pm (return at midnight!) on Saturdays and the evening preceding public holidays from March to September, in addition on Wednesdays from June to September.

This is a favourite trip for the Nantais in a pleasantly green countryside dotted with manor houses. The Erdre widens beyond Sucé to form a lake, Lac de Mazerolles.

NOIRES MOUNTAINS ** (MONTAGNES NOIRES)

Michelin map **230** 19, 20

This district, in the heart of Breton speaking Brittany, will please tourists in search of local colour and those who wish to avoid crowded roads.

With the Arrée Mountains *(p 49)*, the Noires Mountains form what Bretons call the spine of the peninsula. These two little mountain chains, mainly of hard sandstone and quartzite, are not quite alike. The Noires Mountains are rather lower (326 m - 1 043 ft as against 384 m - 1 229 ft); their crest is narrower; their slopes are less steep and their heaths are less extensive.

The name of the chain suggests that it was once covered with forest. As in all inner Brittany, the ground became bare with time. Since the end of the last century reafforestation has been going on, and the fir woods, now numerous, once more justify the name of Black Mountains.

Quarrying of Breton slate is now concentrated on the eastern end of the chain, in the district of Motreff and Maël-Carhaix. The beds of slate bearing schist are worked by means of shafts sunk to a depth of about 100 m - 325 ft. The blocks are extracted by modern machinery and brought to the surface. They are cut up by electric saws into approximately the size of slating tiles and stacked in sheds where the "splitters" work with their long steel blades. Machines then cut these leaves into roofing tiles.

The Breton slate quarries supply about 5% of French production (those of Anjou 45%).

ROUND TOUR STARTING FROM CARHAIX
80 km - 50 miles – about 4 hours – Local map below

Leave Carhaix-Plouguer *(p 68)* to the west by the N 169 which enters the Valley of the Hyères.

St-Hernin. – Pop 826. *4 km - 2½ miles from Port-de-Carhaix.* Church and parish close.

The D769 crosses the Nantes–Brest canal and climbs gradually up the northern slopes of the Noires Mountains. Slate quarries can be seen to the right and left.

On the left a road branches off to the **St-Hervé Chapel** *(1 km - ½ mile)*. A *pardon* is held on the last Sunday in September.

After crossing the crest you run down to Gourin.

Gourin. – Pop 5 526. Once a centre of slate production. Gourin also has white stone quarries, raises horses and cattle and poultry and has large horse and pig markets.

It has a small parish close *(details on closes p 31)* a *pardon* on the first Sunday in July for the "Sonneurs bretons" (Breton "ringers") and the national championship of the Bagadou (bagpipes and bombard players) on 1 May.

After Gourin, you make again for the crest of the Noires Mountains.

Toullaëron Rock*. – ½ hour on foot Rtn. 6 km - 4 miles from Gourin, leave your car. Take a stony lane *(private property, no picnicking)* to the right bordered with young oak trees. At the end of the lane you will see the rock, which you will climb. From the top, which is the highest point in the Noires Mountains, you will see in clear weather a great **panorama***. To the west is the densely wooded Valley of Châteaulin; to the north, the Arrée Mountains. To the south, in the distance, the Breton plateau slopes gently down to the Atlantic.

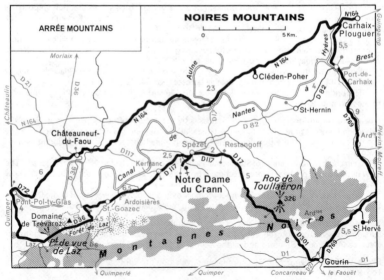

Notre-Dame-du-Crann★. – *Description below*.

After St-Goazec take D 36, which climbs into the fine forest of Laz, skirting the great park of the castle of Trévarez. Coming out of the forest you will reach the viewpoint of Laz.

Trévarez en St-Goazec Forest Park (Domaine de Trévarez en St-Goazec). – *Open 1 May to 30 September, 1 to 7pm. Closed Tuesdays. The rest of the year, open 2 to 6pm Saturdays, Sundays and holidays; only Sundays and holidays in December, January, February and March. Admission: 2F.* This 75 ha - 185 acres forest park is administered by the Finistère authorities. It has signposted paths throughout the woods and a large variety of camellias, azaleas and rhododendrons.

Return to the D 36; after the forest you reach the Laz viewpoint.

Laz Viewpoint★ (Point de vue de Laz). – A splendid view of the Aulne valley to the right, between two groups of rocks.

Go on to the outskirts of Laz, where you will take a picturesque by-road to the right which, at the start, offers a fine view to the right.

Pont-Pol-Ty-Glas. – *Facilities p 44.*

Take the D 72 to the right which crosses the Nantes–Brest canal.

Châteauneuf-du-Faou. – This village is built in very pretty surroundings on the slope of a hill overlooking the Aulne. It is the anglers' delight with salmon swimming up the Aulne from the sea and also pike. *Pardon* on the second Sunday in August.

The road from Châteauneuf to Carhaix is charming for a few kilometres, as it follows the Aulne. On the right, on the horizon, you will see the Noires Mountains.

Cléden-Poher. – Pop 1 011. A small 16C parish close *(details on closes p 31)*. In the church (1694) you will see altarpieces, carved panels and statues. In the cemetery are an ossuary turned into a chapel with a picturesque wooden roof, a fine Calvary (1575) and two curious sacristies with roofs shaped like the keels of capsized boats.

Return to Carhaix by the N 787 and the N 169.

OUR LADY OF CRANN Chapel ★ (NOTRE-DAME-DU-CRANN)

Michelin map **230** 19 – 8.5 km - 5 miles east of Châteauneuf-du-Faou – *Local map p 134*

To visit the church – ¼ hour – ask for the key at the house next door to the chapel or at the presbytery.

The Chapel of Our Lady of Crann (N.-D.-du-Crann), built in 1532, has some remarkable 16C **stained glass windows★★**.

In the south aisle you will see the window of St. Eligius illustrating the legend of the Saint, who is the patron of farriers. At the south transept are the Death and Coronation of the Virgin. Above the south aisle, is the stained glass window of St. James Major, in three bays. The window in the chancel depicts scenes of the Passion in twelve bays. Above are the Last Judgment and the Triumph of Christ. The upper part of a window in the north transept shows the Adoration of the Shepherds, and the lower part, the Adoration of the Magi; another, on the right, shows the Martyrdom of St. Lawrence in three panels. The window in the north aisle represents the Baptism of Jesus Christ.

The high altar is framed between two niches with **shutters★** decorated with carvings; that on the left contains a statue of the Virgin Mother; the carved shutters recall episodes in her life; the niche on the right contains a group of the Trinity.

A *pardon* is held on Trinity Sunday *(p 10)*.

*(After Le Doaré
photo, Châteaulin)*

Detail of a window.

PAIMPOL

Michelin map **230** 8 – Pop 8 498 – *Facilities p 43 – Town plan in the Michelin Guide France*

Pierre Loti's novel *Pêcheur d'Islande, Fisherman of Iceland* and the *Paimpolaise* of the songwriter Botrel, brought Paimpol both literary fame and popularity in France. Life has changed a great deal, however, since those days in the port, which is now large and impersonal: deep sea cod fishing on the Iceland banks is a thing of the past, its place being taken by inshore fishing and pleasure boating. Oyster cultivation, now on a large scale, has also brought riches to the region. Paimpol retains a certain prosperity as a market for early vegetables.

The *pardon* of Notre-Dame-de-Bonne-Nouvelle takes place on the second Sunday in December.

In the centre of the town is the **Place du Martray** containing the 16C house where Loti used to stay, and which he made the home of Gaud, the heroine of *Pêcheur d'Islande*. Go along the Rue de l'Église to see an isolated **bell tower**, all that remains of a former church, in the middle of the Square Botrel. A Merchant Service college (École Nationale de la Marine Marchande) is located in Rue Pierre Loti *(not open to the public)*.

EXCURSIONS

Arcouest Point★★; Bréhat Island★. – *6 km - 4 miles – plus 2-4 hours to cross and visit Bréhat. Leave Paimpol to the north by the D 789.*

Kerroc'h Tower. – *1 km - ¾ mile from the D 789. ¼ hour on foot Rtn.* From the first platform there is a fine **view★** of Paimpol Bay.

Ploubazlanec. – Pop 3 507. In the cemetery is a curious ossuary and a pathetic wall on which the names of men lost at sea are recorded.

Pors-Even. – *2 km - 1 mile to the east of Ploubazlanec.* It was in this village that the fisherman lived who was Loti's model for Yann in *Pêcheur d'Islande.*

Arcouest Point★★. – *Facilities p 43.* On the way down to the creek of Arcouest there are remarkable **views★★** of the bay and of Bréhat. Each summer the place is invaded by a colony of artists and men of science and letters.

Bréhat Island★. – *Description p 60.*

Guilben Point. – *2 km - 1 mile to the east. Leave Paimpol by the D 789, Poulafret and the road to the point which ends in a long tongue of land cutting the cove of Paimpol in two.*

Loguivy-de-la-Mer. – *5 km - 3 miles to the north. Leave Paimpol by the D 786, then take D 15 to the left.* This little lobster fishing port, which has a certain distinction, is simply a creek in which boats are grounded at low tide. Climb the promontory that encloses the creek on the left to get a view of the mouth of the Trieux River, Bréhat and the many islands.

Beauport Abbey; Bilfot Point. – *11 km - 7 miles to the east. Leave Paimpol by the D 786. On leaving Kérity, in a bend to the right, take the road to the abbey on the left.*

Beauport Abbey. – *Open Easter, Whitsun and 1 July to 15 September, 9am to noon and 2 to 7pm. Admission: 3F.*

The large-scale ruins of the Beauport Abbey, which was founded in the 13C by the Premonstratensians, stand in an attractive green setting.

Of the 13 and 14C church only the façade, the nave, the north aisle and the north transept remain. There are some early gravestones. The long chapterhouse with its polygonal apse, lying to the east of the cloisters, is an excellent example of a Norman Gothic chapterhouse. In the northwest corner of the cloisters, to the right of the three fine tiers-point arches which stood above the lavabo, is the dignified entrance to the big refectory which looked out over the sea.

Continue on the D 786, after 1 km - ½ mile turn left towards Ste-Barbe.

Ste-Barbe. – The sea can be seen from the small square of the chapel whose porch is decorated with a statue of St. Barbara. A path, 250 m farther on takes you to a viewing table from where one can see beyond the meadow, Paimpol Bay and its nearby islands, the oyster-beds, Port-Lazo and Lost-Pic Lighthouse.

Return to the D 786. At Plouézec, turn left onto the D 77 and left again to Port-Lazo.

Port-Lazo. – At the end of the road there is a view of Paimpol Bay and Lémenez Island.

Return to the D 77, bear left towards Bilfot Point.

Bilfot Point. – From the viewing table, the **view★** extends westwards to the Talbert Spit and eastwards to Cape Fréhel. Paimpol Bay is enlivened by the trawlers which sail between the Lost-Pic Lighthouse and the Paon Lighthouse at Bréhat.

PAIMPONT Forest ★

Michelin map **230** 38, 39

The Forest of Paimpont – the ancient "Brocéliande" where, according to the songs of the Middle Ages, the sorcerer Merlin and the fairy Viviane lived *(details about Merlin and Viviane, p 22)* – is all that remains in the east of the great forest which, in the early centuries of our era, still covered a large part of inner Brittany extending from Rennes to Carhaix, almost 140 km - 85 miles distant. The cutting and clearing that went on for centuries have reduced the forest so that it now only covers an area of 6 600 ha - 25 sq miles. Recently great areas have been replanted with conifers which will increase the industry of the massif.

A few charming corners remain, especially near the many pools, round which the trees have been left untouched. Such places give us some idea of the forest's former glory.

Situated on the southern edge of the forest is the **Coëtquidan-St-Cyr Camp** at which are based the French military officers' training college of St. Cyr and the Inter-Arms School.

■ SETTINGS AND SIGHTS

Baranton Fountain. – Water from the Baranton fountain spilling over "Merlin's steps" (Perron de Merlin – a stone at the edge of the fountain) was said to unleash wild storms.

Comper Castle. – The castle was said to be the birthplace of the fairy Viviane. Exhibitions of painting and Breton art during the season. *Not open to the public.*

Paimpont. – Pop 1 559. This market village deep in the forest, near a pool surrounded by great trees, dates from the time of the Revolution. It owes its origin to the foundation of a monastery on the site in the 7C. This became an abbey at the end of the 12C and continued until the Revolution. The abbey church built in the 13C has been altered many times. Inside you will see fine wood-work and a 17C high altar, 15, 16 and 17C statues and in the sacristy a statue dating from the 15C, of St. Anne bearing the Virgin Mary and the Infant Jesus, and a 15C silver reliquary. There is also a remarkable 17C

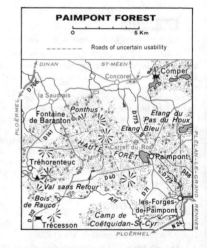

PAIMPONT FOREST

0   5 Km

―――――― Roads of uncertain usability

ivory Crucifix *(the treasure is open from 9am to noon and 3 to 7pm from June to 15 September).* *The 17C north wing of the abbey, which has recently been restored, contains the town hall and the presbytery.*

Les Forges de Paimpont. – A picturesque village by a pool.

Trécesson Castle. – *Not open to the public.* The 15C building, surrounded by its pool, has kept its mediaeval character.

Tréhorenteuc. – Mosaics and pictures in the church and the sacristy depict the legend of the Valley of no Return and the Baranton fountain.

Rauco Wood and Valley of No Return (Bois de Rauco et Vals sans Retour). – Very picturesque settings. In the Valley the witch, Morgane, is said to have entrapped wicked youths to punish them.

PARISH CLOSES ** (ENCLOS PAROISSIAUX)

Michelin map **230** 4, 5, 18, 19

This trip will be of most interest to lovers of church architecture. Among the parish closes, which are a special feature of Breton art, the most interesting are St-Thégonnec, Guimiliau and Lampaul-Guimiliau.

Lovers of fine landscape will also not be disappointed, for the route runs through the picturesque Arrée Mountains and leads to the Trévezel Rock, from which there is the finest view of inner Brittany, as well as going to the remarkable site of Huelgoat.

TOUR

Round tour of 130 km - 81 miles – about 1 day – Local map below

The tour which we describe, with Morlaix as the starting point, can also be made starting from Landerneau or Huelgoat. Part of the ride is through the Armorique Regional Nature Park.

Morlaix*. – *Description p 126.*

St-Thégonnec**. – *Description p 175.*

Guimiliau**. – *Description p 104.*

On the outskirts of Guimiliau, before the bridge under the railway, note lower down on your left a fine fountain decorated with three figures.

Lampaul-Guimilau*. – *Description p 104.*

Landivisiau. – *Description p 113.*

Bodilis. – Pop 1 344. *5 km - 3 miles – plus ¼ hour visit. Leave Landivisiau by the D 32 on the west; after 2 km - 1 mile turn right on D 30.* The **church*** (16C) is preceded by a Flamboyant tower pierced with three openings at the base. The large sacristy, jutting out from the north aisle, is a 17C addition. It is very handsome, with a roof in the shape of an inverted hull, a richly decorated cornice and buttresses ornamented with niches. A fine porch opens on the south side. Inside, the chief decorations are the carved beams and gilded altarpieces. The font is carved from Kersanton granite.

On your way back, avoid Landivisiau and follow D 30 as far as N 12, into which you turn right. In the Élorn Valley the road follows the river, which runs between grassy slopes.

Brézal Mill (Moulin de Brézal). – *½ hour on foot Rtn.* Leave your car at Pont-Christ and take a lane that climbs to the right. The mill, which has an interesting façade with a Flamboyant doorway, stands in a pleasant setting, near a pool.

3 km - 2 miles after Pont-Christ turn left to La Roche.

La Roche*. – *Time: ½ hour.* The village, lying on the flank of a ridge, is dominated by the ruins of a castle. The **parish close*** has a 16C church with a fine **porch*** on the right decorated with grapes and statuettes of saints. There is a good view from the terrace on the left of the building. Inside is a remarkable Renaissance **rood-screen***; behind the altar, a great 16C **stained glass window***. The panelled vault is interesting, with its carved struts and beams. The 17C **ossuary*** is one of the largest in Brittany. It shows Death threatening a group of little figures representing the classes of society. A laconic inscription proclaims: "I'll kill you all."

Turn back and return by the main road to Landerneau.

Landerneau. – *Description p 112.*

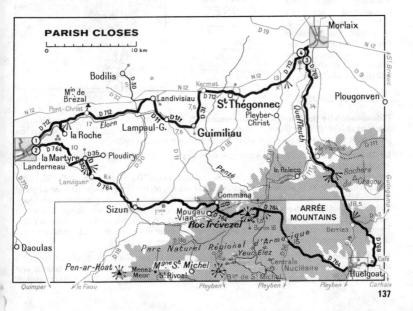

La Martyre★. – Pop 527. *Time: ¼ hour.* The triumphal arch of the **parish close★** is surmounted by a Calvary. The church has a fine **porch★** on its south side and interesting woodwork inside (pulpit, canopy and triumphal arch); also 16C **stained glass windows★**. The ossuary chapel is 17C and stands next to the porch, but is in poor repair. A *pardon* is held on the second Sunday in May and the second Sunday in July.

Ploudiry. – Pop 677. *1.5 km - 1 mile by the D 35 – plus ¼ hour visit.* Ploudiry has an interesting close. The 17C ossuary has a façade ornamented with a Dance of Death. The church has a fine **porch★** (1665) on the south side; Renaissance stalls inside. The high altar, behind which should be noticed the window of the Crucifixion, and the side altars, are good specimens of 17C Breton art.

Soon after La Martyre there is a general **view★** of the Arrée Mountains, ending with the Ménez-Hom on the right. At the crossroads at Lanviguer turn left on D 764.

Sizun★. – Pop 1 871. *Facilities p 44. Guided tour of the parish close every evening at nightfall from 1 July to 15 September.* The most interesting features of the **close★** are the 16C **triumphal arch★** and the 16C **ossuary chapel★**. The 17C church is joined by a passage to the sacristy, which is isolated. The base of the apse is decorated with a sculptured frieze. Inside, at the bases of the panelled vaults, statuettes stand on the decorated carved beams.

Commana. – Pop 1 262. *Time: ¼ hour. Out of season ask for the key at the presbytery.* The village stands on an isolated foothill of the Arrée Mountains. Within the close is a 16-17C **church★** with a fine south porch. Inside are three interesting altarpieces of which the most remarkable is the one on the altar to St. Anne (1682).

Mougau-Vian. – *Take the lane which branches off the D 764 opposite the D 11, coming from Commana.* You will find a fine covered alleyway with pillars carved on the inside.

1 km - ½ mile from the crossroads of the D 764 and the D 785 (going towards Quimper), turn right. Leave the car opposite a bench mark of the French Ordnance Survey.

Trévezel Rock★★. – *Description p 179.*

Return to the D 764 on the right.

Huelgoat★. – *Description p 107.*

3.5 km - 2 miles from Huelgoat, opposite a café, turn left into the D 769. This picturesque road runs through the State forest and affords, after the village of Berrien, a pretty view on the right of the Arrée Mountains, and ahead, of the rugged rocks of Le Cragou. On the northern slope of the Arrée Mountains the road goes down to Morlaix into a pleasant valley.

PERROS-GUIREC ★★

Michelin 230 6, 7 – *Local map p 65* – Pop 7 793 – *Facilities p 43*

This much frequented seaside resort built in the form of an amphitheatre overlooks the fishing and pleasure boat harbour, the anchorage and the two well sheltered beaches of Trestraou and Trestrignel. The gently sloping, fine sand beaches are excellent for children.

Church (A). – Partly Romanesque.

Town Hall (H). – *Apply at the Tourist Information Centre.* Modern paintings and a painting by a local artist, Maurice Denis, in the Council Chamber.

Château Point. – Steep little viewpoint.

Viewing Table (Table d'orientation). – There is a splendid **view★** of the Château Point, the Trestrignel beach, Port-Blanc, Trélevern, Trévou, Tomé Island, the Seven Islands and of the rocks below.

PERROS-GUIREC

0   500 m

Bons-Enfants (R. des) ___ 2
Foch (R. du Mar.) ___ 5
Gaulle (R. du Gén.-de) ___ 6
Joffre (R. du Mar.) ___
Le-Bihan (Bd Joseph) ___ 7
Le-Braz (R. A.) ___ 8
Leclerc (R. du Gén.) ___ 9
Renan (R. Ernest) ___ 20
Rohellou (R. de) ___ 22

EXCURSIONS

Ploumanach by the Sentier des Douaniers★★. – *2½ hours on foot Rtn. Go preferably in the morning at high tide.* Follow the edge of the cliff on foot as far as Pors-Rolland to reach the lighthouse via the Squewel Point. *Description of Ploumanach p 142.*

La Clarté★. – *3 km - 2 miles to the west. Leave Perros by ②, D 788, and 500 m farther on turn left in the Rue de la Clarté.*
The pretty rose granite **Chapel of Notre-Dame-de-la-Clarté** stands 200 m back from the D 788. In the 16C the lord of Barac'h, whose ship was in danger in a fog off the coast, vowed to build a chapel to Our Lady at whatever spot on the coast first emerged from the fog. The promised chapel was built on the height which enabled him to take his bearings; to commemorate the circumstances, it was called Our Lady of Light (Notre-Dame-de-la-Clarté). A *pardon* is held every year *(p 10)*. There is a fine **panorama★** to be seen from the viewing table at the top of a rocky knoll near the chapel *(10 minutes on foot Rtn)*. Nearby are large rose granite quarries.

Signal Station★. – *3.5 km - 2½ miles to the west. Leave Perros-Guirec by ②, D 788.* From the roadside the **view★** extends to the rocks of Ploumanach, seawards to the Seven Islands and backwards to the beaches of Perros-Guirec, and in the distance along the Port-Blanc coastline.

Louannec. – Pop 1 619. *5 km - 3 miles to the east.* In the church *(closed Sunday afternoons),* where St. Yves once was the parish priest, to the right of the altar, there is a carved wood group of the early 15C, showing St. Yves standing between a rich and a poor man. In the presbytery is an ancient chasuble said to have belonged to St. Yves.

The Seven Islands (Sept-Iles — Réserve Chappelier). – *From June to mid-September launches make a tour of the islands starting from Trestraou beach.*

The largest of the Seven Islands is the **Monks' Island** (Ile aux Moines) where you may visit the lighthouse and the fort erected by Vauban. The other islands: Bono, Malban, Plate Island, the Cerf and Rouzic are a sea bird sanctuary *(launches forbidden).* One can see brown and herring gulls, kittiwakes, petrels, a large colony of gannets as well as a few penguins, guillemots, puffins and shags who escaped the *Torrey-Canyon* and *Amoco-Cadiz* disasters.

PLEUMEUR-BODOU

Michelin map **230** 6 – *Local map p 65* – Pop 2 941

This small village between Lannion and Penvern has given its name to an important Earth station for satellite communication, which is situated 2 km - 1 mile to the north.

Space Telecommunications Station of Pleumeur-Bodou★. – *Guided tour (about 1 hour) of the equipment, showing of a working model and film; July and August 9am to noon and 1.45 to 6pm; the rest of the year 9 to 11am and 2 to 4.45pm. Closed from 16 October to Easter and on Tuesdays except in June, July and August. Admission: 4F.*

Built at the request of the National Telecommunications Research Organisation (CNET) the station was to play an important role in the first demonstrations of intercontinental television transmission. The first programmes were received via the satellite *Telstar* on the 11 June 1962. A monument in the form of a menhir commemorates the occasion. Isolated on the Breton heath, the equipment is highly impressive: the great white radar dome big enough to contain the Arc de Triomphe of Paris, transmits the necessary waves and houses a 340 ton antenna.

The centre has been greatly developed since 1962 and the French Post Office (PTT) now has at its disposal five antennae for telephone, telegraph, television and data transmission by means of the satellites at an altitude of 30 000 km - 18 640 miles above the Equator.

PLEYBEN ★★

Michelin map **230** 18, 19 – *Local map p 50* – Pop 3 911 – *Facilities p 44*

The great feature of Pleyben is its magnificent parish close *(details of closes p 32),* built from the 15 to the 17C. *Pardon* on the first Sunday in August.

- ### PARISH CLOSE★★ *time: ½ hour*

Calvary★★. – Built in 1555 near the side entrance to the church, it was displaced in 1738 and given its present form in 1743. Since then new motifs and scenes have been added to the monument: the Last Supper and Washing of the Disciples' Feet date from 1650. The enormous base with its triumphal doorway gives ample space for the harmonious presentation of the figures on top of it and allows them to stand out clearly against the sky. To follow the life of Christ start at the corner with the Visitation where the Virgin is holding Elizabeth's hand and move in an anticlockwise direction to discover the Nativity, the Adoration of the Shepherds, etc.

Church★. – The church is dominated by two belfries, of which that on the right is the more remarkable. It is a Renaissance **tower★★** crowned with a dome with small lantern turrets *(illustration p 28).*

The other tower has a Gothic spire. Beyond the south transept is a curious sacristy, dating from 1719, with cupolas and lanterns.

Inside, the nave is roofed with 16C carved and painted **panelling★**, the beam is decorated with mythological and religious scenes. At the high altar is

(After Dr le Thomas photo)

Pleyben. — The beam.

an altarpiece with turrets and a two storey tabernacle. At the centre of the east end is a **stained glass window★** depicting the Passion. Other items of interest include the pulpit and the organ case (18C), the group representing the Baptism of Christ over the font and the many statues.

Funeral Chapel. – A former 16C ossuary. Exhibitions from June to September.

PLOËRMEL ★

Michelin map **230** 38 – Pop 7 022 – *Facilities p 44*

This little town which was once the seat of the Dukes of Brittany is interesting for its church and old houses. A statue has been raised to Dr. Guérin, citizen of Ploërmel, who devised lint surgical dressings which saved many wounded in the Franco-Prussian War of 1870.

St-Armel★ (*AZ* A). – St. Armel, who founded the town in the 6C, is shown taming a dragon which he leads away with his stole.

The building dates from the 16C. The much carved left **doorway★** is remarkable. Among the scenes depicted are a shoemaker sewing up his wife's mouth, a woman pulling off her husband's cap, a sow playing bagpipes, and the boy who cries and the boy who laughs.

The eight magnificent 16 and 17C **stained glass windows★** of the church have been reset. In the chapel to the north of the chancel are white marble statues of Dukes John II and John III of Brittany (14C). In the south transept, behind the Kersanton granite tomb of Philip of Montauban and his wife, is a fine 14C recumbent figure in white marble.

PLOËRMEL★

Old Houses. – In the Rue Beaumanoir, so-called in memory of the hero of the Battle of the Thirty *(p 108)* are to be found the 16C **Marmousets Mansion★** (AY **B**) adorned with woodcarvings, and the 16C former house of the Dukes of Brittany. Other old houses may be seen in the Rue des Francs-Bourgeois and the Place de l'Union.

Astronomical Clock (AZ **C**). – Placed in the inner courtyard of an abbey founded in 1818 it was created between 1852 and 1855 and was intended for the instruction of the future teachers of the coastal schools.

Duc Pool. – *2.5 km - 1½ miles to the north. Leave Ploërmel by* ⑦, *the D 8.* Locally known as "the lake" it is a popular excursion place. There is an artificial beach and a water sports centre.

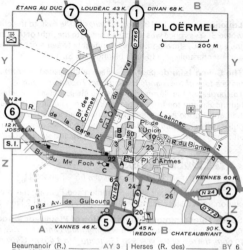

PLOËRMEL

Beaumanoir (R.)	AY 3
Député-J.-de-Rohan (R. du)	AZ 5
Dubreton (R. du Gén.)	AZ 6
Forges (R. des)	BZ 7
Francs-Bourgeois (R. des)	AY 8
Gare (R. de la)	AY
Gaulle (R. Gén. de)	AZ 9
Herses (R. des)	BY 6
Hôtel-de-Ville (Pl. de l')	BZ 10
Lamennais (Pl.)	AY 20
Patarins (R. des)	BZ 22
St-Armel (R.)	BY 24
Sénéchal-Thuault (R.)	BZ 25
Union (R. de l')	AY 32

PLOUGASNOU

Michelin map **230** 5 – Pop 3 368 – *Facilities p 43*

Plougasnou is a small seaside resort with a beach 800 m - ½ mile from the town centre.

Church. – For the most part a 16C building, opening on to the square through a Renaissance porch.

Oratory of Notre-Dame-de-Lorette. – *300 m from the church.* Granite building (1611), with a stone roof.

EXCURSION

Primel-Trégastel★; Térénez. – *Round tour of 16 km - 10 miles – about 1½ hours. Leave Plougasnou by the Ste-Barbe road to the north.*

    Ste-Barbe. – *Description p 147.*

    Primel-Trégastel★ and **Primel Point.★** – *Description p 147.*

Follow the D 46 and the coast where you will come across the Primel oyster-beds.

    Diben Point. – *Description p 147.*

The route passes on the right the attractive Guersit beach and the road down to the beach of St-Samson before reaching Terénez.

    Térénez. – Very pleasant little port which is typically Breton.

Return to Plougasnou by Kerenot.

PLOUGASTEL-DAOULAS ★

Michelin map **230** 17 – *Local maps pp 47, 64 and 141* – Pop 8 223 – *Facilities p 43*

Plougastel is the centre of a strawberry growing district; part of the crop is sent to Great Britain.

Calvary★★. – *Details and illustration p 32.* The Cross was inspired by the Guimiliau Calvary, but is more harmonious, though its 180 figures are perhaps less lifelike. It was built in 1602-4 to commemorate the end of the Plague of 1598. On either side of the Cross, the two thieves are surmounted by an angel and a devil respectively. On the Calvary base an altar is carved.

    The church is built of granite and reinforced concrete; inside it is brilliant with blue, green, orange and violet all used in its decoration. The furnishings include altars and wooden altarpieces.

EXCURSIONS

St-Jean. – *4.5 km - 3 miles to the northeast by D 33[A], D 29 and 500 m from the crossroads, a road leading off to the left (signpost).* The chapel stands in a **setting★** of greenery on the banks of the Élorn. The Dreff fountain nearby was once a Druids' fountain.

Plougastel Peninsula★. – *Round tour of 34 km - 21 miles – about 2½ hours – Local map p 141.* Lying away from main roads, the Plougastel Peninsula is a corner where the Breton countryside may be seen in its traditional guise.

    Narrow, winding roads run between hedges through farming country, characteristically cut up into squares. There are few houses apart from occasional hamlets grouped round their little chapels, where interesting *pardons* are held and collections of little saints, carved in wood, can be seen *(pp 22 and 23)*. Here everything seems hidden away; you are deep in the strawberry country, but you will not see the strawberries, which grow in open fields, unless you get out of your car and look through the gaps in the hedges.

    In May and June, however, when the strawberries are picked, there is plenty of life on the roads; often, at a turning, you will come upon lorries fitted with open racks in which the little baskets of strawberries are carefully packed.

Nowadays only the old women wear the local black dress and scarf, but the tourist who is able to enter the houses will still see Breton furniture in its proper setting standing next to modern furniture and fittings.

Leave Plougastel-Daoulas to the southwest.

Kernisi panorama. – At the entrance to the hamlet of Kernisi, after a group of houses, turn right and follow the signposts along the path. Turn right into a path where the wall bends. About 150 m farther on take the path leading off to the left with a low wall on the right. This brings you to a knoll from which you will see a panorama of the Brest roadstead, the outer harbour and town of Brest, the Élorn estuary and the Albert Louppe Bridge.

Ste-Christine. – *To visit the chapel ask for the key from Mme Perramant.* On the Sunday following 23 July there is an interesting *pardon* here, with a procession in traditional dress. Inside are old painted wooden statues.

Caro Cove (Anse de Caro). – View of the Espagnols Point, which forms the south shore of the Brest Sound.

Kerdeniel panorama**. – *Leave your car directly you are past the houses and walk up the hill.* From left to right you will see the Faou estuary, the Ménez-Hom, the Espagnols Point, Brest and the Élorn estuary. Below are the Armorique Point and Ronde Island.

PLOUGASTEL PENINSULA

St-Adrien. – *To visit the chapel ask for the key from M. Gourmelon.* An interesting *pardon* takes place on the second Sunday in May. Notice, inside, fine woodwork, round the choir two triptychs (one of St. Martin) and old painted wood statues.

St-Guénolé. – *To visit enquire at Mme Runavot's house in St-Guénolé.* In a picturesque setting. There is a *pardon* on the first Sunday in May. Inside, you will see curious painted wood statues characteristic of the chapels in the peninsula.

Keramenez panorama*. – Take an uphill lane which prolongs the road and goes across the fields to the top of the ridge. An extensive panorama *(viewing table)* shows, from left to right, the estuaries of the Daoulas and Le Faou Rivers, the Ménez-Hom, and the Roscanvel Peninsula; in the foreground is the Plougastel Peninsula, with Lauberlac'h cove, the hamlet of St-Adrien, and, beyond, the Armorique Point.

Go back to your car and turn round.

PLOUHA

Michelin map **230** 8 – Pop 4 310

This village has many little villas standing in well kept gardens which belong to Navy pensioners.

EXCURSIONS

Kermaria*; Lanleff*. – *11 km - 7 miles to the west – plus ½ hour visit. Leave by D 21.*

Kermaria*. – *Description p 110.*

Lanleff*. – Pop 88. The **Temple***, a curious circular building, now in ruins, is a former chapel or baptistery built in the 12C on the model of the Holy Sepulchre in Jerusalem. Twelve round arched arcades connect the rotunda with a circular aisle.

Port-Moguer. – *3.5 km - 2 miles to the northwest.*
From the end of the jetty there is a good view of the coast, with cliffs up to 100 m - 320 ft high.

Le Palus-Plage. – *4 km - 2½ miles to the east. Leave by the St-Quay-Portrieux road and turn left into the D 32.*
To the left of the beach a stairway cut in the rock leads to an upper path from which there are good views.

Lanloup; Bréhec-en-Plouha. – *7.5 km - 4½ miles to the north. Leave by the road to Paimpol.*

Lanloup. – Pop 236. The 15-16C church *(closed Sunday afternoons)* has a porch adorned with statues of the Apostles *(details on porches p 29)*. The twelve Apostles in granite precede the doorway dominated by a 14C Virgin. In the cemetery are an old Calvary and the tomb of the composer Guy Ropartz (1864-1955).

The D 54 leads to Bréhec-en-Plouha.

Bréhec-en-Plouha. – *Facilities p 43.* A little harbour and a modest seaside resort. It was at Bréhec that St. Brieuc and the first emigrants from Britain landed in the 5C *(p 20)*.

*With this guide use the **Michelin** map (scale 1:200 000) shown on p 3.*

PLOUMANACH ★★

Michelin map **230** 6 – *Local map p 65* – *Facilities p 43*

This little fishing port, well situated at the mouths of the two picturesque Traouiéros Valleys, has become a well known seaside resort, famous for its piles of rose and grey **rocks**★★ *(details p 64: Geological Notes)*. You will get a good view of them by going to the lighthouse.

Beach. – The beach lies in the Bay of St-Guirec. At the far end on the left, on a rock washed by the sea at high tide, stands the oratory dedicated to St. Guirec, who landed here in the 6C *(p 20)*. A granite statue of the Saint has taken the place of the original wooden effigy which had suffered from a disrespectful tradition: girls who wanted to get married stuck a pin into his nose.

Bastille Promenade. – *Entrance opposite the Chapel of St-Guirec.* This promenade leads to another part of the rocks and gives a better view of the entrance to the harbour. On a small island stands Costaeres' modern manor in which Sienkiewicz, the author of *Quo Vadis*, used to live.

The Lighthouse. – Go down to the beach, pass in front of the Hôtel St-Guirec and follow the uphill path which soon runs along the coast to the lighthouse, passing among splendid **rocks**★★.

Open 2 to 6.30pm in July and August.

From the platform the view extends from Trégastel to the beach at Trestel and beyond it to the coast towards Port-Blanc, taking in the Seven Islands and the Perros-Guirec Peninsula.

Municipal Park★★. – *To get there, turn left, as you come back from the lighthouse, into a path which skirts the fence of a villa.* This park extends from Pors-Kamor, where the lifeboat is kept, to Pors-Rolland. It is a sort of reserve where the rocky site is kept in its original state. The most interesting feature is the Squewel Point, formed of innumerable rocks separated by coves. The Devil's Castle (Château du Diable) also makes a fine picture.

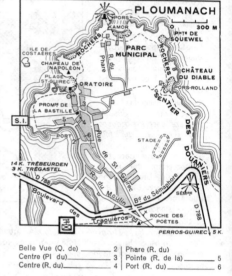

Belle Vue (Q. de)	2	Phare (R. du)
Centre (Pl du)	3	Pointe (R. de la) _____ 5
Centre (R. du)	4	Port (R. du) _____ 6

EXCURSION

Perros-Guirec by the Sentier des Douaniers★. – *2½ hours on foot Rtn. Go preferably in the afternoon at high tide.*

A path along the edge of the cliff leads from Pors-Rolland to Trestraou, the main beach of Perros-Guirec *(p 142)*.

PONT-AVEN ★

Michelin map **230** 33 – Pop 3 561 – *Facilities p 44*

The town lies in a very pleasant setting at the point where the River Aven, after flowing between rocks, opens out into a tidal estuary. The Aven used to drive numerous mills; hence the saying: "Pont-Aven, a famous town; fourteen mills, fifteen houses".

The place has been a favourite resort of painters; the Pont-Aven school, headed by Gauguin, was formed in about 1888. The poet and song writer Théodore Botrel spent a great part of his life there and started the Gorse-Bloom Festival (Fête des Fleurs d'Adjoncs), which draws many visitors *(p 10)*.

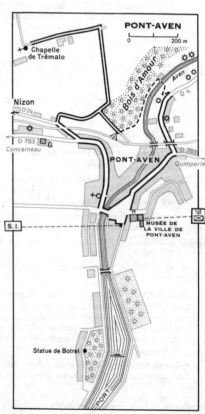

■ **SIGHTS** *time: 1 hour*

Museum. – *Open 16 June to 15 September, 10am to 12.30pm amd 3 to 7pm. Admission: 3F. Go through the town hall courtyard.*

Temporary exhibitions are shown in the four galleries (paintings by the Pont-Aven school and sometimes by Gauguin).

Bois d'Amour★. – *Follow the arrows at the entrance of the viaduct.* All along the walk posts indicate places which inspired painters of the Pont-Aven school. Enter the Bois d'Amour by the path which leads to the Trémalo Chapel and the Rue de la Villemarqué which commands a good view of Pont-Aven. The Bois d'Amour borders the Aven and covers a hill.

Trémalo Chapel. – *Leave Pont-Aven by the D 24 and take an uphill road to the right. Out of season ask for the key at the farm.* The Chapel of Trémalo is a characteristic Breton country chapel, set amid fine trees. It has a lop-sided roof, with one of the eaves nearly touching the ground. Inside is a 16C wooden figure of Christ which was the model for Gauguin's *Yellow Christ.*

EXCURSIONS

Nizon. – *3 km - 2 miles to the west. Leave Pont-Aven by the D 24.* The little Nizon church with its squat pillars has been given fine modern furnishings. The colours of the modern stained glass windows by the master glass maker Guérel are remarkable. The Calvary was also used as a model by Gauguin for his *Green Christ.*
Return by Kerzog and the N 783.

Port-Manech. – *25 km - 15 miles to the west. Leave Port Aven by the Concarneau road (D 783).* After 2.5 km - 1½ miles turn left into the D 77 which goes through **Névez** (in the church is a mural of the Crucifixion by André Even). A road on the left leads to Kerdruc.

Kerdruc*. – *Facilities p 42.* Small harbour in a good setting and still possessing some old thatched cottages.
Return to the D 77, after 650 m turn right towards Kerascoët.

Kerascoët. – This calm hamlet has many thatched farms several of which have been restored.
Continue along the road (track) towards the chapel at Tremorvezen, turn right and then left to reach the D 77 which you take to the right towards Port-Manech.

Port-Manech. – *Facilities p 42.* A charming, quiet and very pleasant resort with a well sited beach on the edge of the woods on the banks of the Aven. A path links the port to the beach.

Belon. – *17 km - 11 miles to the east. Take the D 783 to Riec-sur-Belon then the D 24. 1 km; ½ mile before Moëlan-sur-Mer turn right twice then after 4 km - 2½ miles take the road sign-posted Belon.*

Lying on the south bank of the Belon this locality is famous as an oyster-farming centre *(p 18).* The oyster-beds on the north bank can be seen at low tide.

Place to stay
A wide variety of places to stay
– pleasure boat harbours and resorts –
have been selected to make your holiday more pleasant.
A map on pp 40-41 shows the location of the places listed on pp 41-44.

PONTCHÂTEAU
Michelin map **230** 52, 53 – Pop 6 520

The Church of Pontchâteau, perched on a hill in a region of windmills, overlooks the little town with its houses built in terraces on the banks of the Brivet River.

EXCURSION

The Magdalene Calvary. – *4 km - 2½ miles to the west. Leave Pontchâteau on the D 33.* St. Louis-Marie Grignion de Montfort, a famous preacher, had the Calvary built in 1709. Beside the Calvary, a small chapel *(pilgrimages from June to mid-October)* contains the original wooden statue of Christ (1707).

From the Temple of Jerusalem, an alley crosses the park and leads to Pilate's Court. It is the first station in the Stations of the Cross which, farther on (on the left) are continued and symbolised by large white statues. From the foot of the Calvary the view extends to the Brière, St-Nazaire and Donges.

PONTIVY
Michelin map **230** 22 – Pop 14 323

This little town stands on the Blavet in a green, pleasant and picturesque area. The old town, with its narrow, winding streets, contrasts with the geometrical town plan laid out by Napoléon.

Napoléonville. – Pontivy was a prosperous town and in 1790 declared wholeheartedly for the Republic. Napoleon, who was Consul at the time, knew the local feeling and was interested in the position of this city in the centre of the province; he had a barracks, a town hall, a court and a school built and, to ensure communication with the sea, he had the Blavet canalised.

During the wars of the First Empire coastal navigation between Brest and Nantes was very dangerous because of British cruisers in the Channel. Napoleon therefore decided to build a canal between the two ports. As Pontivy was about halfway between them, the Emperor also decided to develop it into a town that would be the military and strategic centre of Brittany.

From 1806 the straight roads of the new town could be seen as they were dug out of the ground. The grateful townspeople called the city "Napoléonville". But the fall of the Empire stopped the building and Napoléonville became Pontivy once more. It changed again under the Second Empire to Napoléonville but in due course reverted again.

■ **SIGHTS** *time:* ¾ *hour*

Place du Martray (19). – This square, the centre of old Pontivy, is bordered with old houses.

Notre-Dame-de-Joie. – Church in the Flamboyant style (16C).

Old houses. – Rue du Pont; Rue du Fil.

Castle. – *Open 15 April to 15 October, 10am to noon and 2 to 6pm; the rest of the year 2 to 4pm. Closed during November and December and on Mondays and Tuesdays except from June to September. Admission: 2F (not including exhibitions).*

The castle was built in the 15C by Jean II de Rohan *(p 109).* The façade is flanked by two large towers and the ramparts with walls 20 m - 64 ft high are paralleled by a moat.

EXCURSIONS

Guerlédan Lake★★. – *Round tour of 67 km - 42 miles – about 3 hours – Local map p 103. Leave Pontivy by* ① *on the plan, the D 767. After 8 km - 5 miles turn left towards Le Stumo, cross the Nantes–Brest canal on the Stumo bridge. Take the D 156 to the right. At Le Corboulo, turn right; 500 m farther on, at the Quénécan bridge, turn left into the D 31 to St-Aignan. Description p 103.*

Return to Pontivy by the D 767.

Stival. – *3.5 km - 2 miles – about ½ hour. Leave Pontivy by* ⑥ *on the plan, the D 764.* The former St. Mériadec Chapel, now the parish church, dates from the 16C. The fine **stained glass windows★** of the south transept and the chancel, a 16C Virgin and Child and a 17C St. Isidore should all be seen. A copper bell dating from the 7 or 8C and said to have belonged to St. Mériadec, is kept in the sacristy *(apply at the sexton's, opposite the church).* This bell is rung in front of the deaf and it is then put on their heads. *Pardon* on Trinity Sunday.

Caïnain (R.)	2	Leperdit (R.)	16
Couvent (Quai du)	3	Lorois (R.)	17
Fil (R. du)	5	Marengo (R. de)	18
Friedland (R.)	6	Martray (Pl. du)	19
Haucourt (Av. d')	8	Mun (R. Albert de)	20
Iéna (R. d')	9	Nationale (R.)	
Jaurès (R. Jean)	12	Niémen (Quai)	21
Le-Bris (R. Joseph)	13	Pont (R. du)	22
Leclerc (Av. Gén.)	14	Presbourg (Quai)	23
Le-Goff (R.)	15	Viollard (Bd)	28

Blavet Valley. – *Round tour of 40 km - 25 miles – about 2 hours. Leave Pontivy by* ④ *on the plan, the N 168.*

St-Nicomède. – *Time:* ¼ *hour. To visit the chapel, ask for the key at the house abutting on the church apse.* The 16C chapel is preceded by a massive tower with a granite steeple. A Renaissance doorway leading to a 16C staircase opens at the base of the tower which can be climbed. Inside, a cornice carved with angels and musicians runs round the base of the panelled vault. There are altarpieces in the north transept and at the high altar. To the left of the chapel a Gothic fountain discharges into three basins in front of three niches surmounted by richly carved gables. *Pardon* on the first Sunday in August.

Soon you rejoin the D 1 as it winds downhill.

St-Nicolas-des-Eaux. – The little town is built on the side of a hill. With its chapel at the top end of the town, surrounded by the thatched roofs of the houses, St-Nicolas-des-Eaux is certainly unusual. The road crosses the Blavet, and following the tongue of land encircled by the river bends back on itself before crossing to the narrow isthmus which overlooks the inner banks of the loop.

Castennec Site★. – From the belvedere there is a magnificent view of the valley and St-Nicolas-des-Eaux.

Turn left after Castennec.

Bieuzy. – Pop 886. The church with its high, modern tower looks even taller since it stands on an islet. The tall 16C chevet, marred by a war memorial, has Renaissance Gothic ornament. The stained glass windows form an attractive series and the woodwork and beams are also worth looking at.

PONTIVY (EXCURSIONS)

Go to Melrand by the D 156 and La Paule.

Melrand. – Pop 1 883. Turn left then take the D 142 on the right going towards Guémené in order to cross this typically Breton town and reach the Calvary. At the top is the Holy Trinity; the shaft is ornamented with representations of the heads of the Apostles; the base depicts the Entombment and Christ bearing the Cross. The whole stands on another base which bears two more recent statues of the Virgin and St. John.

Follow the D 2 for 6.5 km - 4 miles then turn left.

Quelven. – The chapel was built at the end of the 15C and stands surrounded by old granite houses. It contains a 16C alabaster low relief in the chapel and an opening statue of Our Lady of Quelven which has within it twelve low reliefs depicting the life of Christ. In the chancel are two 16C stained glass windows.
A very popular *pardon* is held on 15 August.

Ste-Noyale; Notre-Dame-de-Timadeuc Abbey. – *Round tour of 41 km - 25 miles – about 1½ hours. Leave Pontivy by the Ste-Noyale road, northeast on the plan.*

Ste-Noyale. – *Under restoration.* Standing in the midst of lawns and trees are Ste-Noyale Chapel, long and narrow *(ask for the key at M. and Mme Pascal Jubin's, Ebéniste-Art)*, the small rectangular Chapel of St-Jean and a granite cross. The group of buildings all date from the 15C and the two chapels are well decorated outside. The west porch of the Ste-Noyale Chapel which supports the belfry is less beautiful than the south which is closed by a grille and leads into a skilfully ornamented arcade. The paintings on the panels inside depict the life of St. Noyale.

Noyal-Pontivy. – Pop 2 731. The large church was built in the 15C and has Flamboyant decoration. The massive square tower set on the south transept is surmounted by a tall polygonal stone spire.

Follow the D 2 and 2 km - 1 mile beyond Rohan turn right into the road leading to the abbey.

Notre-Dame-de-Timadeuc Abbey. – Founded by the Trappist Order in 1841. *No visits to the monastic buildings, but the public can attend services. Slides shown with commentary at the Gatehouse.*

Return to Pontivy by the D 2.

PONT-L'ABBÉ

Michelin map **230** 31, 32 – *Local map p 75* – Pop 7 823 – *Facilities p 42*

This town, which stands at the head of an estuary, owes its name to the first bridge built by the monks of Loctudy between the harbour and the pool. It is the capital of the Bigouden district which is bounded by the estuary of the Odet, the coast of Penmarch and Audierne Bay. Bigouden costume is most original *(p 24)*, and lends a picturesque note to ceremonies, *pardons*, markets and fairs. The *coiffe* is frequently worn on weekdays. A local speciality is embroidery on tulle. Dolls in costumes of all the different provinces of France are made here.
Market gardening is the basis of the region's prosperity.

The "Stamped Paper" Revolt (1675). – The glory that Louis XIV won for France cost a lot of money. In 1675 Colbert decreed that all legal acts must be recorded on stamped paper. He also reimposed taxes on tobacco and pewter vessels which Brittany had taken over, a few years before, at a cost of 2 million livres. Anger was great but repression, in the guise of the wheel and the hangman's noose, was powerful; the Parliament that protested was exiled to Vannes. Pont-l'Abbé, in particular, suffered at the suppression of the rebellion; its castle was pillaged.

■ **SIGHTS** *time: 1½ hours*

Notre-Dame-des-Carmes. – Former 14-15C chapel of the Carmelite monastery.
On the right going in, at the back of the façade, stands an 18C font.
Above the high altar is a 15C stained glass window with a rose 7 m - 23 ft in diameter. To the right is a modern processional banner; in the north aisle a 15C Crucifix and also a statue of the Virgin teaching the Child to walk.
As you come out, turn right to go round the church and look at the apse.
Pardon on the Sunday after 15 July.

Castle. – This 14-17C fortress has a large oval tower with a building attached. Go round the tower to see the belfry turret overlooking the Rue du Château.
Inside you may visit the **Bigouden Museum** which has collections of Bigouden costumes and furniture. *Open 1 June to 15 September, 9am to noon and 2 to 7pm. Closed Sundays and holidays. Admission: 2F.*

Bigoudens' Memorial (Monument aux Bigoudens). – Work of the sculptor F. Bazin.

Ruins of Lambourg Church. – A 13-15C building.

EXCURSIONS

Notre-Dame-de-Tréminou. – *2 km - 1 mile to the west. Ask for the key at the presbytery in Plomeur.*
Standing in a shaded close this 14-16C chapel (restored) has a belfry which is set above the nave. Inside a fine 13C arch with triple covings supports the belfry. Decorative angels adorn the stringers and beams.
A *pardon* takes place on the fourth Sunday in September.
Our Lady is invoked for mentally retarded children.

Plomeur. – Pop 2 263. *5.5 km - 3½ miles to the southwest. Leave Pont-L'Abbé by ③, the D 785.*
The Church of Ste-Thumette dates from 1760 and its massive façade is flanked by low turrets. Inside are several 15C statues and a rather strange pregnant Virgin.

PORNICHET ★

Michelin map 230 52 – Local map p 98 – Pop 5 538 – Facilities p 42

Originally a salt-marsh workers' village, Pornichet became a much frequented seaside resort in 1860. The town was known as a place of rendezvous for Parisian editors. The beach is the continuation of the 8 km - 5 mile long stretch of fine sand which encircles the Bay of Amour. A jetty shelters the pleasure boat harbour. The well known racecourse of the Côte d'Amour region stands on now drained marshland.

EXCURSION

Ste-Marguerite. – 3.5 km - 2 miles to the southeast by the D 292. This village nestled in the verdure, has a rock encircled beach.

Collet (Av.)	2
Gravelais (Av.)	3
Mazy (Av. de)	4
Mer (Av. de la)	5
République (Bd de la)	6
Yolande (Av.)	7

PORT-LOUIS

Michelin map 230 34 – Pop 3 720 – Facilities p 42

Port-Louis is a small fishing port and seaside resort where many of the inhabitants of Lorient may be found. It still has its 16C citadel and 17C ramparts.

Port-Louis was originally called Blavet. During the League the Duke of Mercœur captured it with the help of the Spaniards. The women, who had fought beside their men, feared the treatment they would receive from the victors. Some young girls fled in a ship, but the Spaniards saw them and gave chase. Rather than be taken by them, the "forty virgins of Port-Louis" joined hands and jumped into the sea.

It was under Louis XIII that Blavet took the name of Port-Louis in honour of the King. Richelieu made it a fortified port and the headquarters of the first India Company, which failed. When Colbert founded the second Company, Lorient was built to receive it (p 118). From that time on, Port-Louis declined.

Under Louis-Philippe the town found new life in sardine fishing and canning.

The Port. – Coming from the Avenue Marcel-Charrier, turn to the right just before the Church of St-Pierre.

Naval Museum. – Guided tours 10am to noon and 2 to 6pm (5pm 1 October to 31 May). Closed Tuesdays, 1 May, Easter Sunday, Christmas Day and 1 November to 15 December. Admission: 4F.

The museum is installed in the citadel.

Beach. – View of Gâvres Point, Groix Island and the beach of Larmor-Plage.

Castles, châteaux, churches, parish closes will be more interesting if you read the chapter on pp 27-34 on Breton Art.

Le POULIGUEN ★

Michelin map 230 51 – Local map p 101 Pop 4 303 – Facilities p 42

Lying to the west of La Baule, it is separated from the latter by a channel linking the ocean to the salt marshes behind the town. This former fishing village with narrow streets became a fashionable resort in 1854. The beach is sheltered by a pleasant 6 ha - 15 acre wood and the pleasure boat harbour is upstream from La Baule's.

Ste-Anne-et-St-Julien (A). – Open from June to October, at other times apply to the Curé, 1 Rue Guinel. Standing near a Calvary, this Gothic chapel has a 16C **statue of St. Anne** and a stained glass window representing St. Julien.

The Grande Côte★★. – See also p 79. This stretch of coast goes from the Points of Penchâteau to Le Croisic. Skirted by boulevards of footpaths, the coastline alternates rocky parts with great sandy bays and has numerous caves which are accessible only at low tide.

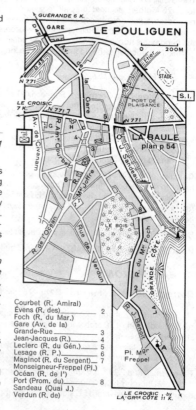

Courbet (R. Amiral)	
Évens (R. des)	2
Foch (R. du Mar.)	
Gare (Av. de la)	
Grande-Rue	3
Jean-Jacques (R.)	4
Leclerc (R. du Gén.)	5
Lesage (R. P.)	6
Maginot (R. du Sergent)	7
Monseigneur-Freppel (Pl.)	
Océan (R. de l')	
Port (Prom. du)	8
Sandeau (Quai J.)	
Verdun (R. de)	

PRIMEL-TRÉGASTEL ★

Michelin map **230** 5

This little seaside resort, with its beach of fine sand, lies in a good setting near a point on which there are piles of rocks comparable with those of Ploumanach and Trégastel.

Primel Point★. – $\frac{1}{4}$ *hour on foot Rtn*. The point is a jumble of pink **rocks**★. From the central spur there is a fine **panorama**★ extending from the Bay of St-Pol-de-Léon to the Trébeurden coast. Out at sea are the Batz Island Lighthouse and the Moines Island (Sept Isles). The end of the point is separated from the rest of the peninsula by a fissure which can be crossed only at low tide at the bottom of which lies a cave.

Ste-Barbe. – *1.5 km - 1 mile to the southeast*. Skirt the beach beyond the Hôtel de la Falaise and follow a by-road which soon begins to climb. Leave your car in the village of Ste-Barbe.

The **view**★ extends from the coast near Roscoff to that of the Bretonne Corniche.

Diben Point. – *2.5 km - 1½ miles to the west – plus ¼ hour on foot Rtn*. Follow D 46 and, after *1 km - ½ mile*, D 46A². At Le Diben, a picturesque fishermen's village, are the big Primel oyster-beds. Pleasure boat harbour. Leave the car to reach the point.

There is a fine view from the rocky point.

QUIBERON Peninsula ★

Michelin map **230** 35, 49

This former island is now attached to the mainland by a narrow isthmus. This natural jetty acts as a breakwater for a great bay which is often used by warships for exercises and firing practice (Polygone de Gâvres).

The landscape of the peninsula varies; the sand dunes of the isthmus are fixed by maritime pines which were greatly damaged during the German occupation in 1944 and 1945. The ocean coast, known as the "Wild Coast" (Côte Sauvage) is an impressive jumble of cliffs, rocks, caves and reefs; to the east and south are wide beaches and two lively fishing ports; in the interior a monotonous landscape of small fields enclosed by uncemented stone walls and low whitewashed houses is broken here and there by an old mill, a chapel or great stones.

Hoche repels the Exiles (July 1795). – Quiberon saw the rout of the Royalists in 1795. The French exiles in England and Germany had made great plans; 100 000 men, led by the princes, were to land in Brittany, join hands with the Chouans and drive out the "Blues". In fact, the British fleet which anchored in the Quiberon roadstead carried only 10 000 men, commanded by Puisaye, Hervilly and Sombreuil. The princes did not come.

The landing began on the beach at Carnac on 27 June and continued for several days. Cadoudal's Chouans *(p 52)* joined them in good time. But the effect of surprise was lost; long preparations and talk among the exiles had warned the Convention; General Hoche was ready, and he drove the invaders back into the peninsula. Driven to the beach at Port-Haliguen, the exiles tried to re-embark. Unfortunately the British ships were prevented by a heavy swell from getting near enough to land. Hoche tried to save them. The Convention refused to pardon them. Some were shot at Quiberon and others were taken to Auray and Vannes and shot there *(p 181)*.

QUIBERON★

Pop 4 723 – *Local map p 148 – Facilities p 42*

A fine sandy beach and a fishing port and departure point for the islands (Port Maria), the proximity of the Côte Sauvage are the tourist attractions of this resort.

The Lighthouse (A). – *Open 10am to noon and 2 to 6pm from 1 June to 31 August*. The lighthouse commands a view of Quiberon and its bay, the coast of the Rhuys Peninsula and the islands of Rhuys Houat, Belle-Ile and Groix.

Port-Maria. – A few pinnaces remain but sardine fishing is decreasing. Some sardines, however, are still sent away to be eaten fresh while the rest are canned in the factories near the harbour.

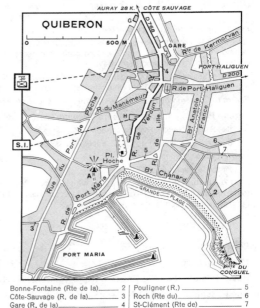

Bonne-Fontaine (Rte de la) ___ 2	Pouligner (R.) ___ 5
Côte-Sauvage (R. de la) ___ 3	Roch (Rte du) ___ 6
Gare (R. de la) ___ 4	St-Clément (Rte de) ___ 7

AROUND CONGUEL POINT

8 km - 5 miles – about 1 hour – Local map p 148

Leave Quiberon by the Boulevard Chanard, skirting the great beach. You pass round the **Thalassotherapy Institute** *(visits reserved to members of the medical profession)* where arthrosis, rheumatism, overstrain and the after effects of injuries are treated by sea water cures.

Conguel Point. – $\frac{1}{2}$ *hour on foot Rtn*. From the tip of the point *(viewing table)* there is a view of Belle-Ile, Houat, Hoëdic, the Morbihan coast and the Quiberon Bay. You can see the Teignouse Lighthouse, near which the battleship *France* sank in 1922 after striking an uncharted reef.

Return to the car to go to Port-Haliguen. When you get to the Fort-Neuf you will notice the bustle on the beach created by the Centre Nautique de l'Éducation Nationale and the Centre Nautique du Touring Club de France. On the left is a local aerodrome. The view opens out over the bay and the Morbihan coastline. You will pass, on your right, an obelisk commemorating the surrender of the exiles.

Port-Haliguen. – *Facilities p 42.* A little fishing and pleasure boat harbour *(now being enlarged)* where regattas are held in summer.

Return to Quiberon by the Rue de Port-Haliguen.

■ THE CÔTE SAUVAGE★★

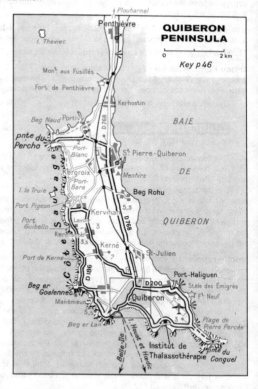

A walk from end to end of the Côte Sauvage, especially along a cliff where caves, crevasses and inlets alternate with little sandy beaches *(dangerous for bathing),* is particularly recommended. Rocks of all shapes and sizes edge the coast, forming passages and labyrinths in which the sea boils and roars.

Tourists passing through quickly who are going to make the tour described below should leave their cars and walk down to the seashore to see the coastline.

Round tour of the Côte Sauvage★★. – *12 km - 8 miles – Local map adjoining.* Go north from Quiberon along the D 768 and, after the station, take the Kerniscob road on the left; 4.5 km - 3 miles on turn left towards the shore. Then walk to Port-Pigeon *(200 m; go down a few steps on the left to come to a freshwater spring on the left of the beach).* Military camp on the right. Turning round you get a good view of the Bull's Cave (Grottes du Taureau), the Window (Fenêtre) and the Old Woman (Vieille). All are marked by pillars.

You can walk north along coastal tracks from Port-Pigeon to Portivy.

Take the D 186 which offers fine views over the Côte Sauvage. Truie Island and, in the distance, Percho Point, can be seen from Kervihan Point. You reach Beg er Goalennec by way of Port Guibello, Scouro Point and Kerné Bay.

Beg er Goalennec. – Go round the oyster-bed keeper's house, and over the rocks to reach the tip of the promontory from which there is a view over the whole length of the Côte Sauvage.

Return to Quiberon by the D 186 along the coast and Port Maria.

Percho Point★. – *7.5 km - 8 miles to the north. Leave Quiberon by the D 768.*

Beg-Rohu. – National sailing school.

St-Pierre-Quiberon. – Pop 2 022. *Facilities p 42.*

Turn left onto the road to Portivy.

Portivy. – *Facilities p 42.*

After 700 m turn left to take a sandy track which leads to **Percho Point★** which offers a good **view★**: to the left the Côte Sauvage, to the right the fort and beach of Penthièvre *(facilities p 42)* and in the distance the islands, Belle-Ile and Groix.

BOAT TRIPS

Belle-Ile★★. – *Description p 56.*

Morbihan Gulf★★. – *Description p 124.*

Houat Island. – Pop 430. An island village; wonderful beaches; fishing.

Hoëdic Island. – Pop 147. Numerous beaches, remains of 17 and 19C forts.

*When visiting London use the **Green Guide "London"***

– Detailed descriptions of places of interest
– Useful local information
– A section on the historic square mile of the City of London
 with a detailed fold out plan
– The lesser known London boroughs – their people, places
 and sights
– Plan of selected areas and important buildings.

QUIMPER ★★

Michelin map **230** 18 – *Local map p 75* – Pop 60 510

A visit to Quimper leaves you with delightful memories of Brittany. The town lies in a pretty little valley at the junction (*kemper* in Breton) of the Steir and Odet Rivers.

This used to be the capital of Cornouaille, and it is here, perhaps, that the traditional atmosphere of the province can best be felt. On market days and at church services you will still find a good number of old costumes, and the Great Festival of Cornouaille *(p 10)*.

St. Corentin's fish. – For centuries the town was called Quimper-Corentin, after its first bishop. According to legend, Corentin lived on the flesh of a single, miraculous fish. Every morning he took half the fish to eat and threw the other half back into the river. When he came back the next day the fish was whole once more and offered itself again to the knife. Corentin was the adviser and supporter of King Gradlon *(p 22)*.

Four men of Quimper. – The statue of Laënnec (1781-1826) commemorates the most illustrious son of Quimper – the man who discovered auscultation (sounding – *see Ploaré, p 88: other memories of Laënnec*).

Streets are named after Kerguelen, Fréron and Madec, three other famous men of Quimper. **Kerguelen** (1734-97) was a South Seas explorer; a group of islands bears his name. **Fréron** (1719-76) was a critic, bitterly opposed to Voltaire and other philosophers.

René Madec (1738-94) was a hero of adventure. As a cabin boy in a ship of the India Company he jumped overboard and landed at Pondicherry. He took service with a rajah and became a successful man. The British had a relentless enemy in him. When he returned to France, enormously rich, the King gave him a title and the Cross of St. Louis, with a colonel's commission.

■ MAIN SIGHTS *time: ¾ hour*

Cathedral★★. – This fine Gothic structure was built from the 13C (chancel) to the 15C (transept and nave). The two towers were erected only in 1856, being modelled on the Breton steeple of Pont-Croix. To pay for their building the Bishop asked the 600 000 faithful of the diocese each to subscribe one *sou* a year for five years. The salt sea air quickly toned down the new stone, and it is difficult to believe that the upper part of the façade is four centuries later than the lower part.

After seeing the north side of the building make for the façade.

Between the spires stands the statue of a man on horseback: this is King Gradlon *(p 22)*. Until the 18C, on 26 July each year, a great festival was held in his honour. A man would climb up behind him, tie a napkin round his neck and offer him a glass of wine. Then he drank up the wine himself, carefully wiped the King's mouth with the napkin and threw the empty glass down on the square. Any spectator who could catch the glass as it fell received a prize of 100 gold *écus*, if the glass was not broken. It used to be said that to save money the Town Council had a few saw-cuts made in the stem of the glass.

Enter by the main door. During the League troubles in the 16C the nave was used as a place of refuge by the inhabitants of the district. Mass was said there among palliasses, boxes and hanging linen. Plague broke out and 1 500 people died.

The first thing that strikes you on entering the church is the fact that the choir is quite out of line with the nave. It is believed that this results from unexpected difficulty encountered during building – subsidence or something of the sort.

The cathedral has a remarkable set of 15C **stained glass★★** in the upper windows. The tourist, going round the fine 92 m - 302 ft long building, will see in the side chapels, tombs, altars, frescoes, altarpieces, statues, old and modern works of art, and in the chapel beneath the south tower an Entombment copied from that in Bourges Cathedral in the 18C.

The cathedral apse can be seen especially well from the ramparts and public gardens.

Old Quarters. – *Follow the route marked on the plan.* After skirting the Odet and crossing the Steir you reach the Place Terre-au-Duc. This was the lay town opposite the episcopal city, and included the law courts, the prison and the Duc de Bretagne market.

Cross the square diagonally, bearing to the right to cross the Steir by a bridge from which there is a picturesque view. Follow the **Rue Kéréon★** (BY 22), a busy shopping street. The cathedral and its spires, between the two rows of old houses, makes a delightful picture.

■ ADDITIONAL SIGHTS

Fine Arts Museum★★ (Musée des Beaux-Arts) (BY M). – *Open 1 May to 15 September, 10am to noon and 1.30 to 7.30pm (2 to 6pm 16 September to 30 April). Closed Tuesdays and holidays. Admission: 2F.*

The museum contains an interesting selection of the paintings of the French and foreign schools from the 16 to the beginning of the 20C: there are works by A. Carracci, Velazquez, Rubens, Maes, Poelenburgh, Mignard, Boucher, Oudry, J. Vernet, Fragonard, Corot, Chasseriau, Boudin, Carrière, Marquet. The Pont-Aven school is represented by Serusier, Maufra, E. Bernard and Max Jacob (drawings and manuscripts). A remarkable 17-18C collection of drawings and engravings is displayed in rotation.

Local Museum★ (BY B). – *Open 1 July to 15 September, 10am to noon and 2 to 6pm (4.30 or 5pm the rest of the year). Closed Tuesdays from 16 September to 30 June and holidays. Admission: 1F.*

This museum is devoted to Finistère history, archaeology and folklore and is installed in the former bishop's palace. The most interesting parts of the palace were built by Bishop Claude de Rohan at the start of the 16C.

Gallo-Roman collections, sculpted wood chests, wardrobes, recumbent figures, everyday objects and pottery will interest many. In the Rohan tower, you will see a great **spiral staircase★** ending under a magnificent carved oak canopy and leading to the Quimper pottery and Breton costume galleries.

Mount Frugy (BZ). – Mount Frugy, a wooded hill 70 m - 224 ft high, overlooks the Place de la Résistance.

St-Mathieu (AY D). – The church is modern, although it incorporates a fine 16C stained glass window halfway up the chancel.

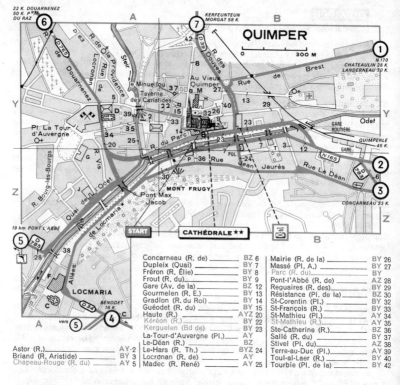

22 K. DOUARNENEZ
50 K. de la PTE
DU RAZ

KERFEUNTEUN
MORGAT 58 K.

QUIMPER

300 M

N 170

CHATEAULIN 28 K.
LANDERNEAU 70 K.

Map labels:

Street	Ref		Street	Ref
Concarneau (R. de)	BZ 6		Mairie (R. de la)	BY 26
Dupleix (Quai)	BY 7		Massé (Pl. A.)	BY 27
Fréron (R. Élie)	BY 8		Parc (R. du)	BY
Frout (R. du)	BY 9		Pont-l'Abbé (R. de)	AZ 28
Gare (Av. de la)	BZ 12		Reguaires (R. des)	BY 29
Gourmelen (R. E.)	BY 13		Résistance (Pl. de la)	BZ 30
Gradlon (R. du Roi)	BY 14		St-Corentin (Pl.)	BY 32
Guéodet (R. du)	BY 15		St-François (R.)	BY 33
Haute (R.)	AYZ 20		St-Mathieu (Pl.)	AY 34
Kéréon (R.)	BY 22		St-Mathieu (R.)	AY 35
Kerguelen (Bd de)	BY 23		Ste-Catherine (R.)	BZ 36
La-Tour-d'Auvergne (Pl.)	AY		Sallé (R. du)	BY 37
Le-Déan (R.)	BZ		Stivel (Pl. du)	AZ 38
Astor (R.)	AY 2	Le-Hars (R. Th.)	BYZ 24	Terre-au-Duc (Pl.)	AY 39
Briand (R. Aristide)	BY 3	Locronan (R. de)	AY	Toul-al-Laer (R.)	BY 40
Chapeau-Rouge (R. du)	AY 5	Madec (R. René)	AY 25	Tourbie (Pl. de la)	BY 42

Notre-Dame-de-Locmaria (AZ C). – Romanesque church, restored.

Pottery (AZ F *and Rue de la Troménie*). – The first Quimper pottery was founded in 1690 by a southerner whose son afterwards went into partnership with a Nivernais and then with a man from Rouen. These various employers brought workers from their respective provinces. The result was a form of decoration inspired by the pottery of Moustiers, Nevers, Rouen and even the Far East. It was about 1880, when labour was recruited at Quimper itself, that pottery with Breton themes appeared and the art became industrialised.

Decoration is now undergoing a change. Specialists interpret flora and marine fauna according to modern taste, and the eye, accustomed to designs in blue with human figures, must adapt itself to this new and successful formula.

Tourists who are interested may visit, in addition to the museum, a working pottery where they will also find exhibits of the work done on the spot *(closed on Saturday afternoons, Sundays and holidays and the last three weeks in August)*.

Old Streets. – **Rue du Guéodet**: a house with caryatids (the ground floor is adorned with figures of men and women in Henri II costumes); **Rue Élie-Fréron; Rue du Sallé; Rue St-Mathieu.**

EXCURSIONS

Kerdévot Chapel; Stangala site*. – *Round tour of 27 km - 17 miles – about 1¾ hours – Local map below. Leave Quimper by ②, the N 165. Take the N 170 on the left then turn right into the D 15. Turn right after 700 m into a road running beside the River Jet and offering views of the wooded countryside and pasturelands.*

3 km - 2 miles beyond the Ergué-Gaberic, turn left at a crossroads into a road going uphill.

Kerdévot Chapel. – *Ask for the key of M. Le Fur in the hamlet of Kerdévot near a metalsmith's shop.* The spacious 15C chapel stands in an attractive setting near a Calvary, which is of a later date and somewhat damaged. Inside, a Flemish **altarpiece*** stands on the high altar. Leave Kerdévot by the road beside the chapel; keep to this until it joins the D 15 and then bear left towards Quimper. After 3 km - 3 miles turn right towards the village of Lestonan. Go through Quelennec and 100 m beyond the village turn

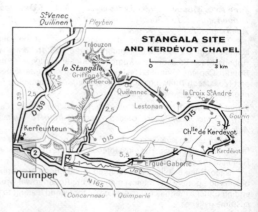

right into a narrow but passable road to the grassy level of Griffonès. Cross the open space and take, on your right, a road that begins between two young oaks and drops down. After 30 m turn left into a road that is both grassy and stony and which soon begins to cross fern covered ground leading directly to Griffonès Point.

Stangala site★. – The site is a remarkable one: the rocky ridge overlooks the Odet from a height of 70 m - 230 ft as the river winds between wooded slopes. Opposite, and slightly to the right, the hamlet of Tréouzon clings to the slopes. Lower, and to the left, you will see the ruins of the Poul mill. Ahead, in the distance, you can easily pick out the mountain of Locronan, with its characteristic outline and the chapel perched on the summit.

To return, take the road on the right towards Quimper, when you leave the narrow road.

Kerfeunteun; Chapels and Calvaries at Quilinen★ and St-Venec. – *Round tour of 30 km - 19 miles – about 1 hour. Leave Quimper by the Rue de Kerfeunteun, the D 39 to the north of the map. Shortly after passing a cemetery on your right as you go into Kerfeunteun, turn right to reach the church.*

Kerfeunteun Church. – A slim bell gable rises above the west wall. It was built in the 16 and 17C, but the transept and the chancel were rebuilt in 1953. The church was modernised with considerable taste when rebuilt and has kept a beautiful 16C stained glass window above the high altar. It shows the Tree of Jesse with a Crucifix above.

Continue along the D 39 for 800 m then take the D 139 on the right and 1.5 km - 1 mile farther on pick up the N 170 on the left. After 7.5 km - 5 miles turn right.

Calvary★ and Notre-Dame-de-Quilinen. – *Ask for the key to the chapel at the house nearby.* Near the main road, hidden by trees, this country church appears with unusual Calvary. Built in 1550, the Calvary reveals a rough and naïve style. The Apostles are grouped at the base of the Cross which becomes more and more slender as it rises to the figure of Christ. Carved on the other side of the Cross is Christ resurrected.

The south portal of the 15C chapel is decorated by a graceful Virgin between two angels. You enter from the nave through a narrow arch and pass under a rood-beam to the chancel which is curiously widened on the north side. Behind the high altar is a Flamboyant window representing Our Lady of Quilinen and St-Guénolé. A *pardon* is held the third Sunday in May.

Return to the N170, 5 km - 3 miles farther on, turn right towards the nearby St-Venec Chapel.

St-Venec. – *Ask for the key at the farm 100 m to the left on the road to Briec.* The Gothic chapel contains many 15 and 16C statues; particularly noteworthy is the group in stone of St. Guen (St. Blanche) and her triplets: St. Guénolé, St. Jacut and St. Venec. The Saint was endowed with three breasts so as to be able to feed her sons simultaneously.

Near the chapel are a 16C Calvary and fountain.

Return to Quimper by the N 170.

Tour of the Odet. – *Round tour of 44 km - 27 miles – about 2 hours – Local map below.* Leave Quimper by ⑤, D 785.

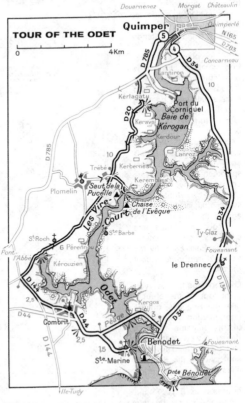

View of the Vire-Court★★. – At the Trébé crossroads turn left towards the Rosulien dock. After 600 m leave your car (end of the metalled road) and walk along the path to a ruined windmill and the dock from which you will have a view of the Vire-Court reach *(description p 152)*.

Combrit. – Pop 2 302. 16C church.

Ste-Marine. – *Facilities p 42.* There is a fine view of the Odet and Bénodet as you cross the river by the Cornouaille Bridge.

Bénodet★. – *Description p 58.*

Take the D 34 for the return journey.

Le Drennec. – Pop 1 206. Standing in front of the chapel beside the road is a charming 16C fountain: in a trefoil niche, beneath a crocket gable, is a Virgin of Pity.

BOAT TRIPS

Down the Odet★★; Bénodet★; Loctudy; Glénan Islands. – *The trip down the Odet to Bénodet takes 1½ hours. Times vary with the tides. Information about continuing the excursion to Loctudy or the Glénan Islands may be obtained from the Tourist Information Centre at Quimper, 3 Rue du Roi-Gradlon, Tel 95 04 69 or from the Vedettes Aigrettes, Tel 91 00 58 at Bénodet.*

The castle woods and the parks, which lie along the river, form a fine, green landscape. The port of **Corniguel**, at the mouth of Kérogan Bay, adds a modern touch to the scene.

Kérogan Bay★. – The estuary at this point looks like a lake.

QUIMPER★★

The Vire-Court★★. – The Odet here winds between high, wooded cliffs. This wild spot has its legends. Two rocks at the narrowest point of the gorge are called the Virgin's Leap (Saut de la Pucelle), referring to the tremendous leap made from one bank to the other by a girl who was being pursued. Another rock is called the Bishop's Chair (Chaise de l'Evêque). Angels are said to have made it in the shape of a seat for the use of a saintly prelate of Quimper who liked to meditate in this lonely place.

A little farther on the river bends so sharply that a Spanish fleet, coming up to attack Quimper, did not dare to go through. After having taken on water at a fountain now called the Spaniards' Fountain, the ships turned back. On the right bank, before Pérennou, ruins of Roman baths can be seen.

Bénodet★. – *Description p 58.*

Up the Odet★★. – *Departures from Beg-Meil or La Forêt-Fouesnant (Port-la-Forêt). Apply to M. R Guillou, Tel 94 97 94 in Beg-Meil.*

QUIMPERLÉ ★

Michelin map 230 34 – Pop 11 712 – *Facilities p 44*

This little town is prettily situated at the junction *(kemper)* of the Ellé and the Isole Rivers, which join to form the Laïta. It consists of an upper town, dominated by the Church of Notre-Dame-de-L'Assumption, and a lower town grouped about the former Abbey of Ste-Croix and the Rue Dom-Morice.

■ SIGHTS *time: 1 hour*

Start from the Place Nationale and take the Rue de la Paix. One skirts the buildings of the former Abbey of Ste-Croix (18C), which houses the Gendarmerie and the Law Courts. Enter the first door on the right to glance at the main staircase and the cloisters with its flowers. This was where Lancelot, one of the "Gentlemen of Port-Royal" and Racine's teacher, died in exile.

Ste-Croix★★ (BY). – The church, which is interesting archaeologically, was first built in the 12C, but had to be rebuilt, except for the apse and the crypt, in 1862, when its belfry collapsed. The new belfry (campanile) stands alone.

The plan is copied from that of the Holy Sepulchre at Jerusalem. It includes a rotunda with three small bays opening into it and a porch, the whole forming a Greek cross.

The **apse★★**, with its vaulting, columns, capitals and windows, is the finest specimen of Romanesque art in Brittany. You will also see a Renaissance stone **altarpiece★** standing against the façade.

You may visit the **crypt★★**, which has remarkable capitals. *Enter by the wrought iron grilles under the chancel.*

Old houses★. – As you come out of the church, take the Rue Ellé, on the right, skirting the left side of the building; from it there is a view of the apse and the belfry. Turn back and take the **Rue Brémond-d'Ars** (BY), on the right. This street includes old houses at nos 8, 10, 11 and 12; at no 15 *bis* is the staircase of the Présidial, a former law court.

Level with the ruins of the Church of St Colomban, at the corner of no 9 turn into the **Rue Dom-Morice★** (BY 3). This narrow alley is flanked by old dwellings with overhanging storeys. No 7, the archers' house, is another remarkable old house. It houses a small museum *(open in summer 10am to noon and 3 to 6pm; closed Sundays; the rest of the year, Tuesdays and Saturdays at the same times).*

Cross the Pont Salé and take the Rue Savary, going up. This leads to the Church of Our Lady of the Assumption on the right.

QUIMPERLÉ

Bourgneuf (R. du)	BZ	Jean-Jaurès (Pl.)	AY	9
Brémond-d'Ars (R.)	BY	La-Tour-d'Auvergne (R.)	BY	10
Carnot (Pl.)	BY 2	Leuriou (R.)	AY	12
Dom-Morice (R.)	BY 3	Lorient (Rte de)	BZ	20
Cornic-Duchesne (R.)	AY 4	Madame-Moreau (R. de)	BY	22
Écoles (Pl. des)	AY 5	Mellac (R.)	AY	
Gaulle (Pl. Charles de)	BY 6	Moulin-de-la-Ville (Pont du)	BY	23
Genot (R.)	AY	Paix (R. de la)	BY	25
Hervo (Pl.)	BY 7	St-Michel (Pl.)	AY	26
Isole (R.)	BY 8	Savary (R.)	BY	

Notre-Dame-de-l'Assumption or **St-Michel** (AY). – A 13 and 15C church, surmounted by a large square tower. Pass under the archway vaulting with a sculptured cornice, magnificent Flamboyant piscinas and, at the back, a 15C font. Among the more interesting wooden statues, note that of Our Lady of Good Tidings and a 12C *Pietà*.

Take the Rue de Madame-Moreau, slowing down and interrupted by steps on its way to the Place Carnot. Turn right into the Rue La-Tour-d'Auvergne, and cross the Moulin-de-la-Ville Bridge. Return to the Place Nationale.

EXCURSIONS

Le Pouldu; Doëlan. – *Round tour of 32 km - 20 miles – about 1 hour – Local map below. Leave Quimperlé by the D 49 which crosses the Carnoët Forest (below).*

Le Pouldu. – *Facilities p 42.* The little port of Pouldu lies at the mouth of the River Laïta. From the beach of the Grands Sables, at the end of D 49, there is a good view of Groix Island and the coast.

The **Notre-Dame-de-la-Paix Chapel** *(open in July and August)* stands in a grassy close whose entrance is flanked by a monument to Gauguin. Transported 26 km - 16 miles and rebuilt here the chapel was consecrated in 1957. The windows have flame and lily shaped tracery with stained glass by Manessier and Le Moal. Below the timber roof the rood-beam carries Christ with a red loincloth and a second group depicting the *Pietà*.

Take the D 124 then the D 24 to the left. At Langlazic turn left again onto the D 16.

Doëlan. – Little fishing port commanding the entrance to a deep estuary where many fishing boats moor. The local cider is excellent.

Return to Quimperlé by the D 316, Clohars-Carnoët and the D 16.

Moëlan-sur-Mer; Kerfany-les-Pins; Belon. – *Round tour of 18 km - 12 miles to the southwest – about ½ hour. Leave Quimperlé by ③, the D 16, then 5 km - 3 miles from the town, take the D 116 to the right.*

Moëlan. – Pop 6 347 *Facilities p 42.* A small Breton museum contains costumes, furniture, minerals *(open 1 April to 30 September and in December, 2 to 7pm. Admission: 3F.).* The Chapel of St-Philibert et St-Roch, 100 m from the village of Moëlan, is picturesquely placed near a Calvary *(pardon* on the second Sunday after 15 August). Alongside is the St-Roch fountain, into which children's shirts used to be dipped to protect them from colic!

Continue along the D 116; 3.5 km - 2 miles farther on there is a view over the Bélon River.

Kerfany. – Standing on the left bank of the Bélon River, this little seaside resort has a pretty site and a sandy beach.

Continue to Lanriot and then turn left.

Belon. – *Description p 143.*

Return to Quimperlé by the D 116.

Carnoët Forest. – *Round tour of 15 km - 9 miles – about 1 hour – Local map adjoining. Some paths are reserved for pedestrians and horse riders.* The State Forest of Carnoët (750 ha - 1 852 acres) is planted with beech and oak and is bounded by the Laïta River. Carnoët Forest is the legendary domain of the Count of Comorre, the Bluebeard of Cornouaille. After hearing a prediction that he would die by the hand of his son he put his first four wives to death as soon as they conceived. The fifth wife, before she died, was able to save her son, who became St. Trémeur. Comorre, meeting the Saint, was struck by his resemblance to his mother and immediately had him beheaded. Then (says the legend) Trémeur picked up his own head, walked towards his father's castle and threw a handful of earth against the building, which collapsed, burying Comorre alive. In his statues, St. Trémeur carried his head in his hands.

Leave Quimperlé by the D 49 which crossed the Carnoët Forest; 9 km - 6 miles from Quimperlé turn left into the D 224.

St-Maurice Bridge (Pont de St-Maurice). – Fine **view*** of the river and its steep banks.

Turn round and after 700 m turn right.

St-Maurice. – The road leads to a green and pleasant **site***: the River Laïta is on the right; on the left is a lake. Close by are remains of the Chapterhouse of the former Abbey of St-Maurice founded in the 12C *(not open to the public).*

Return to the D 224 and then the D 49.

5 km - 3 miles farther on, turn right into a road leading to the Carnoët Château. Leave the car and follow the footpath to the left.

Royal Rock (Rocher Royal). – $\frac{1}{2}$ *hour on foot Rtn.* Shaded walk up to a rocky ridge overlooking the Laïta.

Return to the car and the D 49 to get back to Quimperlé.

QUINTIN

Michelin map **230** 22 – Pop 3 599 – *Facilities p 44*

The old houses of Quintin rise in terraces on a hill at the foot of which the Gouët River forms a fine stretch of water overlooked by the terrace and the 17C wing of the castle. The town was once encircled by ramparts, of which some traces remain (Porte Neuve).

The Basilica. – The relics of St. Thuriau and a piece of the Virgin's girdle, brought from Jerusalem in the 13C by a lord of Quintin, are kept in the basilica *(inquire at the presbytery).* There are also four stoups made of shells from Java and, under the porch, the old crowned statue of Our Lady of Safe Delivery, which is specially venerated by expectant mothers. The *pardon* of Notre-Dame-de-Délivrance takes place on the second Sunday in May.

Old Houses. – There are 16 and 17C houses in the Place 1830, the Place du Martray, the Grande-Rue and the Rue Notre-Dame, where you will also see a pretty 15C fountain.

EXCURSION

Robien Château. – *2 km - 1$\frac{1}{2}$ miles by the road to Corlay. Not open to the public.* The 18C château has taken the place of two others, which were successively destroyed. Of the first, there remain only the ruins of a 14C chapel, 200 m from the present house. The monotony of granite and squared stone façades is relieved by a central rotunda and projecting wings at either end.

RANCE Valley **

Michelin map **230** 11, 25

The Rance estuary lies between St-Malo and Dinard, which are famous for various reasons and are among the places most frequented in Brittany, especially by foreigners. Farther upstream, Dinan is a typical old inland town.

The Rance is a perfect example of a Breton river. It forms a deep gulf between Dinan and the sea, flowing with many branches and inlets over a level plateau. This curious gulf is due to the flooding by the sea of an ordinary but steep sided valley: the stream itself and the bottom of the valley have been "drowned" by a mass of tidal water. All that remains visible of the original valley is its steep sides, sloping into the sea. The Rance proper is a small river without much water, which winds along above Dinan. The exceptional volume of the tides make it the very place for a tidal power station.

BOAT TRIP** leaving from St-Malo or Dinard

4 hours Rtn – not counting the stop and tour of Dinan

For all information apply at the landing stages or to the Tourist Information Centre: St-Malo Tel 40 94 95 or Dinard Tel 46 12 54.

St-Malo*. – *Description p 167.*

The boat follows the same course as the Aleth Corniche (St-Servan) and crosses the Rance estuary at its widest point.

Dinard*. – *A stop giving no time for a visit.*

The boat enters the Rance, passes in front of Vicomté Point and Bizeux Rock and then enters the lock of the Rance dam. You will go up the river, between its great banks, through a series of narrow channels and wide pools. The Rance gets narrower and narrower and becomes a mere canal just as you come within sight of Dinan, perched on its ridge.

Dinan**. – *Description p 81. Your boat will stop for a longer or shorter time according to the tide – 8 hours or only $\frac{1}{4}$ hour. Find out when it will leave.*

The scenes on your way back will be changed by the difference in the direction of the light and its intensity. We would only point out the **landscape** which opens out as you approach the sea, directly you have passed the Bizeux Rock.

ROUND TOUR STARTING FROM ST-MALO*

79 km - 49 miles – about 4 hours – Local map p 156

This tour can be made equally well from Dinan or Dinard.

Leave St-Malo (p 167) by ③ on the map, the N 137. Turn right by the aerodrome into the D 5.

La Passagère. – Fine view over the Rance.

Make for the Chapel of the Boscq and St-Jouan. *The N 137 then the D 117 on the right take you to St-Suliac. Turn left at St-Suliac Church in the direction of Mount Garrot; leave the car 1 km - $\frac{1}{2}$ mile farther on.*

Mount Garrot. – $\frac{1}{4}$ *hour on foot Rtn.* A path to the right leads to an old mill a few yards from the road; go on along the path to the point, passing behind a farm, and noticing the views of the Rance Valley on the way. Go back to your car and continue on the road on which you came until you reach the D 7. Turn right almost immediately. From La Ville-ès-Nonais make a detour to the Port St-Jean Bridge over the Rance from which there is a very good view of the valley.

Return to La Ville-ès-Nonais and there take a road on the right which joins the D 29.

Lanvallay. – Pop 2 901. A remarkable **view*** of the old town of Dinan, its ramparts and its belfries. Below, flows the Rance spanned by a long viaduct.

Dinan**. – *Description p 81.*

By the D 2, which passes under the Dinan viaduct then by the D 12, you return towards Dinard.

After Plouër-sur-Rance and Le Minihic turn right into the D 114 and 250 m later take the D 3.

La Landriais. – The walk along the Hures Promenade, a Customs' patrol path, from the car park and, as it skirts the Rance for 2 km - 1 mile affords fine views.

On your way back, take the D 114 again after 1 200 m - ¾ mile then turn right onto the D 5, a fine coast road. At the end, just before you get to the Jouvente Dock (Cale de la Jouvente), turn back.

La Richardais. – Pop 1 228. The church is dominated by its pierced tower and the Crucifix surmounting it. On the walls of the nave is a fresco depicting the Stations of the Cross by Xavier de Langlais. The greens, browns and ochres of the fresco go well together with the church interior. From the fine wood vaulting with exposed beams, five lamps in the form of wheels hang down. The stained glass is by Max Ingrand.

On leaving La Richardais by the north, you get a viewpoint of the tidal power scheme and the Rance estuary.

Reach Dinard by the D 114 and ① on the map.

Dinard***. – *Description p 84.*

Leave Dinard by the Avenue de la Vicomté and the D 114.

The Rance Tidal Power Scheme (Usine marémotrice de le Rance). – *Time: ½ hour from 8.30am to 8pm. The scheme is explained by a series of luminous panels and dioramas.*

The use of tidal power is nothing new to the Rance Valley. As early as the 12C riverside dwellers had thought up the idea of building little reservoirs which, as they emptied with the ebb tide, drove mill wheels. To double the output of a modern industrial plant it was fascinating to try to work out a means of using the flow as well as the ebb tide. The French electricity authority (EDF), therefore, searched for new technical methods of producing electricity and successfully set up, between the headlands of La Briantais and La Brebis, a hydro-electric power scheme operated by both the flow and the ebb of the tide.

The Rance estuary is closed by a dam 750 m - 800 yds long, making a reservoir of 22 sq km - 8 sq miles. The D 168 which connects Dinard and St-Malo runs along it.

The lock is 65 m - 69 yds long and enables boats to pass through the dam. The road crosses the lock by means of bascule bridges.

From a balcony you get a general view of the generating room. The power station is in a huge tunnel nearly 390 m - 400 yds long in the very centre of the dam. Here, each in a reinforced pit, are the 24 AC generators of a combined capacity of 240 000 kW which can produce 550 million kW per year.

Walk along the dam to the platform. From there the **view*** extends over the Rance estuary as far as Dinard and St-Malo.

The dam lies between the power station and the right bank with its centre on the small Island of Chalibert. There are six sluice gates at the eastern end which can regulate the emptying and filling of the reservoir thus controlling the water supply to the power station.

Return to St-Servan and St-Malo by the direct route (D 168 and N 137).

RANCE VALLEY

0 —— 5 Km.

Key p 46

DINARD

Paramé

St MALO

St Servan-s-Mer

Usine marémotrice

la Richardais   le Boscq

la Passagère

la Jouvente   la Landriais

Pleurtuit   St Jouan-des-Guérets

le Minihic-s-Rance

St Suliac

17,5

M. Garrot

Châteauneuf

la Ville-ès-Nonais

Plouër-s-Rance   Port St-Jean

Mordreuc

14

11,5   la Vicomté

Lanvallay

Dinan

Rothéneuf   Cancale

la Guimorais

Michelin main road maps (scale 1:1 000 000)

986 *Great Britain, Ireland*
987 *Germany, Austria, Benelux*
988 *Italy, Switzerland*
989 *France*
990 *Spain, Portugal*
991 *Yugoslavia*

REDON

Michelin map **230** 38, 39 – Pop 10 159

This river port at the crossing at the Vilaine and the Nantes–Brest canal, has a wet dock which links these two waterways. It is also a local farming centre with its markets on Mondays and fairs. The **Foire Teillouse** *(fourth Saturday in October)* is renowned for its chestnuts. The town's industries include mechanical engineering, plastics, foundries, refrigerated depots and the production of cigarette lighters.

St-Sauveur (A). – This former abbey church was cut off from its 14C Gothic bell tower by a fire in 1780. A remarkable Romanesque **tower★** in sandstone and granite stands at the transept crossing. From the neighbouring **cloister** occupied by the College of St. Saviour, the superimposition of its arcades can be seen. Entering the Rue du Tribunal, one has a good view of the **chevet** with its buttresses.

The **interior** reveals a dimly lit 11C nave with wood vaulting. The 12C vaulting at the transept reveals remains of frescoes. The chancel and the ambulatory date from the 13C.

EXCURSIONS

La Belle-Anguille. – *8 km - 5 miles to the east by the Rue St-Michel, the D 65 and after the first intersection on the road in the direction of Ste-Marie turn right.* Pleasant verdant site on the banks of the Vilaine.

Rieux. – *Pop 2 263. 7 km - 4 miles to the south by ③, the D 775, the D 20 and then the second on the left.*
The **church** (1952) has a slim belfry built against the side of the main vessel. The pointed brick vaulting springs from roughly hewn capitals which are in turn supported by short columns. The unfaced stonework of the walls is interrupted only by the vividly colourful **stained glass windows★** of unevenly cut glass by Job Guével.

REDON

Desmars (R. Joseph) _____ 2	Notre-Dame (R.)
Douves (R. des)	République (Pl. de la)__ 9
Duchesse-Anne (Pl. de la)__ 3	Richelieu (R.)_____ 10
Etats (R. des)_____ 4	St-Michel (R.)_____ 12
Foch (R. du Mar.) _____ 5	St-Nicolas (R.)_____ 13
Franklin (R.) _____ 6	St-Sauveur (Pl.)_____ 14
Gare (Av. de la)_____ 7	Tribunal (R. du)_____ 15
Grande-Rue	Union (R. de l')_____ 16
Moulinet (R. du)_____ 8	Victor-Hugo (R.)_____ 17

RENNES ★★

Michelin map **230** 26 – Pop 205 733

Rennes, considered the capital of Brittany, has changed its face since the Second World War. Once a calm provincial city and the administrative and judicial centre it has now doubled in population and has developed industrially.

The Classical style which prevails in the town centre, give the streets, buildings and houses a rather cold dignity. The mediaeval streets, however, not touched by the 1720 fire *(see below)* warm this quarter with its pretty half-timbered houses. This area (bordered on the south by the Vilaine) is where the people of Rennes congregate: shops, theatre, cinemas and pancake restaurants *(crêperies)*.

The new city on the left bank of the Vilaine includes the coach station, hotels and sports, radio and cultural centres. The new residential quarters around the city are cut by three industrial zones which since 1950 have attracted many plants manufacturing cars, railway equipment, and printing and paper works and refineries.

Recently Rennes has become a centre of the electronics and communications industry. There are three schools specialising in electronics and telecommunications.

Rennes is also a university city: two universities, a medical school, with a total student enrolment of 25 000.

HISTORICAL NOTES

Du Guesclin's Beginnings (14C). – Bertrand Du Guesclin was born in the Castle of La Motte-Broons, southwest of Dinan, which has now disappeared. He was the eldest of ten children, short, dark, flat nosed and broad shouldered and by no means handsome. He never learned to read. On the other hand, he was bursting with energy and good sense. Bertrand spent his childhood among peasant boys whom he taught to fight. In this way he acquired strength, skill and cunning – and rough manners. His family were ashamed of him and kept him out of sight.

In 1337 – when Du Guesclin was seventeen, all the local nobles met for a tournament on the Place des Lices, at Rennes. Our hero went to it in peasant's dress, mounted on a draught horse. He was kept out of the lists. His despair at this was such that one of his Rennes cousins lent him his armour and his charger. Without giving his name, Bertrand unseated several opponents. At last a lance thrust lifted his visor. His father recognised him. Delighted and proud, he exclaimed: "My fine son, I will no longer treat you scurvily!" *Other details pp 21, 52, 81, 99 and 106.*

The Duchess's marriage (1491). – In 1489, when François II died, his heiress, Anne of Brittany, was only twelve, but this did not prevent many wooers from coming forward. Her choice fell on Maximilian of Austria, the future Emperor. The religious marriage was performed by proxy in 1490.

Charles VIII, who had an unconsummated marriage with Margaret of Austria, daughter of Maximilian, asked the Duchess's hand for himself; he was refused, but laid siege to Rennes in August 1491. The starving people begged their sovereign to accept the marriage. She agreed and met Charles VIII. Anne was small and thin and slightly lame, but she had gaiety and charm; she knew Latin and Greek and took an interest in art and letters. Charles was short and ill favoured, with large, pale eyes and thick lips, always hanging open; he was slow witted, too, but he loved power and had a taste for pomp. Quite unexpectedly the two young people took a liking to each other, which grew into love. Their engagement was celebrated at Rennes. Then remained the problem of freeing the fiancés. The Court of Rome agreed and the wedding took place in the royal Castle of Langeais, in the Loire Valley, on 6 December 1491. The marriage united Brittany to France. *See other details about Anne of Brittany pp 126 and 181.*

The great fire of 1720. – At the beginning of the 18C the town still looked as it did in the Middle Ages, with narrow alleys and lath and plaster houses. There was no way of fighting fire, for there was no running water.

In the evening of 22 December 1720, a drunken carpenter set fire to a heap of shavings with his lamp. The house burned like a torch and immediately 1 000 other houses caught fire.

The ravaged quarters were rebuilt to the plans of Jacques Gabriel, the descendant of a long line of architects and himself the father of the Gabriel who built the Place de la Concorde in Paris.

A large part of the town owes its fine rectangular streets, with uniform and rather severely distinguished granite houses, to this event. In order that they might be inhabited more quickly, new houses were divided into apartments or flats which were sold separately.

The La Chalotais affair. – In 1762 the Duke of Aiguillon, Governor of Brittany, clashed with Parliament over the Jesuits. The Jansenist lawyers *(robins)* opposed the Society of Jesus, whose colleges made it very powerful in Brittany – that of Rennes had 2 800 pupils. La Chalotais, the Public Prosecutor, induced Parliament to vote for the dissolution of the Order. His report had a huge success: 12 000 copies were sold in a month. Voltaire wrote to the author: ''This is the only work of philosophy that has ever come from the Bar.''

Aiguillon, who defended the Jesuits, asked Parliament to reverse its vote. It refused. Louis XV summoned the Councillors to Versailles, scolded them and sent three into exile. On returning to Rennes the Members of Parliament resigned rather than submit. The King had La Chalotais arrested and sent him to Saintes; the other Councillors were scattered over various provinces, but the Paris Parliament took the side of the Rennes Parliament and Louis XV hesitated to go further. Aiguillon, lacking support, retired in 1768. The Assemblies had defeated the royal power. Revolution was on the march.

A great mayor: Leperdit. – In 1793, before going to Nantes, where he became notorious *(p 128)*, Carrier was appointed to represent the Convention at Rennes. There he found a Mayor named Leperdit, who was a working tailor and a simple fellow but a man of great character and coolness. The Convention man wanted to execute prisoners wholesale. Leperdit stood up to him bravely. ''No mercy,'' said Carrier; ''those people are outside the law.'' ''Yes,'' answered the Mayor, ''but not outside humanity.'' Fortunately for Rennes and its Mayor, Carrier did not stay long.

In 1794, when Leperdit was addressing a crowd who were demanding bread, stones were thrown and he was wounded on the forehead. Bleeding but still calm, he said to the ruffians: ''I cannot, like Christ, change these stones into bread; as for my blood, I would give the last drop if it would feed you.''

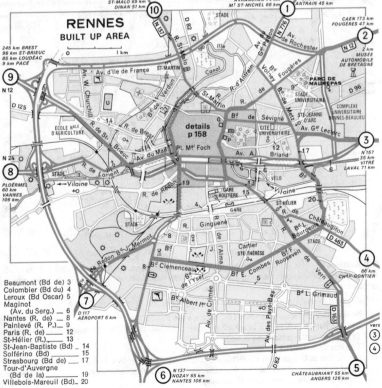

■ **MAIN SIGHTS** time: 2 hours

Law Courts★★ (Palais de Justice) (BY). –Guided tour. Ask the Keeper of the Court, at the end of the right corridor. The Law Courts, the former Houses of Parliament of Brittany, stand in the Place du Palais, a square, lined on its remaining sides by 17 and 18C houses. The building with its sweeping, sober lines is worthy of the powerful assembly that had it built between 1618 and 1655 to the plans of Salomon de Brosse, the architect of the Luxembourg Palace in Paris. Funds for the building were found by levying a tax of one *sol* per litre of wine and three *deniers* per litre of cider (a builder's mate then earned seven to twelve *sols* a day).

The Parliament was the supreme court of the 2 300 Breton tribunals. It also played a legislative and political role. Most of the 100 to 120 Councillors and Presidents were drawn from the noble families of the province. A seat could be bought for a sum equivalent to about 3 000 francs today. Salaries were low, but the judges received the famous ''spices'' (consisting originally of sweets and preserves) from their clients. Members of Parliament were much respected at Rennes; they ruled over thousands of lawyers; by tradition, they had large families: a president to whom his wife presented thirty-two children hardly caused a stir.

Enter the **Hall of the Great Pillars★** (Gros Piliers), a large vestibule with columns.

The tourist goes through a series of magnificently decorated rooms, on which 17C painters such as Jouvenet and Coypel worked. The most impressive is the **Grand'Chambre★★**, the former parliamentary debating chamber. It is 20 m long, 10 m wide and 7 m high - 66 ft by 33 ft by 23 ft. The panelled ceiling, paintings and woodwork are amazingly rich. The walls are covered with ten modern tapestries representing scenes in the history of Brittany, which the Gobelins manufactory took twenty-four years to weave. Charming loggias or boxes, finely decorated, enabled important visitors to follow the debates. Mme de Sévigné came there several times during her visits to Les Rochers (p 161).

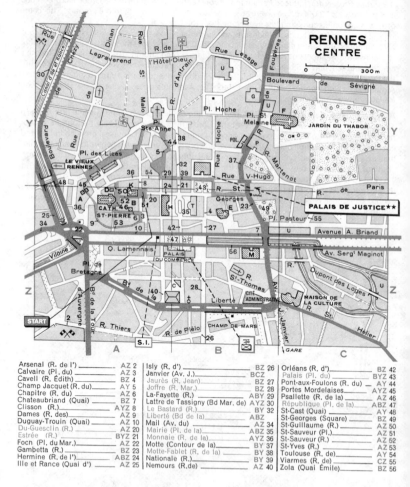

Arsenal (R. de l')	AZ 2	Isly (R. d')	BZ 26	Orléans (R. d')		BZ 42
Calvaire (Pl. du)	AZ 3	Janvier (Av. J.)	BCZ	Palais (Pl. du)		BYZ 43
Cavell (R. Édith)	BZ 4	Jaurès (R. Jean)	BZ 27	Pont-aux-Foulons (R. du)		AY 44
Champ Jacquet (R. du)	AY 5	Joffre (R. Mar.)	BZ 28	Portes Mordelaises		AYZ 45
Chapitre (R. du)	AZ 6	La-Fayette (R.)	ABY 29	Psallette (R. de la)		AZ 46
Chateaubriand (Quai)	BZ 7	Lattre de Tassigny (Bd Mar. de)	AYZ 30	République (Pl. de la)		ABZ 47
Clisson (R.)	AYZ 8	Le Bastard (R.)	BZ 32	St-Cast (Quai)		AY 48
Dames (R. des)	AZ 9	Liberté (Bd de la)	ABZ	St-Georges (Square)		BZ 49
Duguay-Trouin (Quai)	AZ 10	Mail (Av. du)	AZ 34	St-Guillaume (R.)		AZ 50
Du-Guesclin (R.)	AZ 20	Mairie (Pl. de la)	ABZ 35	St-Sauveur (Pl.)		AZ 51
Estrée (R.)	BYZ 21	Monnaie (R. de la)	AYZ 36	St-Sauveur (R.)		AZ 52
Focn (Pl. du Mar.)	AZ 22	Motte (Contour de la)	BY 37	St-Yves (R.)		AZ 53
Gambetta (R.)	BZ 23	Motte-Fablet (R. de la)	BY 38	Toulouse (R. de)		AY 54
Hermine (R. de l')	ABZ 24	Nationale (R.)	BY 39	Viarmes (R. de)		CZ 55
Ille et Rance (Quai d')	AZ 25	Nemours (R.de)	AZ 40	Zola (Quai Émile)		BZ 56

Old Rennes★. – This is the part of the old town which escaped the fire. It contains a maze of 15 and 16C houses with overhanging storeys and lordly mansions with sculptured façades which can be seen as you stroll in the cathedral quarter.

Follow the itinerary indicated on the plan starting from the St-Sauveur Church.

At no 6 **Rue St-Sauveur** stands a 16C canon's residence.

At no 3 **Rue St-Guillaume** a beautiful mediaeval house, said to be the house of Du Guesclin (AZ D), contains the restaurant Ti Koz.

The **Rue de la Psalette** which skirts the cathedral is lined with old houses.

No 22 **Rue du Chapitre** is a Renaissance house, no 8 is the Hôtel de Brie (17C) and no 6 the 18C **Hôtel de Blossac** (AZ B) with a fine staircase (on the left on entering).

Nos 6 and 8 **Rue St-Yves** are 16C houses.

The restored no 10 **Rue des Dames** is the Hôtel Freslon de la Freslonnière.

The **Mordelaise Gate** (Porte Mordelaise) (AZ A) is all that remains of the 15C ramparts. Go through the gate to see the outside face. The Dukes of Brittany passed through it on their way to the cathedral for their coronation. In 1598 the silver-gilt keys of the city were presented there to Henri IV. At this kind of ceremony the Béarnais made a statement which always went down well: "These are beautiful keys," he would say, "but I would rather have the keys to the hearts of your citizens."

The **Place des Lices** (AY) was where jousts and tournaments were held. Nos 26 and 28 are 17C hotels with large staircases capped with domes.

Looking onto the **Place Ste-Anne** (AY) are several 16C houses. Leperdit, the mayor, lived at no 19.

The animated and shopping street, **Rue de Pont-aux-Foulons** is lined with half-timbered houses.

The **Rue du Champ Jacquet** leads to an oddly shaped triangular square. The façade of the Hôtel de Tizy (no 5) gives onto it.

Rue St-Georges (BZ). – All the houses are old. The half-timbered houses, nos 8, 10 and 12 form an exquisite ensemble.

The Hôtel de Moussaye (16C), no 3, has an elegant Renaissance façade with sculpted pilasters.

Museums★★ (BZ M). – *Open 10am to noon and 2 to 6pm. Closed Tuesdays and holidays. Admission: 2.50F.*

The **Breton Museum** (musée de la Bretagne) recalls the history of Brittany. Each gallery evokes a period: geological, prehistoric, Gallo-Roman Armorica, Palaeo-Christian Armorica and Brittany of the *ancien régime*.

In the last gallery, concerned with the period from 1789 to 1914, are displayed costumes, everyday objects, tools and furniture characteristic of Brittany.

The **Fine Arts Museum** (musée des Beaux-Arts) contains paintings of the French and foreign schools from the 16C to the present. Note especially *Nouveau-né* by Georges de la Tour. The museum also contains a rich collection of old drawings, porcelain (18C Rennes) and fine Egyptian, Greek and Etruscan archaeological pieces.

■ ADDITIONAL SIGHTS

St. Peter's Cathedral (Cathédrale St. Pierre) (AZ). – This, the third cathedral built on this site since the 6C, was finished in 1844 after fifty-seven years' work. The previous building collapsed in 1762 except for two towers in the Classical style flanking the façade.

The interior is very rich, its stucco facing covered with paintings and gilding. The cathedral contains a masterpiece: the gilded and carved wood **altarpiece★★** in the chapel before the south transept. Both in size and in execution, this 15C Flemish work is one of the most important of its kind. The scenes represent the life of the Virgin.

The Mordelaise Gate *(see above)* and quarters of the old town *(p 158)* can be seen near the cathedral.

Town Hall (Hôtel de Ville) (AZ H). – *To visit apply to the porter in the left wing.*

The City Hall was built to the plans of Jacques Gabriel in 1734-43, after the fire of 1720. A central tower, standing back from the façade, carries the great clock – "le gros", as the townspeople call it – and is joined by two curved buildings to two large annexes. The right wing contains the Pantheon of Rennes, a hall dedicated to the memory of men who have died for France. *Open from 8am to noon and 2 to 6pm. Closed Saturday afternoons and Sundays.* Provided no official reception is being held, the public are admitted to the left wing of the building and can see the monumental staircase and the 18C Brussels' tapestries. There is a beautiful banqueting hall.

St-Sauveur (AZ K). – 17 and 18C. Inside is a fine gilded wooden canopy. To the right is a chapel consecrated to Our Lady of Miracles who saved Rennes from the English during the siege of 1357.

St-Germain (BZ E). – This Flamboyant church (15-16C) with its 17C gable (on the south side) retains certain characteristics typical of a Breton cathedral: wood vaulting and its beams with sculpted tips. In the south transept the beautiful 16C stained glass window recounts the life of the Virgin.

Notre-Dame or **St-Melaine** (CY F). – This church was rebuilt in the 14 and 17C. All that remains of the church of the former St-Melaine Abbey is the 11C tower and transept. To see the 17C cloisters which adjoin the north side of the church, take the impasse which leads to the Services of Urbanism. Left of the square, is the former bishop's palace (17-18C).

Cultural Centre (Maison de la Culture) (CZ). – *Open noon to the end of the performances. Closed in August.*

Designed by the architects Carlu (he also designed the Palais de Chaillot in Paris, *see Michelin Green Guide to Paris*) and Joly, it contains various halls of different seating capacities: theatre, cinema, conference hall. Also included is an exhibition gallery, a discotheque and a library.

Thabor Garden★ (CY). – *Open, according to the season, till 6 or 9.30pm.*

The former garden of the Benedictine Abbey of St-Melaine formed the nucleus of this park, which now covers nearly 11 ha - 27 acres. It includes a formal French garden; a botanical garden, a landscape garden, a rose garden and rhododendrons.

Maurepas Park. – *Plan p 158.* Go by way of the Rues de Fougères and Paul-Painlevé.

Breton Car Museum (Musée Automobile de Bretagne). – *2 km - 1 mile by ② on the plan. Open 9am to noon and 2 to 7pm. Closed Tuesdays.*

Old car museum.

EXCURSIONS

Vilaine Valley. – *Round tour of 36 km - 23 miles – about 1 hour. Leave Rennes by ⑦ on the plan, the D 177. After going 11.5 km - 7 miles turn right at La Rabine into the D 36 towards Blossac Château (not open to the public).* This castle stands 1.5 km - 1 mile away from where the Vilaine and the Meu flow into one another, and is surrounded by pleasant and peaceful farmland.

Return to the D 177 which crosses the river at Pont-Réan in beautiful surroundings. As you leave the market town, turn left along a road which is soon lined with trees.

Le Boël. – You can go for a short walk beside the river which runs between bare hills. A small lock seems once to have been used to control the water for the old mill on the far bank.

Return to Pont-Réan and after crossing the bridge over the Vilaine, turn right.

Bruz. – Pop 7 358. This country town is an example of successful planning in rural surroundings. The church, which is built of rose veined schist, is beautiful. A pointed spire rises above the square tower that forms the porch at its base. The interior blends well; daylight enters on all sides through square panes of glass decorated with a picture of three fishes within a circle; in the apse through stained glass windows depicting the Seven Sacraments and in the two arms of the transept through windows, to the south of the Crucifixion and to the north of the Virgin Mary. The organ, also incorporated in the decoration, is flanked on either side by the long, narrow stained glass windows of unequal height that can be seen in the façade.

Return to Rennes by the D 44 and the N 137.

La ROCHE-BERNARD

Michelin map **230** 52 – Pop 1 038

A little old town picturesquely sited on the spur of La Garenne, overlooking the Vilaine River. In the 17C its shipyards were famous. The port stands on a tributary of the river. A pleasure boat harbour was created in 1972.

A real Republican. – The town of La Roche-Bernard welcomed the Revolution and opposed the Chouans. In 1793 6 000 "Whites" easily defeated the 150 "Blues" who were defending the town. The Mayor, Sauveur, refused to flee. He was ordered to shout, "Long live the King!" and he replied, "Long live the Republic!" Although knocked down and streaming with blood, he would not give way. Finally he was shot down with a pistol. The Tree of Liberty was set on fire and the dying man was thrown into the flames. The next day his stoical father wrote to the authorities at Rennes: "My son died at his post; the barbarians could not rise to the level of a true Republican."

Bridge★. – The suspension bridge over the Vilaine is a fine engineering feat, standing at the level of the Breton plateau and more than 50 m - 160 ft above the river. Stop at either end or on the corniche roads upstream to see how it blends with the landscape.

Viewpoint★. – From a bend of the D 774, a belvedere dominates the Vilaine Valley extending its views onto the wooden slopes and on the right the suspension bridge, on the left the pleasure boat harbour on the Rodoir.

Old Quarter. – Across the D 774 and in front of a plaque which commemorates the launching of the vessel, *La Couronne* (1634), begins the **Promenade du Ruicard**. Overlooking the port, the promenade leads you through a maze of small streets, some of which are stepped. Houses of the 16 and 17C follow: no 8 is well restored, nos 6 and 11 have interesting doorways, no 12 has a turret. The Passage de la Quenelle with its gable windows surmounted by sculpted pediments leads to the **Place Bouffay** where stood the guillotine in 1793. The Rue de la Saulnerie with a 15C house opens onto the left.

EXCURSIONS

Missilac. – Pop 3 691. *13 km - 8 miles by the N 165 to the southeast and D 2 on the left.* The 19C church in Gothic style contains in its north apsidal chapel a graceful 17C **altarpiece★** with small twisted columns ornamented with angels and Prophets.

Separated from the town, by a small stretch of water beside the wood, the 15C **Bretesche Castle** stands in an outstanding **site★**. *Park and courtyard open 9.30am to noon and 2.30pm to 7pm (6pm 1 October to 30 April). Closed Mondays and also Thursday mornings in season. Admission: 6F.*

Arzal Dam. – *Round tour of 19 km - 12 miles by the N 165 to the northwest and then the D 148 to the left.* This dam on the Vilaine forms a freshwater reservoir thus eliminating the effect of the tides and making the trip easier for the coasting vessels that ply upstream to Redon. It is also an attractive stretch for pleasure craft. The D 139 follows the crest of the dam over the river.

Turn left onto the D 34 to return to La Roche-Bernard.

Branféré Zoological Park; Léhélec Château. – *29 km - 18 miles to the north. Take the N165 in the direction of Muzellac, turn right onto the D 774 and continue to Péaule, then left onto the D 20. Turn right towards Le Guerno and once through the village, right again before taking the avenue on the left to the château.*

Branféré Zoological Park. – *Guided tours from 9am to noon and 2 to 6.30pm (or 1½ hours before sunset in autumn); closed from November to Palm Sunday. Admission: 10F; children: 5F.* The château stands in a parkland of 50 ha - 124 acres, where over 200 species of exotic animals and countless birds roam their homes amidst a series of lakes.

Return to Péaule, then take the D 20 in the direction of Redon and after 8 km - 5 miles turn right.

Léhélec Château. – *Open 2 to 7pm in July and August; closed on Tuesdays; from 15 May to 30 June and 1 to 15 September at weekends only; time: ½ hour. Admission: 4F.* Surrounded by woodland this manor house built of ferruginous schist offers on its south front an attractive perspective of the three courtyards bordered by the 17 and 18C outbuildings (small rural museum). Visitors are admitted to two rooms on the ground floor.

ROCHEFORT-EN-TERRE ★

Michelin map 230 38 – Pop 599 – *Facilities p 44*

A charming small old town in a picturesque **site**★ on a promontory between deep dells. This landscape includes rocks, woods, ravines, orchards and old houses bright with geraniums.

Grande-Rue. – A street of 16 and 17C houses.

Castle. – *Open daily in July and August, 11am to noon and 3 to 6pm; Easter to All Saints' Day, Sundays and holidays, 11am to noon and 3 to 6pm. Admission: 4F.*

The only features that remain of the former feudal buildings are sections of the walls, ruined towers and underground passages. Small local museum.

There is a good view of the Gueuzon Valley from the terrace.

Notre-Dame-de-la-Tronchaye. – The 12, 15 and 16C building includes a fine 18C wrought iron grille, a carved wood organ loft and the remains of an old rood-screen. A 17C altarpiece on the right of the chancel bears the venerated statue of Our Lady of La Tronchaye, which, according to tradition, was found in the 12C in a hollow tree where it was hidden at the time of the Norman invasions. The statue is the object of a pilgrimage on the Sunday after 15 August. In the chancel are 16C stalls and behind them, on the left, a Renaissance altarpiece adorned with painted wood statues. The door facing the altarpiece is 16C.

ROCHE-JAGU Castle ★

Michelin map 230 7

To get to the castle, take a road branching off the D 787 to the right, 5.5 km - 3½ miles from Pontrieux.

Guided tours 1 July to 30 September, 9.30am to noon and 2 to 6pm. The rest of the year, only Sunday and holiday afternoons. Time: about ¾ hour. Admission: 2F or 4F, when exhibitions.

The castle was built in the 15C at the top of the steep wooded slopes which form the left bank of the Trieux River. It was restored in 1967. There is a magnificent view of the **setting**★ of the Trieux from the flat ground in front of the east wall and from the windows facing east and the covered wall walk on the second storey. The river forms a steep sided loop at the foot of the castle.

Notice the ornate chimneys on top of the building.

ROCHERS-SÉVIGNÉ Château ★

Michelin map 230 north of 42

The Rochers-Sévigné Château, which was the home of the Marquise de Sévigné, is a place of literary interest. Admirers of the famous *Letters* will enjoy visiting the castle and park.

The castle avenue branches off the D 88. Guided tours 9am to noon and 2 to 6pm. Closed 1 January, Easter Sunday, 1 November and 25 December. Admission: 4F. Time: ¾ hour. Ring the bell by the small door in the back wing.

The Marquise de Sévigné at Les Rochers. – The Marquise used to stay frequently at the château, largely to save money as her husband and her son had spent three-quarters of her fortune, and after 1678 she virtually lived there until she died in 1696 – although it was not at the château that she died.

Her letters give a picture of life as it was led at Les Rochers. Up at eight o'clock, Mass in the chapel at nine, a walk and then lunch. In the afternoon, needlework, another walk, talks and letter writing. Charles, the lady's son, used to read learned books aloud: Montaigne, Virgil, Pascal and the Jansenists. Sometimes the readings would go on for five hours; one wonders which to admire the more, the reader's vocal powers or the patience of his audience. Dinner at 8pm. After dinner Charles would read again, this time from amusing books "to keep himself awake". The circle broke up at 10pm, but Mme de Sévigné went on reading or writing in her room until midnight.

The only variety in this country life was that created by the visits of local ladies and gentlemen or a little trip to Vitré when the legislative bodies of the district met there. The Marquise describes, sometimes with a touch of malice, the provincial nobility, their dress, their airs and graces and their faults. The official banquets, at which 400 bottles of wine were emptied, filled her with astonishment. "As much wine passes through the body of a Breton", she wrote, "as water under the bridges."

The noble lady took an interest in repairs to the building. She felt dizzy when she saw carpenters perched on the roof: "One can only thank God", she wrote, "that some men will do for 12 *sous* what others would not do for 10 000 *écus*." That did not prevent her from keeping a sharp eye on the accounts and deploring the high cost of living.

Château. – The château was built in the 14C and remodelled in the 17C. It consists of two wings set at right angles. On the left, as you enter, is the chapel (1671), built by the "very good" Abbot of Coulanges, the Marquise's maternal uncle.

The only parts open to visitors are the chapel and two rooms in the big north tower: the room on the ground floor was known as the Green Room *(Cabinet Vert)*. It contains Mme de Sévigné's furniture, personal possessions, family pictures and her portrait by Mignard; there is a collection of autographs and other documents in a glass case. The 16C chimneypiece is adorned with the Marquise's initials (Marie de Rabutin-Chantal – MRC).

Garden. – The garden, laid out by Le Nôtre, contains cedars planted in 1806. At the end of the main avenue, at the Place Coulanges, is the semicircular wall that Mme de Sévigné called "that little wall that repeats words right into your ear" because of its double echo (stones mark the places where the two conversationalists should stand).

Park. – Beyond the garden is the large, wooded park, crossed by avenues named by the Marquise: the Mall, the Lone Wolf, Infinity, the Holy Horror, My Mother's Whim, My Daughter's Whim, Royal Avenue.

ROSANBO Château ★

Michelin map 230 6 – 8 km - 5 miles west of Plouaret

The château stands on the site of a former fortified castle built on a rock overlooking the Bo – hence the name: *ros*=rock, *an*=on the, Bo=the name of the stream.

The road to the castle branches off to the right from the D 32, west of Lanvellec. Open Easter to 30 September, 10am to noon and 2 to 7pm. Admission: 6.50F.

As you enter the courtyard you see all the different periods of construction.

The oldest part is 14C and consists of the buildings on the right of the courtyard up to the tower; the part opposite is 17C and that on the left, 19C.

The ground floor rooms contain fine Breton and Florentine Renaissance furniture, pewter dishes bearing royal coats of arms and tapestries. Church and sacristy furnishings have been assembled in a great hall and, in the billiard room, which has been transformed into a museum, are to be found ivory tusks, a bronze door knocker, a writing desk, etc. A second room displays valuable castle documents. The library, which is in the modern part, looks on to a terrace ornamented with a pond. A second terrace, communicating with the first, is decorated with a formal garden of box hedging whose geometrical design was outlined by Le Nôtre. From this terrace there is a sheer drop to the Bo valley.

On the entrance side and sweeping away into the distance is the French **garden**★ also designed by Le Nôtre. It is terraced and consists of lawns. The end of the garden, shaded by trees, is divided into "green halls"; there is a Hall of the Four Seasons, each represented by a cherub, the "triangle" with Tuscan vases, a former open-air theatre beneath a fine arch of trees and a level lawn known as "the lawn of the lion overcoming the serpent" after the statue by Barye which stands upon it. The whole is divided off from the main garden by two arbours between which is a bridle path.

On the lawn before the 14C façade is a modern statue of a wild boar cut in rose granite.

ROSCOFF ★

Michelin map 230 5 – Pop 3 732 – *Facilities p 43*

Roscoff is a much frequented seaside resort and a medical centre using sea water treatment; it is also a fishing port for lobsters, a pleasure boat harbour and a great vegetable market and distribution centre to England. The University of Paris owns a laboratory in the town for oceanographic and biological research.

■ SIGHTS *time: 1¾ hours*

Notre-Dame-de-Kroaz-Baz★ (A). – Built in the 16C, this church has a remarkable Renaissance **belfry**★, one of the finest in Finistère. The outside walls and the tower are adorned with sculptured ships and cannon, for Roscoff was once a base for privateers as well as a trading port. Inside note the seven 15C alabasters in the **altarpiece**★ by the altar in the south aisle; the church has other altarpieces – particularly interesting is the one at the high altar.

In the church close are two ossuaries. The larger is in early 17C style.

Charles Pérez Aquarium★ (D). – *Open April to 31 May, 2 to 7pm; 1 June to 17 September, 10am to noon and 2 to 7pm. Admission: 5F.*

The aquarium has a central pool and several aquaria in which most of the creatures to be found in the Channel are shown in their natural state. On the first floor, history of the biological centre and oceanographic research.

The great fig tree (B). – *Ring at the entrance of the Maison, 6 Rue des Capucins.*

The tree was planted about 1625 by Capuchin monks. It is carefully propped and covers an area of 600 m² - 720 sq yds. Some years it produces as much as 400 kg - 880 lb of figs.

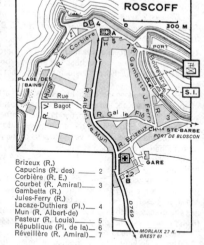

Brizeux (R.)
Capucins (R. des) ___ 2
Corbière (R. E.)
Courbet (R. Amiral) ___ 3
Gambetta (R.)
Jules-Ferry (R.)
Lacaze-Duthiers (Pl.) ___ 4
Mun (R. Albert-de)
Pasteur (R. Louis) ___ 5
République (Pl. de la) ___ 6
Réveillère (R. Amiral) ___ 7

Old Houses. – The houses in the Place Lacaze-Duthiers (4) and Rue Amiral-Révellière (7) date from the 16 and 17C.

Ste-Barbe. – *Go preferably at high tide.* Go round the old port and follow the Rue Amiral-Courbet. At the end of the road leave your car and go up the steps on the left.

On going round the chapel you will get a fine view of the coast and the islands. At the foot of the chapel you will see lobster pens.

EXCURSION

Batz Island. – Pop 807. *Boat trip, crossing: ¼ hour.*

Access: *See the current Michelin Guide France.*

This treeless island is shielded to the north by a belt of reefs. At its highest point (23 m - 75 ft) stands a lighthouse 41 m - 135 ft high. *Apply to the keeper to go up to the platform,* which commands a wide view of the coast. At Batz the men are either sailors or farmers; the women help to cultivate market produce and collect seaweed. The climate is mild (the tropical garden on the southwest point proves this) and it has many sandy beaches. On one of these there is a modern life saving station.

ROSPORDEN

Michelin map **230** 33 – Pop 4 389

This little town stands by a pool formed by the Aven River, in which the east end of the church is reflected.

Church. – The 14-17C building has a fine bell **tower***. Inside are a few old statues and a carved and gilded high altar depicting the Entombment.

RUNAN

Michelin map **230** 7 – 5 km - 3 miles west of Pontrieux

Runan, which stands on a Trégorrois plateau, possesses a large church that belonged first to the Knights Templar and then to the Hospitallers of St. John of Jerusalem.

Church. – The 14-15C church, one of the most remarkable in the district, is richly decorated. The south side has four gables pierced with broad windows with clearly designed tracery and façades covered with coats of arms, unfortunately disfigured by hammer blows. The porch gable is adorned with a sculptured lintel depicting the Annunciation, and a Descent from the Cross with St. John and Mary Magdalene on either side. The superimposed figures of the twelve Apostles join to form the keystone of the vaulting.

The ossuary adjoining the church dates from 1557; the outdoor pulpit from the time of St. Vincent Ferrier *(p 182)*.

Inside the building, roofed with panelled vaults resting on decorated beams, the Commandery Chapel (right) contains sculptured pillars of great variety and delicacy. The furnishings are remarkable: the great stained glass window of the east end (1423) is beautifully designed. The old altarpiece of the font chapel is of the same period; it is not Breton work but is made of bluish Tournai stone and includes exceptionally delicate figures. It depicts five scenes from the lives of Christ and the Virgin.

> *The age of great Gothic cathedrals in France was heralded by the construction of*
> *St-Denis (c 1136), Sens (c 1140) and Notre-Dame in Paris (1163);*
> *followed by Strasbourg (c 1176),*
> *Bourges (c 1185), Chartres (1194),*
> *Rouen (1200), Reims (1211),*
> *Amiens (1200) and Beauvais (1247).*

ST-BRIEUC *

Michelin map **230** 8, 9 – Pop 56 282

The town is built 3 km - 2 miles from the sea on a plateau deeply cleft by two watercourses: the Gouëdic and the Gouet. Bold viaducts span their valleys. The Gouet is canalised and leads to the commercial and fishing port of Légué. St-Brieuc is the administrative, commercial and industrial centre of the department. The markets and fairs of the town are much frequented, especially the Fair of St. Michael on 29 September.

An industrial zone has been established, where there are already many factories and great refrigerated depots intended for the storage of local products such as meat and the early vegetables of the Léon district.

The *pardon* of Notre-Dame-d'Espérance takes place the last Sunday in May.

■ MAIN SIGHTS

St. Stephen's Cathedral* (Cathédrale St-Étienne) (BZ). – This great building of the 13 and 14C has been reconstructed several times; its mass bears striking witness to its original role of church fortress. The front is framed by two great towers complete with loopholes and machicolations and supported by stout buttresses. The two arms of the transept jut far out and are protected by towers with pepper-pot roofs.

Go into the church through the Gothic porch in the front.

Inside, note the 18C pulpit; in the south aisle, several tombs, including that of Bishop St. Guillaume who died in 1234, the 18C carved wood altar in the Chapel of the Annunciation, the 15C rose window in the south transept, and, in the apsidal chapel, a 15C statue of the Virgin in alabaster.

The organ loft is 16C, the Stations of the Cross by Saupique are modern.

Aubé Hill* (Tertre Aubé) (CY). – The hill commands a fine **view*** of the Gouet Valley, crossed by the viaduct which carries the road to Paimpol; also of the port of Légué, below, and, to the right, of the Bay of St-Brieuc. On a hill to the right is the ruined tower of Cesson.

Rond-point Huguin (CYZ). – From the roundabout, on which stands a monument to the folklorist, Anatole Le Braz, there is a view of the Gouëdic Valley, St-Brieuc Bay and the coast as far as Cape Fréhel. The village and tower of Cesson can be seen perched above the Gouëdic Valley.

■ ADDITIONAL SIGHTS

Grandes Promenades (CZ). – These walks encircle the Law Courts. Among the statues are a bust by Élie Le Goff Sr. of the writer Villiers de l'Isle-Adam, who was born at St-Brieuc, *Form arising from Matter* by Paul Le Goff and *La Bretonne du Goëlo* by Francis Renaud.

Notre-Dame-de-la-Fontaine and St-Brieuc Fountain (AZ A). – The fountain, which is sheltered by a 15C porch, stands against the apse of the chapel which was rebuilt in the 19C.

Rue Fardel (BZ 9). – To the right (going up), at the corner of an alley, is the 15C Le Ribeault mansion; left at no 15 is the Hôtel des Ducs de Bretagne (1573).

Tour du Saint-Esprit (BZ). – *To see it, apply to the caretaker at the Préfecture. The interior is not open to visitors.*

The tower is an interesting Renaissance structure, restored in 1962.

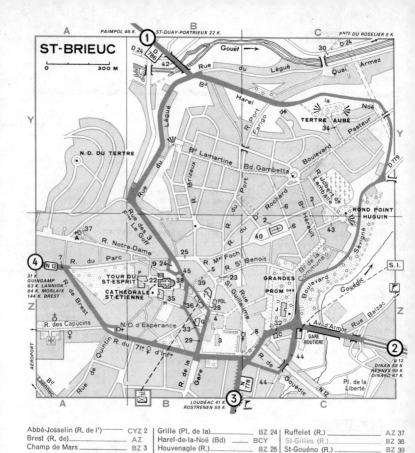

ST-BRIEUC

EXCURSIONS

Le Roselier Point*. – *Round tour of 17 km - 11 miles – about 1 hour. Leave St-Brieuc to the north by the Légué port, follow the quay on the left bank.*
You cross St-Laurent-de-la-Mer, a popular place for aquatic sports.

Turn right in La Ville-Agan. 400 m beyond Le Manoir, on your left, park the car (car park) and take a lane to the left.

The narrow path, without a parapet, skirts the steep Roselier Cliff and affords extensive views of St-Brieuc Bay.

Les Rosaires Beach. – *7.5 km - 4½ miles – about ¼ hour. Leave by ① on the plan and at Plérin take the D 1ᴮ.*
The beach is framed between wooded cliffs nearly 100 m - 320 ft high. The view includes the whole of the Bay of St-Brieuc from St-Quay Point to Cape Erquy.

ST-CAST-LE-GUILDO ★★

Michelin map **230** 10, 11 – *Local map p 90* – Pop 3 232 – *Facilities p 43*

This seaside resort, which is much frequented, is formed by three settlements: Le Bourg, l'Isle and La Garde.

A fine beach, which attracts numerous tourists in summer, is bounded by La Garde and St-Cast Points.

■ **SIGHTS** *time: 1½ hours*

St-Cast Point★★. – There is a superb **view★★** of the Emerald Coast from the point *(viewing table beside the signal station).* A monument to the Escaped Prisoners of France at the point can be reached by a cliff path which follows the shore, passes the monument to the crew of the lightship *Laplace,* mined in 1950, and rejoins the St-Cast road at La Marre beach. A similar path joins the point to the port of St-Cast.

La Garde Point★★. – At the end of this point there is a very fine **view★★** of the beaches of St-Cast and Pen Guen; also a statue of Notre-Dame-de-la-Garde by Armel Beaufils. A tourist path starts from the Hôtel Ar Vro, passes near the oratory, follows the cliff along the point and, on the south shore, joins the road leading to the dock near the oratory.

Commemorative column (A). – The column is surmounted by a greyhound for France, trampling the English leopard. It recalls the failure of a British attack on St-Malo in 1758, during the Seven Years War, when 13 000 British troops returned to embark in warships anchored in the Bay of St-Cast. They were attacked by the Duke of Aiguillon, Governor of Brittany, and lost 2 400 men. The Duke directed the battle from the mill of Anne de la Vieuxville and covered himself with glory, which on hearing the Procurator of the Rennes Parliament, La Chalotais *(p 157)*, commented sardonically, "Yes, and also with flour."

Church *(at Le Bourg – B)*. – The modern church contains a 16C font and some 17C statues. A modern stained glass window depicts the Battle of St-Cast.

Ste-Blanche *(at L'Isle – D)*. – Above the high altar is an old statue of St. Blanche, the mother of St. Guénolé, St. Jacut and St. Venec *(p 151)*, which is an object of great veneration.

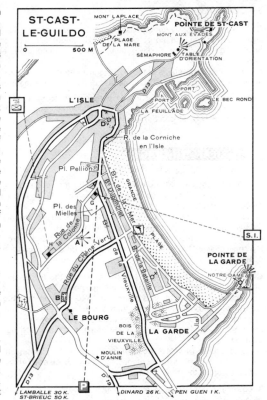

ST-CAST-LE-GUILDO

ST-GEORGES-DE-GRÉHAIGNE

Michelin map **230** 13

The Benedictine church was built in the 15C on the hilltop on the former site of a chapel that had been dedicated to St. George in 1030. The interior, with its oak roof which was restored in 1942, is adorned by several large statues the oldest being one of St. Samson. The central aisle paved with commemorative stones leads to the narrower chancel lit by a 15C window showing the Virgin as a Breton peasant. On looking between the trees behind the church one can distinguish Mont-St-Michel beyond a distant row of poplar trees.

ST-GILDAS-DE-RHUYS

Michelin map **230** 50 – *Local map p 124* – Pop 1 010 – *Facilities p 42*

This village owes its origin to a monastery founded by St. Gildas in the 6C. The most famous of the abbots who governed it was **Abélard** in the 12C. It was after the adventures, by which his name is linked, with that of Héloïse, that the learned philosopher tried to find peace in this Breton solitude. His disillusion was quick and cruel: "I live", he wrote to Héloïse, "in a wild country whose language I find strange and horrible; I see only savages; I take my walks on the inaccessible shores of a rough sea; my monks have only one rule, which is to have none at all. I should like you to see my house; you would never take it for an abbey; the only decorations on the doors are the footmarks of various animals – hinds, wolves, bears, wild boars – or the hideous regurgitations of owls. Every day brings new dangers; I always seem to see a sword hanging over my head." However, the monks used poison, not a sword, to get rid of their Abbot. It was a wonder he survived and managed to escape through a secret passage in 1140.

Church★. – *Time: ½ hour*. This is the former abbey church built at the end of the 11C and largely rebuilt in the 16 and 17C. The Romanesque apse has pure, harmonious lines.

Inside, the Romanesque **chancel★** is remarkable. Behind the high altar is the tomb of St. Gildas. Other tombs in the north transept and the ambulatory are lit by modern stained glass windows. There are also the gravestones of St. Goustan (6-7C) and the children of Brittany (13C). At the end of the nave are stoups carved from old capitals. The **treasury★** contains valuable and well displayed old pieces: shrines, reliquaries containing the arms and legs of St. Gildas, and his embroidered mitre, a 17C silver-gilt cross bejewelled with emeralds, etc. *Open in July and August, 10am to noon and 3 to 6pm. Closed Sundays and holidays. Admission: 1F.*

ST-GUÉNOLÉ

Michelin map **230** 31 – *Local map p 77* – *Facilities p 42*

Small seaside resort. The modern church is charming though a little dark; it stands near the old square tower that is all that remains of the former church. Behind the fishing port (coastal fishing: sardines, mackerel) are the famous rocks against which the sea breaks furiously.

Finistère Prehistorical Museum★. – *Open 1 June to 30 September, 10am to noon and 2 to 6pm; the rest of the year, apply to the caretaker. Admission: 2F.*

A series of megaliths and Gallic steles or obelisks called *lec'hs* stand around the museum. By going round clockwise you will see the exhibits in chronological order, from the Stone Age to the

Gallo-Roman period: a large polisher, polished axes of rare stone, wonderfully finely shaped arrowheads in flint, and bronze weapons, in the south hall; in the other hall, two reconstructions of Iron Age cemeteries, Gallic pottery with Celtic decorations and a Gallic stele with spiral carving.

The museum contains all the prehistoric antiquities discovered in Finistère, except for those displayed in the Museum of National Antiquities at St-Germain-en-Laye.

Pors-Carn Beach. – Opposite St-Guénolé's prehistorical museum, on the other side of the road, the sandy beach of Pors-Carn extends along La Torche Bay. The telephone cable linking France to the U.S. ends in Pors-Carn.

ST-JEAN-DU-DOIGT ★

Michelin map **230** 5, 6 – Pop 688

This picturesque village owes its name to the relic kept in its church since the 15C. It celebrates its *pardon,* which is attended particularly by people suffering from ophthalmia, the last Sunday in June.

In the parish close *(time: ¾ hour)* are to be seen a triumphal gateway whose Gothic arch is the largest left to us and, on the left, a pretty Renaissance **fountain★**. To the right of the church porch is a small chapel (1577) adorned inside with a frieze and sculpted beams.

Church★. – St. John's finger, which was brought to the Chapel of St. Meriadoc by a young man from Plougasnou in 1437, worked miracles. A great church was started in 1440, but the building went slowly and was finished only thanks to the generosity of Anne of Brittany in 1513. The Queen came there on a pilgrimage in 1505 and from that date contributed a yearly sum until the building was complete.

The church *(under restoration inside)* is in the Flamboyant style with two small ossuaries at the base of the tower; one *(on the right)* is Gothic, the other Renaissance.

Treasury★★. – *Apply to M. le Curé.* The treasury contains several reliquaries, one of which holds the first joint of the forefinger of St. John the Baptist (this relic is dipped into the Sacred Fountain several times a year to bless the water). There are also a monstrance, chalices and patens and a **processional cross★**. The finest piece is a silver-gilt Renaissance **chalice★★**.

(After Arthaud photo, Grenoble)

The chalice.

ST-LUNAIRE ★★

Michelin map **230** 11 – *Local map p 91* – Pop 1 585 – *Facilities p 42*

This smart resort has two beaches: that of St-Lunaire, which is the more frequented, and that of Longchamp, which is the larger.

■ **SIGHTS** *time: ½ hour*

Walk to Décollé Point★★. – The point is joined to the mainland by a natural bridge crossing a deep fissure and known as the Cat's Leap (Saut du Chat); the Décollé Promenades are laid out beyond the bridge.

To the left of the entrance to the Décollé Pavilion, take the road leading to the point, on which there is a granite cross. The vantage point affords a very fine **view★★** of the Emerald Coast, from Cape Fréhel to the Varde Point.

The Sirens' Cave★ (Grotte des Sirènes). – From the bridge crossing the cleft through which it opens to the sea, you can see the bottom of the grotto. The wash of the sea at high tide is spectacular.

Old Church (A). – *Out of season, ask for the key at the presbytery.* The church, which has an 11C nave, contains various tombs with reclining figures; three are 12C and four 14 and 15C. The tomb of St. Lunaire is among the later group. There is an annual *pardon* in July *(second or third Sunday).*

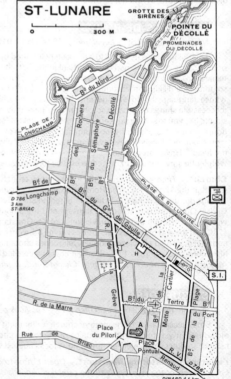

The excursions listed under Dinard – 4.5 km - 3 miles away – may be made equally well from St-Lunaire *(p 85).*

ST-MALO ★★★

Michelin map 230 11 – Local maps pp 80 and 155 – Pop 46 270

St-Malo, St-Servan, Paramé and Rothéneuf *(facilities p 43)* have joined together to form a continuous settlement. The **site**★★★ of St-Malo is unique in France and makes it one of the great tourist centres of Brittany. St-Servan and Paramé are pleasant seaside resorts on either side.

The Port. – The port has four wet docks (Vauban, Duguay-Trouin, Bouvet and an inner dock) and an outer harbour. Imports of coal, fertilisers, wood and pulp for paper, wine, foodstuffs for cattle and building materials keep it busy. Its main export is wheat from the hinterland.

It is the only Breton port still to have a cod fishing fleet *(details p 17)* and is the port from which passengers cross from France to the Channel Islands and England.

Hovercraft service to Jersey and Guernsey. Car ferry service to Jersey. Apply to Morvan, 4 Rue des Cordiers, Tel 56 42 29. Car ferry service to Plymouth and Portsmouth. Apply to Brittany Ferries, Nouvelle Gare Maritime, Tel 56 42 29.

A port for pleasure boating has been made in the Vauban dock and another is being built in the Sablons Bay *(p 41)*.

HISTORICAL NOTES

Origin. – St. Malo, returning from Wales in the 6C, converted Aleth (St. Servan) and became its bishop. The island on which the town of St-Malo is built today was then uninhabited. Later, people settled there because it was easy to defend, and it became important enough for the Bishopric of Aleth to be transferred to it in 1144. It took the name of St. Malo while Aleth put himself under the protection of another local saint – St. Servan.

The town belonged to its bishops, who built ramparts round it. It took no part in provincial rivalries. At the time of the League, St-Malo declared itself a republic and was able to keep its independence for four years. This principle is reflected in the device: ''Ni Français, ni Bretons, Malouins suis'' (I am neither a Frenchman nor a Breton but a man of St-Malo).

Famous men of St-Malo. – Few towns have had as many famous sons as St-Malo.

Jacques Cartier left in 1534 to look for gold in Newfoundland and Labrador: instead he discovered the mouth of the St. Lawrence River, which he took to be the estuary of a great Asian river. As the word Canada, which means ''village'' in the Huron language, was often used by the Red Indians he encountered, he used the word to name the country. Cartier took possession of the land in the name of the King of France in 1535, but it was only under Champlain that the colonisation of Canada began and that Quebec was founded (1608).

Porcon de la Bardinais, who had been charged in 1665 by the St-Malo shipowners to defend their ships against the Barbary pirates, was captured and taken before the Dey of Algiers. The Dey sent him to Louis XIV with peace proposals on condition that if these were not accepted he would return to Algeria. The Dey's proposals were refused, so Porcon went to St-Malo to put his affairs in order, said farewell to his family and returned to Africa, where he was executed by being blown from the mouth of a cannon.

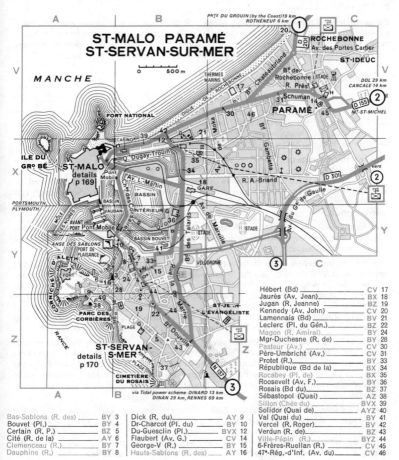

Hébert (Bd)		CV 17
Jaurès (Av. Jean)		BX 18
Jugan (R. Jeanne)		BZ 19
Kennedy (Av. John)		CV 20
Lamennais (Bd)		BV 21
Leclerc (Pl. du Gén.)		BZ 22
Magon (R. Amiral)		BY 24
Mgr-Duchesne (R. de)		BY 28
Pasteur (Av.)		CV 30
Père-Umbricht (Av.)		CV 31
Protet (R.)		BY 33
République (Bd de la)		BX 34
Rocabey (Pl. de)		BX 35
Roosevelt (Av. F.)		BY 36
Rosais (Bd du)		BZ 37
Sébastopol (Quai)		AZ 38
Sillon (Chée du)		BVX 39
Solidor (Quai de)		AYZ 40
Val (Quai du)		BY 41
Vercel (Av. Roger)		BV 42
Verdun (R. de)		BZ 43
Ville-Pépin (R.)		BYZ 44
6-Frères-Ruellan (R.)		CV 45
47e-Rég.-d'Inf. (Av. du)		CV 46

Bas-Sablons (R. des)	BY 3	Dick (R. du)	AY 9		
Bouvet (Pl.)	BY 4	Dr-Charcot (Pl. du)	BY 10		
Certain (R. P.)	BZ 5	Du-Guesclin (Pl.)	BVX 12		
Cité (R. de la)	AY 6	Flaubert (Av. G.)	CV 14		
Clemenceau (R.)	BY 7	George-V (R.)	BY 15		
Dauphine (R.)	BY 8	Hauts-Sablons (R. des)	AY 16		

Duguay-Trouin (1673-1736) and Surcouf (1773-1827) are the most famous of the St-Malo privateers. These bold seamen received "letters of marque" from the king which permitted them to attack warships or merchantmen without being treated as pirates, that is, hanged from the mainyard. In the 17 and 18C the privateers inflicted heavy losses on the English, the Dutch and the Spanish.

Duguay was the son of a rich shipowner and had been destined for the priesthood; but by the time he was sixteen the only way to put an end to his wild living was to send him to sea. His gifts were such that at twenty-four he entered the so-called Great Corps of the French Navy as a commander and at thirty-six he was given a peerage. When he died he was a Lieutenant General in the seagoing forces and a Commander of the Order of St. Louis.

Surcouf's history is completely different, but quite as outstanding. He answered the call of the sea when very young and soon began a prodigious career of fabulous exploits. First as slaver then as privateer he amassed an enormous fortune. At thirty-six he retired! He continued, however, to make money by fitting out privateers and merchantmen.

Chateaubriand and Lamennais brought the flavour of the Romantic Movement to their native St-Malo.

François-René de Chateaubriand (1768-1848) was the tenth and last child of a very noble Breton family who had fallen on evil times. His father went to America in search of fortune and was able, on his return, to set up as a shipowner at St-Malo. The future poet spent his early years in roaming about the port, then went in succession through the schools of Dinan, Dol, Rennes and Brest, dreaming sometimes of the priesthood, sometimes of the sea. He spent two years in exile at Combourg *(details p 72)* with his father, his mother and his sister Lucile. It was through the profession of arms that he began, in 1786, the adventurous career which ended in 1848 in the solitary grandeur of Grand Bé *(p 169)*.

Lamennais (1782-1854), another St-Malo shipowner's son, also had a place in the Romantic Movement. He was early an orphan and was brought up by an uncle at the Castle of Chesnaye, near Dinan. At twenty-two he taught mathematics in the College of St-Malo before entering the seminary of that town. He was ordained a priest in 1816 and had a great influence on Lacordaire and Montalembert. His writings and violent quarrels got him into trouble with Rome and even led him to throw up the Church. He retired to Chesnaye and published, in 1834, the famous *Paroles d'un Croyant* (Words of a Believer). Owing to his advanced political ideas he was sentenced to a year's imprisonment in 1840 but won a seat in the National Assembly in 1848.

To the famous men of St-Malo already mentioned should be added Mahé de la Bourdonnais (1699-1753), a great colonist and the rival of Dupleix in the Indies; Broussois (1772-1838), who transformed the medical science of his time; Gournay (1712-59), the economist to whom the formula "laissez faire, laissez passer" (let it be, let it go) is attributed; and finally that saintly figure of André Desilles. In 1790 the garrison of Nancy, to which this twenty-three-year-old Lieutenant belonged, revolted against the National Assembly. Troops were sent to subdue it. To prevent the fraticidal struggle, Desilles threw himself in front of the guns and fell, mortally wounded.

As Chateaubriand commented of his home town: "It's not a bad record for an area smaller than the Tuileries Gardens".

Destruction and Renaissance of St-Malo. – St-Malo and the area around was turned into an entrenched camp by the Germans and became the prize for which a merciless battle raged from 1 to 14 August 1944. The town was left in ruins. With a great sense of history, its restorers were determined to bring the old city back to life. They have been completely successful.

■ **MAIN SIGHTS** *time: 2 hours*

Leave your car on the St-Vincent esplanade.

St-Malo, now restored, is once again a picturesque town, surrounded by ramparts, bringing back memories of great privateers and shipowners.

The statue near the esplanade, at the entrance to the Casino garden, is of Chateaubriand by Armel-Beaufils. It was set up in 1948 on the centenary of his death.

Tour of the Ramparts★★★. – Pass under the St. Vincent Gate (Porte St-Vincent), which consists of twin gates; then take the staircase to the right leading to the ramparts.

The ramparts, started in the 12C, were enlarged and altered up to the 18C and survived the wartime destruction. The rampart walk commands magnificent views especially at high tide which runs from 8 to 14 m - 25 to 45 ft completely altering the shoreline and appearance of the islands in the bay.

From the St-Vincent Gate to the St-Louis Bastion. – Directly after the Grande Gate (Grande Porte), which is crowned with machicolations, the view opens out over the narrow isthmus which joins the old town to its suburbs, the harbour basins and, beyond, St-Servan.

From the St-Louis Bastion to the St-Philip Bastion. – The rampart skirts the houses of the rich shipowners of St-Malo; two, near the St-Louis Bastion, are still intact but the following walls and façades are reconstructions. The fine group including the high roofs, surmounted by monumental chimneys, standing up from the ramparts, once more gives this part of the town its old look.

The view extends over the outer harbour; to the Aleth Rock, crowned by the Cité Fort, and the mouth of the Rance estuary; to Dinard, with the Prieuré beach and the Vicomté Point.

From the St-Philip Bastion to the Bidouane Tower. – A very fine view of the Emerald Coast west of Dinard, and of the islands off St-Malo. To the right of the Moulinet Point you can see part of the great beach at Dinard, the Étêtés Point separating Dinard from St-Lunaire, the Décollé Point, the Hébihens Archipelago, the St-Cast Point and Cape Fréhel; nearer, on the right, are Harbour Isle and, farther to the right, the Grand Bé *(p 169)* and Petit Bé Islands; then, in the background, Cézembre Island and Conchée Fort.

From the Bidouane Tower to the St-Vincent Gate. – From this point you can see the National Fort *(p 169)* and the great curve which joins St-Malo to the Varde Point, passing through the beaches of Paramé, Rochebonne and Le Minihic.

At the end of the ramparts take the stairway going down near the St-Thomas Gate (Porte St-Thomas) – this gate opens on the main beach which joins the immense Paramé beach.

Aquarium, – *Open 1 July to 15 September, 9am to 11pm; the rest of the year, 10am to noon and 2 to 6pm. Admission: 6F.*

A gallery with some 100 aquariums, built into the walls of the ramparts in the Place Vauban near the St. Thomas Gate, contains a collection of salt and freshwater specimens, particularly fish and fauna native to the St-Malo Bay, North Sea, Mediterranean coasts and coral reefs. Note a blue lobster, a couple of king crabs, seahorses and a collection of anemones.

Quic-en-Groigne*. – *Open Easter to 20 September, 9am to noon and 2 to 6pm. Admission: 6F.*

This tower which is located in the left wing of the castle, bears the name Quic-en-Groigne from an inscription Queen Anne had carved on it in defiance of the bishops of St-Malo: "Qui-qu'en-groigne, ainsi sera, car tel est mon bon plaisir." (Thus it shall be, whoever may complain, for that is my wish.) It contains reconstructions of historic scenes, the celebrities of St-Malo being represented by wax figures (waxworks museum).

Return to the St-Vincent esplanade.

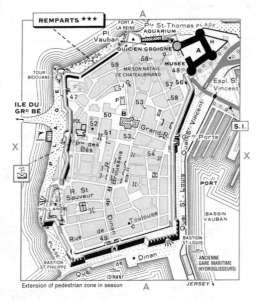

ST-MALO

0 —————— 200 m

Extension of pedestrian zone in season

■ ADDITIONAL SIGHTS

Castle** (AX A). – *You can enter the courtyard and see the façades of the former 17-18C barracks (now the town hall), the well, the great keep and the redoubt.*

The little keep was built as part of the ramparts in 1395. The great keep (1424) and corner towers were constructed in the 15 and 16C. The Galley dates from the 17C.

St-Malo Museum. – *Open 1 June to 30 September, 9.30am to noon and 2 to 6.30pm. The rest of the year, 9.45am to noon and 2 to 6pm. Closed Tuesdays in winter. Admission: 2F.*

The museum which is installed in the great keep and records the development of the city of St-Malo and its celebrities (Jacques Cartier, Duguay-Trouin, La Bourdonnais, Surcouf, Chateaubriand, Lamennais). To end the visit climb up to the watch towers of the keep, from which you will see an impressive panorama of the town and the sea.

St-Vincent Cathedral (AX B). – The building was started in the 11C and completed in the 18C. The nave is roofed with diagonal ribbed vaulting typical of the Angevin style; dark and massive it contrasts with the slenderly built 13C chancel. Lit by magnificent **stained glass windows*** by Jean Le Moal, the chancel becomes a kaleidoscope of colours. In the transept restored in the 17C style are the stained glass windows, muted in colour while in the side aisles the windows by Max Ingrand are brighter. The north side aisle has preserved its original vaulting.

The Chapel of the Sacred Heart (south side) is a very successful piece of reconstruction with its wooden vault and granite altar. A 16C Virgin, Notre-Dame-de-la-Croix-du-Fief, is kept in the second chapel north of the ambulatory together with the remains of Duguay-Trouin. The neighbouring chapel houses the tomb of Jacques Cartier.

Grand Bé Island** and **Chateaubriand's Tomb** (AX – *plan p 167*). – ¾ *hour on foot Rtn. Only at low tide. Leave St-Malo by the Champs-Vauverts Gate and cross the beach diagonally to the causeway. Follow the road that skirts the right-hand edge of the island.*

Chateaubriand's tomb is on the seaward side; it is a plain, unnamed flagstone surmounted by a heavy granite cross. Edouard Herriot, based an interesting character sketch of Chateaubriand on the loneliness of this place. "He was a giant of letters, living in splendid isolation. And though it may surprise us at first, we can understand why he wished to be buried on his lonely rock, with nothing around him but the sea that inspired his first dreams. At the meeting-point of two centuries he stands like an island, destined to know the convulsions of war even after his death, rugged by nature, remote from ordinary men, preferring to their society, which he scorned, the lofty pleasures of communion with his friend the Ocean."

From the top of the island there is a panorama of the entire Emerald Coast.

Cross the open space, go down a few steps and turn left along a road leading back to the causeway by which you came.

National Fort* (AV – *plan p 167*). – *Access by the Plage de l'Éventail at low tide, ¼ hour on foot Rtn. Admission: 4F.*

Built by Vauban in 1689, the Royal Fort became the National Fort after the Revolution and then private property. Built on the rock, this stronghold assured the protection of the city. The **view**** of the ramparts is remarkable. The fort commands extensive views of the coast: St-Malo, St-Servan, the Rance estuary, the Grand and Petit Bé Islands, Harbour Island, the Grand Jardin Lighthouse, the Conchée Fort and in the distance the Chausey Islands.

The fort played an important part in 1692 against the English and Dutch fleet.

BOAT TRIPS

Dinard★★★. – P 84.

Cruise to Cape Fréhel★★★. – P 85.

Dinan the Rance★★. – P 154.

Cézembre Island. – P 85.

ST-SERVAN-SUR-MER★

The resort of St-Servan-sur-Mer is gay with many gardens, in striking contrast to the walled town of St-Malo. Its main beach is around by the Sablons Bay, although there are also smaller beaches along the Rance.

The town has three ports: the Bouvet dock, a trading and a fishing port, linked with that of St-Malo, the Solidor, a former naval base, and the Saint-Père.

Jeanne Jugan, humble servant of the poor (1792-1879). – The name of Jeanne Jugan, which has been given to a street in St-Servan-sur-Mer, recalls a humble, devoted life, a faith to move mountains and an admirable work of charity.

Jeanne Jugan was born in 1792. She was the daughter of a Cancale fisherman who lost his life at sea, leaving a widow and seven children. Jeanne found a place as a domestic servant with an old maiden lady at St-Servan-sur-Mer, and while taking care of her for eighteen years she helped the poor and lonely old people of the neighbourhood. In 1835 her mistress died, leaving her 400 francs. The great hearted serving woman bought a hovel in which she sheltered old people with the help of three friends who were also domestics or working women. In 1840 these holy women formed a sort of religious society of which the Vicar of St-Servan-sur-Mer, the Abbé Le Pailleur, became chaplain. The society, in due course, became the Congregation of the Little Sisters of the Poor.

To feed her people Jeanne went out begging every day, in all weathers, with her basket on her arm, well received by some, rebuffed by others. One day an angry boor struck her. "The blow is for me, my good man," she said with a smile, "now give me something for my paupers." By the rules of the Congregation, this daily quest is still its only means of subsistence. Jeanne Jugan died at the age of eighty-six. Today the 6 500 Sisters are scattered all over the world, in more than 300 establishments where they shelter and care for 50 000 old people.

Aleth Corniche★★ (AY). – This walk, with the magnificent **views★★** it offers, is the chief attraction of St-Servan.

Leave your car in the Place St-Pierre, where in a garden stand the ruins of the former cathedral of Aleth. Take the street on the right going north and follow the corniche pathway.

First comes a remarkable view of St-Malo. Farther to the left can be distinguished the Petit Bé, the Grand Bé and Cézembre Islands. Bear left and skirt the seashore. Go round the fort. The whole harbour is now visible: to the right of Cézembre Island, in the distance, is the fortified Island of Grande Conchée; on the left, the Grand Jardin Lighthouse, Harbour Island and its fort and, in the distance, Cape Fréhel and the Décollé Point, followed by a maze of reefs. Finally there is a very fine view of the Rance estuary, barred by the Bizeux rock, on which stands a statue of the Virgin, and beyond, of the tidal power scheme.

Solidor Tower★ (Tour Solidor) (AZ). – This tower, which commands the Rance estuary, was built in 1382 on foundations which were probably Roman. It consists of three contiguous towers and its three storeys were long used as a prison. It now houses the International Museum of Cape Horn Vessels.

International Museum of Cape Horn Vessels★ (Musée International du Long-Cours Cap Hornier). – *Guided tours every hour from 10am to noon and 2 to 6pm, 1 June to 30 September; the rest of the year 2 to 5pm. Closed Tuesdays in winter. Admission: 2F.*

The life of the great navigators (16-20C) who sailed to Cape Horn is recounted in the museum. Throughout the galleries life on board is evoked. Note the model of *Victoria*, the first ship which sailed round the world in 1 084 days from 1519 to 1522. A succession of exhibits at different levels leads to the wall walk which commands a view of the estuary, St-Servan-sur-Mer, St-Malo, Dinard and the Rance.

Corbières Park★ (Parc des Corbières) (ABZ). – *Open 1 April to 30 September 8am to 8pm; the rest of the year 9am to 5pm.*

Still bearing left, follow the cliff path which goes round Corbières Point, affording fine **glimpses★** of the Rance estuary and the tidal power station.

City Fort (Fort de la Cité) (AY). – *Start from the Place St-Pierre.*

The City Fort was built in 1759 on the orders of the Duke of Aiguillon. It was modernised and used by the Germans in the last war. Around the inner courtyard, where an open-air theatre has since been built, is a chain of blockhouses joined by over a mile of underground passages, which also serve the barracks, the hospital and all the offices of this little town, built on several storeys *(not open to the public).* From the top of the bastions of the old fort there are fine general views of the harbour and the Rance estuary.

Ste-Croix (BZ A). – The church is in the Greco-Roman style. The interior is decorated with frescoes.

Rosais Cemetery (BZ B). – This little marine cemetery on the side of a cliff overlooking the Rance contains the tomb of the Count and Countess of Chateaubriand, the writer's parents. **View★** of the Bizeux rock and Vicomté Point.

St-Jean-l'Évangéliste. – 1964. In the form of a Mauritanian tent the triangular façade of this church is adorned by a fresco.

PARAMÉ★★

Paramé, a much frequented seaside resort, possesses a salt-water thermal establishment. It has two magnificent beaches extending for 2 km - 1½ miles: the Casino Beach, which continues that of St-Malo and the Rochebonne Beach. The splendid seafront promenade, 3 km - 2 miles long, is the chief attraction for the passing tourist.

ROTHÉNEUF

This seaside resort has two beaches which differ widely. That of the Val is wide open to the sea. That of Rothéneuf Cove lies on an almost landlocked bay like a large lake surrounded with dunes, cliffs and pines; it is a favourite place for lovers of aquatic sports.

Near Rothéneuf is **Le Minihic**, with its own beach and villas.

Sculptured Rocks (Rochers sculptés). – Some rocks along the coast have been sculptured with patience by a priest, the Abbé Fouré, who spent twenty-five years of his life on the task. *Private property. Admission: 4F.*

Salt-water Aquarium. – *Open in summer 8am to 8pm; in winter 8am to noon and 2 to 5pm. Admission: 4 F.*

This has interesting specimens of live salt-water creatures and a big collection of shells.

ST-MATHIEU Point ★★

Michelin map 230 16 – *Local map p 47*

St-Mathieu, which was an important town in the 14C, is now only a village known for the ruins of its abbey church, its site and its lighthouse.

The Lighthouse. – *Open 9am to noon and 2 to 7pm (5pm in winter).*

The lighthouse has a considerable system of lights; two auxiliary lights are reserved for air navigation. There is also a radio beam. The main light is served by a 1 500 watt lamp, giving it an intensity of about 5 000 000 candlepower, with a range of 55 to 60 km - 34 to 37½ miles.

From the top *(167 steps)* there is a superb **panorama★★**: from left to right – the mouth of the Brest Sound; the Crozon Peninsula; Raz Point; Sein Island (in clear weather); the Pierres Noires reef; and the Islands of Béniguet, Molène and Ushant. Beyond Béniguet, 30 km - 18½ miles away, you can sometimes distinguish the Jument lighthouse.

Ruins of the Abbey Church★. – The ruins are the remains of a monastery founded in the 6C which, according to legend, had as a relic the head of St. Matthew, brought from Africa by seamen. The 13C chancel, which has ogive vaulting, is flanked by a square keep. The nave with rounded or octagonal pillars, has a single aisle on the north side and two 16C aisles on the south side.

At the tip of the point a column erected to the memory of the French sailors who died in the First World War is the work of the sculptor Quillivic. There is a magnificent view from the edge of the cliff.

At a point 300 m from St-Mathieu are two Gallic steles surmounted by a cross and known as the Monks' Gibbet (Gibet des Moines).

Renards Point. – Jutting out not far from the beach of Le Conquet this headland offers fine views of St-Mathieu Point, Ushant and Molène.

A visit to St-Nazaire, which is above all a great shipbuilding centre, is particularly interesting for tourists who are familiar with shipping and industrial questions. The town developed rapidly when large ships, finding it difficult to get up to Nantes, stopped at its deep water port. The 4 000 inhabitants of 1846 had become 25 000 by the beginning of the 20C.

HISTORICAL NOTES

St-Nazaire during the War. – St-Nazaire, a little, almost insignificant town, which suddenly became a large port in the 19C, was the obvious target for aerial bombardment between 1940 and 1945. In addition, like Lorient, the town got caught up in the fighting for the St-Nazaire Pocket and consequently was just as desolate when finally liberated.

A monument to commemorate the Surrender of the St-Nazaire Pocket stands at Bouvron, a place on the N 771 between Savenay and Blain, 36 km - 22 miles from St-Nazaire.

St-Nazaire today. – Rebuilt after the war, the town is now divided into two distinct quarters: to the east is the **harbour and industrial zone** and to the west the **residential quarter** opened with wide avenues. In the town centre, the town hall (1969) stands amidst a fine square decorated with fountains. Farther west the Avenue Léo-Lagrange separates the **park** from the **sports ground**. Near the coast, modern buildings have been built in the Kerledé quarter.

To the east of St-Nazaire, near the mouth of the Brivet the **St-Nazaire-St-Brévin Bridge*** *(toll)* spans the Loire, a distance of more than 2.5 km - 1½ miles, and it stands 61 m - 200 ft above mean high water at midpoint. It links the town of St-Nazaire to the Retz country, the Vendée and the Charentes.

■ THE PORT *time: 1½ hours*

Tourists may walk along the harbour roadways (BY) *but it is particularly difficult to do so when the men of the naval yards are coming in to work or leaving.*

The **St-Nazaire Basin** (9 ha - 22 acres) was established in 1856, when St-Nazaire was only an annexe of Nantes. The port was freed from this limitation in 1879. Two years later the magnificent **Penhoët Basin** (22 ha - 54 acres), one of the largest in Europe, was opened. The port is governed jointly with that of Nantes by the Autonomous Port Authority of Nantes-St-Nazaire.

Three works deserve attention: the entrance lock, the submarine base and the exit for submarines.

The **entrance lock, Louis-Joubert** (Forme-écluse Louis Joubert), which was built between 1929 and 1932, to allow for the increase in tonnage of great Atlantic liners such as the *Normandie*.

The lock has a treble function: first as a dry dock for the repair and careenage of very large ships; second as a lock allowing ships drawing not more than 12.50 m - 40 ft to pass from the Penhoët dock directly to the Loire estuary at high tide; finally the lock can also serve as a loading and unloading berth.

This lock supplements, for the larger ships, the lock at the southern entrance to the port. This measures 210×30 m - 675×96 ft.

The **submarine base*** (Base sous-marine), which was built by the German Todt Organisation, during the occupation, is a very large reinforced concrete structure covering an area of 37 500 sq m - 44 830 sq yds and measuring 300×125 m - 960×400 ft. It had fourteen bays, which together could take some twenty submarines. Machine shops were installed at the back of the bays. In spite of much bombing the base came through the war undamaged and is now the site of various industries.

The **submarine exit*** (Y A), opposite the base, is a covered lock. This was to provide shelter from air attack and to allow the German submarines to enter and leave the base in secret (it is no longer used). It adjoins the former entrance to the port (53 m long by 13 m wide - 170×42 ft) which is now used for the Loire river traffic and for fishing craft.

The panoramic terrace commands a full view of the town, the port and the estuary *(viewing table)*. Open June to September 9.30am to 8pm. Admission: 2F.

The shipyards (BXY). – Between the Penhoët Basin and the Loire lies the Atlantic Dock-yard, made up of the former Loire workshops and dockyard and the Penhoët dockyard which have all been linked together. Among the ships which have come from the Atlantic Dockyard are the battleship *Jean Bart,* the liner *Normandie* and the liner *France.* Cargo boats, container ships, ore carrying ships and tankers for French and foreign use are also built in the yards.

The Atlantic Shipyards (Chantiers de l'Atlantique) are equipped to build several ships simultaneously. This method substitutes for the conventional slipway, a huge dry dock divided into sections in which stand the ships under construction. Launching the completed ship is achieved by filling the section with water and floating her out. A new dock enables ships of 500 000 tons to be built.

Apart from building ships for the French Navy, the Atlantic Shipyards also produce diesel engines for ships and railways, steam turbines, compressors.

■ ADDITIONAL SIGHTS

Lighthouse (BZ B). – Standing on the old pier, the lighthouse commands a view of the shipyards and the Loire estuary.

Dolmen (AY C). – In a little garden two high stones support a granite table. Alongside is a menhir.

Ste-Anne. – The church stands between the Rue du Soleil-Levant and the Boulevard Jean-Mermoz, which you reach from the Rue du Commandant-Gaté (AY). The only thing that makes one think St. Anne's is a church is the belfry standing separately to the left of the façade. The entrance is surrounded by great mosaics by Paul Colin depicting work in the St-Nazaire naval dockyard. Inside the stained glass windows contrast vividly with the bare concrete walls; to the left, the chapel with blue stained glass windows, contains a statue of St. Anne.

St-Nazaire (AZ). – This vast 19C Gothic style church with its slate topped belfry, was restored in 1945. Sculpted round the side aisles is a way of the Cross with a series of expressive figures. The transept is lit by fine rose windows with modern stained glass.

Beaches. – The Grand and Petit Traict sand beaches extend for over 2 km - 1 mile between the outer harbour *(avant-port)* jetty and the Ville-ès-Martin Point. They are skirted by the Président-Wilson and Albert I Boulevards and separated by a rock. The view from the beach extends over the Loire estuary to the south as far as St-Gildas Point.

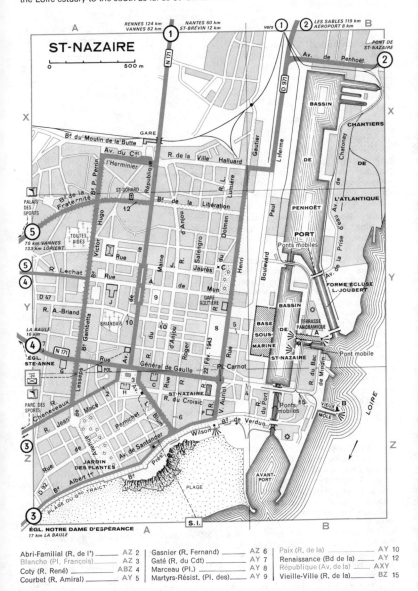

Abri-Familial (R. de l')	AZ 2	Gasnier (R. Fernand)	AZ 6	Paix (R. de la)		AY 10
Blancho (Pl. François)	AZ 3	Gaté (R. du Cdt)	AY 7	Renaissance (Bd de la)		AY 12
Coty (R. René)	ABZ 4	Marceau (Pl.)	AY 8	République (Av. de la)		AXY
Courbet (R. Amiral)	AY 5	Martyrs-Résist. (Pl. des)	AY 9	Vieille-Ville (R. de la)		BZ 15

Botanical Gardens (Jardin des Plantes) (AZ). – With their shaded alleys and colourful flower beds the gardens offer a pleasant resting spot near the Grand Traict beach.

Notre-Dame-d'Espérance. – Standing to the south of Place Pierre-Bourdan, near the Rue de Pornichet (AZ) this 1965 church has a white façade with oblique buttresses and a bare interior showing uncovered stonework.

EXCURSION

From St-Nazaire to La Baule by the coast*. – *Round tour of 38 km - 24 miles – about 1¼ hours. Leave St-Nazaire by ③, D 92. Turn left onto the D 292. The road in the reverse direction is described on p 55.*

The perfect companions to this guide:

Michelin Guide France
hotels and restaurants, garages, town plans, prices

Michelin Guide Camping Caravaning France
sites, access, facilities, charges

Michelin map 230 at a scale of 1:200 000
sightseeing, principal sights, viewpoints, road conditions.

Michelin map 230 5 – Pop 8 750

This little town, which St. Paul, known as the Aurelian, made the first bishopric in Lower Brittany, offers the tourist two of the finest buildings in Brittany: the former Cathedral (the bishopric did not survive the Concordat) and the Kreisker Belfry.

From January to September, during the season for cauliflowers, artichokes, onions and potatoes, St-Pol is extremely busy. Numerous farm carts, vans and tractors with trailers arrive, bringing these famous Breton products to the market for many transporters and agricultural co-operatives.

■ MAIN SIGHTS time: 1¼ hours

Former Cathedral★★ (Ancienne Cathé-drale). – The cathedral was built in the 13 and 14C (nave, aisles, façade and towers) and in the 15 and 16C transept, chancel and apse). The building is neither very large nor very tall (80 m - 256 ft long and 16 m - 51 ft high) but it is beautifully proportioned and plainly elegant. The architects were inspired by the cathedral at Coutances and used Norman limestone to build the nave; the traditional granite was used for the façade, the transept and the chancel. The Breton stamp can be found in the bell turrets on the transept crossing and also in the porches (p 29).

Exterior. – From a small public garden, on the north side between the church and the former bishop's palace (now the town hall), is a view of the north transept wall with Romanesque characteristics. The south side which faces the main square has a fine porch. The transept contains a remarkable rose window with above it a sort of pulpit from which sentences of excommunication used to be read.

The façade is dominated by two towers each 50 m - 160 ft high. The spires differ slightly, the smaller turrets on the left tower being joined by a balustrade, and the general outline slenderer. The terrace which surmounts the porch was used by the bishop to bless the people; the small door under the right tower was reserved for lepers.

Interior. – Enter the church through the south porch. To the left is a Roman sarcophagus which serves as a stoup. Starting the tour from the right, note a Renaissance stained glass window and in the transept the rose window. Around the chancel are tombs of local bishops and two 17C altarpieces. The carved **stalls★** of the chancel date from the 16C. Over the high altar, a palm tree in carved wood bent in the shape of a crozier, bears a ciborium for the Host.

In wall niches against the chancel, the wooden reliquaries contain thirty-five skulls exhumed from either the church or the cemetery. Opposite, kept in a gilded bronze shrine are bones of St. Pol.

Kreisker Chapel★★. – *Visit and ascent to the tower: during spring school holidays, 2 to 4pm; in June and September, 9.30am to noon and 2 to 6pm; in July and August, 9.30am to 6.30pm.* It was, at one time, in this 14-15C chapel that the town council used to meet; today it is the college chapel. What makes it famous is its magnificent **belfry★★** *(illustration p 28)*, 77 m - 246 ft high. This was inspired by the spire of St. Peter's at Caen (destroyed during the war), but the Breton building in granite surpasses the original. Vauban expressed his admiration as an engineer for "this marvel of balance and daring". The Kreisker belfry has served as a model for many Breton towers.

The chapel aisles are formed of a series of gables over fine, tall windows. The west front and the flat east end are pierced with very large bays of glass.

Enter through the north porch, a specimen of 15C architecture surmounted by a statue of Notre-Dame-de-Kreisker. The church is roofed with wooden cradles. The only stone vault joins the four huge uprights which support the belfry at the transept crossing.

You may climb the tower *(169 steps)*. From the platform you will get a circular **view★★** of Batz Island, the coast as far as the Bretonne Corniche and the Arrée Mountains inland.

Rue Général-Leclerc. – Old houses nos 30, 12 and 9.

■ ADDITIONAL SIGHTS

Cemetery. – Small arched ossuaries are built into the walls. In one corner is the Chapel of St. Peter in the Flamboyant style. Opposite the porch is a war memorial by Quillivic, backed by a semicircular wall adorned with low reliefs.

Prébendal House (A). – This was the 16C residence of the canons of Léon.

The Rue de la Rive starts from one corner of the house and leads by a shaded walk to the Champ de la Rive. At the far end is a hillock from the top of which there is a fine view of Carantec, the Taureau Castle and Morlaix Bay *(viewing table)*.

EXCURSION

Kérouzéré Castle. – *8 km - 5 miles by ③ on the plan, the D 788, then the D 10 to the right – plus ½ hour sightseeing. Visit after application in writing (or Tel 69 11 06). Closed Sundays. Go along the castle avenue and apply at the small door in the northwest tower.*

This granite feudal castle is an interesting specimen of 15C military architecture. You visit the armoury, chapel, stairs, wall walk and watchman's tower (view over the sea).

Map labels:
ANCIENNE CATHÉDRALE★★ ① 5 K. ROSCOFF
ST-POL-DE-LÉON
0 300 M.
R. de la Rive
S.I.
③ R. du Pont-Neuf
23 K. LANDIVISIAU
31 K. BRIGNOGAN
CHAPELLE DU KREISKER★★
GARE ROUTIÈRE
Plage
③ GARE
CARANTEC 11 K.
MORLAIX 23 K. ②

Budes-de-Guébriant (Pl. A.) 2
Colombe (Pl. Michel) 3
Colombier (R. du) 4
Croix-au-Lin (R.) 5
Parvis (Pl. du) 6
4 Août 1944 (R. du) 7

ST-QUAY-PORTRIEUX ★★

Michelin map 230 8, 9 – Pop 3 559 –
Facilities p 43

This much frequented resort has four
sandy beaches. The liveliest is that of
St-Quay with its casino and sea-water
swimming pool.

The little port of Portrieux used to be
a deep sea fishing base; it still sends out
lobster boats to the St-Quay Islands. A
coast road starting from Portrieux passes
near the signal station *(viewing table)*,
from which there is a very fine **view**★★ of
the Bay of St-Brieuc from Bréhat to
Cape Fréhel. The road goes on for 3 km -
2 miles along a rugged and picturesque
coast.

EXCURSION

**Étables-sur-Mer and Binic; Notre-
Dame-de-la-Cour.** – *Round tour of
22 km - 14 miles – about ¾ hour.* Take
the D 786 towards St-Brieuc. The road
goes towards the coast which it finally
overlooks and follows closely.

    Notre-Dame-de-L'Espérance. – *Open
in July and August 2 to 7pm; the
rest of the year Sunday afternoons.*
Built after the cholera epidemic of
1850, the Chapel of Our Lady of
Hope, decorated with stained glass
windows in blue tonalities, stands
on the Étables cliff, overseeing
St-Brieuc Bay.

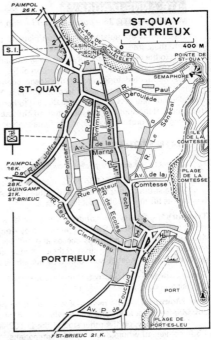

Gaulle (Av. Gén.-de) _____ 2	Plage (Pl. de la) _____ 5
Jeanne-d'Arc (R.) _____ 3	République (R. de la) _____ 6
Leclerc (Av. du Gén.) _____ 4	Victoire (R. de la) _____ 8

After the road has left the shore and Étables on its right, you get a good view of Binic.

    Étables-sur-Mer. – Pop 2 041. *Facilities p 43.* The town, built on a plateau and possessing a
fine public park, overlooks the quiet, family resort on the coast. The two parts of the town are
linked by an avenue with villas built on either side. There are two sheltered, sandy beaches.

    Binic. – Pop 2 361. *Facilities p 43.* A delightful bathing resort. Cod fishing schooners used to
anchor in the port but today it is only used by pleasure boats and merchantmen. From a
belvedere on the jetty there is a pleasant view of the beach and the port.

Leave Binic by the D 786; after 500 m take the D 4 on the left.

    Notre-Dame-de-la-Cour. – *Out of season, apply at the nearby grocer's (M. Burlot) for the key.*
The chapel is a fine 15C building with stone vaulting. Magnificent Flamboyant canopies
occupy all the upper part while beautiful stained glass at the back of the high altar depicts the
life of the Virgin in eighteen panels. The tomb of Guillaume de Rosmadec is in Kersanton
granite. A 13C calvary stands in the small square. *Pardon on 15 August.*

Return to St-Quay by Lantic and Plourhan.

ST-THÉGONNEC ★★

Michelin map 230 5 – *Local map p 137* – Pop 1 986

    This village has a magnificent parish close *(details on parish closes and illustration p 31)*, the
ossuary and the church being the key features of this rich 16-17C Renaissance group.

■ PARISH CLOSE ★★ *time: ½ hour*

Triumphal Arch★. – A rounded arch surmounted by small lanterns (1587).

Ossuary★. – The ossuary was built from 1676 to 1682 and later turned into a chapel. Inside is a
17C altarpiece with spiral columns. In the crypt, under the altar, is a **Holy Sepulchre**★ with figures
carved in relief and painted (1699-1702), the work of a Breton sculptor, Jacques Lespaignol.

Calvary★★. – The Calvary was erected in 1610. On the base are groups of figures depicting the
Passion. Below, a small niche shelters St. Thégonnec with the wolf he harnessed to his cart after
his donkey had been devoured by wolves. The platform is surmounted by a double armed cross
bearing figures. Notice the angels collecting blood running from Christ's wounds.

Church★. – The church has been rebuilt several times. The only trace of the old building is the
gable belfry (1563) on the left of the tower. The Renaissance tower is crowned with a lantern
dome with corner turrets. Over the porch is a statue of St. Thégonnec; in niches in the corner
buttresses are statues of the Annunciation, St. John and St. Nicholas; inside the porch, four
statues of Apostles. The end door is surmounted by a statue of the Virgin and Child.

    Inside, the **pulpit**★★ is one of the masterpieces (1683) of Breton sculpture. The corners are
adorned with the four Cardinal Virtues, while the Evangelists are depicted on the four panels. On
the medallion at the back, God is giving the Tables of the Law to Moses. The canopy (1732),
decorated with cherubs and roses, is surmounted by The Angel of Judgment blowing a trumpet.

    Over the pulpit St. Thégonnec stands in a niche with shutters bearing low reliefs illustrating
the Saint's life. Opposite is a statue of the Virgin carrying the Child Jesus, framed in a Tree of
Jesse. The apse and both arms of the transept are covered with 17 and 18C **woodwork**★ recently
restored. In the left arm is the **Rosary altarpiece**★: below it, in the centre, the Virgin and the Child
Jesus are giving a rosary to St. Dominic and St. Catherine; above, the Virgin and St. Lawrence
give Christ a soul saved from the flames of Purgatory.

Michelin map **230** 36 – *Local map p 53* – Pop 1 502

Ste-Anne is the outstanding Breton place of pilgrimage. The first *pardon* takes place on 7 March; then, from Easter until Rosary *(the first Sunday in October)*, there are parish pilgrimages. Up to the beginning of July they are made really interesting by the religious fervour of the pilgrims and the local costumes. The *pardon* of St. Anne on 26 July *(p 10)* and on 15 August is the most frequented, together with the Rosary *(details on pardons p 24)*.

In 1623 St. Anne appeared to a ploughman, Yves Nicolazic, and asked him to rebuild a chapel which had previously been dedicated to her in one of his fields. On 7 March 1625, Yves unearthed, at the spot she had indicated, an old statue of St. Anne. A church was built there the same year. The present basilica, in the Renaissance style, took its place in the 19C.

■ MAIN SIGHTS *time: ½ hour*

Visitors to the pilgrimage closes must respect local traditions and be circumspectly dressed.

Basilica. – Built from 1866 to 1872, it took the place of the 17C chapel.
At the south transept is a modern statue of St. Anne; part of the face of the original statue, which was burnt in 1796, is set in the base.

Treasury★. – *To visit, pass under the 17C cloisters. Admission: 3F.*
It contains a relic of St. Anne presented by Anne of Austria in thanks for the birth of Louis XIV. There are also goldsmiths' pieces and processional banners, the Processional Ark of the miraculous statue, with the cloak of the old statue, and, in a glass case in the centre, ornaments given by Anne of Austria, surrounded by numerous votive offerings.

Scala Sancta. – Old doorway from the square with a double staircase which pilgrims climb up on their knees.

War Memorial. – The memorial was raised by public subscription all over Brittany to the 250 000 Breton soldiers and sailors who died in the First World War.
Not far away, on the other side of the D 102, a national cemetery contains the graves of 1 338 soldiers of whom 370 were Mohammedans.

Miraculous Fountain. – The fountain consists of a basin and a column adorned with smaller basins and surmounted by a statue of St. Anne.

■ ADDITIONAL SIGHTS

St. Anne Diorama (Historial de Sainte Anne). – *Guided tours 1 May to 30 September, 9am to 7pm.* This retrospective exhibit, which includes wax figures in period costume, brings the visitor into the atmosphere of old Brittany and shows the origins of the annual pilgrimage.

Nicolazic Museum. – *To the right of the war memorial. Admission: 3F.* Old statues and dolls in Breton costumes.

House of Nicolazic. – *To visit, apply to the caretaker on the spot or the house next door.*
It was in this house that St. Anne appeared to the pious peasant. Inside are a chapel and some old furniture.

SEIN Island ★

Michelin map **230** 15, 16 – Pop 607

Sein Island makes a picturesque excursion. It is less than 1 km² - ½ sq mile in area and lies very low; the sea sometimes covers it as it did in 1868 and 1896.
Access: *See the current Michelin Guide France.*

HISTORICAL AND GEOGRAPHICAL NOTES

Men and their work. – For centuries the island was an object of superstitious dread. In the 18C its few inhabitants lived in almost total isolation, even remaining pagan until finally converted by Jesuit Fathers. The islanders were great wreck looters. Today they are among the most active lifesavers, but they still draw profit from the sale of goods and equipment from ships wrecked on their coast. Nearly all the furnishings in their houses come from this source.
The island is bare: there are no trees or even bushes; a few tiny fields of barley or potatoes are enclosed by low, drystone walls. The small white houses of the village stand along alleys barely a yard wide in which there is just enough room to roll a barrel.
The women do all the manual labour, the men are sailors or fishermen. Fishing is the island's only means of livelihood.

A fine page of history (1940-44). – Directly after General de Gaulle's appeal of 18 June 1940, the men of Sein Island (altogether 130 sailors and fishermen), the youngest of whom was fourteen, put to sea and joined the troops of Fighting France in England. Moreover, nearly 3 000 French soldiers and sailors also reached the island and embarked for England. When the Germans arrived on Sein they found only women, children, old men, the Mayor and the priest. For several months fishing boats brought or embarked Allied officers. Of the sailors from the island who went to England twenty-seven were killed on the world's battlefields. General de Gaulle came in person in 1946 to award the Liberation Cross to the Island.

TOUR

By climbing to the top of the lighthouse you will get an extensive view of the island, the coast and the Sein reef. This last group of rocks, some submerged, some visible, prolongs the island towards the open sea. It took fourteen years of superhuman effort to erect the Ar Men lighthouse on one of these rocks, which is constantly pounded by the sea. It was completed in 1881; its light has a range of 55 km - 34 miles to warn seamen off the rocks. The port provides a good shelter for pleasure craft.

TOUL GOULIC Gorges *

Michelin map **230** 21 – 11 km - 7 miles northwest of St-Nicolas-du-Pélem

Go along the D 87 from Lanrivan to Trémargat then, near the village of St-Antoine, take the D 110 which brings you to a flat but rocky piece of ground overlooking the wooded Blavet Valley. Take the path facing you (*¼ hour on foot Rtn*), it is a continuation of the road. The path drops steeply and will lead you to the cleft in which the Blavet River disappears. The river is still full at the beginning of the cleft (north side), but has entirely vanished by the time you reach the middle of the cleft and flows, rumbling, beneath a mass of huge rocks.

TRÉBEURDEN *

Michelin map **230** 6 – *Local map p 65* – Pop 2 901 – *Facilities p 43*

This seaside resort has several beaches, the two chief are well situated and separated by the rocky peninsula of Le Castel: the Pors-Termen beach which is a continuation of the Trozoul, which faces the harbour and the Tresmeur which is much larger and more frequented (*illustration p 13*).

■ WALKS

The Castel*. – ½ *hour.* Follow a path along the isthmus between the two beaches. Le Castel commands an extensive **view*** of the coast and the Milliau, Molène, Grande and Losquet Islands. In clear weather you can see the north coast of Finistère as far as St-Pol-de-Léon.

Bihit Point*. – *Round tour of 4 km - 2½ miles.* The Porz-Mabo road overlooks the Tresmeur beach and offers views of the Grande, Molène and Milliau Islands. From the roundabout on the road to the Bihit Point there is a **view*** of the coast from Batz Island and Roscoff right over to Grande Island and the Triagoz lighthouse out to sea.

The road, which has already covered a quarter circle, goes on to Porz-Mabo from where you can see Locquémeau and Séhar Point.

A road goes from the beach to Trébeurden.

Christ's Chapel. – Near a monolithic cross of 1697. A fine view of the coast.

TRÉGASTEL-PLAGE **

Michelin map **230** 6 – *Local map p 65* – Pop 2 013 – *Facilities p 43*

The resort of Trégastel rivals Ploumanach for the beauty and strangeness of its **rocks****.

■ WALKS

Coz-Pors Beach. – To the right of the beach and behind, near the Armoric-Hôtel, on a mass of enormous rocks known as the Tortoises, stands a statue of the Eternal Father. Beneath the rocks there are caves in one of which a prehistorical museum has been installed containing stone axes, pottery, etc., and a sea water aquarium.

The White Shore* (Grève Blanche). – *1 hour.* Rock enthusiasts will go there from Coz-Pors. The path, which starts from the left end of the latter beach, follows the cliff edge around a promontory from the end of which can be seen the White Shore, Rabbits' Island and, out at sea, the Triagoz Islands. The path near the foot of a rock called the Corkscrew (Tire Bouchon) continues and reaches the end of the White Shore, dominated by a great rock known as King Gradlon on account of its resemblance to a crowned head.

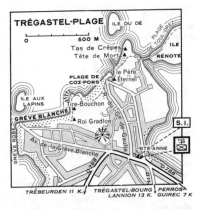

Take the road to the left that passes behind the Hôtel de la Grève Blanche to get back to the village. If you wish to extend your walk go on to the Grève Rose, which is a continuation of the Grève Blanche but lies at right angles to it. Follow the Rue de la Grève Blanche. Bear left at the D 788 crossroads and you come to a viewing table.

Viewing table. – This permits a circular view of the coast and the hinterland: the White Shore, Grande Island, the aerial of Losquet Island, the Seven Islands, Ploumanach, the radar dome of Pleumeur-Bodou and the bell towers of Pleumeur-Bodou and Trébeurden.

Rénote Island. – *2 km - 1 mile.* By following the coast from Coz-Pors beach to the right you reach a small beach beside two rocks, the Death's Head (Tête de Mort) and the Pile of Pancakes (Tas de Crêpes – *both on the right*). This last rock, which appears to lie in folds, is a good example of wind erosion.

Beyond a sandbank are a mass of rocks, among which is the Thimble (Dé). Leaving the sand bar you will find opposite you Rénot Island, formed of huge blocks of granite and now connected with the mainland. Follow the road that crosses the island. You pass Touldrez beach on your left and approach the Great Chasm (Grand Gouffre), a cavity in the middle of a mass of rocks which can be reached at low tide. As you walk amidst the rocks to the very end of the peninsula, you get good views of the horizon out to sea and of the Seven Islands looking north; of the Ploumanach coast to the east and the Bay of St. Anne to the south. To return follow the shoreline.

Trégastel-Bourg. – *3 km - 2 miles – plus ½ hour visit.* An interesting 12-13C church and 17C ossuary. 500 m beyond the village, on a knoll, is a Calvary from which there is a fine **view*** of the Côte de Granit Rose.

TRÉGUIER ★★

Michelin map 230 7 – Pop 3 718 – *Facilities p 43*

The town, a former episcopal city, was built in terraces on the side of a hill overlooking a wide estuary formed by the junction of the Jaudy and Guindy Rivers.

The port, which provides a magnificent anchorage for yachts, is deep enough to receive big ships.

One of the great Breton *pardons* takes place in the town of St. Yves on 19 May *(p 23)*. This is the "pardon of the poor", as well as that of advocates and lawyers. The procession goes from the cathedral to Minihy-Tréguier *(p 179)*.

■ MAIN SIGHTS *time: 1¼ hours*

Place du Martray (12). – The square, where fairs and markets are held, is the heart of the town. It has kept picturesque old houses. A statue of Ernest Renan (1823-92) was erected in the square in 1903 to commemorate the writer's birth in Tréguier and his attendance at the local college until he was fifteen *(p 35)*.

St-Tugdual Cathedral★★. – The cathedral, which dates from the 13 to the 15C, is one of the finest in Brittany. The transept is surmounted by three towers; the tower of the south arm roofed by an 18C pierced spire rises 63 m - 202 ft. At its base under a fine Flamboyant **window★** is a 15C porch. Every fifteen minutes five bells peal St. Yves' canticle. The Gothic tower of the sanctuary, uncompleted, rises above the crossing. The Romanesque Hastings Tower is all that is left of the 12C church.

Enter by the main porch. Steps lead down towards the luminous nave with its Gothic arches worked delicately in the granite. A sculpted frieze runs under the triforium. The ribbed vaulting in the Tudor style is lit by the tall clear glass windows. The magnificent 15C windows made from the Tréguier workshops were broken in 1793. They were replaced for the most part in 1971 by modern stained glass, the work of the master glazier Hubert de Sainte-Marie, portraying Biblical themes (to the left scenes from the Old Testament, to the right scenes from the Gospel).

From the north aisle, you will see the tomb of St. Yves (1890) which represents the monument built by Jean V, Duke of Brittany, in the 15C. The recumbent figure of Jean V sculpted in 1945 is located in the Holy Sacrament Chapel, lit by

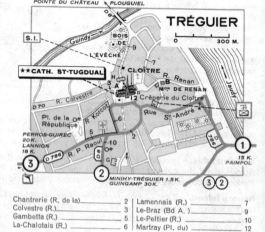

Tréguier. — The cathedral and cloister.

stained glass donated in 1937 by American, Belgian and French lawyers. The doors of the sacristy and cloisters open under handsome Romanesque arches which rise above a heavy pillar, coupled by columns with sculpted capitals and pilaster strips.

In the ambulatory, the third chapel houses a 13C Christ carved in wood. The chancel with slender columns has 18C painted vaulting. It holds forty-six Renaissance **stalls★**.

The **stained glass window★** brightens the south transept. It recounts the story of the Vine (symbol of the Church) which winds round the founders of the seven Breton trades. Near the south doorway an interesting 15C group carved in wood represents St. Yves between the Rich and the Poor.

The sacristy *(admission: 1F)* contains the treasure: the head reliquary (19C) of St. Yves and other reliquaries, a 17C vestiary, old statues and a 15C rampart.

The 15C **cloisters★★** *(admission: 2F)* abut the former bishop's palace and the cathedral chancel cuts across the north gallery. The Flamboyant arches in Breton granite, roofed with slates, frame a cross amidst a lawn flowered with hydrangeas. Under the wooden vaulting are 15 to 17C recumbent figures.

Chantrerie (R. de la) _____ 2	Lamennais (R.) _____ 7
Colvestre (R.) _____ 3	Le-Braz (Bd A.) _____ 9
Gambetta (R.) _____ 5	Le-Peltier (R.) _____ 10
La-Chalotais (R.) _____ 6	Martray (Pl. du) _____ 12

Renan's House (Maison de Renan). – *Open Easter to 31 October, 9am to noon and 2 to 7pm. Admission: 3F; Sundays and holidays: 1.50F.*

The house has been turned into a museum, and there you may see the room where Renan was born, his room as a schoolboy, a reproduction of his study at the Collège de France and his library. A gallery has been arranged in honour of Renan's *Prayer on the Acropolis* following a visit by the philosopher to Greece.

■ **ADDITIONAL SIGHTS**

War Memorial (A). – A sober and moving work by F. Renaud.

The Trégor hand-weaving workshop (B). – *Open 9am to noon and 2 to 6pm (7pm 15 June to 5 September). Closed 20 December to 10 January and Sundays except from 15 June to 5 September.*

This is installed in a 17C house that has been restored.

Bois de l'Évêché. – The wood ove...ooks the Guindy River and contains a monument to the writer Anatole Le Braz.

EXCURSIONS

Minihy-Tréguier. – Pop 673. *1 km to the south - ½ mile. Leave Tréguier by ② on the plan, the D 8.* Shortly after coming out of the town, turn left. Minihy-Tréguier, the birthplace of St. Yves, is the scene of a *pardon* on 19 May. This is called locally "going to St. Yves"; the local priest is even known as the "Rector of St. Yves". The 15C church is built on the site of the former chapel of the manor of Kermartin, where Yves Hélori was born and died (1253-1303 – *p 23*). His will is written in Latin on a painted canvas kept in the chapel. A 13C manuscript kept in the presbytery is called the *Breviary of St. Yves.* In the cemetery is a 13C monument pierced in the middle by a very low archway, under which the pilgrims pass on their knees. This is called the "tomb of St. Yves", but is probably an altar belonging to the original chapel.

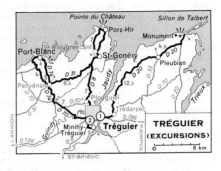

Tour of Château Point and Port-Blanc. – *Round tour of 35 km - 22 miles – about 1¾ hours – Local map above.*
Leave Tréguier by the road to Plouguiel, D 8. At Plougrescant turn right.

Round tour of Château Point by way of Porz-Hir. – Ahead lies the mouth of the Tréguier River, a view which opens out later, on the left, over the sea beyond Château Point. You go through **Porz-Hir**, with its small harbour built between great rocks near a little cove.

Return to the D 8.

St-Gonéry★. – *Time: ¼ hour.* The chapel *(visit: 2F)* dates from the 15C and has a curiously leaning lead steeple above a 10C tower. Inside are painted wooden vaults representing the Old and the New Testament. There is a piece of 16C **sacristy furniture★** in the chapel on the right. At the entrance to the chapel on the left is the 16C **mausoleum★** of a bishop of Tréguier. At the beginning of the nave on the north side is a Virgin in alabaster.
A Calvary and a pulpit stand in the old cemetery.

Make for Port-Blanc by D 31 and D 74, passing through Penvénan.

Port-Blanc★. – *Facilities p 43.* A small fishing port and seaside resort.
To reach the chapel of Notre-Dame-de-Port-Blanc, go to the Rocher de la Sentinelle, which overlooks the beach. Follow this for 100 m then leave the car in the car park. The 16C chapel *(¼ hour)* has a roof that comes down to the ground. Inside, to the right of the chancel, is a group showing St. Yves between a rich man and a pauper. There is a Calvary in the enclosure. *Pardon* on 8 September. *Ask for the key at the presbytery.*

Return to Tréguier by the D 74 and D 70.

Pleubian and Talbert Spit. – *17 km - 10½ miles – about 1 hour – Local map above. Leave Tréguier by ①. D 786, then take D 20 to the left.*

Pleubian. – Pop 3 401. Near the church you will see a carved granite pulpit (15C).

Talbert Spit. – This long, narrow tongue of land, surrounded by reefs, consists of sand and shingle. Blue thistles grow on it thickly. Continue for 500 m when, from near the war memorial, there is a fine view *(viewing table).*

TRÉVEZEL Rock ★★

Michelin map 🔟 19 – 15 km - 9 miles northwest of Huelgoat – *Local maps pp 50 and 137*

This rock escarpment, which juts up on the skyline (384 m - 1 228 ft), is in a remarkably picturesque spot in a truly mountainous setting *(illustration p 14).*
Leave your car on the D 785. Take the path *(½ hour on foot Rtn)* which begins alongside a boundary stone of the French Ordnance Survey. Ahead rise three groups of rocks; go between the middle group and the one on the left, cross a small heath, bearing to the right, and make for the most distant rocky point.
From here the **panorama★★** is immense. To the north the Léon plateau appears, bristling with spires; in clear weather you can see the Kreisker Spire at St-Pol-de-Léon and, to the east, Lannion Bay; to the west, the end of the Brest roadstead; to the south, the mountain of St-Michel and, beyond it, the dark line of trees on the Noires Mountains.

La TRINITÉ-SUR-MER

Michelin map 🔟 35, 49 – Pop 1 404 – *Facilities p 42*

The village, built on a height, now extends some 800 m down the slope to the harbour and Crach River estuary which is lined with oyster-beds. There is a good **view★** of the estuary and the pleasure boat harbour *(p 41)* from the Kerisper Bridge.

Michelin map ❷❸❶ 1 – Pop 1 450

An excursion to Ushant by sea is of the greatest interest, particularly to those who are good sailors since it enables you to see the Brest Channel, the St-Mathieu Point, the Four Channel, the famous Black Stones (Pierres Noires) reef and that of the Green Stones (Pierres Vertes), the Islands of Béniguet and Molène, and the Fromveur Channel. The island itself is extremely curious.

Access: – *See the current Michelin Guide France.*

On the way to Ushant the boat usually calls at **Molène**. There the pastures on the rare patches of earth in this archipelago are so small that, according to a local jest, a Molène cow who has her four feet in one field, grazes from another and manures a third.

GEOGRAPHICAL NOTES

Nature. – Ushant is 7 km - 4 miles long and 4 km - 2½ miles wide and its highest point is 65 m - 213 ft above sea level. It is famous in marine history for the danger of its waters due to frequent fog, strong currents and countless reefs. There have been innumerable wrecks. In winter the wind is master and hurls the waves against the broken and rocky shores with the utmost fury for as much as ten days on end. The scene is often sinister when the fog comes down and the mournful howl of the foghorns mingles with the roar of the storm. Few tourists know the island in this guise, for summer brings calm and a quieter atmosphere, similar to that of the coasts of Brittany. The climate is mild. In January and February, Ushant has the highest mean temperature in France.

The colonies of sea birds that nest on the island's cliff and on the neighbouring islets are particularly numerous in the autumn when the migrants from northern Europe and sometimes even from America fly in.

The Armorique Regional Natural Park, to which Ushant has been attached since 1969, helps maintain its traditional character.

The men and their work. – The women work on the land while the men ply the seas in the Navy, the Merchant Marine or in lobster boats. Only one-fiftieth of the island can be cultivated; there are a few fields of potatoes and barley and a little wheat.

Small sheep, some with brown wool, crop meagre salt pastures; their meat is good. They live in the open and take shelter from northwesterly or southwesterly gales behind low walls built in a star formation. Though in spring and summer they are tethered in twos to a stake they wander freely the rest of the year, their owner's mark being nicked on their ears.

Tradition. – The important part played by the women of Ushant in family life was recognised by an old custom by which it was the girls who proposed marriage. Women's dress is severe: it is made of black cloth and consists of a short skirt and a small *coiffe*; the hair is combed back and falls on the shoulders.

The character of the people is reflected in the customs observed when a member of a family is lost at sea. The friends and relatives meet at the man's home to pray and watch over a little wax cross that stands for him; the sad vigil goes on all night. The next day, at the funeral service, the cross is deposited in a reliquary in the church. Later, at some major ceremony, it will be put in a mausoleum in the cemetery where the crosses of all the missing are assembled. These little wax crosses are called *Proëlla* or *Broëlla* crosses. The word means "the homecoming of souls".

TOUR

The steamer enters the port of Lampaul when the sea is perfectly calm, or, more often, the Baie du Stuff. In the latter case there is a bus service to Lampaul.

The Northwest Coast. – The coast with its extraordinarily broken **rocks**★★★ is very impressive.

Pern Point. – This, the westernmost point of the island, extends into the sea in a series of rocks and reefs lashed by the rollers.

Notre-Dame-de-Bon-Voyage. – The Chapel of Our Lady of Safe Return stands near Loqueltas village. The people of Ushant come here as pilgrims every two years for the island's *pardon (the first or second Sunday in September).*

Créac'h Lighthouse. – *Not open to the public.* The platform commands a wonderful view of the rocks of the northwest coast.

This lighthouse, with that of the British at Land's End, marks the entrance to the English Channel. The light is cast by four lamps, giving a total of 16 million candlepower and an average range of more than 60 km - 37 miles.

Niou. – *Open 1 June to 30 September, 10am to noon and 2 to 7pm; April and May, 2 to 5pm. Closed Sundays and holidays. Admission: 3F.*

Two houses have been restored and rearranged. Visitors will see in them furniture typical of the island and an exhibit of farm implements.

Lampaul. – This is the island's capital. Note the old houses kept in excellent repair. A small monument containing the *Proëlla* crosses stands in the cemetery south of the church. The tiny port, facing west, is picturesque, while the sandy beach of Le Corce extends to the south.

■ ADDITIONAL SIGHTS

Ty-Corn Road. – The twisting and hilly, but very picturesque road affords many views over Lampaul Bay and its north coast, and of the Jument lighthouse in the distance.

Stiff Point. – From the lighthouse *(open 10am to noon and 2pm to one hour before lighting up time)* you get a very good view of the islands and the mainland.

Arland Point. – Beautiful spot by the sea on the west side of the island.

Cadoran Point. – View over Beninou Bay and Keller Island.

Le VAL-ANDRÉ ★★

Michelin map 230 9 – Local map p 90 – Facilities p 43

The resort has one of the finest sand beaches on the north coast of Brittany.

Tour of Pléneuf Point★★. – ½ hour on foot Rtn by a path which goes round the Cape northwards.
This very pretty walk on a cliff path overlooking the sea affords superb **views★★** of St-Brieuc Bay and the beach and resort of Le Val-André.
The path comes out in the Rue de la Corniche above a small harbour.

The Watch-path Walk★ (Promenade de la Guette). – ½ hour Rtn on foot. At the southwest end of the quay at the juncture with the Rue des Sablons, two arrows point the way to the Guette pathway, the Corps de Garde and the Batterie.
Go round the Anse du Pissot, down to the beach and along the Corps de Garde which is now in ruins. Soon after there is an extensive **view★** of St-Brieuc Bay. From the statue of the Virgin, go down to **Dahouët**, a fishing port and pleasure boat harbour.
Follow the Quai des Terre-Neuvas until you reach a post to the left which indicates: *"Plage par les hauteurs, Val-André, piétons"*, then return by crossing the moor and you will come to the Val-André quay.

EXCURSION

Bienassis Château; St-Jacques-le-Majeur. – *Round tour 19 km - 12 miles – about 1 hour. Leave Le Val-André by the D 786, towards Erquy. After 5 km - 2½ miles turn right.*

Bienassis Château. – *Open June and September, 10am to noon and 3 to 6pm; July and August, 10am to 12.30pm and 2.30 to 6.30pm. Closed Sundays and holidays. Admission: 4.50 F. Leave the car in the car park.* At the park entrance *(signpost)* take the main avenue which affords good views of the building as it leads up to the 17C château. The ground floor, which is open, includes a grand salon, the former guardroom and the dining room. The courtyards, the surrounding walls and the French garden are also open.

1 km - ½ mile beyond the D 17 crossroads turn left for St-Jacques-le-Majeur.

St-Jacques-le-Majeur. – This little Gothic Chapel of St. James the Major stands at the crossroads. Enter an elegant doorway *(ask for the key in the farm, opposite the side doorway).*
In the bare interior, note a charming statue of the Virgin and Child known locally as Our Lady of Safe Return (Notre-Dame-du-Bon-Voyage).

Return to Le Val-André by the D 17 and the D 786.

VANNES ★★

Michelin map 230 36, 37 – Local map p 124 – Pop 43 507

Vannes is built in the shape of an amphitheatre at the head of the Morbihan Gulf. The town, an important agricultural centre, is also developing industrially.
The old quarter, enclosed in its ramparts and grouped around the cathedral, is picturesque.

HISTORICAL NOTES

Nominoé, founder of Breton unity (9C). – Nominoé, a modest Breton, was discovered by Charlemagne, who made him Count of Vannes. Becoming Duke of Brittany (826) under Louis the Pious, he had decided to unite all the Bretons in an independent kingdom under his rule *(p 20)*. When Louis died, he went into action. In ten years unity was achieved: the Duchy reached the boundaries which were to be those of the Province until 1789. From the first Vannes was the capital of the new Breton kingdom, which reverted later to the status of a Duchy.

The union with France (16C). – Anne of Brittany, who married successively Charles VIII *(details p 157)* and Louis XII, remained the sovereign of her duchy.
When she died in 1514 at the age of thirty-seven without leaving a male heir, Claude of France, one of her daughters, inherited Brittany. A few months later Claude married the heir to the throne of France, François of Angoulême, and after a few months, on 1 January 1515, became Queen of France. The King easily persuaded her to yield her duchy to their son, the Dauphin. Thus Brittany and France would be reunited in the person of the future king. The last step was taken in August 1532. The States (councils), meeting at Vannes, proclaimed "the perpetual union of the Country and Duchy of Brittany with the Kingdom and Crown of France". The rights and privileges of the duchy were maintained: taxes had to be approved by the States; the Breton Parliament kept its judicial sovereignty and the province could maintain an army.

The Bishop's Hat (Revolution). – After the disaster at Quiberon in 1795 *(details p 147)* some of the Royalist prisoners were sent to Vannes. Twenty-two of the best known were shot on the Promenade de la Garenne. Standing against the wall with his hands tied, Mgr. de Hercé, Bishop of Dol, asked that someone should remove his hat so that he might say his last prayers. As a Blue (Republican) came up, Sombreuil, one of the leaders of the expedition, and also a prisoner said: "Leave it! You are not worthy." And he pulled off the Bishop's hat with his teeth. Three hundred and fifty other Royalists died near Vannes.

■ **MAIN SIGHTS** *time: 1 hour*

Start from the Place Henri-IV.

Place Henri-IV★ (BY 20). – The square is lined with 16C gabled houses.

St. Peter's Cathedral★ (Cathédrale St-Pierre) (BY). – Men worked on this building from the 13 to the 19C. The only trace of the 13C construction is the north tower of the façade, which is surmounted by a modern steeple. Return to the Place Henri-IV and take the Rue des Chanoines to the right, which skirts the north side of the cathedral. The chapel, whose rotunda juts out, was built in 1537 in the style of the Italian Renaissance, which is rare in Brittany.

Enter the church by the fine transept door (Flamboyant Gothic, with Renaissance niches). In the rotunda chapel, the Chapel of the Holy Sacrament, is the tomb of **St. Vincent Ferrier**, a Spanish monk who was a great preacher and died at Vannes in 1419. He was canonised in 1455. At the entrance to the chapel (left) is a picture showing the healing of a paralytic; fine tapestries depict the miraculous cures made by Vincent and his canonisation.

In the apsidal and nave chapels you will see altars, altarpieces, tombs and statues of the 17 and 18C. The 15C nave has lost some of its original character: the heavy 18C vaulting has reduced its height by almost one third and masked the panelled woodwork.

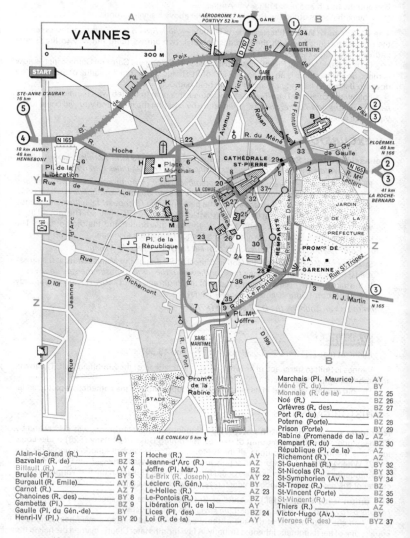

The cathedral **treasure** is exhibited in the old chapterhouse which is ornamented with 18C woodwork. A remarkable painted 12-13C chest forms part of the treasure. *Open 15 June to 15 September 10am to noon and 3 to 6pm. Closed Sundays and holidays. Admission: 1F. Staircase leading to the treasure near the sacristy.*

Leave the church by the south transept.

Take the Rue St-Guenhaël on the right then the downhill Rue de la Monnaie. This passes by the foot of the Constable's Tower (Tour du Connétable) and leads to Postern Gate (Porte Poterne) and ramparts.

Ramparts★ (BZ). – After crossing a small bridge, go to the left-hand parapet, from which you can look down on some old wash houses with very curious roofing.

Before you enter the Promenade de la Garenne, take the Rue A.-Le-Pontois to the right to enjoy a very pleasant glimpse of the old Hermine Ducal Castle (rebuilt about 1800), with a pretty flower garden in front of it. From the railings of the lower alley of the Promenade de la Garenne, you will get a **view**** of the most picturesque corner of Vannes, with the stream that flows at the foot of the ramparts (built in the 13C and remodelled repeatedly until the 17C), the formal gardens and the old houses with the cathedral in the background.

When you reach the end of the promenade, follow the Rue A.-Le-Pontois, which leads to the 15C Prison Gate (BZ **29**), flanked by a machicolated tower; this is where Sombreuil and Mgr. de Hercé were imprisoned *(p 181)*.

Pass through the gate. The cathedral apse now comes into full view. Follow the Rue St-Guenhaël, with its old houses, to the Place St-Pierre.

To the left of this square, a passage leads you to the picturesque Rue des Malles, crossing La Cohue, a market place from the 12 to 14C and where until 1840 fairs were held. On the first floor, the courtroom dating from 1550, was the seat of the Presidial court of justice.

Continue on the Rue des Halles, turn right towards the Place Henri-IV and return to your car.

■ ADDITIONAL SIGHTS

Gaillard Château (Musée archéologique de la Société Polymathique du Morbihan) (BZ **A**). – *Open 9.30am to noon and 2 to 6pm. Closed Sundays and holidays. Go through the gate and apply to the caretaker. Admission: 5F.*

A former 15C House of Parliament arranged as an archaeological museum. The museum is rich in prehistoric specimens, most of which come from the first megalithic excavations made in Morbihan, at Carnac, Locmariaquer and on the Rhuys Peninsula.

Limur Mansion (Hôtel de Limur) (AZ **K**). – A fine late 17C town house.

Oyster Museum (Musée de l'huître) (AZ **M**). – *Guided tours from 9.30am (10am in July and August) to noon and 2.30pm (3pm in July and August) to 6pm. Closed Saturdays, Sundays and public holidays. Admission: 3F.*

In the premises above the Tourist Information Centre the museum deals with all aspects of oyster cultivation: raising or capturing the larvae, their maturation and final purification.

Town Hall (AY **H**). – This building in the Renaissance style, erected at the end of the 19C, stands in the Place Maurice-Marchais, which is adorned with the equestrian statue of Constable de Richemont, one of the great figures of the 15C, for it was he who created and commanded the French army which defeated the English at the end of the Hundred Years War. He became Duke of Brittany, succeeding his brother in 1457, but died the following year.

From the campanile overlooking this building you may enjoy, in fine weather, a view of Vannes and the Morbihan Gulf. *The campanile is open every day except Saturdays, Sundays and holidays between 10am and noon and 2 and 5pm. Apply to the caretaker.*

St-Patern (BY **B**). – This church was rebuilt in the 18C.

House of St. Vincent Ferrier (Maison de Saint Vincent Ferrier) (BZ **E**). – Remodelled in the 16C.

House of Vannes (Maison de Vannes) (BZ **D**). – An old dwelling adorned with two carved wood busts of jovial peasants known as "Vannes and his wife".

Promenade de la Garenne (BZ). – The park of the former ducal castle of Vannes was arranged as a public promenade in the 17C. The view of the ramparts *(p 182)*, especially the Constable's Tower, is attractive. In the upper part of the garden, on a wall, to the left of the War Memorial, a marble tablet recalls the shooting of the Royalists *(details p 181)*.

EXCURSIONS

Conleau Island*. – *5 km - 3 miles – plus ½ hour on foot Rtn. Leave Vannes by the Promenade de la Rabine.* After 2 km - 1 mile a good view of the Morbihan Gulf unfolds before you. Cross the estuary of the Vincin on a causeway to reach Conleau Island. Leave your car *(car park)*.

Turn right in the woods on to the path skirting the Vincin.

Conleau. – *Facilities p 42.* A small port well placed at the mouth of the Vincin. From the beach there is a good view over Boëdic Island between Langle Point, on the left, and Kerguen Point on the right.

Return by the road to your car.

Elven Towers*; Lanvaux Moors; St. Avé. – *Round tour of 55 km - 34 miles – about 3 hours. Leave Vannes by ② on the plan, N 166.*

After 14 km - 9 miles turn left to the Elven Towers.

Elven Towers* (Tours d'Elven). – *Description p 89.*

After Elven turn left into the D 1. The road crosses the Lanvaux moors.

Lanvaux Moors (Landes de Lanvaux). – Contrary to what the name *landes* – moors – implies, this long crest of flaking rock-land, which was not even cultivated last century, is now a fertile region rich in trees and agricultural crops. There remain, however, many megalithic monuments which are worth seeking on foot, particularly around St-Germain, to the left of the road.

Trédion. – Pop 915. After turning left you go along the banks of a pool which surrounds a most attractive Breton manor house. Looking straight ahead, turn right and cross the built up area then left into the D 133, above the square. The road drops into the rural Valley of the Claie and its tributary the Callac stream.

Callac. – Turn left. On the left of the road before a crossroads a Lourdes' grotto has been hollowed out. To the left of the grotto a path climbs steeply: on either side are Stations of the Cross consisting of groups of figures carved in granite. The path leads to a Calvary. The descent is by another path which passes near the chapel.

On the other side of the road a stream flows swiftly at the foot of a hillock at the top of which stands a cross. It is a pleasant spot.

Take the left-hand road. When it reaches the D 1, turn left, and 600 m later bear right. After 2 km - 1 mile take the D 126 on the left, which will bring you back to Vannes.

St-Avé. – The Chapel of Our Lady of Le Loc (Notre-Dame-du-Loc) stands by the old lie of the D 126. *Ask for the key at the presbytery.* A Calvary and a fountain stand before the 15C building. Inside, note the carving on the beams; in the centre of the nave stands a Calvary with figures, surmounted by a wooden canopy. There are alabaster panels on the high altar and 15C granite altarpieces at the right and left hand altars. The statues date from the 15, 16 and 18C and include a 15C Virgin in white stone.

The Morbihan Gulf (and possibly the Auray River) by boat★★. – *Description p 124.*

Trémohar Château. – *17 km - 11 miles. Leave by ③, the N 165. After 10 km - 6 miles turn left onto the D 7. Burnt by the Spanish, rebuilt in 1720, sacked again during the Revolution this stately house was restored in 1802.*

VITRÉ ★★

Michelin map **230** 28 – Pop 12 883

This is the best preserved old world town in Brittany: its strong castle, its ramparts and its little streets have remained just as they were 400 or 500 years ago and make a picturesque and evocative picture which is long remembered.

The old enclosed town is built on a spur commanding the deep Valley of the Vilaine on one side and a railway cutting on the other. The castle stands proudly on the extreme point.

From the 16 to the 18C, Vitré was one of the most prosperous of Breton cities; it made hemp and woollen cloth and cotton stockings which were sold not only in France but in England, Germany, Spain and even America and the Indies.

This prosperity dwindled rapidly in the 19C, but is now reviving with the establishment of knitting mills, tanneries, boot and shoe and agricultural machinery factories and a factory making beds and metal furniture.

The career of Pierre Landais (15C). – About the middle of the 15C, Pierre Landais, a tailor was noticed by Duke François II, who made him his wardrobe master. Being clever and enterprising, he worked his way up and became Grand Treasurer and Counsellor to the sovereign of Brittany. But the nobles and the clergy hated this conceited upstart who encouraged bourgeois representation in the councils and had feudal rights abolished. With the support of the King of France, a plot was hatched which compelled the Duke to sacrifice his Counsellor: Landais was seized in the castle at Nantes. Under torture he admitted all the charges against him, and died by hanging in 1485.

(After Yvon photo, Paris)

Vitré. — The castle.

Arrival at Vitré★★. – Vitré Castle and the houses at its foot are a fine sight. Motorists should pause before going into the town.

Coming from Fougères: there is a magnificent view of the town coming down the hill on the D 178.

Coming from Rennes: there is a view of the castle from the bend in the road from Brest, N 157. Tourists should make for the Tertres Noirs from which they will see a panorama of the town *(p 185)*.

■ **MAIN SIGHTS** *time: 1¾ hours*

Start from the Place de la Liberté. Follow the Rue Garangeot. You will cross the Rue de la Poterie, the most picturesque part of which is on the right. Go as far as the crossroads and then return to the Rue Garangeot. At the end of this street turn right into the Rue Notre-Dame.

Notre-Dame★ (AY). – The church is 15-16C. Outside, the most curious part is the south side, with its seven gables decorated with pinnacles and its pulpit from which preachers addressed the congregation assembled on the small square.

Inside, you will see many altarpieces and a fine Renaissance stained glass window in the south aisle (third bay). In the sacristy *(apply to the Sacristan in the church or at no 24 Rue Notre-Dame)* is a fine **triptych★** adorned with thirty-two Limoges enamels.

The Rue de Paris, which opens on the Place de la République, contains many old houses.

Ramparts★ (BY). – From the beginning of the Rue de la République you will see one of the old rampart towers. On the south side of the town the walls follow the line, at a little distance, of the present Rue de la Borderie and the Promenade St-Yves and then join the castle. Only fragments remain, built into private properties. On the north and east sides the ramparts are still intact.

Go through the gate in the Val Promenade to circle the ramparts. At the end of the alley, after passing a gate, take the ramp to the left which passes under the St-Pierre postern; follow the Rue du Four uphill and turn right in the square, then right again into the Rue Notre-Dame.

Castle★★ (Château). – The castle was rebuilt in the 14 and 15C and is an impressive building. The town bought it in 1820 for 8 500 francs and has since restored it.

The present square used to be the castle forecourt where the stables and outbuildings were. The fortress is triangular in plan. The entrance is guarded by a sturdy redoubt flanked by two big machicolated towers. At the south corner stands the main keep or St. Lawrence Tower; at the northeast corner stands the Archives Tower, and at the northwest corner, the Montafilant Tower. These various works are linked by a wall, reinforced by other towers.

As you enter the courtyard you will see, on the right, the modern town hall abutting on the north front. In front of you is the Oratory Tower with an elegant Renaissance loggia.

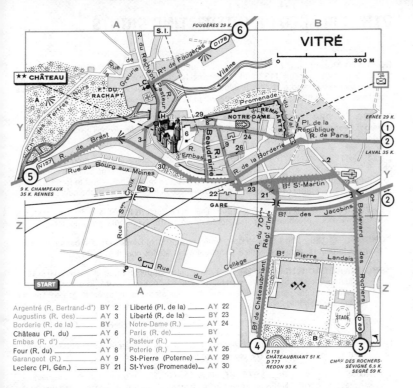

VITRÉ

FOUGÈRES 29 K.

S.I.

★★ CHÂTEAU

F^te DU RACHAPT

Ch. des Tertres Noirs

N 157

R. de Brest

5

9 K. CHAMPEAUX
35 K. RENNES

START

ERNÉE 29 K.

Pl. de la République
R. de Paris

LAVAL 35 K.

NOTRE-DAME

REMPARTS

GARE

Bd St-Martin

des Jacobins

Boulevard des Rochers

Bd Pierre Landais

STADE

Bd de Châteaubriant

Rue du Collège

Rue Ste-Croix

4

D 178
CHÂTEAUBRIANT 51 K.
D 777
REDON 93 K.

3

CH^au DES ROCHERS-
SÉVIGNÉ 6.5 K.
SEGRÉ 59 K.

Argentré (R. Bertrand-d')	BY 2	Liberté (Pl. de la)	AY 22
Augustins (R. des)	AY 3	Liberté (R. de la)	BY 23
Borderie (R. de la)	BY	Notre-Dame (R.)	AY 24
Château (Pl. du)	AY 6	Paris (R. de)	BY
Embas (R. d')	AY	Pasteur (R.)	AY
Four (R. du)	AY 8	Poterie (R.)	AY 26
Garangeot (R.)	AY 9	St-Pierre (Poterne)	AY 29
Leclerc (Pl. Gén.)	BY 21	St-Yves (Promenade)	AY 30

Museum. – *Open 10am to noon and 2 to 5.30pm (only afternoons in winter). Closed on Tuesdays and in November. Admission: 2F.*

The museum in the castle contains 15-16C sculpture, coffers, 16-17C tapestries and engravings of old Vitré as well as documents on the castle.

There is a good view of the town from the wall walk.

Take the Rue Notre-Dame again and turn right into the Rue Beaudrairie.

Rue Beaudrairie★★ (AY). – This is the most curious street in Vitré. At the second crossing, glance at the picturesque Rue d'Embas, which used to end at a gate in the ramparts.

Return to the Place de la Liberté by the St-Yves Promenade.

■ ADDITIONAL SIGHTS

Tertres Noirs★★ (AY A). – There is a fine **view★★** of Vitré, its site and its castle.

Public garden★ (BZ B). – A pleasant well kept garden.

Faubourg du Rachapt (AY). – During the Hundred Years War this suburb was occupied for several years by the English, while the town and the castle resisted all their attacks. The people of Vitré paid the invaders to go away: hence the name of the suburb *(Rachapt=rachat= repurchase)*.

This suburb, lying at the foot of the castle, crosses the Vilaine Valley and rises on the north hill slope. The Rue Pasteur, which affords picturesque views of the town and river, leads to the hospital and the 15C **chapel of St-Nicolas** (AY C). Enter by the little door on the left and follow the outside corridor, skirting the chapel. At the end, on the right, go through a pretty door beneath a basket handle arch into the chapel where there is an 18C high altar.

The Rue du Rachapt is lined with old houses.

Ste-Croix (AY D). – The church, rebuilt in 19C, has an 18C high altar.

EXCURSIONS

Rochers-Sévigné Château★. – *6.5 km - 4 miles to the southeast. Leave Vitré by ③, D 88. 6 km - 4 miles from the town, on coming out of a wood, take the château drive on the left. Description p 164.*

Champeaux★. – *9 km - 5½ miles to the west. Leave Vitré by ⑤, N 157. 2 km - 1 mile from the town turn right onto the D 29. Description p 70.*

185

OTHER PLACES OR INTERESTING SIGHTS

BOQUEN (Abbey) – 🗺230 24 – 23 km - 14 miles southeast of Lamballe. The abbey was founded by the Cistercian Order in 1137 and grew considerably. But it began to decline under the commendam system and then the Revolution; there followed pillage of the building materials and it was to a ruin that the first monk returned to in 1936. You can see the church.

BURGO-EN-GRAND-CHAMP (Notre-Dame-du) – 🗺230 36 – 2 km - 1 mile east of Grand-champ. *The approach road branches off the D 133 at Locméren-des-Prés.* The chapel is prettily sited in the woods.

CAST – 🗺230 18 – Pop 1 573 – 7 km - 4 miles southwest of Châteaulin. Standing in front of the church is an attractive sculpture, known locally as St. Hubert hunting. The Saint, accompanied by his squire and two basset hounds, is kneeling beside a minute horse and in front of a stag bearing the cross. Statue of St. Tugen *(illustration p 22)* in the courtyard of the new presbytery.

CHÂTEAUGIRON – 🗺230 41 – Pop 2 343. The castle, built in the 15 and 18C, stands on a mound while its keep, which is separate, looks down on the road from a great height.

CORSEUL – 🗺230 25 – Pop 1 955 – 9 km - 6 miles northwest of Dinan. A ruined octagonal tower of Roman stonework, assumed to be a Temple of Mars, stands near the N 794.

KERGORNADEAC'H (Castle) – 🗺230 4 – 9 km - 6 miles south of Plouescat. It was built in 1630 and is the last fortified castle to have been built in France. Though it is now in ruins you can still see the original square plan with the round, machicolated towers at each corner. The tall chimneys are still standing.

KERGROADÈS (Château) – 🗺230 2 – 8 km - 5 miles northwest of St-Renan – *Local map p 47.* The château was built in the 17C and has been restored. The court of honour is closed on one side by a crenellated gallery and is surrounded on other sides by an austere main building and two wings built at right angles. *Only the outside can be seen.*

LOCMINÉ – 🗺230 36 – Pop 3 574 – *Facilities p 44.* This little town (Locminé=*lieu des moines*=place where the monks are) owes its name to an abbey which was founded here in the 7C. The Chapel of St. Columban abuts on the 16C church, and behind stands the Chapel of Our Lady of Plasker (Notre-Dame-du-Plasker), decorated in the Flamboyant style. There is an old house on the Place de l'Église.

MAILLÉ (Château) – 🗺230 4 – 4 km - 2½ miles south of Plouescat. This stately home in granite is flanked by a Classical wing. The west front has an elegant mansard roof with a pediment in the form of a pagoda or scroll. *Only the outside can be seen.*

MONTAUBAN (Château) – 🗺230 25 – 1.5 km - 1 mile north of Montauban. Standing before the main building and flanking the narrow entrance, are tall towers with pepper-pot roofs. The chapel is on the left: the severity of its appearance makes it quite impressive. *Open 9am to 7pm. Admission: 5F.*

La MOTTE-GLAIN (Château) – 🗺230 56 – 2 km - 1 mile south of La Chapelle-Glain. Two great towers with pepper-pot roofs flank the entrance fort. This and the seignorial living quarters are the most interesting parts. The walls overlooking the courtyard and the vegetable garden are ornamented with dormer windows topped by very pointed gables.

PLOËRDUT – 🗺230 21 – Pop 1 842 – 7 km - 4 miles northwest of Guémené-sur-Scorff. The church nave is very fine and like the aisles is Romanesque. The rounded arches come down on to solid square capitals. Note the ossuary abutting the church. 3 km - 2 miles from Guémené, 17C chapel of **Notre-Dame-de-Crénénan** *(pardon, p 10).*

PLOUESCAT – 🗺230 4 – Pop 4 067 – *Facilities p 43.* Old covered market where the ancient roof is supported by wonderful old beams, held up on oak supports.

PONT-SCORFF – 🗺230 34 – Pop 1 762. Picturesque market town. The town hall was once a Renaissance mansion (1511). There is a pleasant walk up the Scorff Valley above the town.

QUESTEMBERT – 🗺230 37, 38 – Pop 4 890. In the market town you will see old covered market halls and houses; standing in the cemetery is a Calvary and a 15-16C Chapel to St. Michael.
    A pyramid recalls the victory of Alain-le-Grand over the Normans in 888 near Questembert – he reunited under his own authority the Brittany once held by Nominoé *(p 181: Historical Notes).*

Le QUILLIO – 🗺230 22 – Pop 657 – 11 km - 7 miles northeast of Mur-de-Bretagne on the D 35. Fine church of Notre-Dame-de-Délivrance with painted roof and porch. The chancel woodwork is 18C. Outside stand a Calvary and a remarkable *Pietà.*

La ROCHE DU FEU – 🗺230 18 – 1.5 km - 1 mile south of Gouézec in front of a Calvary *(car park)* take a path to the right. You will get an extensive view from the top of the hill (281 m - 899 ft – ¼ hour on foot Rtn. Viewing table.)

ROSTRENEN – 🗺230 21 – Pop 4 814. Rostrenen is situated on a hillside and is a pleasant little town. The church of Notre-Dame-du-Roncier, has a beautiful porch decorated with statues of the Apostles. Close by is a 16C sacred fountain.
    Rostrenen makes a good centre from which to make a trip up the cutting of the Nantes–Brest canal *(5 km - 3 miles – plus ½ hour on foot Rtn).* Take the N 164 towards Carhaix and after 3.5 km - 2 miles – turn left into the D 3. At the canal bridge, walk along the tow path going west. This follows the deep canal cutting. Between the canal bridge and Carhaix port a series of forty-four locks enables boats to climb or descend 120 m - 384 ft – in 17 km - 10½ miles.

ST-AUBIN-DU-CORMIER – 230 27 – Pop 3 158. St-Aubin-du-Cormier was a fortress of the Breton marchland and its walls looked down, in 1488, on the decisive battle that brought Brittany within the kingdom of France *(p 20)*. The impressive fortress, which was largely destroyed by Charles VIII, stands, still an imposing ruin, between the pool and the deep ravine which formed its natural defences.

ST-JUST – 230 39 – Pop 1 121. This little town lies at the centre of an area rich in megaliths which will provide walks of great interest for tourists curious about prehistory.

ST-MÉEN-LE-GRAND – 230 24 – Pop 3 514. There are the remains of an abbey founded in the 6C by St. Méen and reconstructed several times up to the 18C. In what was once the abbey and is now the parish church, can be seen many old tombs, including St. Méen's.

ST-NICOLAS-DU-PÉLEM – 230 21 – Pop 2 449. The town includes a 15C church with a fine stained glass window in the apse. Nearby is a 17C fountain to St. Nicholas *(illustration p 29)*. In the 17C Ruellou Chapel is a carillon wheel which is rung by the faithful seeking a blessing from heaven.

La TRINITÉ-LANGONNET – 230 20 – 13 km - 8 miles east of Gourin. Fine Flamboyant church. The most interesting parts of the church are the south door and the richly ornamented chancel. Note also the beams and timbering, the doors, piscinas, the vestry and the brackets. A sacred fountain, which is of the same period (1502), stands 200 m away (invisible from the road).

TRONJOLY (Manor) – 230 4 – 8 km - 5 miles northeast of Plouescat. This gracious manor house was built in the 16 and 17C and was made even more attractive by the addition of tall Renaissance dormer windows. A massive square tower stands in one corner of the court of honour which is enclosed by the living apartments and a terrace with a stone balustrade. *Only the exterior may be viewed.*

(After TCF Records photo, Paris)

Mont-St-Michel.

INDEX

Nizon . . . . Towns, beauty spots and tourist regions
Cléder . . . . Other towns or places referred to
Audierne . . . . The red underlining indicates that a town is
Cabellou (Le) . . . . mentioned in the Michelin Guide France
Du Guesclin . . . . . . Main references to historical events, persons and
                           particular terms appearing in the text.

The Department is given in brackets after the town, see abbreviations below :

C.-du-N. : Côtes-du-Nord   N Finistère : Nord Finistère
I.-et-V. : Ille-et-Vilaine   S Finistère : Sud Finistère
L.-Atl. : Loire-Atlantique

NOTES